KW-392-427

ELIZABETH I AND THE CULTURE OF WRITING

90 0758095 5

WITHDRAWN
FROM
UNIVERSITY OF PLYMOUTH
LIBRARY SERVICES

Un

Sub

h

ELIZABETH I AND THE CULTURE OF WRITING

Edited by

PETER BEAL & GRACE IOPPOLO

The British Library
2007

First published 2007 by
The British Library
96 Euston Road
London NW1 2DB

© The Contributors, 2007

British Library
Cataloguing in Publication Data
A CIP record for this volume is
available from The British Library

ISBN 978-0-7123-0678-2

Designed by John Trevitt
Typeset in England by
Norman Tilley Graphics, Northampton
Printed in England by
Cromwell Press, Trowbridge, Wilts

UNIVERSITY OF PLYMOUTH

9007580955

CONTENTS

ILLUSTRATIONS

PREFACE

Elizabeth I (1533-1603), who reigned for nearly forty-five years as Queen of England, Ireland and Wales from 1558 to 1603, lived immersed in a culture of writing, one in which she herself participated and which to some degree she helped to create. She wrote works, both original and in translation, in verse and in prose, including personal poems, treatises, prayers, devotions, and speeches, some of them written in her earlier years in semi-calligraphic script for presentation to her family. She also wrote letters, both personal and official, and signed innumerable documents on state affairs – of sometimes remarkable historical import.

She was the recipient of a huge number of books and manuscripts, presented to her, usually as New Year's Gifts, by courtiers, kinsmen, friends, diplomats, foreign potentates, and other worthies, dignitaries and supplicants. This was in addition to her receiving a huge number of letters from correspondents throughout Europe on foreign and domestic political, legal, commercial and administrative affairs, and handling state documents virtually every day of her long reign. Various entertainments were presented before her, a number of them in her honour when she was on her elaborate Progresses in various parts of her realm. She was the subject of countless eulogistic or gratulatory poems and dedications, as well as of allegorical representations in various literary genres; and she was, from an early age, a voracious reader, fluent in several foreign languages, including Greek and Hebrew. Her courtiers included notable poets and prose writers such as Sidney, Edward Dyer, Fulke Greville, Ralegh, John Harington, Bacon, Essex and Oxford, and, besides all else, she lived in a flourishing national literary culture, in which both printed and manuscript writings abounded.

The four-hundredth anniversary of Elizabeth's death has just been resoundingly commemorated around the world, not least by the spectacular exhibition at the National Maritime Museum, Greenwich (on the site of the house where she was born). This celebration of her reign coincided with renewed interest in her own work following the appearance of the first major attempt to publish the Queen's diverse writings (in the Chicago *Collected Works* edition). The contributors to the present volume believe that it is therefore time to pursue aspects of the culture of writing to which she belonged and which was, indeed, an essential part of her life and reign. The volume gathers together essays that examine such features as the Queen's handwriting; letters written by and to her; her representation in a popular romance, initially only circulated in manuscript; an entertainment acted before her, with a related manuscript presented to her; songs performed before her; the books and manuscripts given to her as New Year's gifts; particularly consequential examples of warrants she was obliged, albeit unwillingly, to sign; and the prayers, as well as letters of condolence, she wrote, some of which would become her most enduring literary legacy in printed books of the seventeenth century. These essays shed light on the roles she played in this culture – as sovereign and ultimate arbiter, spectator and protagonist, friend and confidante, creator and recipient, and muse and literary icon, as well as a woman. They also bring to light a number of newly discovered or little-known documents relating to Elizabeth. These remind us of the wealth of archival evidence that remains to be investigated by both historical and literary researchers in this 'golden' period of British culture.

NOTES ON CONTRIBUTORS

PETER BEAL is Senior Research Fellow at the Institute of English Studies, University of London, where he is building an AHRC-funded on-line *Catalogue of English Literary Manuscripts 1450-1700* (*CELM*). He is a Consultant to Sotheby's, where he was formerly English Manuscript Expert and a Director. His publications include *Index of English Literary Manuscripts 1450-1700* (4 vols, 1980-93) and *In Praise of Scribes: Manuscripts and their Makers in Seventeenth-Century England* (1998). He also co-edits the series *English Manuscript Studies 1100-1700* (12 vols to date, 1989-2005) and is currently completing for Oxford University Press *A Dictionary of English Manuscript Terminology*.

KATHERINE DUNCAN-JONES is Senior Research Fellow of Somerville College, Oxford, and Honorary Research Fellow of University College London. Her biography *Sir Philip Sidney: Courtier Poet* was published in 1991; her Arden 3 edition of Shakespeare's *Sonnets* in 1997; and her biographical study *Ungentle Shakespeare* in 2001. She is currently working with Henry Woudhuysen on an Arden 3 edition of Shakespeare's *Poems*.

JOSHUA ECKHARDT is Assistant Professor of English at Virginia Commonwealth University. He is completing a study of early-seventeenth-century manuscript verse miscellanies.

GABRIEL HEATON completed his doctoral thesis at the University of Cambridge in 2003. He has published articles on early modern manuscripts and on court entertainments. He is an Associate General Editor on the John Nichols Project, for which he has edited a number of Elizabethan progress entertainments, including Woodstock. He now works as a manuscript expert at Sotheby's.

GRACE IOPPOLO is Reader in English and American Literature at the University of Reading. She is the author of *Revising Shakespeare* (1991) and *Dramatists and their Manuscripts in the Age of Shakespeare, Jonson, Middleton, and Heywood* (2006). She has also edited plays by Shakespeare and by Middleton. She currently holds a two-year Research Fellowship from The Leverhulme Trust and a Larger Research Grant from The British Academy to direct a project to digitise the Philip Henslowe-Edward Alleyn archive at Dulwich College, London.

JANE A. LAWSON is an independent researcher and Senior Research Project Coordinator at Emory University. She is preparing a fully annotated edition of the New Year's gift rolls of Queen Elizabeth I, an interdisciplinary reference work which includes transcriptions of the extant gift rolls, biographical sketches of the participants, and a listing of the gifts exchanged.

STEVEN W. MAY is adjunct Professor of English at Emory University, Atlanta. He has published books and articles on Tudor verse, Sir Walter Ralegh, the Earl of Essex, Sir Edward Dyer, and other Elizabethan courtier poets. His edition of *Queen Elizabeth I: Selected Works* and *Elizabethan Poetry: A Bibliography and First-Line Index of English Verse, 1559-1603* (3 vols) both appeared in 2004.

BLAIR WORDEN is Research Professor of History at Royal Holloway College, London. He has taught at the Universities of Cambridge, Oxford, and Sussex and has been Literary Director of the Royal Historical Society and British Academy Research Professor. His publications include *The Rump Parliament 1648-1653* (1974); *The Sound of Virtue: Philip Sidney's* 'Arcadia' *and Elizabethan Politics* (1996); *Roundhead Reputations: The English Civil Wars and the Passions of Posterity* (2001), and a series of essays on the literature and political and religious thought of seventeenth-century England.

H. R. WOUDHUYSEN is Professor of English at University College London. Among his publications are *Sir Philip Sidney and the Circulation of Manuscripts, 1558-1640* (1996) and an edition of *Love's Labours's Lost* for the Arden Shakespeare third series (1998), for which he is also co-editing the narrative and other poems.

THE QUEEN'S OWN HAND
A PRELIMINARY ACCOUNT

H. R. Woudhuysen

Of course, it is deeply presumptuous to offer an essay on Queen Elizabeth's own hand: she was a queen and therefore her writing was beautiful. Furthermore, the subject raises a number of questions, not all of which can yet be answered in full. In pursuing it I have been surprised that very little has been said about her handwriting, and that what has been said relates mainly to her early years. The appearance of the *Collected Works* of Queen Elizabeth I has prompted renewed interest in what the Queen wrote and anyone interested in that subject might like to think about how she wrote as well.[1] The *Collected Works* has had some mixed reviews, and I do not want to criticise the volume further; it has now been joined by the companion old-spelling volume, but both raise an essential question about how we can be certain or might be certain as to what are the Queen's works.

The one thing we all know about Elizabeth's hand is that, when a princess, she was taught writing by Roger Ascham. Ascham, John Strype says in his life of Sir John Cheke (1702), 'for his exquisite hand, was the person appointed to teach the Lady Elizabeth to write. So that fair writing and good learning seemed to commence together.'[2] It is hard not to believe that Ascham's fine italic hand had an influence on the young princess's, but he himself does not claim to have taught her to write. Elizabeth's earliest English tutor, as far as we know, was the Greek scholar William Grindall, who came to teach the eleven-year-old princess at court in the winter of 1544, but died of the plague in January 1548. Grindall was Ascham's favourite pupil, as he had been Sir John Cheke's: all three were fellows of St John's College, Cambridge. I have so far found no specimen of Grindall's hand, but we shall see what sort of penmanship his young pupil practised under his instruction. On Grindall's death he was replaced by Ascham, despite

This paper was originally given at a PERDITA conference, 'Standards of Manuscript Description', on 14 July 2001. I am grateful for comments on it from members of the conference, and especially to Peter Beal and Jonathan Gibson. In addition to them I should like to thank Simon Adams, Patrick Collinson, Katherine Duncan-Jones, Helen Hackett, and Anne Lake Prescott for help and advice.

1 *Elizabeth I: Collected Works: Speeches, Letters, Verses, and Prayers*, ed. Leah S. Marcus, Janel Mueller, and Mary Beth Rose Rose (Chicago & London, 2000); this has been followed by *Elizabeth I: Autograph Compositions and Foreign Language Originals*, ed. Janel Mueller and Leah S. Marcus (Chicago & London, 2003).

2 Alfred Fairbank and Berthold Wolpe, *Renaissance Handwriting: An Anthology of Italic Scripts* (London, 1960), p. 31.

the wish of Catherine Parr and the Protector Seymour that the post should go to the Queen's lawyer and gentleman of her privy chamber, Francis Goldsmith, who was himself an accomplished penman.[3] Ascham tutored her first at Chelsea Palace and later between 1548 and 1550 mainly at Sir Anthony Denny's house in Cheshunt, Hertfordshire. Before he took up the post he sent a silver pen to her governess Catherine Ashley and repaired the princess's own silver pen.[4]

If he did not in the literal sense of the phrase teach the princess to write, Ascham was enormously proud of the way in which she could write. 'Nothing,' he boasted to his friend the educationalist Johann Sturm in a letter written from Cambridge on 4 April 1550, 'can be more elegant than her handwriting whether in the Greek or Roman character.'[5] In the posthumously published *Scholemaster* of 1570, he described how 'she hath obteyned that excellencie of learnyng, to vnderstand, speake, & write, both wittely with head, and faire with hand, as scarse one or two rare wittes in both the Vniuersities haue in many yeares reached vnto'.[6]

On 11 April 1562 he wrote again to Sturm sending a single word written by the Queen: 'That you may yourself see how elegantly she writes, I send you inclosed in this letter a slip of paper, in which you have the word "quemadmodum" written in the queen's own hand. The upper one is mine, the lower the queen's.' Ascham asked Sturm whether 'the sight is pleasant to you and the present an acceptable one'.[7] As always, the sense of presence conveyed by that phrase 'the queen's own hand' includes both a measure of royal or monarchical power and of a more personal and intimate association.[8] Ascham's tutoring was rewarded by the new Queen's allowing him to keep his post as Latin secretary: Queen Mary had initially appointed him to the secretaryship. He served Elizabeth in other ways, by continuing to read classical authors with her, before and after she came to the throne, and by helping her develop her much-admired facility with foreign languages.

Certainly, it is easy to make the obvious connection between Ascham and Elizabeth's hand, but since he only took responsibility for teaching her from Grindall's death in January 1548, when she was fourteen, and her hand was already formed, other influences may be detected. Alfred Fairbank thought one of these might have been Edward VI's French tutor, the appropriately named Jean Belmain or Balmain, 'who grounded her and her brother Edward in fine penmanship'.[9] He seems to have believed this because of the translation from the French of Marguerite of Navarre's *The Glass*

3 Susan E. James, *Kateryn Parr: The Making of a Queen* (Aldershot, Brookfield (Vt), Singapore, & Sydney, 1999), pp. 140, 194-5, 322. For Goldsmith's hand, see, for example, British Library, Lansdowne MS 97, fol. 43r.

4 Lawrence V. Ryan, *Roger Ascham* (Stanford & London, 1963), p. 104.

5 Fairbank and Wolpe, p. 38; *The Whole Works of Roger Ascham*, ed. J. A. Giles, 3 vols in 4 (London, 1864-5), I, 191, and translation on p. lxii.

6 *The Scholemaster* (London, 1570), sig. $H1^r$.

7 *The Zurich Letters (Second Series)*, ed. Hastings Robinson (Cambridge, 1845), p. 68.

8 For ideas and attitudes about autographs before the Renaissance, see David Ganz, '"Mind in Character": Ancient and Medieval Ideas about the Status of the Autograph as an Expression of Personality', in *Of the Making of Books: Medieval Manuscripts, their Scribes and Readers: Essays Presented to M. B. Parkes*, ed. P. R. Robinson and Rivkah Zim (Aldershot & Brookfield, Vt, 1997), pp. 280-99.

9 Fairbank and Wolpe, pp. 64, 66-7.

of the Sinful Soul. In fact Belmain's influence extended far beyond his teaching her French: his italic hand supplied the model for three of her four formal presentation manuscripts, which she produced in 1544-5.[10] In contrast to Belmain whose work survives among the Royal Manuscripts in the British Library and elsewhere, no specimen of the hand of her Italian tutor, Giovanni Battista Castiglione, has come to light with which to compare it.[11] Perhaps we should look elsewhere and consider the interest there was in italic handwriting, the script of humanism, in the early Tudor court, where it seems that the key figure was Henry VIII's last queen, whom he married in 1543, Catherine Parr.[12] Her old-fashioned secretary hand does not seem to have influenced the young princess directly: rather, it was her concern for her step-children's general education which was so important.[13]

The italic style was fostered by Prince Edward's masters John Cheke, appointed tutor in 1544, and by Richard Cox, the future Bishop of Ely. In this atmosphere good writing and book making were considered essential parts of humanist education. The nine-year-old Prince Edward even told Richard Cox in 1546 of his pleasure ('Literae enim sunt meliores thesauris') in letters.[14] A few months later he wrote to Catherine Parr, complimenting her on her italic hand and joking that his tutor thought a recent letter from her was written by a secretary until he saw that she signed her name equally. Edward clearly admired his step-mother's writing and praised the individual letter-forms, contrasting them with his lack of ability in this area.[15] Ascham was proud of his royal pupil and boasted in a letter to Stephen Gardiner, written at the end of 1553, that 'I was sent for many times to teach the king to write, and brought him before a xi years

10 Belmain's hand can be found in: BL, Royal MS 20 A. XIV, his translation into French of the second Prayer Book of Edward VI, presented to the King in 1554; BL, Royal MS 16 E. I, an undated translation of Basil the Great's letter to St Gregory on the solitary life, presented to Princess Elizabeth (cf. David Starkey, *Elizabeth: Apprenticeship* (London, 2000), pp. 86-7, who dates it to around 1548); in a French glossary, dedicated to King Edward VI in 1554, formerly owned by Lord Kenyon and offered for sale at Sotheby's, 24 July 1995, lot 374; and in a manuscript translation of Catherine Parr's *Lamentations of a Sinner* into French at Hatfield House, Cecil Papers 314.

11 For Castiglione, see Felix Pryor, *Elizabeth I: Her Life in Letters* (London, 2003), p. 137. BL, Add. MS 35831, fol. 119r, is a letter addressed to Castiglione. In a letter from Sir Henry Bedingfield to the Council, from Woodstock, 27 May 1554, he mentions a John Picton, 'who taught her many tongues in her youth'; this is cited from the Bedingfield Papers (*Norfolk Archaeology*, 4 (1855)) in Frank A. Mumby, *The Girlhood of Queen Elizabeth* (London, 1909), p. 137; the Council replied on 31 May, 'we know not the man' (Mumby, p. 140).

12 Cf. James Kelsey McConica, *English Humanists and Reformation Politics Under Henry VIII and Edward VI* (Oxford, 1965), pp. 7-8, 10-11, 215-34; John N. King, 'Patronage and Piety: The Influence of Catherine Parr', in *Silent But for the Word: Tudor Women as Patrons, Translators and Writers of Religious Works*, ed. Margaret P. Hannay (Kent, Ohio, 1985), pp. 43-59. The question of Parr's learning is canvassed by James, *Kateryn Parr*, pp. 22-39.

13 Fairbank and Wolpe, pp. 67-8 and pl. 29, reproduce a letter (BL, Cotton MS Vespasian F. III, fol. 37r), which they date 20 September 1544, as written by Catherine Parr. However, James in *Kateryn Parr*, p. 32 and n.41, points out correctly that the letter was written by 'Princess Elizabeth, acting as her stepmother's amanuensis', and that it belongs to 1547. Nevertheless, Fairbank and Wolpe cite the powerful evidence (from BL, Harley MS 5087, fols 3v-4r (cf. also fol. 17v), and 6986, fol. 15r) of Prince Edward's praise of Parr's italic hand and her beautiful writing, which suggests she could have been an accomplished scribe.

14 Fairbank and Wolpe, pp. 64-5 and pl. 25, from BL, Harley MS 5087, fol. 2r.

15 Fairbank and Wolpe, pp. 67-8.

old to write as fair a hand, though I say it, as any child in England.' He added that this can be proved 'as a letter in his own hand doth declare, which I kept as a treasure for a witness of my service'. This intimate association with Edward – he taught him in his 'privy-chamber' – was a valuable mark of Ascham's own status.[16]

The importance of handwritten books in this culture is made explicit in one of Hugh Latimer's sermons preached before Edward, now king, in 1549. The text was from Romans 15:4 'Whatsoever things are written aforetime, are written for our learning; that we through patience and comfort of scripture might have hope':

> What must he [the king] do then? He muste be a studie*n*t. He must wryte Goddes boke hym selfe ... yet a Kynge maye take hys pastyme in haukinge or huntynge or such lyke pleasures. But he muste vse the*m* for recreation ... and this is called pastime with good companye. He must wryte out a boke hymselfe. He [St Paul] speaketh of wrytynge bicause printynge was not vsed at th*a*t tyme.
>
> And shall the Kynge wryte it out hymselfe? He meaneth he shall se it wrytten, and rather then he shoulde be wythout it, wryte it hym selfe.[17]

Edward and Elizabeth were not the only pupils to come out of this rather intense culture in which good handwriting was seen as the mark of a good Protestant. Ascham also taught the Duke of Suffolk's young sons Henry and Charles Brandon, Rudolph Radcliffe, and John Whitney. He may also have taught Lady Jane Grey with Princess Elizabeth.[18] Lady Jane Grey's hand is perhaps the most distinguished of this group, as in a letter of 1552 to the reformer Henry Bullinger.[19] The place to see some of these children at work under Ascham's care is in Edward VI's exercise-book in the Bodleian Library, Oxford. This contains extracts and phrases from Cicero's *De officiis*, made by Edward between 4 January and 14 August 1548, but there are three other hands at work in the volume: one of them (fols 63r-66r) is most probably that of the young King's whipping-boy, Barnaby Fitzpatrick.[20] Another would seem to be that of Princess Elizabeth. It is very difficult to distinguish the hands at work in this volume; however, it is possible that the part of the manuscript sometimes assigned to her (fols 73r-78v, and perhaps 72v) is not in fact hers, but that she wrote an earlier part of it (fols 56r-62v).[21] If we cannot speak with complete confidence of a royal school-room or scriptorium, Elizabeth's own accomplishments with her pen can be put in a context in which fine writing was valued: it was expected that the royal and aristocratic children should take trouble over their letters and lessons and that the materials they used should match their position.

16 Fairbank and Wolpe, p. 33, n.1; Ryan, *Roger Ascham*, p. 107.

17 Hugh Latimer, *The seconde sermon* (London, 1549), sigs $C5^v$-$C6^v$; for a modernised version, see Hugh Latimer, *Sermons*, ed. H. C. Beeching (London & New York, [1906]), p. 102.

18 Alfred Fairbank and Bruce Dickins, *The Italic Hand in Tudor Cambridge*, Cambridge Bibliographical Society Monograph, No. 5 (1962), p. 4; Ryan, *Roger Ascham*, p. 107; cf. Ascham, *The Scholemaster*, sigs $E3^v$-$E4^r$.

19 Fairbank and Wolpe, pp. 70-1 and pl. 33.

20 For the later development of Fitzpatrick's hand, see Fairbank and Wolpe, pp. 69-70 and pl. 32, and BL, Cotton MS Caligula E. IV, fols 296r-301r.

21 Bodleian, MS Autogr. e. 2 (SC. 3071).

Most examples of Queen Elizabeth's writing probably survive in the form of her royal signature on official documents and letters – the 'Elizabeth R.', suitably flourished, which was made famous in the television series of that name or on the covers of innumerable books about her, such as David Starkey's. It would be possible, and possibly quite interesting, to put together a collection of these signatures in chronological order, but signatures, signs manual, and royal signatures in particular, are formal pieces of penmanship and conform more or less to a set pattern.[22] Yet even with a collection of royal signatures beginning in 1558, little would be revealed about her other writings. Unlike her father, she does not appear to have made much practical use of the small number of books which can now be identified as belonging to her.[23] Among the exceptions to this general rule might be included a remarkable sextodecimo volume in the Bodleian Library, containing the Litany and first fifteen Psalms printed on vellum at London in 1563. This has been decorated in red, blue, and gold, had a calendar and prayers added in manuscript, and has the end of a prayer in what may well be her hand. Another volume, a sextodecimo New Testament of about 1579 with an inscription on the endpaper of a saying attributed to St Augustine, may be related to this one, and is also in the Bodleian.[24] In the Royal Library at Windsor, there is a psalter, printed in France, which contains a four-line autograph poem signed by 'Your louinge maistres. Elizabeth'.[25]

The main source for any detailed study of the Queen's hand must be her correspondence. Her more or less 'private' correspondence, which might include semi-official letters to other monarchs and rulers, was often written in her own hand. Her official duties led to the production of a vast number of documents which she simply signed with her name, but there were also many occasions when she would add a subscription and a more personal autograph message to the recipient, which might consist of only a few words but might also be much longer. The identities of the secretaries and scribes, many of them employed in the Signet Office, who produced the

22 See the sequence of signatures in Pryor, *Elizabeth I*, pp. 12-13. Pryor (p. 14) points out that on 10 March 1570 the Queen 'issued a warrant authorizing Sir William Cecil to affix her signature by stamp to a series of letters sent into the shires to raise levies against the Rebellion of the Northern Earls'; the draft warrant and an accompanying specimen letter are in the National Archives, SP 12/67, fol. 30v. For an example of such a letter with the stamped signature, sent to Thomas Knyvett of Ashwellthorpe, see Maggs, catalogue 926 (1970), item 50 and pl. VII.

23 Cf. T. A. Birrell, *English Monarchs and their Books: From Henry VII to Charles II*, The Panizzi Lectures 1986 (London, 1987), pp. 24-6.

24 Bodleian, MS Arch. A g. 17, which seems to be *STC* 16455; MS e Mus. 242 (SC. 3701). I have not seen the second of these books, but cf. John N. King, *Tudor Royal Iconography: Literature and Art in an Age of Religious Crisis* (Princeton, 1989), pp. 109-12. A French dialogue on life and death printed in civilité types in 1558, with an eight-line poem in French in what may possibly be the Queen's hand, is contained in MS Bodl. 660 (SC. 3007); the poem is, however, written as by a man. For this volume's extremely beautiful binding, see Giles Barber, *Textile and Embroidered Bindings*, Bodleian Picture Books: Special series, No. 2 (Oxford, 1971), pl. 10.

25 See *Elizabeth: The Exhibition at the National Maritime Museum*, ed. Susan Doran (London, 2003), p. 201. Pryor, *Elizabeth I*, p. 141, suggests that the inscription may date from about 1549 and relate to the Seymour affair.

fair copies of these official documents and letters have not yet received the attention they deserve.[26] The names of some of the more famous scribes, such as Ascham himself, the French secretaries Nicasius and Charles Yetsweirt and the Latin secretary Sir John Wolley, are relatively well known, but the personnel and duties of most of the secretariat await detailed investigation.[27] Although many of the documents, which they produced for the Queen, are unsigned, it may be possible to attribute some groups of letters to scribes on the basis of handwriting alone. On some occasions, especially when they were producing official letters, which took the form of broadsides, scribes would sign their work in the lower margin, usually on the right-hand side.[28]

Without a full inventory or calendar, estimates of the numbers of the Queen's letters which survive can only be approximate, and will be affected by definitions of what exactly constitutes a letter. Susan Doran believes that 'Elizabeth wrote well over 3000 letters' and notes that G. B. Harrison, who produced the only modern collection of her letters covering the whole of her life, claimed to have read between two and three thousand of them.[29] One aspect of her scribal practice was her habit of terminating her signature with what has been described as 'a paraph similar to the quatrefoil flourish used by her father'.[30] There are a number of problems here. Elizabeth's paraph is similar to, but not formed in exactly the same way as, her father's mark, yet seems to imitate it. When Henry VIII's mark is examined against Henry VII's signature it becomes clear that the son is imitating his father's form of majuscule *R* for 'Rex': both men form the letter in exactly the same way, although the results are different.[31] If there is a direct relationship between Elizabeth's paraph and her father's *R*, then the fact that she used it before she was crowned might be taken to suggest that she was clearly conscious of

26 On the Signet Office, see Penry Williams, *The Tudor Regime* (Oxford, 1979), pp. 39-45, and for the earlier period J. Otway-Ruthven, *The King's Secretary and the Signet Office in the XV Century* (Cambridge, 1939).

27 For the Yetsweirts, see Charles Angell Bradford, *Nicasius Yetsweirt: Secretary for the French Tongue* (London, 1934): there is a copy of this pamphlet in the BL. For Wolley, see H. R. Woudhuysen, *Sir Philip Sidney and the Circulation of Manuscripts, 1558-1640* (Oxford, 1996), pp. 67, n.1, 77, 80.

28 See, for example, Queen Elizabeth to Sir Thomas Cawarden, 3 January 1559, in Washington, Folger Shakespeare Library, MS L. b. 33, reproduced in David M. Bergeron, 'Elizabeth's Coronation Entry (1559): New Manuscript Evidence', in *The Mysteries of Elizabeth I: Selections from 'English Literary Renaissance'* (Amherst & Boston, Mass., 2003), pp. 21-30, at p. 29, and cf. the endorsement by Nicasius Yetsweirt that he has examined a warrant in Pryor, *Elizabeth I*, pp. 84-5. The various volumes of the Calendar of State Papers Foreign occasionally note the name of the scribe at the end of individual entries.

29 Susan Doran, 'Elizabeth I's Religion: The Evidence of her Letters', *Journal of Ecclesiastical History*, 51 (2000), 699-720 (p. 701).

30 Pryor, *Elizabeth I*, p. 12; her use of it before she came to the throne is shown on pp. 20, 24, and by Fairbank and Wolpe, *Renaissance Handwriting*, pl. 28. For a theory that Henry VIII's terminal letter is in fact an *H* and that Elizabeth's paraph is related to then fashionable knots and affirms her Tudor identity, see Lisa M. Klein, 'Your Humble Handmaid: Elizabethan Gifts of Needlework', *Renaissance Quarterly*, 50 (1997), 459-93 (p. 481).

31 A particularly clear example of Henry VII's royal signature with the final *R* is reproduced from a letter of 16 November 1500, mainly in the hand of his Latin Secretary, Petro Carmeliano, in Martin Breslauer, catalogue 100 (n.d.), item 19 and pl. on p. 35. On Carmeliano, see also Otway-Ruthven, *The King's Secretary*, pp. 190-1. On Henry VIII's ways of signing his name, see *The Letters of King Henry VIII: A Selection*, ed. M. St Clare Byrne (London, 1936), pp. xvi-xviii, 50-2, and Seth Lerer, *Courtly Letters in the Age of Henry VIII: Literary Culture and the Arts of Deceit* (Cambridge, 1997), pp. 87, 93.

her royal status. It would be interesting to know exactly when she replaced the paraph with the more familiar form of *R*.[32]

Throughout Elizabeth's life she had the maddening habit of not dating her letters, but study of the evolution and development of her handwriting would allow many of her undated letters to be placed in some sort of chronological order. From the earlier years, two sorts of hand can be clearly distinguished, one which is used in formal letters and one in presentation manuscripts. If we look at what may be one of her earliest letters, dating from 20 September 1547 according to the editors of her *Collected Works*, that is just before January 1548 when Ascham came to be her tutor, certain distinctive features are already present. In it she congratulates her younger brother Edward, who had been crowned at the beginning of the year, on his recovery from illness. Apart from the more obvious flourishes, the two sorts of ampersand, the initial downstroke of *v*, sometimes reflected in the *L* and *N*, the *t* with a bar only on the right, the ornamented bowl of the *e*, the ligatured *ss*, the crossed *I* are characteristic (PLATE 1).[33] This shows Elizabeth's formal and fairly careful handling of Latin. When writing an English comment on Sir Robert Tyrrwhitt's interrogation of her, just a few months later in February 1548/9, some of these features are present, but it seems as if she consciously wrote in a slightly different but still quite elaborate style.[34] An even more formal letter, addressed to Edward Seymour, Duke of Somerset, from Hatfield House on 21 February 1548/9, shows her extraordinarily controlled mastery of italic.[35]

In a letter written a few years later, on 21 April 1552, again congratulating her sickly brother on his recovery from illness, the decoration is slightly more restrained, except in the subscription and signature; but even allowing for the change into the vernacular, the forms are not much altered.[36] If the dates of these two letters are correct, one was written before Ascham became her tutor, the other after.

A third early example can be precisely dated 17 March 1553/4, and shows a rather different appearance: there is still some ornamentation and a remarkable degree of control, but, especially after the tenth line, the hand is looser, slightly bolder and perhaps rather coarser – 'knowen' in line 22 stands out in both respects. The plain *I* has given way to an ornamented one. The difficulty here in assessing the development of the hand is that the Princess Elizabeth is writing to her half-sister Queen Mary, in the aftermath of Wyatt's rebellion, begging her to believe that she is not a traitor and to spare her from the Tower.[37] In other words, has the hand actually changed or is

32 A letter to Sir Edward Saunders written on 20 November 1558, three days after she succeeded to the throne, bears the paraph: see Julian Browning, catalogue 18 [1997], item 28. The Folger document, dated 3 January 1559, days before her coronation, is signed with the flourished *R*: see Bergeron, 'Elizabeth's Coronation Entry', p. 29.

33 BL, Harley MS 6986, fol. 21r; Fairbank and Wolpe, pp. 66-7 and pl. 28; *Elizabeth I: Collected Works*, Letters 6, pp. 14-15.

34 Hatfield House, CP150/89-90, fol. 90r, illustrated in *Elizabeth*, ed. Doran, p. 20.

35 Pryor, *Elizabeth I*, pp. 20-1.

36 See *2,000 Years of Calligraphy: A Three-Part Exhibition Organised by The Baltimore Museum of Art, The Peabody Institute Library, The Walters Art Gallery* (Baltimore, 1965), No. 103.

37 NA, SP/11/4/2, fol. 3r-v. *Tudor Royal Letters: Elizabeth I and the Succession*, ed. C. J. Kitching, Public Record Office Museum Pamphlets No. 3 (London, 1972), No. I; for the date, see Pryor, *Elizabeth I*, p. 138.

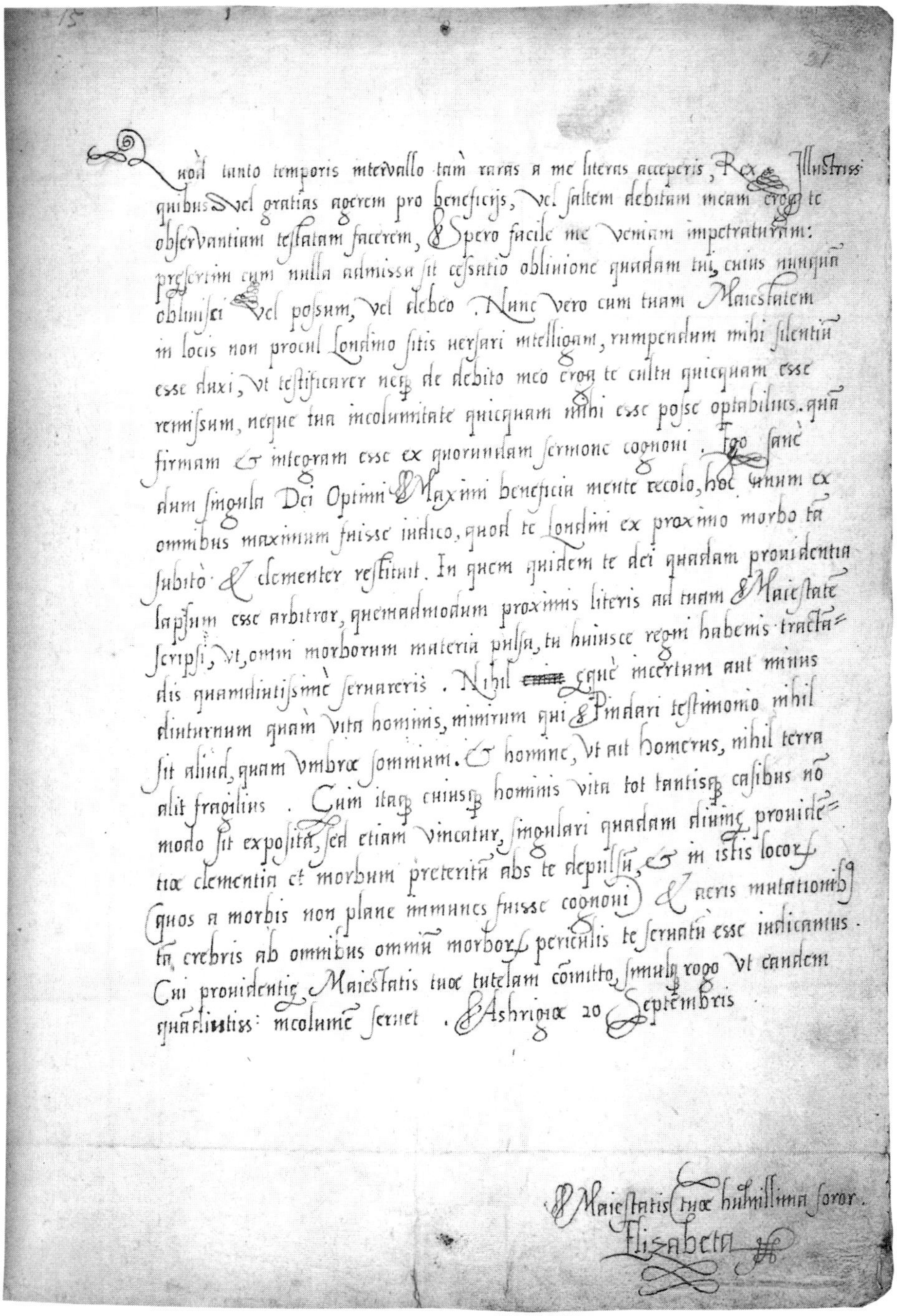

Quod tanto temporis intervallo tam raras a me literas acceperis, Rex Illustriss:
quibus vel gratias agerem pro beneficijs, vel saltem debitam meam erga te
observantiam testatam facerem, spero facile me veniam impetraturam:
presertim cum nulla admissa sit cessatio oblivione quadam tui, cuius nunquam
oblivisci vel possum, vel debeo. Nunc vero cum tuam Maiestatem
in locis non procul Londino sitis versari intelligam, rumpendum mihi silentium
esse duxi, vt testificarer neque de debito meo erga te cultu quicquam esse
remissum, neque tua incolumitate quicquam mihi esse posse optabilius. quam
firmam et integram esse ex quorundam sermone cognovi. Ego sane
dum singula Dei Optimi Maximi beneficia mente recolo, hoc vnum ex
omnibus maximum fuisse iudico, quod te Londini ex proximo morbo tam
subito et clementer restituit. In quem quidem te dei quadam providentia
lapsum esse arbitror, quemadmodum proximis literis ad tuam Maiestatem
scripsi, vt omni morborum materia pulsa, tu huiusce regni habenis tracta-
dis quamdiutissime servareris. Nihil ~~enim~~ [illegible] incertum aut minus
diuturnum quam vita hominis, nimirum qui et Pindari testimonio nihil
sit aliud, quam umbrae somnium. et homine, vt ait homerus, nihil terra
alit fragilius. Cum itaque cuiusque hominis vita tot tantisque casibus non
modo sit exposita, sed etiam vincatur, singulari quadam divinae provide-
tiae clementia et morbum preteritum abs te depulsum, et in istis locorum
(quos a morbis non plane immunes fuisse cognovi) et aeris mutationibus
tam crebris ab omnibus omnium morborum periculis te servatum esse iudicamus.
Cui providentiae Maiestatis tuae tutelam committo, simulque rogo vt eandem
quamdiutiss: incolumem servet. Ashridgiae 20 Septembris

Maiestatis tuae humillima soror.
Elizabeth

1 Autograph letter signed by Princess Elizabeth, to King Edward VI, Ashridge, 20 September [1547] (BL, Harley MS 6986, fol. 21r)

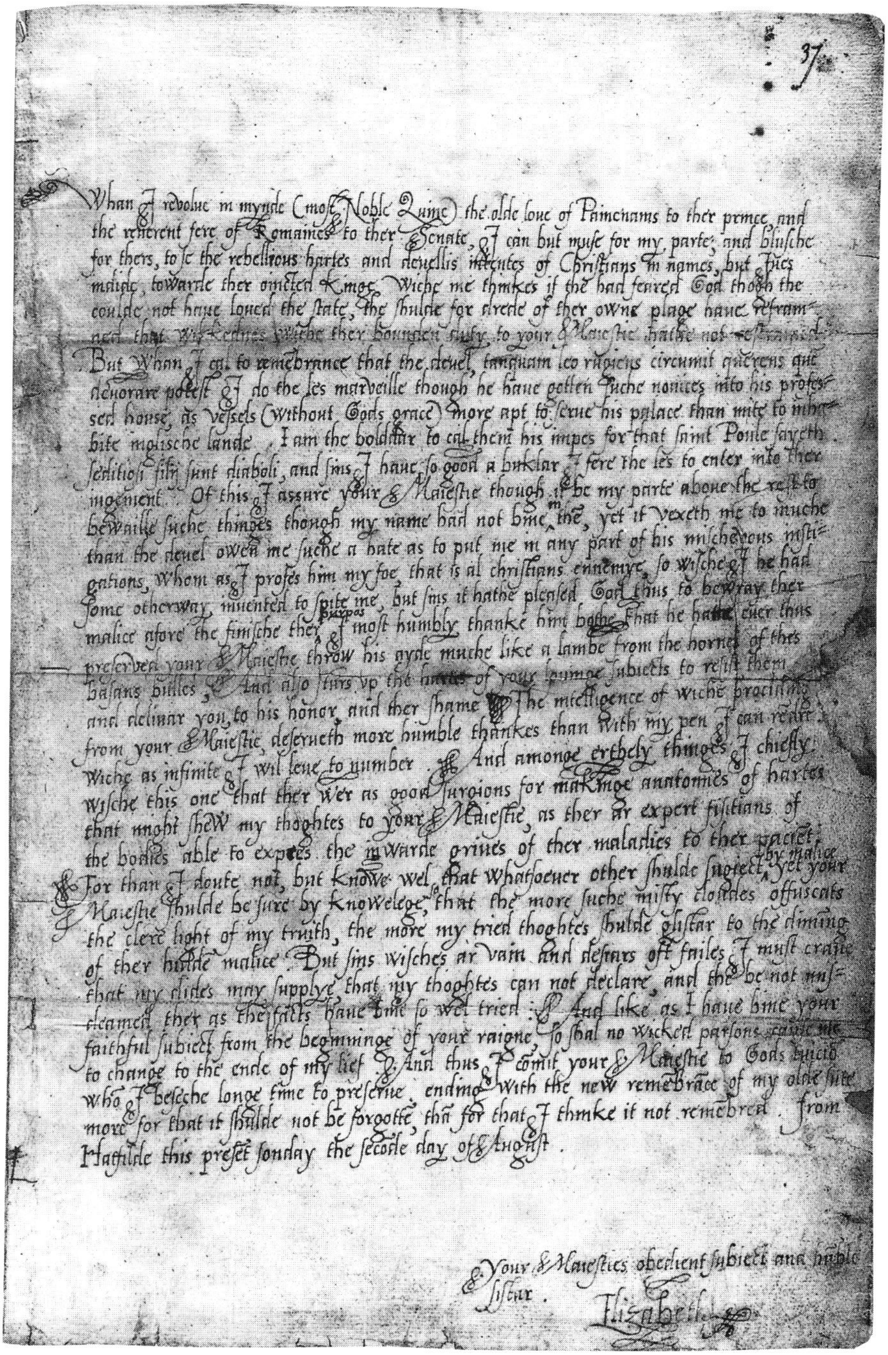

When I revolue in mynde (most Noble Quene) the olde loue of Paynims to ther prince, and the reuerent fere of Romaines to ther Senate, I can but muse for my parte, and blusche for thers, to se the rebellious hartes and deuellis intentes of Christians in names, but Iues in dide, towarde ther oincted Kinge. Wiche me thinkes if the had feared God though the coulde not haue loued the state, the shulde for drede of ther owne plage haue refrained that wickednes wiche ther bounden duty to your Maiestie hathe not restrained. But when I cal to remembrance that the deuel, tanquam leo rugiens circumit querens quem deuorare potest, I do the les marveille though he haue gotten suche nouices into his professed house, as vessels (without Gods grace) more apt to serue his palace than mite to inhabite English lande. I am the boldar to cal them his impes for that saint Paule sayeth seditiosi filii sunt diaboli, and sins I haue so good a buklar I fere the les to enter into ther iugement. Of this I assure your Maiestie though it be my parte aboue the rest to bewaille suche thinges though my name had not bine in them, yet it vexeth me to muche than the deuel owith me suche a hate as to put me in any part of his mischeuous instigations, whom as I profes him my foe, that is al christians enemye, so wische I he had some other way inuented to spite me, but sins it hathe plesed God thus to bewray ther malice afore the finische ther purpos I most humbly thanke him bothe that he hathe euer thus preserued your Maiestie throw his aide muche like a lambe from the hornes of thes Basans bulles, and also stirs vp the hartes of your louinge subiects to resist them and deliuer you to his honor and ther shame. The intelligence of wiche proceding from your Maiestie deserueth more humble thankes than with my pen I can rendre wiche as infinite I wil leue to number. And amonge erthely thinges I chiefly wische this one that ther wer as good surgions for makinge anatomies of hartes that might shew my thoghtes to your Maiestie, as ther ar expert fisitians of the bodies able to expres the inwarde griues of ther maladies to ther pacient. For than I doute not, but know wel, that whatsoeuer other shulde suggest by malice, yet your Maiestie shulde be sure by knowelege, that the more suche misty cloudes offuscats the clere light of my truth, the more my tried thoghtes shulde glistar to the dimming of ther hidde malice. But sins wisches ar vain and desires oft failes I must craue that my dides may supply that my thoghtes can not declare, and the be not misdeamed ther as the facts haue bine so wel tried. And like as I haue bine your faithful subiect from the beginninge of your raigne, so shal no wicked parsons cause me to change to the ende of my lief. And thus I comit your Maiestie to Gods tuition who I besech longe time to preserue, ending with the new remembrance of my olde sute more for that it shulde not be forgotten, than for that I thinke it not remembred. From Hatfilde this present sonday the seconde day of August.

Your Maiesties obedient subiect and humble sistar.
Elizabeth

2 Autograph letter signed by Princess Elizabeth, to Queen Mary, 2 August 1556 (BL, Lansdowne MS 1236, fol. 37r)

it revealing the pressures which lie beneath it? The answer is almost certainly the second of these, for order and control are restored nearly two and a half years later in another letter to Queen Mary, dated 2 August 1556. However, some forms prominent in the earlier letter have been retained, in particular the flourished *I* and the rather prominent *k* (PLATE 2).[38]

Four surviving early presentation manuscripts, all written on vellum, show a quite different sort of development. The earliest is the translation of Marguerite of Navarre's *The Glass of the Sinful Soul*, which was dedicated to Queen Catherine Parr at Ashridge on 31 December 1544.[39] The English script is really quite crude and clumsy, but of course it must be remembered that the Princess was only eleven when she wrote it, and the vellum may not have been of the highest quality. I cannot agree with David Starkey that 'her handwriting declined' as she wrote the volume because she was pressed for time having left the copying 'to the last minute'.[40] Again, a year later, it is hard to judge whether the hand has improved or whether it is responding to the different demands of Latin, in her copying of Catherine Parr's prayers or meditations, which she translated into Latin, French, and Italian. This was dedicated to Henry VIII from Hertford Castle, Hertfordshire, on 30 December 1545 (PLATE 3).[41] It is worth pointing out that the first word of the dedication here is 'Quemadmodum', the same one Ascham sent to Sturm.[42] It might be supposed that the Latin as well as the dedication to her father put her on her best calligraphic behaviour; but a comparison with the companion volume, a translation of Calvin's *Institution of Christian Religion* into English, presented at the same time to the Queen, reveals that this is not the case: both books are written with equal care (PLATE 4).[43] The hand has improved: 'In place of the rather unformed script of the previous year,' as Starkey says, 'she wrote in a muscular, regular italic that was the equal of her best subsequent efforts.'[44] The italic hand used in these manuscripts is evidently based on that of her half-brother's tutor Jean Belmain, who must now be seen as an important influence on the future queen, or at least on the development of her hand (PLATE 5). The same hand appears in what seems to be Elizabeth's earliest

38 BL, MS Lansdowne 1236, fol. 37r; *Elizabeth I: Collected Works*, Letters 23, pp. 43-4; W. W. Greg *et al.*, *English Literary Autographs, 1550-1650*, 3 vols (Oxford, 1925-32), No. XCI.

39 Bodleian, MS Cherry 36. There are two facsimiles of the manuscript of which the first is superior in the quality of the reproduction to the second: *The Mirror of the Sinful Soul: A Prose Translation from the French of a Poem by Queen Margaret of Navarre, Made in 1544 by the Princess (Afterwards Queen) Elizabeth Reproduced in Fac-Simile*, ed. Percy W. Ames (London, 1897) and Marc Shell, *Elizabeth's Glass with 'The Glass of the Sinful Soul' (1544) and 'Epistle Dedicatory' & 'Conclusion' (1548) by John Bale* (Lincoln, Nebr. & London, 1993). See also Frances Teague, 'Princess Elizabeth's Hand in *The Glass of the Sinful Soul*', *English Manuscript Studies*, 9 (2000), 33-48.

40 Starkey, *Elizabeth*, p. 49.

41 BL, Royal MS 7 D. X. The embroidered binding of this manuscript is reproduced in *Elizabeth*, ed. Doran, p. 15.

42 Jonathan Goldberg, *Writing Matter: From the Hands of the English Renaissance* (Stanford, 1990), p. 122, believes that Ascham sent Sturm 'a page on which the queen (then princess) practiced the first word of the dedicatory letter to Henry VIII' before the book of prayers.

43 Edinburgh, National Archives of Scotland, RH 13/78. Margaret H. Swain, 'A New Year's Gift from the Princess Elizabeth', *The Connoisseur*, 183 (1973), 258-66.

44 Starkey, *Elizabeth*, p. 52; he does not refer to the translation of Calvin.

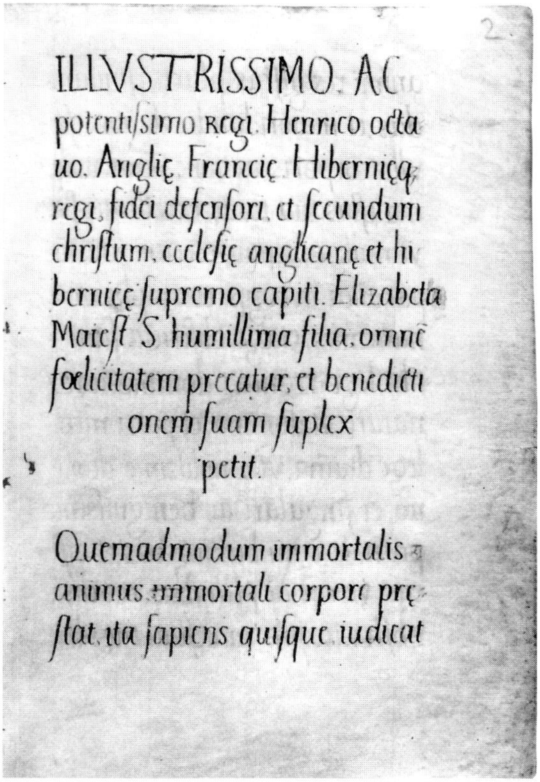
ILLVSTRISSIMO AC
potentissimo regi Henrico octa
uo. Angliæ Franciæ Hiberniæq;
regi, fidei defensori, et secundum
christum, ecclesiæ anglicanæ et hi
berniæ supremo capiti. Elizabeta
Maiest S humillima filia, omnē
foelicitatem precatur, et benedicti
onem suam suplex
petit.
Quemadmodum immortalis
animus immortali corpore præ
stat, ita sapiens quisque iudicat

3 Catherine Parr's Prayers or Meditations, written by Princess Elizabeth (BL, Royal MS 7 D. X, fol. 2r)

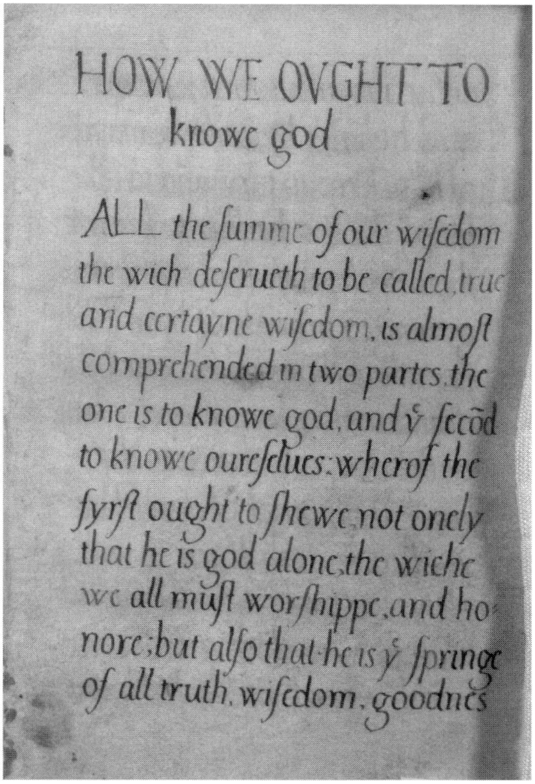
HOW WE OVGHT TO
knowe god
ALL the summe of our wisedom
the wich deserueth to be called true
and certayne wisedom, is almost
comprehended in two partes, the
one is to knowe god, and ye secōd
to knowe ourselues: wherof the
fyrst ought to shewe not onely
that he is god alone, the wiche
we all must worshippe, and ho
nore; but also that he is ye springe
of all truth, wisedom, goodnes

4 Princess Elizabeth's autograph translation of Jean Calvin's *Institution of Christian Religion* (Edinburgh, National Archives of Scotland, RH 13/78, fol. 16r)

surviving letter, written on 31 July 1544, in Italian to her stepmother, Queen Catherine Parr.[45]

Once her debt to Belmain is recognised, then the significance of the change seen in her next known presentation manuscript becomes clear. The last of these four volumes, dedicated to King Edward from Enfield on 30 December, a translation into Italian of Bernardo Ochino's *Sermo de Christo*, shows an unmistakable move away from her old French master, some calligraphic mastery, and considerable skill. The formal italic hand of the letters, complemented by capitals and headings in a red ink, the text within a red-ruled frame, has replaced the unwieldy hand found in the other manuscripts. The volume is usually dated 1547 and if that is correct, then she was no more than fourteen and Ascham had yet to appear on the scene. David Starkey, however, would place it as late as the end of 1552, and on calligraphic grounds, this is probably more or less when

45 Pryor, *Elizabeth I*, pp. 16-17.

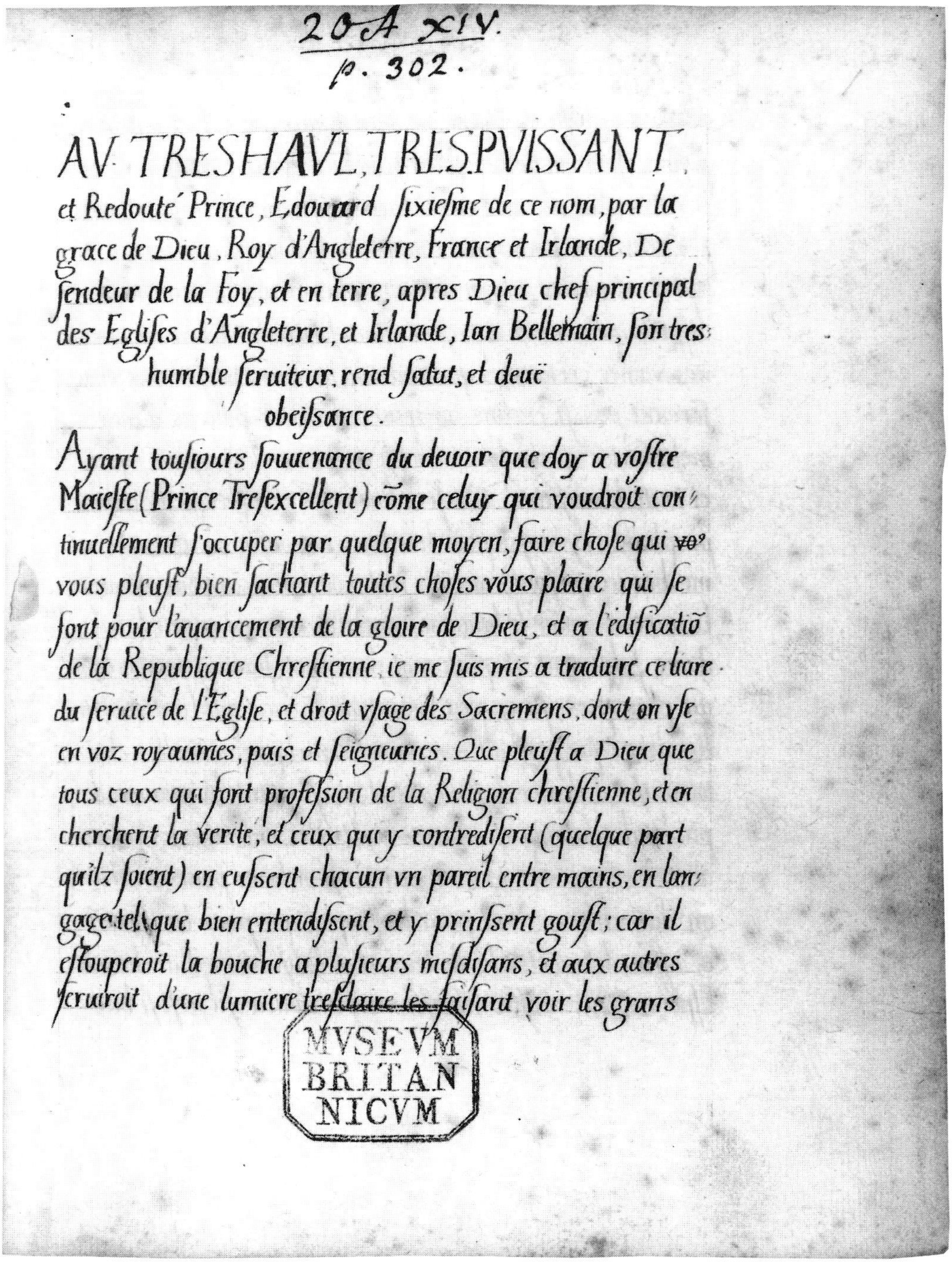
20 A XIV.
p. 302.

AV TRESHAVL, TRESPVISSANT
et Redoute' Prince, Edouard sixiesme de ce nom, par la grace de Dieu, Roy d'Angleterre, France et Irlande, Defendeur de la Foy, et en terre, apres Dieu chef principal des Eglises d'Angleterre, et Irlande, Ian Bellemain, son tres humble seruiteur, rend salut, et deuë obeissance.

Ayant tousiours souuenance du deuoir que doy a vostre Maieste (Prince Tresexcellent) cõme celuy qui voudroit continuellement s'occuper par quelque moyen, faire chose qui vous pleust, bien sachant toutes choses vous plaire qui se font pour l'auancement de la gloire de Dieu, et a l'edificatiõ de la Republique Chrestienne, ie me suis mis a traduire ce liure du seruice de l'Eglise, et droit vsage des Sacremens, dont on vse en voz royaumes, pais et seigneuries. Que pleust a Dieu que tous ceux qui font profession de la Religion chrestienne, et en cherchent la verite, et ceux qui y contredisent (quelque part quilz soient) en eussent chacun vn pareil entre mains, en langage tel que bien entendissent, et y prinssent goust; car il estouperoit la bouche a plusieurs mesdisans, et aux autres seruiroit d'une lumiere tresclaire les faisant voir les grans

MVSEVM BRITANNICVM

5 The first page of Jean Belmain's autograph translation into French of the second Prayer Book of Edward VI (BL, Royal MS 20 A. XIV, fol. 1r)

the manuscript was written (PLATE 6).[46] The hand is closer to the italic of the almost exactly contemporary letters, but shows some distinctive, different forms. One of the most obvious of these is the spacing of the *ct* and *st* ligatures; the *g* forms are unlike those in the letters, the *x* seems to be made of two *c*s back to back rather than two intersecting diagonal strokes, the *e*s are not flourished and some of the *t*s appear to have bars extending very slightly to the left. In other words, Belmain's French italic has given way to Ascham's italic Cambridge hand.

The exact later development of Elizabeth's hand is not easy to reconstruct. What seems to have happened is that at some point, probably due to the pressure of government and business, she developed a much more informal cursive mixed italic and secretary hand. This co-existed with her formal italic hand, especially in signatures, subscriptions, and postscripts, but eventually the looser style of writing took over more or less completely.

This looser mixed cursive can be seen as early as 1563, in a reply to a parliamentary petition concerning her marriage (PLATE 7).[47] The hand here has loosened up a great deal and become almost cursive: the *k* is still distinctive, the flourished terminal *l* looks almost like a majuscule and majuscule *T* is also flourished and written like a *C*. At the same time, there are a number of secretary-hand forms, such as *A*, *e*, *h*, and *s*. The hand is still relatively clear: it would seem that the Queen is correcting and revising a fair copy she has herself made: this accounts for the piece's messy appearance. We can perhaps see her actually in the act of composition a few months earlier in her angry note written at the end of a bill which would allow her government the subsidy only on the condition that the Queen settle the question of the succession (PLATE 8).[48] Similarly, the brief note Elizabeth sent to Burghley on 11 April 1572 deferring the Duke of Norfolk's execution shows her probably composing and writing at the same time: the hand is fairly free, with some initial and final letters quite heavily inked, suggesting pauses for thought or *currente calamo* revision.[49]

There can be no doubt that the quality of her script began to deteriorate, probably from when she acceded to the throne. The obvious inference is that her new responsibilities made her write a great deal more and that her hand suffered, perhaps literally as well as metaphorically. In a French postscript to Henri II of France written on 8 January 1558/9, she says 'My fingers prevent my writing the words with which my heart is full', but it is not clear whether she is speaking figuratively.[50] In the last couple

46 Bodleian, MS Bodl. 6 (SC. 27877); Frederick Chamberlin, *The Private Character of Queen Elizabeth* (1921), pl. opposite p. 21; W. D. Macray, *Annals of the Bodleian Library Oxford*, 2nd edn (Oxford, 1890), pp. 460-1; Starkey, *Elizabeth*, p. 86. A letter to Edward VI, dated in *Elizabeth I: Collected Works*, p. 21, summer or autumn 1548, is written from Enfield.

47 BL, Lansdowne MS 94, fol. 30r; *Elizabeth I: Collected Works*, Speeches 6, pp. 79-80 and plate on p. 78; also reproduced in Pryor, *Elizabeth I*, pp. 42-3.

48 BL, Lansdowne MS 1236, fol. 42r; *Elizabeth I: Collected Works*, Speeches 9D, p. 103; plate in J. E. Neale, *Elizabeth I and her Parliaments 1559-1581* (1953), opposite p. 162.

49 Bodleian, MS Ashmole 1729, fol. 13r, reproduced in *Elizabeth*, ed. Doran, p. 219, and Pryor, *Elizabeth I*, pp. 64-5; *Elizabeth I: Collected Works*, Letters 33, p. 131.

50 Mumby, *The Girlhood of Queen Elizabeth*, p. 294; the postscript is apparently in French, and is cited from Patrick Forbes, *A Full View of the Public Transactions in the Reign of Elizabeth*, 2 vols (London, 1740-1).

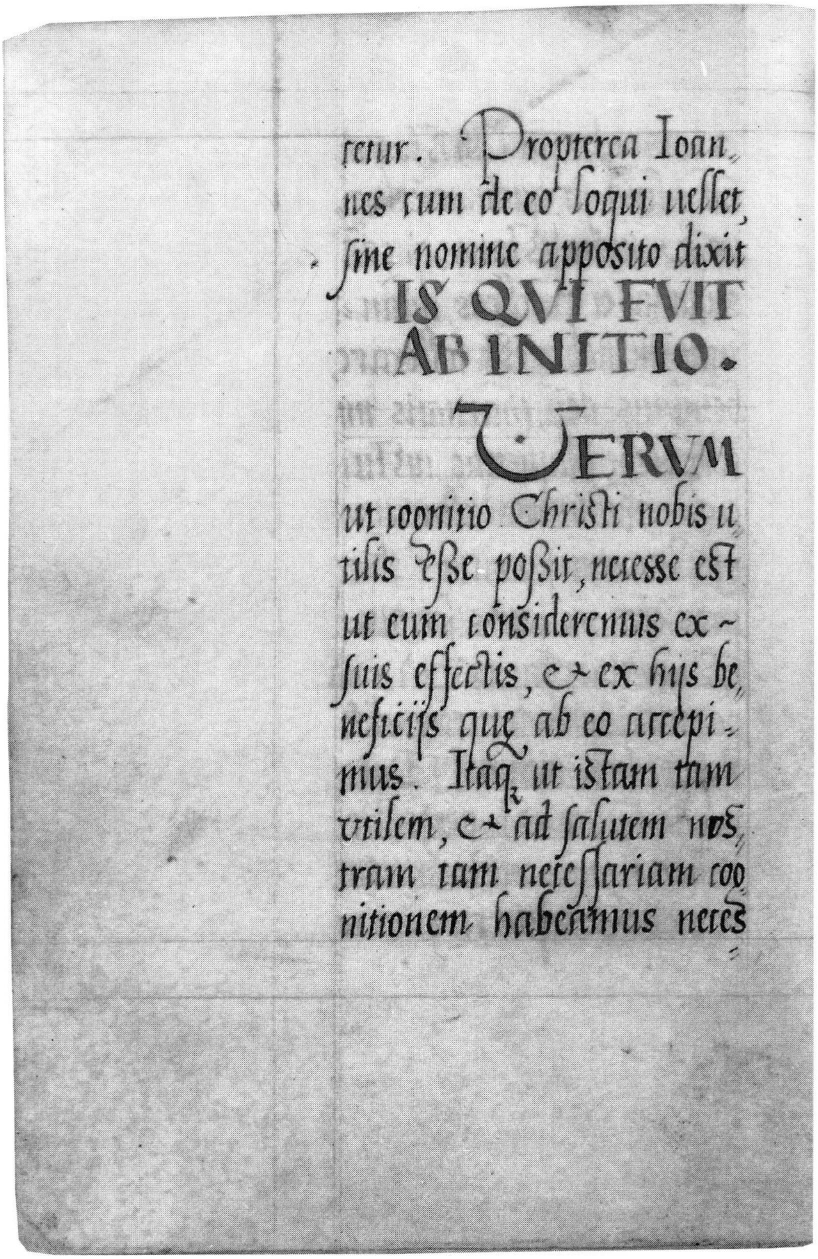
retur. Propterea Ioan-
nes cum de eo loqui nollet,
sine nomine apposito dixit
IS QVI FVIT
AB INITIO.
VERUM
ut cognitio Christi nobis u-
tilis esse possit, necesse est
ut eum consideremus ex
suis effectis, et ex hijs be-
neficijs que ab eo accepi-
mus. Itaque ut istam tam
utilem, et ad salutem nos-
tram tam necessariam cog-
nitionem habeamus neces

6 Princess Elizabeth's autograph translation of Bernardo Ochino's *Sermo de Christo* (Oxford, Bodleian Library, MS Bodl. 6, fol. 4v)

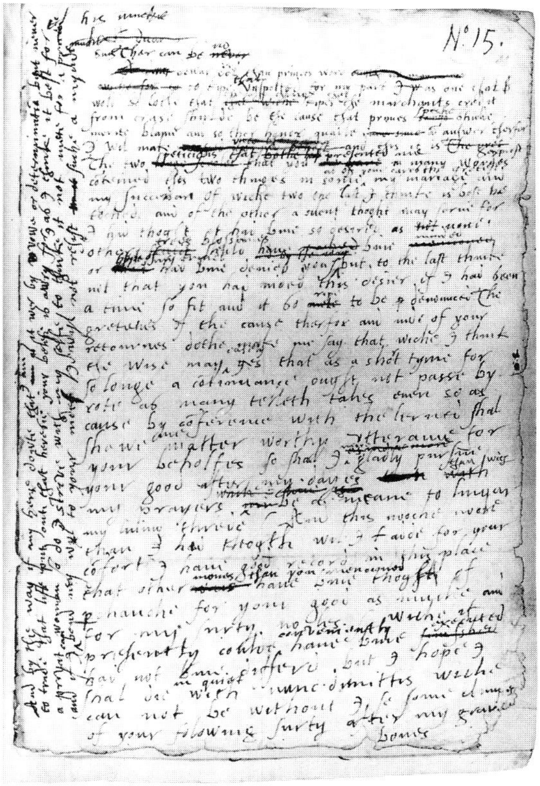

7 Autograph manuscript of Queen Elizabeth's reply to a parliamentary petition, 1563 (BL, Lansdowne MS 94, fol. 30r)

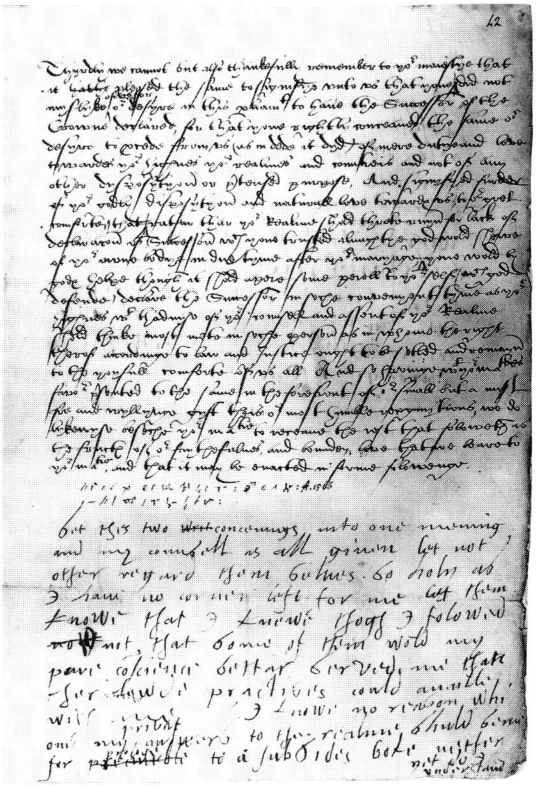

8 Queen Elizabeth's autograph note at the end of a copy of a parliamentary bill (BL, Lansdowne MS 1236, fol. 42r)

of years of her reign she was afflicted with gout and rheumatism. 'I have heard it credibly reported', wrote John Clapham in 1603, 'that, not long before her death, she was divers times troubled with gout in her fingers whereof she would never complain, as seeming better pleased to be thought insensible of the pain than to acknowledge the disease.'[51] What may have been meant figuratively at the beginning of her reign had become literally the case by the end of it.

Autograph materials are relatively scarce for the rest of the 1570s until the Alençon courtship began towards the end of the decade: a few holograph letters at Hatfield survive relating to the affair.[52] In the mid-1580s the correspondence with her cousin James VI of Scotland, preserved in the British Library, supplies rich resources: their family relationship, their royal status, and the nature of the correspondence itself all

51 *Elizabeth of England: Certain Observations Concerning the Life and Reign of Queen Elizabeth by John Clapham*, ed. Evelyn Plummer Read and Conyers Read (Philadelphia & London, 1951), pp. 89-90; *Letters of Queen Elizabeth I*, ed. Harrison, p. 292.

52 See, for example, Pryor, *Elizabeth I*, pp. 72-3.

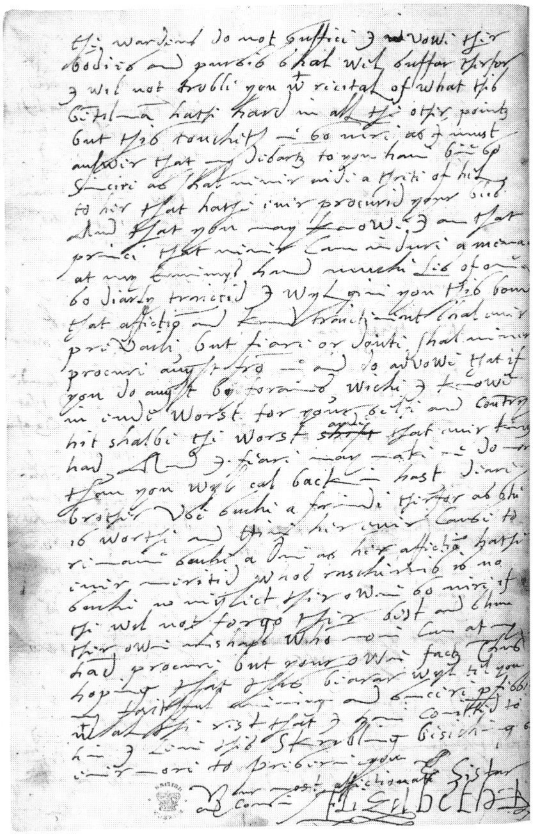

9 Autograph letter by Queen Elizabeth, to James VI of Scotland, May 1594 (BL, Additional MS 23240, fol. 132v)

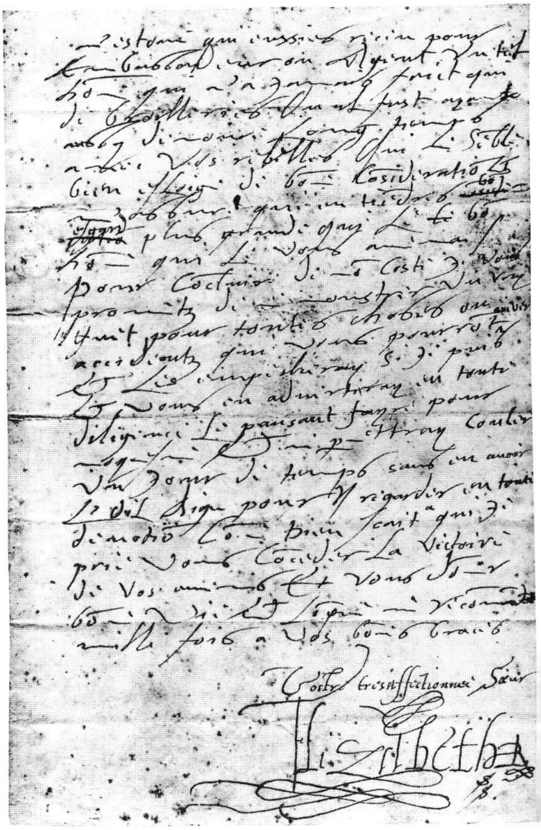

10 Autograph letter by Queen Elizabeth, to Henri IV of France, in French

demanded that the queen should write in her own hand.[53] Yet the hand is constantly in danger of degenerating into a scrawl. Nevertheless, the Queen always seems to have more control of her hand than James VI or his mother have of theirs: to modern eyes James's writing looks distinctly childish. A letter sent to James in May 1594 illustrates some of this: the features and forms noted earlier have become more exaggerated (PLATE 9).[54] What has changed is that the pen has a tendency to move horizontally for some words and letters with almost no vertical movement. Furthermore, the Queen's

53 See BL, Add. MS 23240, and *Letters of Queen Elizabeth and King James VI. of Scotland*, ed. John Bruce, Camden Society, 46 (1849).

54 BL, Add. MS 23240, fol. 132v; *Elizabeth I: Collected Works*, Letters 90, p. 379. A similar letter from the correspondence, dating from about March 1593 (Folger, MS X. d. 397), is illustrated and discussed in Jean F. Preston and Laetitia Yeandle, *English Handwriting 1400-1650: An Introductory Manual* (Binghampton, NY, 1992), pp. 64-6; see also *'The Pen's Excellencie': Treasures from the Manuscript Collection of The Folger Shakespeare Library*, ed. Heather Wolfe (Washington, D.C., 2002), pp. 53-4.

idiosyncratic spellings, such as the terminal *z* for *s* in lines 4 and 6, pose problems of their own. These features, which render her hand hard to read, are further complicated when she writes in French, as she does here to Henri IV of France towards the end of her reign (PLATE 10).[55]

This is the hand that appears in the twenty-seven stanzas in French which Steven W. May and Anne Lake Prescott published from the Hatfield manuscripts.[56] As May and Prescott show this has one further, characteristic feature, the use of a Greek *phi* for the letters *ph*. Some of these idiosyncratic spellings and forms can also be found in her English translations of Boethius's *The Consolation of Philosophy*, made between 10 October and 5 or 8 November 1593, of the first 178 lines of Horace's 'Art of Poetry', and of Plutarch's *De Curiositate*, made in 1598 and now in the National Archives. This sudden and late interest in translation is undoubtedly curious. In the Boethius most of the metres are autograph, but the proses are scribal and have been identified as in the hand of Thomas Windebank, who seems to have taken them down from dictation.[57] If this division of labour does point to dictation, it was a habit the Queen was known to favour. As evidence of this there is the famous pair of letters, preserved among the Harington family papers, which 'the Queene's Majesty *wrote*, whylest she gave instructions for the other that followith, and hearing a tale which she made answer unto'.[58]

Yet it is important to note that the Queen's own hand could vary a great deal. If we look again at the subscription to the letter to Henri IV, it is clear that the Queen has by no means lost her ability to write an italic hand. In fact, if one looks through her correspondence she regularly wrote the subscription, or the address, or a further few lines, or a combination of the three, in her formal italic hand. There is a good early example of this in the *Collected Works*: a scribal letter dated 25 June 1577 to the Earl and Countess of Shrewsbury with a fine italic autograph addition – a subscription as a superscription.[59] This is what makes me revise my initial belief that the prayer on the Azores expedition in July 1597, the very last item in the *Collected Works*, is scribal, to

55 Unlocated: the plate comes from the Sotheby's sale catalogue, 12 June 1911, of the Huth collection of Autograph Letters, lot 66; the letter, probably dating from the 1590s, sold for £365. For a similar letter in French to Henri IV of about the same date, see '*The Pen's Excellencie*', ed. Wolfe, pp. 51-2, 233-5: this letter is Folger, MS V. b. 131.

56 Hatfield House, Cecil Papers 147, fols 207r-13r: Steven W. May and Anne Lake Prescott, 'The French Verses of Elizabeth I (Text)', *English Literary Renaissance*, 24 (1994), 9-43; *Elizabeth I: Collected Works*, Poems 15, pp. 412-21.

57 *Queen Elizabeth's Englishings*, ed. Caroline Pemberton, Early English Text Society, OS 113 (1899), p. xi; see also Pryor, *Elizabeth I*, pp. 112-13, and for a page, with prose and verse entirely in a scribal hand, Maria Perry, *The Word of a Princess: A Life of Elizabeth I from Contemporary Documents* (Woodbridge, 1990), p. 299. For a political reading of these translations, see Kevin Sharpe, 'The King's Writ: Royal Authors and Royal Authority in Early Modern England', in *Remapping Early Modern England: The Culture of Seventeenth-Century Politics* (Cambridge, 2000), 127-50, esp. pp. 131-4; the essay also appeared in *Culture and Politics in Early Stuart England*, ed. Kevin Sharpe and Peter Lake (London, 1994).

58 *Nugæ Antiquæ: Being a Miscellaneous Collection of Original Papers by Sir John Harington*, ed. Henry Harington and Thomas Park, 2 vols (London, 1804), I, 115-18.

59 London, Lambeth Palace Library, MS 3206, fol. 819r; *Elizabeth I: Collected Works*, Letters 41, p. 28.

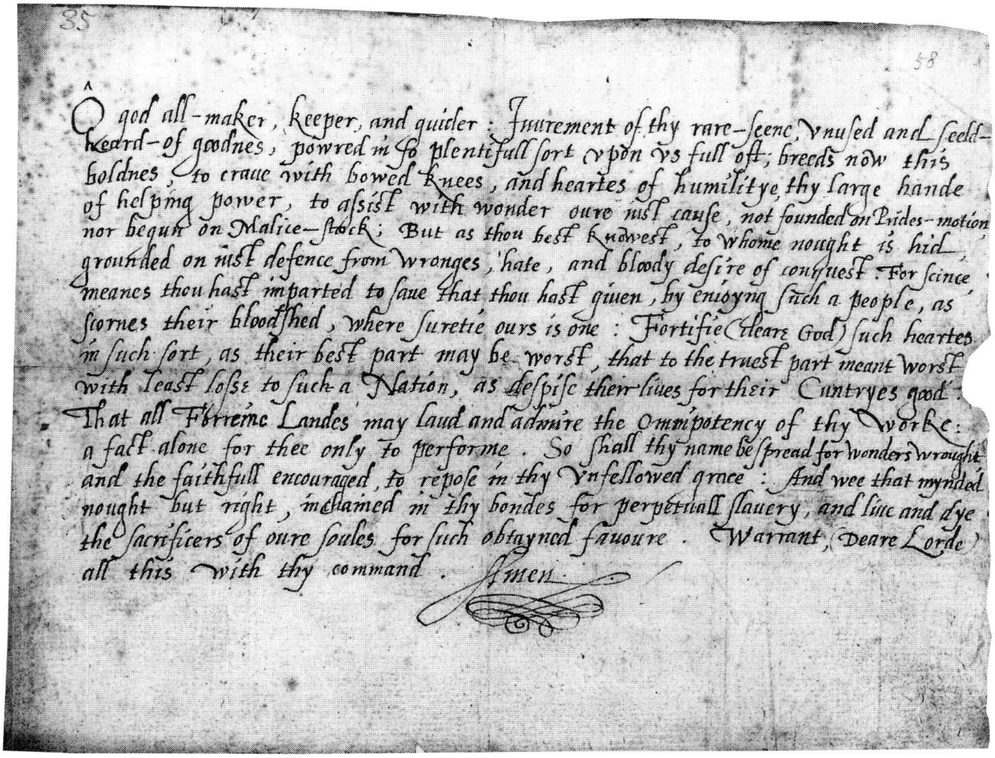
85 58

O god all-maker, keeper, and guider: Inurement of thy rare-seene, vnused and seeld-heard-of goodnes, powred in so plentifull sort vpon vs full oft; breeds now this boldnes, to craue with bowed knees, and heartes of humilitye, thy large hande of helping power, to assist with wonder oure iust cause, not founded on Prides-motion nor begun on Malice-stock; But as thou best knowest, to whome nought is hid, grounded on iust defence from wronges, hate, and bloody desire of conquest. For scince meanes thou hast imparted to saue that thou hast giuen, by enioying such a people, as scornes their bloodshed, where suretie ours is one: Fortifie (deare God) such heartes in such sort, as their best part may be worst, that to the truest part meant worst with least losse to such a Nation, as despise their liues for their Cuntryes good. That all Forreine Landes may laud and admire the Omnipotency of thy worke: a fact alone for thee only to performe. So shall thy name be spread for wonders wrought and the faithfull encouraged, to repose in thy vnfellowed grace: And wee that mynded nought but right, inchained in thy bondes for perpetuall slauery, and liue and dye the sacrificers of oure soules for such obtayned fauoure. Warrant, (Deare Lorde) all this with thy command. Amen

11 Prayer possibly by Queen Elizabeth on the Azores expedition (BL, Harley MS 6986, fol. 58r)

being almost but not quite willing to believe that it is autograph (PLATE 11).[60] The difficulty with this piece is that although some of the letter-forms are superficially like her italic hand, on closer examination they are not; the final flourish at the end of 'Amen' is also uncharacteristic, and the prayer has none of the Queen's distinctive orthographic forms.

If an element of doubt lingers here, it is almost possible to be resolved of all ambiguities in one final case. This is in relation to a little prayer-book (about three by two inches), containing prayers in English (two of these), French, Italian, Latin, and Greek, each one copied in an appropriate hand (PLATE 12). It was beautifully written, with majuscules decorated in gold, and was supplied by Nicholas Hilliard with miniatures of the Queen and her suitor the Duc d'Alençon. Unfortunately, the manuscript has been lost for the past century or so, and its appearance is known only from a facsimile made by its then owner, J. W. Whitehead, in 1893. The facsimile on vellum was supposed to be limited to only forty copies; there is a copy in the BL Department

60 BL, Harley MS 6986, fol. 58r; *Elizabeth I: Collected Works*, Prayers 39, pp. 426-7; Fairbank and Wolpe, p. 82 and pl. 55.

of Manuscripts, which did not acquire it until 1916. The prayers are certainly composed as if to be said by the Queen, with references to her reign, her subjects, her royal status, the throne, sceptre, and crown, and have been printed and discussed as hers. For example, the editors of the *Collected Works* print all the prayers (in translation) as hers and describe the manuscript as 'in Elizabeth's own hand'.[61] The author of the most scholarly article on this volume, William P. Haugaard, is more cautious about who wrote the manuscript: he wonders 'if, in the midst of the pressures of her office, she would have sought her recreation in such painstaking handwork', and goes on to suggest that 'Perhaps she assigned that task to a clerk of her chapel staff or to one of her ladies-in-waiting with the requisite talent'. He is more certain that she composed the prayers, on the basis of 'their highly personal character and their distinctive style', and because there is no evidence that she did not compose them. The argument of his whole account of the *Book of Devotions*, as the volume is generally known, is that it supplies 'A Neglected Clue to the Queen's Life and Character'.[62]

I have had doubts about the hand of the *Book* for some time.[63] It is hard to know whether the hand that wrote the prayers in English, Italian, and Latin was also responsible for the prayers in French and Greek, but the main hand of the manuscript was certainly not the Queen's. Instead, it can be associated with a Cambridge academic called John Palmer. He was educated at Westminster School, went up to Trinity College, Cambridge, in 1575, became a fellow in 1582, a royal chaplain, Archdeacon of Ely ten years later, and died in 1614. In the 1580s and 1590s he wrote official letters on behalf of the university and may have been the man of that name who contributed verses to the Cambridge memorial volume for Sir Philip Sidney.[64] (His *alter ego* was a slightly older man, who was at St John's, where he was a noted actor, and became Master of Magdalene and Dean of Peterborough; he was accused of stripping the lead from the roof of his cathedral, and died in gaol in 1607, a prisoner for debt.) In one of the younger John Palmer's most elaborate productions, a letter to Burghley dated 2 September 1581 seeking his aid to secure a Trinity fellowship, it is possible to see several features reminiscent of the *Book of Devotions* (PLATE 13).[65] Among these are

61 BL, MS Facsimile 218; *Elizabeth I: Collected Works*, Prayers 30-5, p. 311, n.1.

62 William P. Haugaard, 'Elizabeth Tudor's *Book of Devotions*: A Neglected Clue to the Queen's Life and Character', *Sixteenth Century Journal*, 12 (1981), 79-105 (p. 81). Patrick Collinson, 'Windows in a Woman's Soul: Questions about the Religion of Queen Elizabeth I', in his *Elizabethan Essays* (London & Rio Grande, Ohio, 1994), pp. 90-2, discusses the volume and seems at first sceptical that it is autograph or the prayers her own, but concedes that it is 'very probable that these were Queen Elizabeth's own prayers'. Susan Doran, 'Elizabeth I's Religion', pp. 699-700, 720, discusses the volume and concludes 'Whether or not the queen wrote the prayers within it herself is immaterial; they expressed a Protestant faith and religious outlook she evidently held.'

63 Helen Hackett, *Virgin Mother, Maiden Queen* (London, 1995), p. 253, n.71.

64 Both men appear in *ODNB*, in John Venn and J. A. Venn, *Alumni Cantabrigienses*, pt 1 from the Earliest Times to 1751, 4 vols (Cambridge, 1922-7), III, 300; Charles Henry Cooper and Thompson Cooper, *Athenæ Cantabrigienses*, 2 vols (Cambridge, 1861), II, 457-8. Palmer's hand is illustrated and discussed in Fairbank and Dickins, *Italic Hand in Tudor Cambridge*, p. 27 and pl. 24, and in Fairbank and Wolpe, p. 80 and pl. 51; a further example of his hand is BL, Lansdowne MS 45, fol. 121r. For the verses on Sidney, see *Lachrymæ* (Cambridge, 1587), sigs C2^{v}-3^{r}.

65 BL, Lansdowne MS 33, fol. 74r; Fairbank and Wolpe, p. 80 and pl. 51; see also BL, Lansdowne MS 45, fol. 121r, and Fairbank and Dickins, *Italic Hand in Tudor Cambridge*, pl. 24.

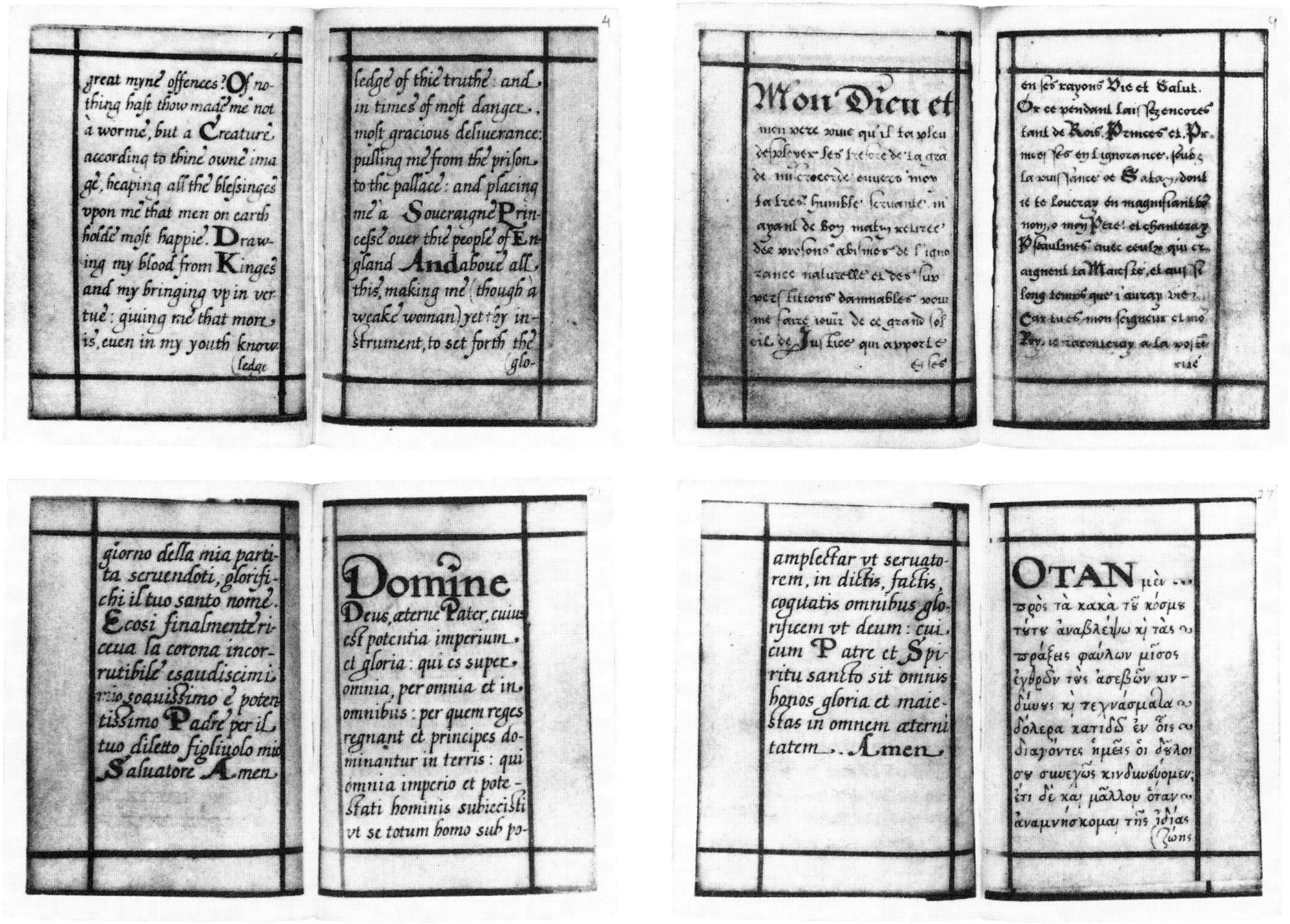

12 Four openings from the *Book of Devotions* possibly by John Palmer (BL, MS Facsimile 218, fols 3v-4r, 8v-9r, 20v-21r, 26v-27r)

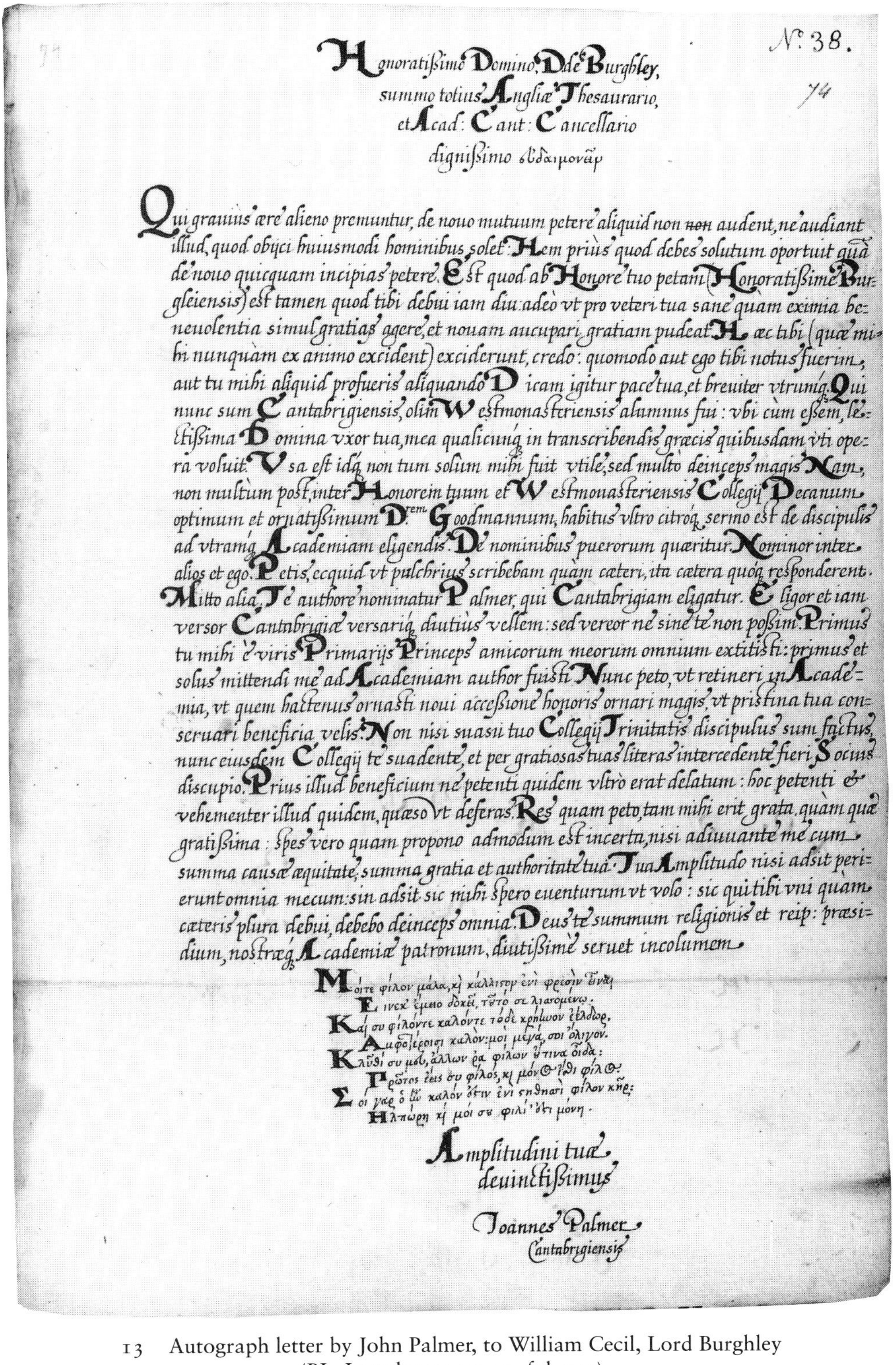

Honoratissimo Domino, D. de Burghley,
summo totius Angliae Thesaurario,
et Acad: Cant: Cancellario
dignissimo εὐδαιμονεῖν

Qui grauius aere alieno premuntur, de nouo mutuum petere aliquid non ~~non~~ audent, ne audiant illud, quod obijci huiusmodi hominibus solet: Hem prius quod debes solutum oportuit quam de nouo quicquam incipias petere. Est quod ab Honore tuo petam (Honoratissime Burgleiensis) est tamen quod tibi debui iam diu: adeo vt pro veteri tua sane quam eximia beneuolentia simul gratias agere, et nouam aucupari gratiam pudeat. Haec tibi (quae mihi nunquam ex animo excident) exciderunt, credo: quomodo aut ego tibi notus fuerim, aut tu mihi aliquid profueris aliquando. Dicam igitur pace tua, et breuiter vtrumque. Qui nunc sum Cantabrigiensis, olim Westmonasteriensis alumnus fui: vbi cum essem, lectissima Domina vxor tua, mea qualicunque in transcribendis graecis quibusdam vti opera voluit. Vsa est idque non tum solum mihi fuit vtile, sed multo deinceps magis. Nam, non multum post, inter Honorem tuum et Westmonasteriensis Collegij Decanum optimum et ornatissimum D.rem Goodmannum, habitus vltro citroque sermo est de discipulis ad vtramque Academiam eligendis. De nominibus puerorum quaeritur. Nominor inter alios et ego. Petis, ecquid vt pulchrius scribebam quam caeteri, ita caetera quoque responderent. Mitto alia. Te authore nominatur Palmer, qui Cantabrigiam eligatur. Eligor et iam versor Cantabrigiae versarique diutius vellem: sed vereor ne sine te non possim. Primus tu mihi e viris Primarijs Princeps amicorum meorum omnium extitisti: primus et solus mittendi me ad Academiam author fuisti. Nunc peto, vt retineri in Academia, vt quem hactenus ornasti noui accessione honoris ornari magis, vt pristina tua conseruari beneficia velis. Non nisi suasu tuo Collegij Trinitatis discipulus sum factus, nunc eiusdem Collegij te suadente, et per gratiosas tuas literas intercedente fieri Socius discupio. Prius illud beneficium ne petenti quidem vltro erat delatum: hoc petenti et vehementer illud quidem, quaeso vt deferas. Res quam peto, tam mihi erit grata, quam quae gratissima: spes vero quam propono admodum est incerta, nisi adiuuante me cum summa causae aequitate, summa gratia et authoritate tua. Tua Amplitudo nisi adsit perierunt omnia mecum: sin adsit sic mihi spero euenturum vt volo: sic qui tibi vni quam caeteris plura debui, debebo deinceps omnia. Deus te summum religionis et reip: praesidium, nostraeque Academiae patronum, diutissime seruet incolumem.

Μοῖτε φίλον μάλα, καὶ κάλλιστον ἐνὶ φρεσὶν εἶναι
Εἵνεκ' ἐμεῖο δοκεῖ, τοῦτο σε λισσόμενος.
Καὶ σὺ φιλοῦντε καλοῦντε τόδε χρήιζων ἔελδωρ.
Ἀμφοτέροισι καλόν· μοὶ μέγα, σοὶ ὀλίγον.
Κλῦθι σύ μευ, ἄλλων γὰρ φίλων οὔτινα οἶδα·
Πρῶτος ἐεὶς σὺ φίλος, καὶ μόνος ἴσθι φίλος.
Σοὶ γὰρ ὁ ἐμῶν καλόν ἐστιν ἐνὶ στήθεσσι φίλον κῆρ·
Ἠλπώρη καὶ μοί σὺ φίλ' ἔστι μόνη.

Amplitudini tuae
deuinctissimus

Joannes Palmer
Cantabrigiensis

13 Autograph letter by John Palmer, to William Cecil, Lord Burghley
(BL, Lansdowne MS 33, fol. 74r)

the ligatures, the flourished and clubbed terminal *e* and *s* – the clubbed ascenders and descenders are unusually early – the 'open' *D* and *P*, as well as the form of the *E*. Above all the gilt decoration of the capitals in the letters looks very like the decoration in the manuscript. I am not a competent judge, but the Greek scripts in both pieces look similar to me. The French one is more puzzling.

Alfred Fairbank and Berthold Wolpe thought Palmer might have been a pupil of the writing-master Peter Bales, who seems to have begun his career at Oxford. Bales was back in London by 1575 and might have taught Palmer while he was still a pupil at Westminster.[66] There are some similarities between Bales's hands and Palmer's, but they do not seem particularly closely related.

Of course, it is one thing to suggest, with all the usual hesitations and qualifications and with the added caution of the difficulty of an attribution based on a facsimile, that Palmer may have written the prayers – or some of the prayers – in the *Book of Devotions*, and quite another to decide what are the implications of this. The presence of the Hilliard miniature of Alençon suggests that the volume must have been bound before the end of the courtship in 1582.[67] The prayers could have been composed any time before then, but the volume as a whole looks as if it was prepared in the late 1570s or early 1580s in connection with the courtship. It may in fact be the 'book of gold with claspes all garnished ouer with small Diamonds & Rubies, hauing the Picture of Queen Elizabeth & of Mounsieur in it, with a booke of Praiers written in parchment', which appears in an inventory of Queen Anne's jewels. If it is this and is identical, as Jane Lawson suggests, with the 'litle boke of golde' in an elaborate binding 'with a ring of golde to hang it by' which Robert Dudley, Earl of Leicester, gave the Queen as a New Year's gift in 1582, then the origins of the manuscript become slightly less obscure.[68] In these circumstances, it seems rather unlikely that the prayers in Leicester's gift were written by the Queen herself: just as literary scholars now take it for granted that the 'I' of poems or sonnet sequences should not necessarily be identified with the author ('I am not I: pity the tale of me'), it is possible to argue that these prayers could have been composed using an authorial persona.

Although its precise significance is hard to determine, the small book of prayers, with its portraits of monarch and suitor, presumably played a part in the complicated relations between Leicester and the Queen during the Alençon courtship. Leicester's choice of scribe for the volume (if it was his and his choice) is puzzling. Palmer was an obscure and very young Cambridge student or don: his hand is quite good, but there were better writing-masters in London. If no certain link can be made between Palmer and the Earl, the key to the volume perhaps lies in finding some sort of association between the miniaturist Hilliard and the volume's scribe. One can be made, but it takes us back to Bales, Palmer's putative teacher, who is known to have been associated with Hilliard, but only for certain as late as 1617.[69]

66 Woudhuysen, *Sir Philip Sidney*, pp. 32-3.
67 Haugaard, 'Elizabeth Tudor's *Book of Devotions*', p. 96.
68 See below, p. 147.
69 Woudhuysen, *Sir Philip Sidney*, pp. 35-6. A 'Mr Palmer' was paid the relatively large sum of £20 on 15 June 1585 'at [h]is going into Scotland' as part of the diplomatic campaign to influence James VI: see

The humanist court culture in which Elizabeth learned to write and then practised her penmanship left her with a considerable interest in the subject. In contemporary images she was never depicted writing, but she was presumably right-handed.[70] In her progresses and public entertainments, she does not seem to have written anything in the general sight of her subjects. It is possible that her courtiers and foreign ambassadors, as well as her government staff, observed her set pen to paper, but instances of her writing in front of others seem rare. In about 1600 Robert Sidney described the aged Queen's behaviour: 'she walketh out but little, meditates much alone, and sometimes writes in private to her best friends'.[71] On the other hand, her calligraphic ability seems to have been recognised in her own lifetime. For example, Paul Hentzner in 1598 noted among the books on display in the royal library at Whitehall a translation into French by the Queen, when princess, of Erasmus's *Dialogus fidei*, dedicated to her father.[72] In the same place Hentzner saw two small and beautifully made silver cabinets in which the Queen kept her paper, and which she used for writing-boxes ('*Cistae duae* sive arculae *argenteae* magna arte elaboratae, in quas Regina papyrum reponere, & ijs ceu atramentarijs, uti solet'). On at least one occasion the Queen was given a silver-gilt standish, with boxes for ink, dust, and counters as a New Year's Day gift.[73] On another she was given a chair, two long and two short cushions, and 'a wrytynge borde'; these made up a matching set, for they were all covered in purple velvet and were presumably designed to make writing more comfortable for the Queen. Over the years, she also received a number of writing-tables of various types, but these were probably of more decorative than practical use.[74] In these circumstances, her interest in writing was more publicly acknowledged. She can be associated, for example, with two books produced by professional writing-masters. A copy in a gilt armorial binding of Clemens Perret, *Exercitatio alphabetica nova* ([Antwerp], 1569) in London, the Victoria and Albert Museum, may have been presented to her; it was later claimed on Perret's behalf that, as her secretary, he taught the Queen to write the italic hand and that she rewarded him with a pension of about one hundred pounds.[75] Perret was born in about 1551 and was dead by 1591, so any possible instruction he gave the Queen was almost certainly during the 1570s or 1580s.

Household Accounts and Disbursement Books of Robert Dudley, Earl of Leicester, 1558-1561, 1584-1586, ed. Simon Adams, Camden Society, 5th Ser., 6 (1995), p. 263.

70 On the symbolism connected with her using her hands, see Julia M. Walker, 'Bones of Contention: Posthumous Images of Elizabeth and Stuart Politics', in *Dissing Elizabeth: Negative Representations of Gloriana*, ed. Julia M. Walker (Durham, NC, & London, 1998), 252-76 (pp. 263-5).

71 *Nugæ Antiquæ*, ed. T. Park, I, 314.

72 Paul Hentzner, *Itinerarium Germaniae, Galliae, Angliae, Italiae* (Nuremberg, 1612), sig. Q4^r; *England as seen by Foreigners in the days of Elizabeth and James the First*, ed. William Brenchley Rye (London, 1865), pp. 133, 165, 171, 282. See also *The Diary of Baron Waldstein a Traveller in Elizabethan England*, trans. and ed. G. W. Groos (London, 1981), p. 51.

73 See John Nichols, *The Progresses and Public Processions of Queen Elizabeth*, new edn, 3 vols (London, 1823), II, 53; the gift came from Elizabeth Dale, the wife of Valentine Dale, the Master of Requests, in 1576-7.

74 For the writing-board, see the 1581 New Year's Gift roll, Eton College MS 192: *OED* records the word from *c.*1440. Nichols records the writing tables in *The Progresses and Public Processions of Queen Elizabeth*, II, 250, 452, III, 13, and cf. II, 1.

75 Woudhuysen, *Sir Philip Sidney*, p. 32, n.14.

At around the same time the scribe William Teshe thought that a handwritten, illustrated and coloured copy of John Baildon and Jean de Beauchesne's printed writing manual, the first in English, would make a good gift for the Queen.[76] Later in her reign, an obscure scribe called Jeremy Delahay also seems to have thought an album of ornamental writing in gilt and colours, with decorated grotesque initials, would make a suitable gift for her.[77]

In an age where diplomacy relied heavily on what was written by hand, she was also concerned with the practical difficulties caused by bad handwriting. On 4 June 1565 Adam Zwetkovich, Baron von Mitterburg, wrote to the Emperor Maximilian II from London about his interview with the Queen the previous May. The subject was her proposed imperial marriage, and the ambassador tried to smooth over current difficulties about which of his grandchildren the Queen was to marry, by explaining that the previous Emperor Ferdinand I 'had consequent upon his great age erroneously written the name of Ferdinand instead of Charles' in a recent letter. The Queen, to coin a phrase, was not amused, and 'here rejoined that she had seen many bad handwritings, but that none had caused her so much discomfort as that of the late Emperor'.[78]

But it was her own bad and deteriorating handwriting which caused her some unhappiness. As early as 1563 she referred to 'my scribbling hand', and went on throughout her reign to end her letters with apologies for 'these scribbled lines', 'so rude scribbling', 'too long scribbling', 'my tedious scribbling', her 'scribbling in haste', 'suche skribled Lines', and in one of her last letters, written in January 1603, to 'my skrating hand', the obsolete form of the verb 'to scrat' or scratch.[79] 'And thus I leave to molest your eyes with my scribbling', she wrote six months earlier. And she refers often to what she describes as 'my pen's labour', 'My pen ... so long dry', and her pen's touching paper. All this might well seem to modern readers to be merely a modesty trope, but there is evidence that her handwriting did cause her subjects great difficulties. When she sent Charles Blount, Lord Mountjoy, an encouraging letter, Robert Cecil enclosed a fair copy with it 'lest you cannot read it'.[80]

This contrasts with the considerable elegance and absolute clarity of her earlier penmanship. In the conclusion to *A godly medytacyon of the christen sowle*, John Bale had reported in 1548 that Elizabeth sent him sentences written in four different

76 Woudhuysen, *Sir Philip Sidney*, pp. 31-2.

77 BL, Royal MS 17 A. XXVIII; Delahay gives his address as 'by the Artillerie yard neere Bishopsgate streete'.

78 *Queen Elizabeth and Some Foreigners*, ed. Victor von Klarwill, trans. T. H. Nash (London, 1928), p. 215.

79 *Letters of Queen Elizabeth I*, ed. Harrison, pp. 46, 164, 202, 224, 240, 288, and Preston and Yeandle, *English Handwriting 1400-1650*, p. 64. For the 'skrating' hand (Harrison, p. 288), see Wilfrid Blunt, *Sweet Roman Hand* (London, 1952), fig. 23b on p. 23, and Pryor, *Elizabeth I*, pp. 128-9; the original is BL, Add. MS 18738, fol. 40v. *OED* cites this usage, without identifying the author, in scrat *v.* (scratting *vbl. sb.* and *ppl. a*). In an earlier letter to James VI, written in July 1593, she apologises for molesting his eyes with 'my scrattinge': see *Letters of Queen Elizabeth and King James VI. of Scotland*, ed. John Bruce, p. 84. Similar apologies for scribbled letters can also be found in Catherine Parr's correspondence: see *Letters of the Queens of England 1100-1547*, ed. Anne Crawford (Far Thrupp, Stroud, 1994), pp. 216, 220.

80 *Elizabeth I: Collected Works*, Letters 101, p. 403, copy; *Letters of Queen Elizabeth I*, ed. Harrison, pp. 125, 192, 218, 289.

languages: 'The written clauses are these, whych she wrote first with her owne hande moch more fynely than I coulde with anye prentynge letter set them fourth.'[81] Her hand was finer and by implication more legible than what was possible in print. Of course, some of this could be put down to the familiar strategies of royal panegyric, but there is something more to it than this. It is that sense that what is written is somehow deeply personal, that it conveys presence, and that the private writings of public individuals, especially divinely ordained royal ones, are particularly powerful.[82] The idea of the Queen's own hand was an important one, conveying intimacy as well as authority. That phrase occurs again and again in relation to her correspondence, and she used it herself on some occasions such as in 1572 on one of the letters to Burghley staying the execution of the Duke of Norfolk.[83] In 1597 the French ambassador De Maisse reported that she: 'signs with her own hand at the head of the *placet* or the *request* which is presented to her; and none dare on peril of life counterfeit her signature, not even the Secretary of State'.[84]

A document signed by her or a letter entirely written by her were precious possessions, but to own one of her writings was exceptional. John Harington was involved in the theft of one of her most famous poems. He sent a lady a copy of 'a precious jewel', Queen Elizabeth's poem 'The doubt of future foes'. 'Lady Wiloughby', he said: 'did covertly get it on her Majesties tablet, and had much hazard in so doing; for the Queen did find out the thief, and chid [her] for spreading evil bruit of her writing such toyes'.[85] Compositions by the Queen and in her own hand were bound to be treated in some sense as precious relics. Yet the reasons for, and the course of, the actual decline of her hand into what Sir Edward Maunde Thompson called 'the well-known straggling scrawl that confronts us in her letters written as queen' remain largely unexplored.[86]

The development of Queen Elizabeth's writing shows how radically a hand can change. In another context, perhaps few people would recognise that the same person produced her late scribbling and her childish italic. Her handwriting shows the constant importance of bearing in mind or trying to reconstruct the circumstances under which

81 Cf. Shell, *Elizabeth's Glass*, p. 95.

82 On these subjects, see Harold Love, *Scribal Publication in Seventeenth-Century England* (Oxford, 1993), esp. pp. 141-8, 160-73.

83 *Letters of Queen Elizabeth I*, ed. Harrison, pp. xiii, 104, 309, 311, 312 (*bis*); *Elizabeth I: Collected Works*, Letters 88, p. 372. Cf. *The Memoirs of Robert Carey*, ed. F. H. Mares (Oxford, 1972), p. 17, 'She delivered me a letter, written with her own hand to my Lord', and Mumby, *The Girlhood of Queen Elizabeth*, p. 169, Bedingfield to the Council, 20 September 1554, 'her Grace did write with her own hand'.

84 *De Maisse: A Journal of All that was Accomplished by Monsieur de Maisse Ambassador in England from King Henri IV to Queen Elizabeth Anno Domini 1597*, trans. and ed. G. B. Harrison and R. A. Jones (1931), p. 88.

85 *The Arundel Harington Manuscript of Tudor Poetry*, ed. Ruth Hughey, 2 vols (Columbus, Ohio, 1960), II, 388; the original of the letter does not survive. This seems to mean that Lady Willoughby got or put on a writing tablet of some kind or a small volume which might be worn as a piece of jewellery, containing the text of the poem. Cf. Woudhuysen, *Sir Philip Sidney*, p. 35.

86 'Handwriting' in *Shakespeare's England: An Account of the Life and Manners of his Age*, 2 vols (Oxford, 1917), I, 288.

a document of any kind was written. The example of the *Book of Devotions* suggests that one ought to try to draw a careful distinction between what is written and what is composed. Few literary critics continue to believe in an entirely innocent 'I', and scholars looking at documents which are generally thought of as non-literary – recipes, journals, tracts, and even prayers – should perhaps bear that sceptical approach in mind. These matters run the risk, of course, of being ideologically determined. In the magnificent catalogue of the even more magnificent collection of autographs formed in the second half of the nineteenth century by Alfred Morrison there is a letter from Queen Elizabeth to Catherine de'Medici. It is undated but carefully and quite beautifully written in an italic hand; it is rather more elaborately flourished than the Queen's own hand sometimes is, but it could be entirely by her. The catalogue describes the letter as written and signed by Ascham, and dates it 1574 with a question-mark; this is puzzling since Ascham had been in his grave for six or so years by then. It is almost as if the cataloguer took it for granted that such a piece of calligraphy was beyond a woman's ability and it had to be written by a man.[87]

It is hard for anyone who is interested in manuscripts of the English Renaissance not to hear that first line 'Why do I use my paper, ink and pen', probably by Henry Walpole, almost every time they open a handwritten volume.[88] People interested in handwriting are mainly concerned with ink and pen, which could be said to represent – in reverse order – the contents of what is written and the form of the script in which it is written. But what of paper? If scholars and historians wish to date Elizabeth's letters, then watermarks and groups of watermarks can supply an essential piece of evidence. The pieces written within Catherine Parr's humanist circle by Elizabeth and Edward share a number of related marks. When she was Queen, Elizabeth apparently became the first person in England to have a personalised watermark in the paper she used.[89] It was made by John Spilman, a German goldsmith to the Queen, who is known to have been producing paper at his mill on the river Darent in a royal manor at Dartford, Kent, in 1588, an event commemorated by Thomas Churchyard in a celebratory poem. The next year, Spilman was granted a royal patent for eight years giving him a monopoly of paper-making. When that ended in 1597, he was granted another patent, this time for fourteen years, which permitted him to make white writing-paper. James I knighted him when he visited the mill in 1605.[90]

87 A. W. Thibaudeau, *Catalogue of the Collection of Autograph Letters and Historical Documents Formed between 1865 and 1882 by Alfred Morrison*, 6 vols (London, 1883-92), II, 78 and plate 70. The attribution to Ascham is noted on the plate itself and on the errata leaf, p. 361. The reference to Mauvissière in the letter suggests a date of 1566 when he visited this country and went to Scotland.

88 For the poem and its authorship, see Louise Imogen Guiney, *Recusant Poets: I. Saint Thomas More to Ben Jonson* (London & New York, 1939), No. 58.

89 George Walton Williams, *The Craft of Printing and the Publication of Shakespeare's Works* (Washington, D.C., London & Toronto, 1985), pl. 21; Pryor, *Elizabeth I*, endpapers and pp. 9, 142; and cf. Edward Heawood, 'Sources of Early English Paper-Supply: II. The Sixteenth Century', *The Library*, 4th Ser., 10 (1929-30), 427-54 (p. 443 and fig. 146).

90 Dard Hunter, *Papermaking: The History and Technique of an Ancient Craft*, 2nd edn (London, 1956), pp. 119-21. For further indications of the range of Spilman's papers, numbering perhaps as many as eight, see Allan Stevenson, 'Tudor Roses from John Tate', *Studies in Bibliography*, 20 (1967), 15-34 (pp. 25-6). I hope to write more fully on Spilman and his papers at a later date.

It is his paper which is used in the 1592 translation of Cicero (Bodleian, MS Bodl. 900) along with 'a crowned eagle looking left with wings spread within a shield-shaped border'.[91] I have not found the ER watermark in letters generally dated before August 1588 or after October 1594, but the subject needs further investigation.[92] One additional reason which makes me continue to have doubts about the Azores prayer is that it is on paper with a common-or-garden pot watermark. The paper on which works are written deserves close attention and may have a great deal to reveal about the circumstances in which manuscripts were made.

91 This is similar to Charles Moise Briquet, *Les Filigranes: Dictionnaire Historique des Marques du Papier, The New Briquet – Jubilee Edition*, ed. Allan Stevenson, 4 vols (Amsterdam, 1968), no. 224.

92 The dates are respectively: *Elizabeth I: Collected Works*, Letters 79; BL, Add. MS 23240, fols 77-8 and fols 136-7.

ELIZABETH I AND HER 'GOOD GEORGE'

UNPUBLISHED LETTERS

KATHERINE DUNCAN-JONES

ELIZABETH I'S SURVIVING LETTERS span fifty-seven years. They present huge variations and developments in penmanship, style and epistolary genre. The earliest of all, addressed to her stepmother Catherine Parr, accompanied the eleven-year-old Princess's translation of Margaret of Angoulême's *Miroir de l'ame Pecheresse* on 31 December 1544. It is almost painful in its careful non-cursive italic script and laboured wording. Later letters are considerably more fluent, though Elizabeth's prose style continued to be rather laborious – she could never resist a parenthesis – and her diction old-fashioned, with many words and word-forms derived from her father Henry VIII. However, she was a compulsive and voluminous letter-writer. As early as 1552 she remarked to her sister Mary, then sick, that 'you may well see by my writing so oft, how pleasant it is to me'.[1] Once she became Queen the volume of her correspondence hugely expanded, and her cursive italic hand soon deteriorated. Nevertheless, on top of a great deal of official and political correspondence, she still found time, throughout her reign, to write substantial personal letters to favourite courtiers when they were in trouble. A good example is her letter to Lady Norris, 'Mine own Crow', condoling with her on the death of her son, Sir John Norris, in Ireland in 1597.[2] Three of the four letters edited here come into the category of 'letters to courtiers in trouble'. By her final years, aware of the virtually illegible quality of her hand when writing *currente calamo*, Elizabeth generally made use of amanuenses, including some whose pretty italic slightly resembled her own as it was back in the 1550s. Perhaps she made a deliberate choice of scribes on this basis. Yet as Letters 2 and 3 in the present collection show, even in the last summer of her life, with hands that were said to be gouty or arthritic, she could still pen quite a free and graceful superscription and signature.

The four letters discussed and edited below[3] were catalogued and quoted, though not in full, by I. H. Jeayes in his *Descriptive Catalogue of the Charters and Muniments of*

1 *Elizabeth I: Collected Works*, ed. Leah S. Marcus, Janel Mueller and Mary Beth Rose (Chicago & London, 2000), p. 38 (referred to henceforth as *Collected Works*).

2 *Collected Works*, pp. 389-90.

3 Berkeley Castle Muniments: Select Letters, Warrants &c., 7, 8, 9, 10. These letters are edited and reproduced by permission of the Trustees of the Berkeley Will and with the co-operation of the Archivist, David J. H. Smith.

the Right Hon. Lord Fitzhardinge of Berkeley Castle (Bristol, 1892), pp. 322-4. This volume was trawled by the compilers of the original *Oxford English Dictionary*. The letter here numbered 3 was quoted under 'squash *v* 2b., To splash or dash (water) *upon* a person. To wet by splashing. *Obs.* Rare.' Elizabeth's jocular expression of anxiety about her Lord Chamberlain, 'I somewhat still doute that ther hath bene to greate abundance of the same [= water] squasshed upon you', provides the first of only two supporting quotations. The second is taken from Robert Forby's *The Vocabulary of East Anglia* (1825). The absence of Jeayes's catalogue from the revised *OED*'s bibliography of 'most commonly quoted texts' suggests that it did not furnish many more words or usages. The location of these letters at Berkeley Castle, in Gloucestershire, combined with the obscurity of the printed references to them, may explain their absence both from G. B. Harrison's *The Letters of Queen Elizabeth I* (London, 1935) and from the recent *Elizabeth I: Collected Works* edited by Leah S. Marcus, Janel Mueller and Mary Beth Rose (Chicago & London, 2000).[4] To my knowledge, none of the many biographers of Elizabeth has ever drawn on them, presumably for the same reasons.

The letters may have arrived at Berkeley Castle when George Berkeley, grandson of Sir George Carey, second Lord Hunsdon, succeeded his paternal grandfather as Baron Berkeley in 1613. Alternatively, and perhaps more probably, they may have been brought to Berkeley from Cranford, in Middlesex, after the death of George Berkeley's mother there in 1635. All four letters are of some interest for the light they shed on Elizabeth's relationship with her close kin the Lords Hunsdon. The first is a formulaic 'warrant' letter, summoning Sir Henry Carey, first Lord Hunsdon, together with Sir Henry Sidney, to assist the installation of Charles Howard as a Knight of the Garter by serving as his 'Compagnons'. Hunsdon himself had been installed on 8 May 1561, and Henry Sidney on 14 May 1564. By 1575, therefore, both men already enjoyed some seniority as Garter Knights. Other documents confirm that they were in attendance at the ceremony, and did indeed perform the important role of Knights-Companions, or Assistants, to Howard.[5] Their function was to lead the closing ceremonies of a new Knight's installation in St George's Chapel, Windsor: 'The last thing to be done at this great solemnity, is setting up the *Helm*, *Crest*, *Sword*, *Banner* and *Plate* of the newly installed Knight, over his stall in the chappel of St. *George*.'[6]

Although Letter 1 is merely formal, taken in conjunction with Letters 2-4 it contributes something to the existing body of evidence testifying to Elizabeth's special affection for her Carey kin. As Mary Boleyn's children, Henry Carey and his younger sister Catherine were the Queen's first cousins. The death of the latter, in February 1602/3, was believed by some observers to be the immediate trigger for Elizabeth's terminal decline. Henry Carey was born on 4 March 1525/6, so was eight years older than his cousin Elizabeth. There is no doubt that Henry VIII had had an affair with

4 The letters that I have numbered 2-4 are included in Steven W. May's volume of selections from Elizabeth's writings published in 2004. However, he has arranged the letters differently, and reaches different conclusions about their dates.

5 See Oxford, Bodleian Library MS Ashmole 1116, fol. 58r.

6 Elias Ashmole, *The History of the most Noble Order of the Garter* (1715), p. 350.

Mary Boleyn, and that her marriage to his Esquire of the Body William Carey was a somewhat rushed and face-saving union. According to a footnote in *The Complete Peerage*, the King 'is even supposed to have been the father of Henry Carey'.[7] If Henry Carey was not only Elizabeth's first cousin but also her elder half-brother, her unfailing and generous favour towards him would be fully explained. During the earliest weeks of her reign he was first knighted, and then created Baron Hunsdon. In 1562, when it appeared that she might be dying from smallpox, one of her most urgent concerns was that the Council should take special care of Hunsdon. Because of their iconic character, Tudor portraits cannot be taken as wholly reliable evidence for physical appearance. Nevertheless, it is noticeable that in their portraits[8] both Henry Carey and his eldest son do resemble Henry VIII in *his* portraits, being rubicund, wide-faced, and small-eyed. Some further support for the hypothesis that Henry Carey was Elizabeth's brother may be discovered here, if we wish, in Elizabeth's closing address to his son in Letter 4 as 'one whom for many respectes wee hold so neere and deere unto us', at least if we read the phrase 'for many respectes' as suggesting 'because of our extremely close blood relationship'. However, the consensus among historians is that their undisputed Boleyn descent is sufficient to explain Elizabeth's strong and unstinting affection for the Careys. Even as first cousins, they were her closest living blood relations.

The dates of Letters 2 and 3 must be conjectural. Their similar format and style suggest that they were written close in time to each other. The scribal italic hand in which they are written resembles that of the copy of a letter sent by Elizabeth to the King of Scots on 4 July 1602, though not so closely that it can be stated with certainty that the scribe is the same.[9] My guess is that they belong to the first two or three weeks of July 1602, when Elizabeth was planning, as she had done also in the summers of 1600 and 1601, to take her Progress into Hampshire (the Earl of Hertford at Elvetham) and north Wiltshire (Lord Chief Justice Popham at Littlecote). Writing on 8 July 1602, John Chamberlain reported:

> We have speech of a progresse to begin toward the latter end of this month: first to Sir John Fortescues in Buckinghamshire, then to the erle of Hartfords and the Lord Chiefe Justice, where there were jewels and presents provided the last yeare that would not be lost: and so to Bath and Bristow to visit the Lord Chamberlain that lies there for help.[10]

Letters 2 and 3 are unlikely to relate to Hunsdon's previous visit to Bath, in May 1600.[11] In this year he was back at Court again by late June, being thought at first to look 'well' after his treatment.[12] This would not fit with Elizabeth's proposal, in Letter

7 G.E.C., *The Complete Peerage* (revised edition, 1926), VI, 627.
8 Portraits of both men are to be seen at Berkeley Castle. A full-size painting of Henry Carey hangs in the Great Hall; that of his son George is a charming Hilliard miniature dated 1601.
9 The copy of Elizabeth's letter is reproduced in David Loades, *Elizabeth I: The golden reign of Gloriana* (The National Archives, 2003), p. 103. Peter Beal is inclined to identify this scribe with that of Berkeley Castle Letters 2 and 3; Henry Woudhuysen is sceptical.
10 *The Letters of John Chamberlain*, ed. N. E. McClure (Philadelphia, 1939), I, 156-7.
11 He became seriously ill towards the end of 1599 (Old Style): see HMC, *De L'Isle and Dudley*, II, 448, 453, 466. Allusions to pain in the head and severe mobility problems suggest that he may have suffered a stroke.
12 See the letter by Rowland Whyte to Robert Sidney, 25 June 1600: HMC, *De L'Isle and Dudley*, II, 471.

3, to visit him in the West Country by extending her progress by twenty or thirty miles, since he had returned to Court before the progress have even begun. I shall therefore proceed on the assumption that they do indeed belong to 1602.

Letter 3 indicates that, as in the summer of 1601, Elizabeth was seriously considering travelling as far as Somerset, perhaps to Bath and Bristol, or to nearby Dauntsey in north Wiltshire, where Sir George Carey and his wife were staying during July.[13] George Carey's younger brother Edmund, who had been knighted by the Earl of Leicester in the Netherlands in 1585, had married, as his second wife, the widowed Lady Danvers, Elizabeth née Neville, who retained possession of her late husband's Dauntsey estate. This included a large medieval manor house with a mid-fifteenth-century oratory and a '14th century hall range running north and south, with a raised cruck roof of three bays on rubble walls'.[14] Elizabeth's 1601 progress had been cut short because of the arrival of a French delegation. In the event, the 1602 progress was cut shorter still, lasting little more than three weeks. It turned out to be a very wet summer, and there were rumours of pox. 'The Quenes progres went not far ... the causes that withheld her from the earle of Hartfords and the Lord Chiefe Justices were the fowle weather, and a generall infection of the small pockes spred over all the countrie.'[15]

Culturally, the most remarkable part of the 1602 progress was the Queen's reception by Lord Keeper Egerton at Harefield, Buckinghamshire, where she stayed from 31 July to 3 August. A player disguised as the 'guiltless Saint', St Swithun, reputed herald of rain, presented her with a dress embroidered with rainbows, declaring that the torrential downpours that marred her visit were not his fault, but that of the goddess Iris. From the second half of August, as Letter 4 shows, the Queen was resident at Oatlands Palace in Surrey, where she was to remain until early October. This 'large and splendid house' had been acquired by Elizabeth's father in 1537. It was adapted towards the end of his reign so that Henry could go hunting there even after he had 'waxed hevy with sicknes, age and corpulences of body, and might not travayle readyly abrode'.[16] Because of these adaptations, which included a ramp and special blocks to enable the unfit and overweight king to mount his horse, Elizabeth may have thought Oatlands particularly suitable for her ailing Lord Chamberlain. As we would now put it, the palace offered 'disabled access'. It may also have contained some of the wheelchairs which had been specially made for Henry VIII.

Letters 2-4 offer an interest that extends well beyond the specific question of Elizabeth's relations with her Carey kin. Stylistically, they are exceptionally relaxed, even playful. G. B. Harrison remarked of Elizabeth's style in her familiar letters that 'Her sense of humour was not very subtle, but her sense of irony was keen'.[17] What

13 HMC, *Salisbury MSS*, XII (1910), 219, 226, 266.

14 *A History of Wiltshire*, ed. D. A. Crowley (Victoria County History, vol. XIV, 1991), pp. 68-9. However, Lady Danvers's second husband is here wrongly alluded to as Sir Edward, not Edmund, Carey. For a useful account of Sir Edmund Carey's marriages and descendants, along with those of Sir John Danvers, see *The Herald and Genealogist*, ed. J. G. Nichols, IV (1867), p. 42 (grateful thanks to Steven May for this reference).

15 *Letters of John Chamberlain*, I, 160.

16 Simon Thurley, *The Royal Palaces of Tudor England* (New Haven & London, 1993), p. 60.

17 G. B. Harrison, *The Letters of Queen Elizabeth I* (London, 1935), p. xv.

Harrison terms her 'irony' we might call 'heavy sarcasm'. It is certainly lacking in subtlety. This sarcasm is first in evidence in Letter 2, in which she pretends to fear that her Lord Chamberlain may be 'rather drowned than otherwise' as a result of his excessive exposure to the supposedly therapeutic waters of Bath. In Letter 3 she suggests, paradoxically, that her 'present choler against those extreame waterpourers' may actually prevent her from coming to see for herself how her 'good George' is faring after his treatment. In both 2 and 3 there is a sense that a front of anger and severe disapproval, which almost resembles that of an aunt in a P. G. Wodehouse story, has been assumed to veil deep personal anxiety. Unreasonably, she is cross with him for still being unwell, and writes almost as if she can badger him back into good health.

Letter 4 is less jocular and more explicitly affectionate. It is also in this letter that Elizabeth, whose management of her own health was remarkably successful, presents herself most explicitly as what might now be called a health guru. As Letter 2 indicates, she had already set out her own personal 'prescription' for Good George's preparation for taking the waters. In Letter 4 she takes control of his treatment further, issuing what is virtually a royal command to her Lord Chamberlain to leave 'that close place' where he is staying – perhaps his brother's Dauntsey Manor, perhaps his own manor of West Drayton in Middlesex – and to come into her presence, and under her direct care, at the salubrious Oatlands. Assuming the ancient mythic role of sovereign as healer, she also suggests that her own love for George, even when they are physically far apart, functions as a kind of sacramental therapy: 'yett is there not any medicine so soveraigne and comfortable vnto you, as the daylie aprehension and feeling you have of our earnest care and longing after your good recovery at the least the ease and mitigation of your infirmitie'.

As an anointed monarch, it seems, Elizabeth believed that she could heal someone she loved simply with the power of her own concern and affection. There is other evidence for Elizabeth's particular, 'hands-on', involvement with the health of those closest to her. When Lord Burghley was sick unto death in 1598, for instance, she sat at his bedside and herself fed him pap with a spoon. Yet none of her previously published writings reach quite the level of tenderness expressed here in Letter 4. Letter 4 also differs from 2 and 3 in the form in which it has survived. It is a scribal copy, rather than the original. A possible explanation for this oddity is that this was Elizabeth's last such letter to her 'good George', and that a copy was made, perhaps after her death, so that the original could be especially treasured by Lord Hunsdon.

It is also interesting to trace the development, in Letters 2-4, of Elizabeth's distinctly secondary concern for Lady Carey, who had evidently also taken the waters. In Letter 2 she sends greetings to her, 'whose estate though I wolde were better, Yet I wish yours were no worse'. In Letter 3 she seems to be refusing to worry much about 'my Lady, of whom I am very sory that she hath receauid so little benefitt by the water as I hear she hath, yet doo I hope to heare of better by this gentleman'. In Letter 4 Elizabeth no longer pretends to be in the least interested in Lady Carey's health, being now concerned only with her role as her husband's nurse, a role she believes she herself can perform better. She explicitly proposes that her George should come to her as soon as possible, 'though my Lady remayne behinde some fortnight after'. She was probably right not to be too much worried about the health of Lady Hunsdon, who was to live on until March 1618. In her closing promise that 'in what place soeuer you be, you shall finde us a Mother and a wife to minister unto you' the Queen presents herself as all the family George needs.

We do not know whether Lord Hunsdon did, in fact, leave his wife behind in the West Country in order to put himself in the healing presence of his cousin and Queen. Judging by a much earlier letter, in which he tells his wife about his considerable resentment at being compelled to hang around at Court to take part in Elizabeth's Accession Day junketings, he may have been reluctant to do so.[18] In any case, he seems have been still too unwell to travel except with great care, especially after a further physical setback – perhaps a mini-stroke – that he suffered on 31 July.[19] This was not his first such setback. On 7 July 1602 Sir William Browne described Hunsdon as having becoming unconscious 'having eaten too great a meal', and receiving treatment with a suppository. He was eventually revived, after three and a half hours, by having 'spirit of sack' poured into his mouth by a faithful servant.[20] According to John Chamberlain, in the letter of 2 October 1602 from which I have already quoted, 'The Lord Chamberlain is come home from the Bath, but neither much better nor worse then when he went out.' 'Home' in this instance was his Middlesex manor of West Drayton, where the Queen visited him on 2 October.[21] In December she visited him again, at Carey Court, his large residence in the Blackfriars, where she saw a play.[22] Circumstantially, it is probable that the play was one written by Shakespeare, who was, jointly with Richard Burbage, the leading Lord Chamberlain's man. Perhaps it was his new comedy *Twelfth Night*, in which it is declared that 'care's an enemy to life'. Merriment is preferable to mourning even when, as the Fool sings at the close, 'the rain it raineth every day', as it had done during that year's summer.

Six months after she wrote Letter 4, Elizabeth, so confident of her own expertise in health matters, would die. Less than six months after that, on 9 September 1603, her 'good George' also died.

TEXTS

In the following transcriptions I have expanded abbreviations, but otherwise retain the spelling of the originals.

18 See K. Duncan-Jones, '*Christs Teares*, Nashe's "forsaken extremities"', *Review of English Studies*, NS 49 (1998), 167-80. In a letter of November 1593 quoted in full in this article, Sir George Carey complains of his 'weeresum kneelinge' before the Queen, and says that she assumed, wrongly, that he had come to honour her Accession Day, 'my good manors not permittinge me to deny it'. But he is impatient to return as soon as possible to 'My sweete soule', his wife.

19 See Lady Hunsdon's letter to Robert Cecil written 31 July 1602: HMC, *Salisbury*, XII, 266.

20 Ibid., 598.

21 E. K. Chambers, *The Elizabethan Stage* (Oxford, 1923), IV, 115.

22 Ibid.

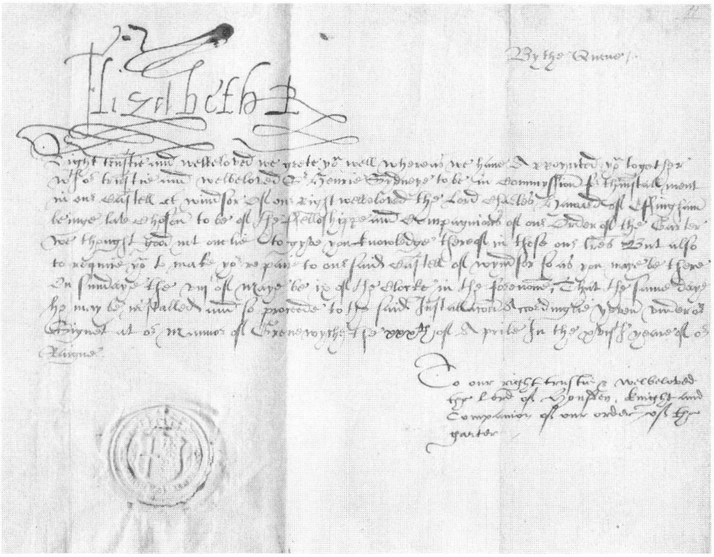

1 Letter 1 signed by Queen Elizabeth, to Sir Henry Carey, Lord Hunsdon, the text in the hand of a secretary, 30 April 1575 (Berkeley Castle Muniments, Select Letters, Warrants &c., No. 7)

LETTER 1

Queen Elizabeth to Sir Henry Carey, first Baron Hunsdon, from Greenwich, 30 April 1575, requesting him to attend the Garter ceremonies at Windsor; written in the hand of a secretary, but signed by the Queen at the top left.

By the Quene/.

Elizabeth R

Right trustie and welbeloved we grete you well. Whereas we have Appoynted you together with our trustie and welbeloved Sir Henrie Sydney to be in commyssion for thinstallment in our castell at windsor of our right welbeloved the Lord Charles Haward of Effingham beinge late Chosen to be of the Felloshippe and Compagnons of our Order of the Garter we thought good not onelie to give you knowledge thereof in these our le*tte*res: But also to require you to make your repaire to our said Castell of Wyndsor so as you may be there On Sunday the viiith of Maye be ix of the clocke in the forenoone, That the same daye he may be installed and so proceede to the said Installacion Accordinglie

Yeven vnder our Signet at our Mannor of Grenewich the xxxth of Aprile In the xviith yeare of our Raigne

To our right trustie welbeloved
the Lord of Honsden, Knight and
Companion of our order of the
garter/

[*Endorsed*]

A Comyssion to the Lorde of
Hunsdon and S*ir* Henrie
Sydney for thinstallinge of
the Lo*rd* Haward of Effingham
the 30 of Aprill A*nn*o R*egni* R*eg*inae
Eliz. 17°

LETTER 2

Queen Elizabeth to Sir George Carey, second Baron Hunsdon, probably written in July 1602: autograph superscription and signature in Elizabeth's italic hand; the rest in an italic hand by an amanuensis; with seal and traces of gold silk ties; some damage to lower left-hand margin; conjectural letters and words are placed between curled brackets {}.

Your most Affectionate Lovinge
Souveraine

Elizabeth R

Good George, I can not but render all laude and thankes to God, for that since your com*m*ing to Bath I understand you haue so well obseruid all such good order both for dyett & otherwise as was prescribed you before your going thither: for your perfourming wherof I doo not only giue you my particular thanks in that you shew therby a care to please me, by observing such prescription as my self had a care to giue you, but doo allso still out of the {s}ame Care & loue, aduise you, yea charge you to contynue the same good {c}ourse. And glad I am to heare that you doo use the aduise of such as {are s}skillfull & experimented there, theyr Judgments being best to be liked. {But I} can {not} but wonder, considering the great nomber of Payles of water {that I} hear haue bene powred upon you, that you are not rather drowned than otherwise, But I trust all shallbe for your better meanes to helth. {Y}our sending to me vpon Satterday hath prevented me who was purposed to haue sent to you upon Monday. Commend me to your Lady and Companyon whose estate though I wolde were better, yet I wish yours were no wors. Thus good George as we receaue very great contentement by our hope to heare of good succes to your helth. So take ye comfort both you and she by my Loue, w*hi*ch with my contynuall prayers to the Allmighty God for you both, shall neuer fayle you.

[*Addressed on verso*] To my good George Lord
Hunsdon, my L*ord* Chamberlen

[*Endorsed*] from the Queenes most Excellent Matie./

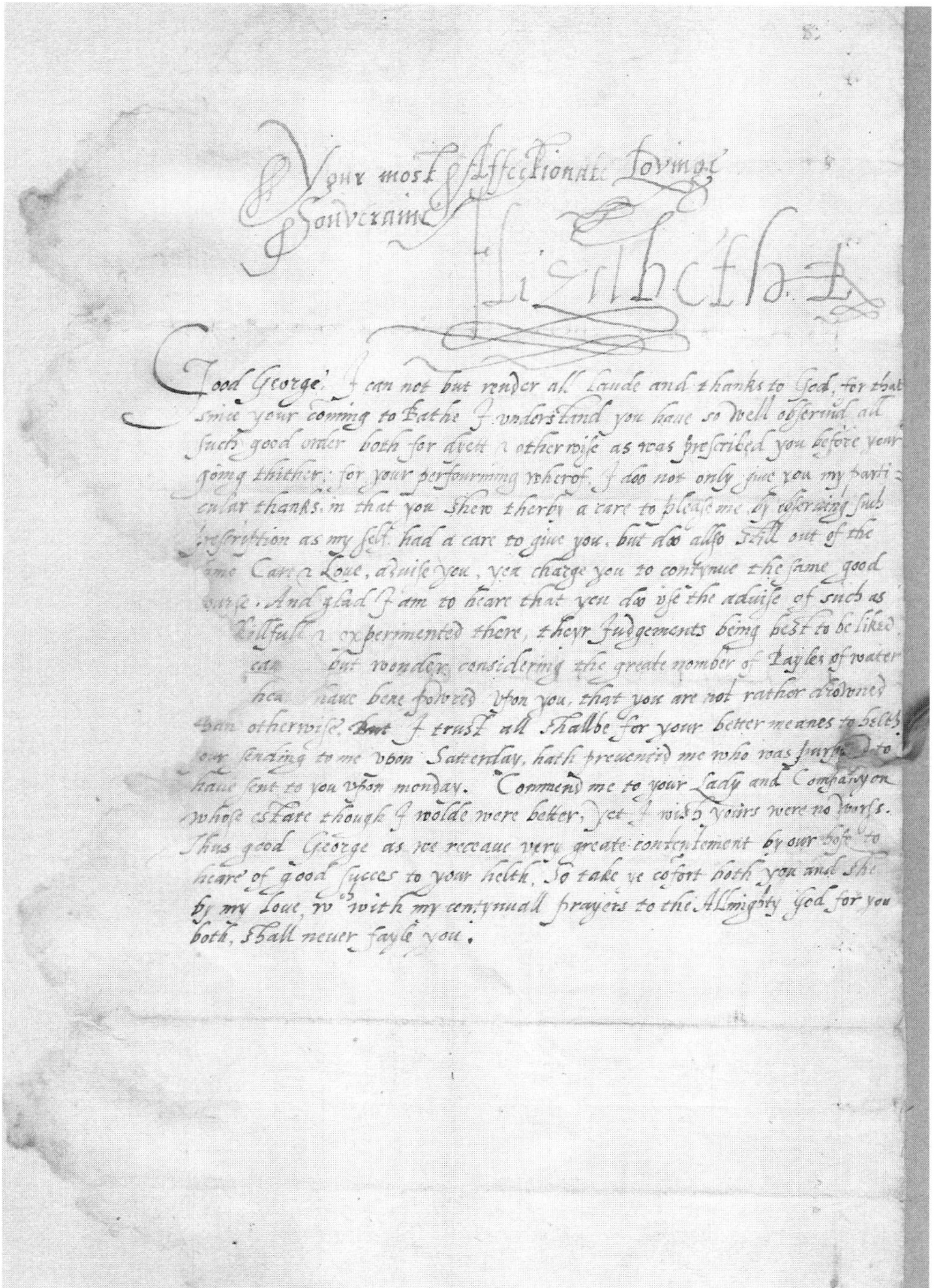

Your most Affectionate Louinge Souveraine

Elizabeth R

Good George: I can not but render all laude and thanks to God, for that since your coming to Bathe I understand you haue so well obserued all such good order both for diett & otherwise as was prescribed you before your going thither: for your performing wherof I doo not only giue you my particular thanks in that you shew therby a care to please me by obseruing such prescription as my self had a care to giue you, but doo allso still out of the same Care & Loue, aduise you, yea charge you to continue the same good course. And glad I am to heare that you doo use the aduise of such as skillfull & experimented there, theyr judgements being best to be liked. can but wonder considering the greate nomber of Payles of water haue bene powred vpon you, that you are not rather drowned than otherwise. But I trust all shallbe for your better meanes to helth. Your sending to me vpon Satterday, hath preuented me who was purposed to haue sent to you vpon monday. Commend me to your Lady and Companyon whose estate though I wolde were better, yet I wish yours were no worse. Thus good George as we receaue very greate contentement by our host to heare of good succes to your helth, So take ye cofort both you and she by my loue, which with my contynuall prayers to the Allmighty God for you both, shall neuer fayle you.

2 Letter 2 signed by Queen Elizabeth, to Sir George Carey, second Baron Hunsdon, the text in the hand of a secretary, probably July 1602 (Berkeley Castle Muniments: Select Letters, Warrants &c., No. 8)

3 Verso of Letter 3 by Queen Elizabeth, to Sir George Carey, second Baron Hunsdon, inscribed by a secretary, undated (Berkeley Castle Muniments: Select Letters, Warrants &c., No. 9)

LETTER 3

Queen Elizabeth to Sir George Carey, Lord Hunsdon, undated: autograph superscription and signature, the rest in the italic hand of an amanuensis; with seal and traces of gold silk ties.

Your most Affectionate
Souveraine

Elizabeth R

Good George. Because I haue hard that before your departing fro*m* Bathe, neyther your speech was becom much better, nor your leges any stronger and being still carefull and desirous to know that you are rather amended since your coming from thence, I haue sent this gentleman the bearar hereof (who we know shall not be a little wellcom unto you) purposely to see you, and to bring me word of your state how it is since y*our* coming from Bathe hoping by him to heare that good effect wrought in you w*hi*ch is saide by such as haue experience of the nature & operation of that Water doth com*m*only ensue & \more/ appeere after som tyme past of leaving the vse therof, although as yet I somwhat still doute that ther hath bene to great abundance of the same squasshed upon you, which I wolde haue restraynid, if my self might haue bene w*i*th you,for therin wold I haue bene bolde to haue playd the parte of a Phisician to you & my Lady, of whom I am very sory that she hath receauid so little benefitt by the water as I hear she hath, Yet doo I hope to heare of better by this gentleman, I am gladd you are no furder from the waye of my intended Som*m*er iourney, for that it may be I shall not stick to make xx or xxx myles Compass to visit you except my present choler against those extreame Waterpowrers doo stay me, for that indeede I wold rather com to finde you amended than otherwise for w*hi*ch as I will daily pray so I assure you good George of all comfort that we can giue both to your self and to my Lady your second self & best companion, to whom I pray you com*m*end me, as I com*m*end you both to Gods holy protection.

[*Addressed on verso*] To my good George, the Lord Hunsdon, my Lord Chamberlen

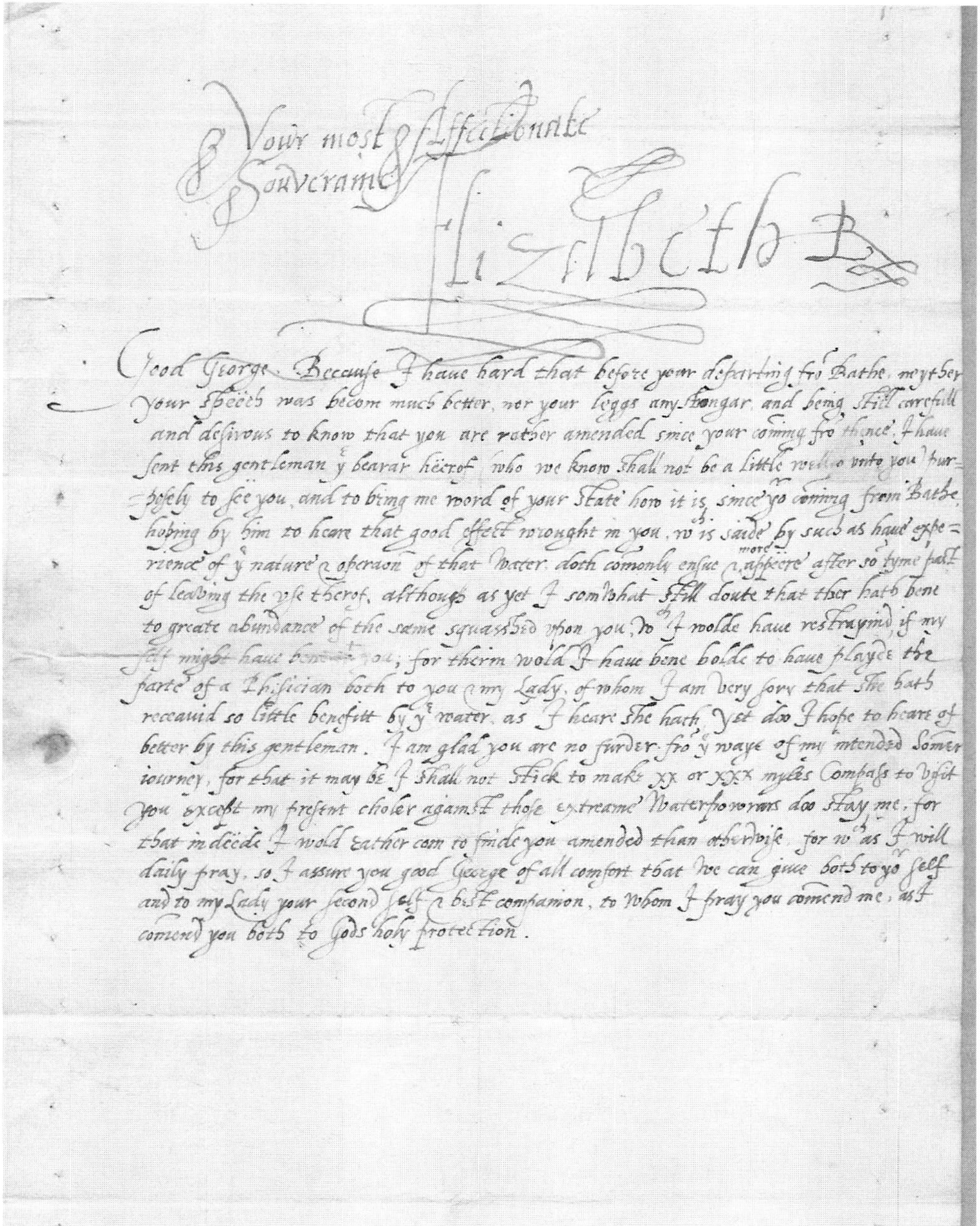

Your most Affectionate Souveraine

Elizabeth R

Good George. Because I haue hard that before your departing fro Bathe, neyther your speech was becom much better, nor your leggs any stronger, and being still carefull and desirous to know that you are rather amended since your comming fro thence, I haue sent this gentleman ye bearar heerof who we know shall not be a little welcome unto you pur=posely to see you, and to bring me word of your state how it is since yor comming from Bathe, hoping by him to heare that good effect wrought in you, wch is saide by such as haue expe=rience of ye nature & operaon of that water doth comonly ensue & appeere more after so tyme past of leaving the vse therof, althoughe as yet I somwhat still doute that ther hath bene to greate abundance of the same squasshed vpon you, wch I wolde haue restrayned if my self might haue ben wth you; for therin wold I haue bene bolde to haue playde the parte of a Phisician both to you & my Lady, of whom I am very sory that she hath receaued so little benefitt by ye water, as I heare she hath, yet doo I hope to heare of better by this gentleman. I am glad you are no furder fro ye waye of my intended Somer iourney, for that it may be I shall not stick to make xx or xxx myles compass to visit you except my present choler against those extreame waterpowrers doo stay me, for that indeede I wold rather com to finde you amended than otherwise, for wch as I will daily pray, so I assure you good George of all comfort that we can giue both to yor self and to my Lady your second self & best companion, to whom I pray you comend me, as I comend you both to Gods holy protection.

4 Letter 3 signed by Queen Elizabeth, to Sir George Carey, second Baron Hunsdon, the text in the hand of a secretary, undated (Berkeley Castle Muniments: Select Letters, Warrants &c., No. 9)

LETTER 4

Queen Elizabeth to Sir George Carey, second Baron Hunsdon, from Oatlands, 20 August 1602: a *scribal copy throughout, in a secretary hand.*

Your verie affectionate Soueraigne

Elizabeth Re./

Good George, Wee cann but give you our hartie thanckes for your visiting vs soe often by your Messengers, as being desirous owt of your kind affection, to heare of the continuance of our happie estate, soe espetiallie in that you lett vs understand, what alteracion you finde in the state of your owne boddy. For the bettering whereof though you have experimented many and sondry meanes, yett is there not any medicine soe soveraigne and comfortable vnto you, as the daylie aprehension and feeling you have of our earnest care and longing after your good recovery at the least the ease and mitigation of your infirmitie. This indeed wee hope you will euer rest most assured of, and soe continewe in the meditacion of the manifold testimonies wee have herof geven vnto you. And for that amongst other impedimentes to the furtherance of your wellfare, wee accompt none to be of more importance, then the want of the freenes of the ayre: Wee are therefore very carefull, and w*i*thall most earnestlie wish, that assoone as you mai you wold come owt of that close place, and make triall of some better ayre. And albeit my lady be alsoe most carefull in her place to omitt nothing that may tende to your good: yett seeing you weare the rather drawen thether by some other occasions, for which shee may have cause yett to make some further staie there: yett wee think it nedefull that your selfe shold presentlie remove from thense, though my Lady remayne behinde some fortnight after. And this to thende you might the sooner tast \of/ the benefitt wee hope shall arise unto you by this chaunge and freshnes of the ayre. Herein we shalbe desirous to heare of your resolucion And though it hath soe fallen out, that hetherto wee cold not see you wheare you are, yett wee nothing doubt but shortelie to see you wheare wee may. And in what place soeuer you be, you shall finde us a Mother and a wife to minister unto you all the best effectes of that tender and kinde affection, which wee maie possiblie extende to one whom for many respectes wee hold soe neere and deere vnto us. And soe recommending our care and wellwishing vnto you, wee betake you to the Almighties keeping, and recommende vs to my lady your better parte in the all=effectuall sort wee maie. Given vnder our Signett at our Mannor of Oatelandes the xxth of August in the 44.yeare of our Raigne.

To our right trustie and welbeloved
Cousin the Lo*rd* Hunsdon ^*our*^ Lo*rd* Chamberlane./

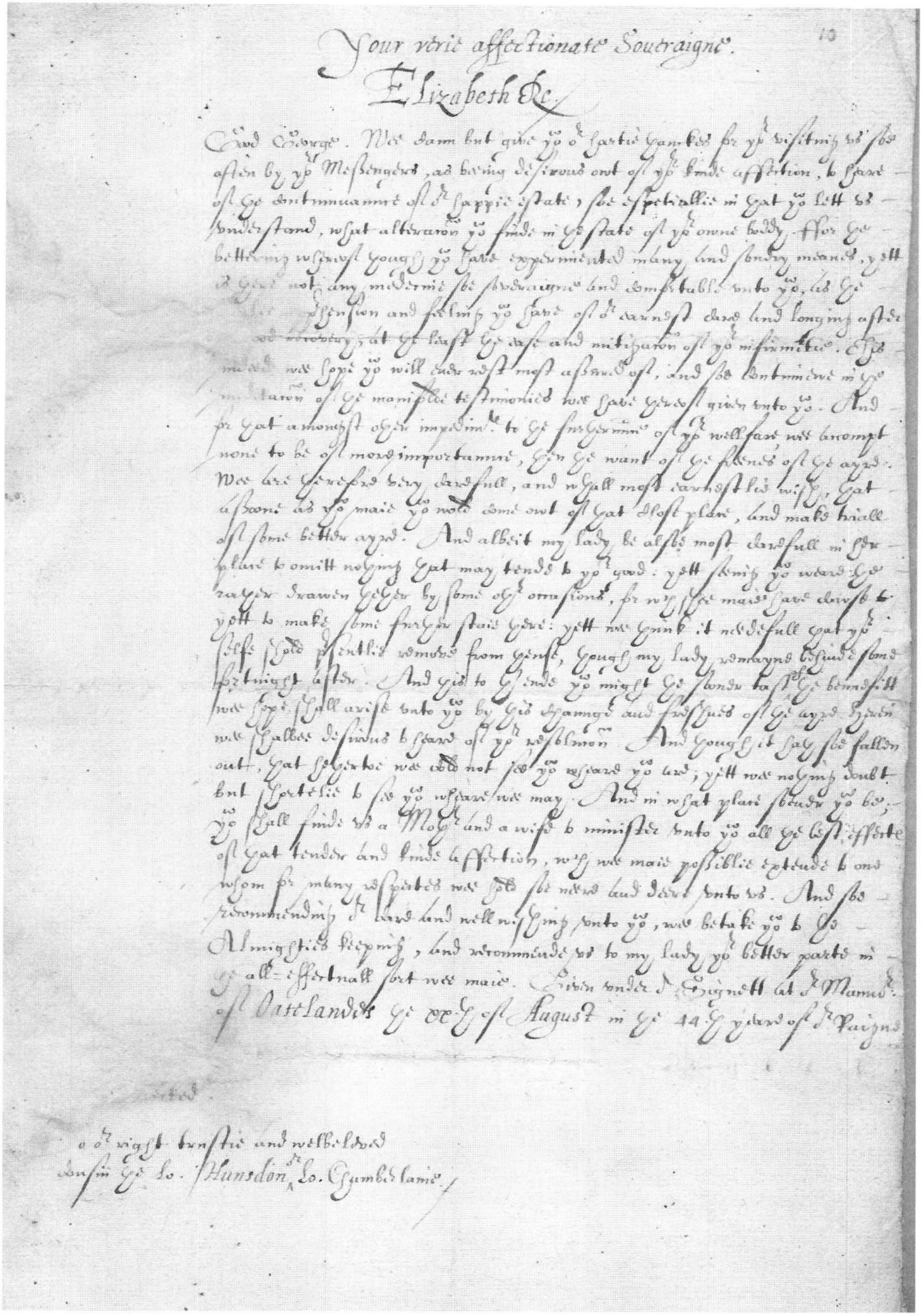
Your verie affectionate Soveraigne.
Elizabeth R.

[illegible]

o our right trustie and welbeloved
cosin the Lo. Hunsdon our Lo. Chamberlaine

5 Letter 4 by Queen Elizabeth, to Sir George Carey, second Baron Hunsdon, 20 August 1602, a scribal copy (Berkeley Castle Muniments: Select Letters, Warrants &c., No. 10)

'YOUR MAJESTIES MOST HUMBLE FAYTHFULLEST AND MOST AFFECTIONATE SERUANT'

THE EARL OF ESSEX CONSTRUCTS HIMSELF AND HIS QUEEN IN THE HULTON LETTERS

GRACE IOPPOLO

Nether will I liue an hower to want your fauor. nor dy more constant in my fayth then in my affection to your Majestie. Deere Lady. I wish your sacred self all the happy ioyes thatt can be thought of and myself no higher fortune then to be your most esteemed, as I am, your Majesties most humble faythfullest and most affectionate seruant, R. Essex.

ROBERT DEVEREUX, second Earl of Essex (1565-1601), lived a simultaneously public and private life. In private, he was a man who humbly and faithfully 'most esteemed' his Queen, Elizabeth I; in public he often appeared to most esteem himself. Such contrary representations of his private and public selves are not unusual in his time or our own. As Jürgen Habermas argued in 1991, 'the virtues, whose catalogue was codified by Aristotle, were ones whose text lies in the public sphere and there alone receive recognition'. Thus words like 'excellence, highness, majesty, fame, dignity, and honor seek to characterize this peculiarity of a being that is capable of representation'.[1] Philippe Ariès controversially claimed in 1989 that such beings were constructed uniquely in England within the private sphere, because the popularity of English diaries and memoirs in the late sixteenth century marked England as 'the birthplace of privacy' and private representation.[2] Yet Ariès and his fellow contributors to Volume 3 of *The History of Private Life* neglected to test their theories against the circulation of personal letters as the pretext or context for private representation. Habermas's belief that Aristotelian virtues can be represented only in the public sphere, and Ariès's implication that such virtues existed in early modern England only within an increasingly private, and separate, sphere can be tried against an extraordinary set of 43 original autograph

1 Habermas, *The Structural Transformation of the Public Sphere: An Inquiry into a Category of Bourgeois Society*, trans. Thomas Burger (Cambridge, Mass., 1991), pp. 4, 7.

2 Ariès, Introduction, *A History of Private Life*, Vol. III *Passions of the Renaissance*, gen ed. Philippe Ariès and Georges Duby, trans. Arthur Goldhammer (Cambridge, Mass., 1989), pp. 1-11. See also Lena Cowen Orlin, *Private Matters and Public Culture in Post-Reformation England* (Ithaca, NY, 1994), pp. 1 *et seq.*

letters from Essex to Elizabeth. Never printed in whole and largely neglected by modern scholars, these letters offer remarkable new insight not simply into private and public 'representation', but into the construction and self-construction of two of the most powerful figures in early modern England: Essex and his patron, monarch, and private correspondent, Elizabeth. Their relationship, previously constructed through gossip, hearsay, and other second- or third-hand reports by members of Elizabeth's circle, can finally be constructed through Essex's own words. In speaking for himself, Essex also comes to speak loudly and incontrovertibly for the Elizabeth he helps to create, sustain and, ultimately, desolate.

I. 'TELL NO TALES': ESSEX AND THE HULTON LETTERS

In theory, letters between two people are always private; in practice, letters are almost always liable to be made public, or, at least, subject to others' mediation, interference, interception, report, and, possibly, copying, annotation, emendation, and even forgery. Unlike conversations, letters are preserved in a potentially permanent, material form. In the early modern age, before the use of envelopes, letters were folded and sealed with wax and sometimes tied with ribbons, with the recipient's address on the outermost sheet, and very little stood between the document and even the bearer entrusted with it. This is especially the case with letters to and from the English monarch which, destined after receipt to be read and filed in the State Papers Office, could never truly be private even if the letters were personal. Even before receipt, such letters could be intercepted and read, or simply withheld. This was reported to be the case in January 1592, when Queen Elizabeth sent through Sir Henry Unton, her ambassador to France, a letter that she had written to Essex, who was leading an English army to assist the Protestant Henry of Navarre in his campaign against the French Catholics. In an accompanying letter to Unton, Elizabeth requested that he withhold her letter to Essex until Unton could gauge whether Essex would obey a previous letter from the Queen ordering him home immediately. If Essex did not obey, Unton was instructed to give Essex the new letter, in which the Queen demanded that Essex explain why he had disobeyed her. However, things did not go as the Queen had planned. As Unton later took pains to explain, perhaps less than truthfully, to Burghley, Elizabeth's Lord Treasurer:

> the letters were lefte by Painter the messenger at darnestalle. and sent me by one of the Earle of Essex servantes ... and in his L*ordshi*ps [i.e. Essex's] p*re*sence delyuered me those letters, whereuppon he requyred me to open the paquett, and said he hoped I had letters for him ... uppon the openinge of the letters, his L*ordship* snatched her Ma*jes*ties letters to him out of my handes before the readinge of anie of myn.[3]

3 British Library, Additional MS 38137, fol. 99. This letter is one of the many scribal copies that Unton had made of his correspondence, and this volume of manuscripts has several other letters about this distressing affair. The letter is transcribed in *Correspondence of Sir Henry Unton*, ed. Joseph Stevenson (London, 1847), p. 294. See also pp. 251, 263-4, and 276 for the other letters.

The Queen, furious that Unton had disobeyed her and allowed Essex to snatch and read her letter, had Burghley censure the hapless ambassador.[4] That this private letter to Essex was only conditionally private and that it had to be kept in reserve by a third party mediator, away from its intended recipient, reminds us of the factors which can complicate the distinction between the private and the public spheres in Elizabeth's age. It also gives us some idea of the nature of her relationship with Essex.

Both his lineage and character marked Essex out for anything but a quiet, private, life. His stepfather, Robert Dudley, Earl of Leicester (*c.*1532-88), was Elizabeth's cherished favourite, and probably her one true love, and towards the end of his life, Leicester eagerly pushed Essex into usurping his own role. Thus, from the late 1580s until his death in 1601, Essex replaced his stepfather in offering Elizabeth his private services as suitor, confidant, courtly lover, and chief favourite, as well as his public services as courtier, soldier, naval hero, and statesman. In return, Elizabeth rewarded Essex with a wealth of private gifts and public renown, naming him Master of the Horse, Privy Councillor, Master of the Ordnance, Commander of her army and navy (whence he became the conqueror of Cadiz in 1596), Earl Marshal of England, Chancellor of Cambridge University, and Lieutenant and Governor-General of Ireland, among other prestigious and powerful titles. Essex was known to have been 'highly beloued' by her, and no person other than Elizabeth was 'more deare to the people'.[5] He eventually betrayed her; she eventually executed him. Yet long before the destruction of their relationship, judging by the depth of distrust between them evident in the 1592 letter and others, we would be hard pressed to say that their relationship was ever truly 'private'. Even if they shared remarkable intimacy, intimacy with a monarch could not and did not guarantee privacy.

In addition to his prowess as a courtier and soldier, Essex had impeccable literary credentials, not just as a poet but as a patron or protegé of other poets. These included Edmund Spenser, Ben Jonson, George Peele, Gabriel Harvey, Sir John Harington, Samuel Daniel, George Chapman, Barnabe Barnes, Sir Fulke Greville, Sir Henry Wotton, Sir Francis Bacon, Anthony Bacon, and even John Donne, who served under Essex in his successful raid on Cadiz. These poets were bound to Essex through personal friendship, political exigency, or financial need, not only in life but death. For example, Essex was reported to have paid for Spenser's burial and interment in Poets' Corner in Westminster Abbey on 20 January 1599.[6] Essex, apparently the model for Spenser's Calidore,[7] the hero of Book V of *The Faerie Queene*, had, according to

4 For the context in which Essex's letters were written, sent, and read, see Paul E. J. Hammer's edition of Cecil's letters to Hatton in 1591, in I. W. Archer (ed.), *Religion, politics and society in 16th century England* (Camden Society, 5th series, vol. 22, 2003).

5 William Camden, *The Historie of the Most Renowned and Victorious Princesse Elizabeth* (London, 1630), IV, 168.

6 Camden, IV, 135.

7 See Ray Heffner, *The Earl of Essex in Elizabethan Literature: An extract from a Dissertation* (Baltimore, 1934). He also notes that allusions to Essex appear in the Mutability Cantos in *The Faerie Queene* and *Protholamion*; that he was celebrated in poems by Peele, Harvey, Daniel among others, and he was commended for his writing ability by Wotton and Jonson.

Jonson, tried to send the dying Spenser '20 pieces' of coin to alleviate his poverty, which Spenser sadly refused on the grounds that he would be dead before he could spend the money.[8]

Essex's coupling with the great English neo-Petrarchan and neo-Platonic sonneteers reached its climax in his relationship with Sir Philip Sidney, his step-cousin through the marriage of Sidney's uncle, Leicester, to Essex's mother, Lettice Knollys. On the day of his death in 1586 from gangrene at Arnhem, after the battle of Zutphen, Sidney added a codicil to his will to include a bequest to 'give to my beloved and much honoured lord the Earl of Essex, my best sword'.[9] An apocryphal story also has Sidney on his deathbed willing Essex something else of best quality, for he reportedly extracted Essex's promise that he would marry Sidney's wife, Frances, daughter of Queen Elizabeth's spymaster, Sir Francis Walsingham, in order to provide for Frances and her daughter. Essex's secret marriage to Frances came to Elizabeth's attention in late summer or early autumn of 1590 when Frances's pregnancy could no longer be concealed. H. R. Woudhuysen has argued that Frances and Essex married as early as the spring of 1587, only months after her first husband's funeral. If so, the marriage occurred around the time of the preparation of the publication of Sidney's works, including *Astrophil and Stella* and *The Arcadia*, the manuscripts of which were left in the care of Fulke Greville and Sidney's sister, the Countess of Pembroke.[10] Judging from surviving letters in her hand, Frances was moderately literate, at best,[11] so she probably did not participate in the publication of her first husband's works. But it is intriguing to wonder if Essex, himself a poet, read Sidney's works in manuscript at this time, thereby appropriating not just Sidney's life and wife, but his art. Essex was, after all, a scholar, and the first major collection of books donated to the newly formed Bodleian Library in 1600 consisted of two hundred volumes from Essex's own collection, including those he had seized during

8 In 'Conversations with Drummond' (in *Ben Jonson*, ed. C. H. Herford and Percy Simpson [Oxford, 1925], p.137), Drummond claims that Jonson told him that 'the Irish having Robd Spensers goods & burnt his house & a little child new born, he and his wyfe escaped, & after he died for lake of bread jn King street and refused 20 pieces sent to him by my Lord of Essex & said he was sorrie he had no time to spend them'. Camden repeats this story.

9 *Miscellaneous Prose of Sir Philip Sidney*, ed. Katherine Duncan-Jones and Jan Van Dorsten (Oxford, 1973), 152.

10 H. R. Woudhuysen, *Sir Philip Sidney and the Circulation of Manuscripts, 1558-1640* (Oxford, 1996), pp. 374-5.

11 A number of her autograph letters can be found in the Cecil Papers at Hatfield House. See, for example this letter, CP 63/84 (transcribed in *HMC, Salisbury*, IX, 286), which reads in full: 'dere lo I did thenke thes berer wold haue gone soner w.ch made me make redy thes enclosed lettar 4 dayes ago and sens that time I haue had the good fortune to reseue to lettars from you. the forst came when I wase so seke that I could not spake w*ith* m[r] darei w*hi*ch braft it bot the Ioye w*hi*ch I toke in reseuing nuse from you ded deleuar me out of a feuar w*hi*ch held me 03 ours w*ith*out ani entarmening in grett extremety bot noue I thanke my god am fre from it bot so mouch wekend by it that I am not abell to com of my bede: none that sese me none wold beleue I ware w*ith* child for I am lese then I wase to months ago. your sone Robin is bettar then euar he wase. I fer I shall neuer reseue so grett comfort of my other lettel one. onles I quekly mend. I will for thes time take my leue being not abell to endur longe writting. bot by the nex mesingar I hope to writt you word of my amendment. from Bar the 11 of Agoust / your fathfull wife / Fra Essex.' The address reads, 'To my dere husband the Erle of Essex'. In another hand appears the note, '1598 The La: of Essex to ye Lo: in Irland'. See PLATE 3.

his raid on Cadiz.[12] Frances's body was not the only female body that Sidney and Essex had carnally or symbolically shared, for Essex's beloved sister, Penelope Devereux, later Lady Rich, was Sidney's Stella, and possibly his mistress.

Essex's dexterity in lightening the deathbeds and ensuring the poetic legacies of two great English Renaissance poets, one who patronised him and the other whom he patronised, was not his only claim to poetic fame, for he wrote lyrics, sonnets, and longer poems himself. Steven W. May's edition of Essex's poetry shows Essex drawing on the types of conceits common in the period, as in this opening of a 1595 sonnet:

> Seated betweene the olde world and the newe,
> A Land there is no other lande may touche,
> Where regnes a Queen in peace and honor true;
> Storyes or fables doe describe noe suche.[13]

Not surprisingly, Essex's Stella is not Frances or even Penelope, but Queen Elizabeth, to whose Nonsuch Palace Essex here alludes; in fact, Elizabeth gave Essex his own rooms in that and other palaces for a period of years. Elizabeth is the third woman who came to be shared between Sidney and Essex. Essex cannot quite appropriate Sidney's skill, however, for his poems are not particularly masterful or original but derivative, indebted to the very authors whose lives, wives, and deaths he seems to have had occasion to usurp.

The contemporary historian William Camden noted that Essex fatally failed to moderate his 'youthfull heat, his swelling affectation of glory, and the fortitude of his inuincible courage neuer sufficiently to bee commended, with aduised moderation and a mature prolonging of time, which are thought to be singular parts of Military discipline'.[14] If Essex adopted senior poets' literary conceits, junior poets could adopt the political conceits that Camden notes, as apparently did William Shakespeare, whose private relationship with Henry Wriothesley, Earl of Southampton, may well have extended to Southampton's closest and most dangerous political ally and mentor, Essex. Blair Worden has recently argued that the play about King Richard II that Shakespeare's company, the Lord Chamberlain's Men, was paid to stage on the eve of Essex's rebellion in February 1601 was based on John Hayward's historical narrative of 1599.[15] Yet the likelihood remains that the play staged and described as 'old' was Shakespeare's play, printed in 1597 and in performance before that time, rather than a new adaptation of a book by an author who was still imprisoned for alleged treason on the eve of the rebellion. Even if Shakespeare did not capture Essex's attention in his play about Richard II, Essex's rise and fall seemed to have captured Shakespeare's in

12 Paul E. J. Hammer, 'Myth-Making: Politics, Propaganda and the Culture of Cadiz in 1596', *The Historical Journal*, 40 (1997), 637; see also Camden, who reports of the Cadiz expedition, 'A Library well furnished was lefte behinde, and fell to *Essex* as prize' (IV, 94).

13 *The Poems of Edward De Vere, Seventeenth Earl of Oxford and of Robert Devereux, Second Earl of Essex*, *Studies in Philology*, 5 (1980), p. 44.

14 Camden, *The Historie of the Most Renowned and Victorious Princesse Elizabeth*, IV, 95.

15 Worden, 'Which play was performed at the Globe theatre on 7 February 1601?', *London Review of Books*, vol. 25, no. 13 (10 July 2003), 22-4.

Henry V, and possibly *Hamlet*, *Troilus and Cressida*, and *All's Well that Ends Well.*[16] Perhaps this is why Essex, imprisoned on his unauthorised return from Ireland in 1599, complained in a letter to Elizabeth in 1600,

> I am gnawed on & torne by ye vilest & basest creatures vpon earth. The prating tavern hunter speaks of me what he list: the frantick libeller writes of me what he list; already they printe me, & make speak to ye world; and shortlye they will play me in what formes they list upon ye stage.[17]

Essex was no stranger to sponsoring theatrical productions; for example, after a banquet given at his home, Essex House, on 14 February 1598, Essex and his guests 'had 2 plaies which kept them up till 1 aclocke after midnight'.[18] That Essex was being represented *publicly* does not appear to be the source of his anger in this 1600 letter; rather it is that he is being represented in such low-class media as tavern gossip, tawdry pamphlets, and cheap drama. What he does *not* complain of here is the myriad public representations of him in the years before 1600 in others' poems, as well as elegant dedications to him of books of poems. In fact, Essex's attempt to court fame during the politically charged years of 1599 and 1600 would suggest that he valued such public representations in poems and books, if not on the stage.[19] If Essex did not become a major poet in his lifetime, it was not due to his lack of familiarity, influence, association, or intimacy with the most important poets of his time.

Essex's letter of complaint about his libellous public representation was copied by his secretary, Edward Reynolds, and can be found among the State Papers in the National Archives at Kew. It is one of a series of official copies of his letters, together with at least fifteen autograph letters by Essex to Elizabeth, still preserved at the National Archives, the British Library, and Hatfield House,[20] the last being the house eventually acquired by Lord Burghley's son, Sir Robert Cecil, Elizabeth's later Secretary of State. Numerous autograph letters by Essex addressed to other people also survive in these libraries and elsewhere, including Lambeth Palace and the Bodleian Library, Oxford. However, the bulk of Essex's original and private letters to Elizabeth has had relatively little attention, largely because the letters were kept, at least since the late seventeenth century, in the private archive of the Hulton family in England. The letters apparently came into their possession after being acquired by the lawyer William Jessop, who was employed by the third Earl of Essex (*d.*1646) as his executor, and whose daughter married into the Hulton family. In the nineteenth century, the letters to Elizabeth, as well as seven other letters relating to the Essex family, were bound into a volume with facing-page transcriptions of each. After nearly three hundred years, the Hulton family loaned the letters to the British Library in 1945, where they were, ostensibly at any rate, available

16 See Heffner, *The Earl of Essex in Elizabethan Literature: An extract from a Dissertation* (Baltimore, 1934).

17 National Archives, SP 274/138.

18 *HMC, De L'Isle*, II, 322.

19 On this point, and for his reading of this essay, I am grateful to Paul E. J. Hammer, whose essay, 'The smiling crocodile: the earl of Essex and late-Elizabethan "popularity"', will be published in a collection forthcoming in 2006.

20 See Sotheby's catalogue 'Elizabeth and Essex The Hulton Papers' (14 December 1992), p. 11. See also Phillips's catalogue 'The Earl of Essex to Elizabeth I' (11 June 1999).

to scholars. After being withdrawn for sale in 1992, the Hulton letters passed through two auction houses before being sold to the British Library in 1999.

This Hulton collection (British Library, Additional MS 74286) comprises 43 letters from Essex to Elizabeth. Most of the letters from Essex's relatives, including his mother and stepfather, originally in the collection, were removed and sold separately. Other letters were removed from the collection prior to 1945, including one from Essex to a nobleman and another to Essex from his mother, and were donated to a private school in Lancashire. Yet other Hulton letters to or from Essex may be housed elsewhere. The letters still bound in the British Library volume are in excellent condition and many still carry the original wax impressions and ribbons used by Essex to seal them. Previous to 1945, the collection remained substantially private, as only 35 of the 43 Hulton letters from Essex to Elizabeth were printed in whole, in part, or in summary, and not always accurately, in Walter Devereux's *Lives and Letters of the Devereux*, which remains the standard edition of Essex's letters.[21] As eight of the Hulton letters have apparently never been printed, a comprehensive understanding of the nature of Essex's intimate correspondence with Elizabeth was obscured for nearly four hundred years, even by Lytton Strachey, whose book attempted to chronicle Essex and Elizabeth's relationship,[22] before the letters were deposited in the British Library.

In a few Hulton letters, Essex's rapid cursive hand suggests that he is writing *currente calamo*, that is, in the heat of writing, in his usual 'ragged Romane', or rough italic hand, with little correction or revision before they were sent to the Queen (PLATE 1). In comparison, the rest of the letters would *seem* to be Essex's fair copies, that is rewritings of his foul-paper drafts or originals. However, in a 1585 autograph letter to his mother (BL Add. MS 32092, fol. 48), which is not part of the Hulton archive, Essex writes in an extraordinarily neat calligraphic hand to acknowledge her 'displeasure' at his recent 'vndutifullnes'[23] (PLATE 2). This hand differs substantially from the one he uses in what appear to be fair (or at least fairer) copy letters to Elizabeth found in the Hulton archive and written between 1590 and 1600. This difference may be due to Essex's younger age in the letter to his mother, or even to his painstaking attempt at that time to prove in both content and style that he was truly seeking his

21 W. B. Devereux, *Lives and Letters of the Devereux, Earls of Essex, in the Reign of Elizabeth, James I, and Charles I*, 2 vols (London, 1853).

22 Strachey, *Elizabeth and Essex* (London, 1928).

23 The letter reads in full: 'My very good L*ady* and mother. As I finde by your L*adyshi*ps displeasure conceaued, that I am thought in sorte to haue offended, so I desire to deliuer myself ether wholy, or in some parte from the same faulte. The w*hi*ch some will hardly terme vndutifullnes to your L*adyshi*p, others carelesnes of mine owne good, and many thinke me inconsiderate, in not makinge your L*adyshi*p more acquainted with my determinacions. The name of vndutiufllnes as a sonne I vtterly abhorre, my purposed course to do well I hope shall deliuer me from the suspicion of carelesnes of mine owne estate, and yf in your L*adyshi*ps wise censure I be thought inconsiderate, I pleade as a yonge man pardon for that fault whereto of all others our age is most subiect ~~vnto~~. And yf ether by sorow for that which is past, or duty hereafter, I may repaire that w*hi*ch your L*adyshi*p may thinke by desert is impared, I shall thinke my self (as much as for any thinge in this world) most happy: / Thus humbly crauinge your L*adyshi*ps blessinge I dayly pray for your L*adyshi*ps most honorable and happy estate. Lanfey this xij of Aprill 1585 Your L*adyshi*ps most obedient sonne R. Essex I haue returned this berer accordinge to your L*adyshi*ps commaundement every way to vsed at your L*adyshi*ps honorable pleasure.'

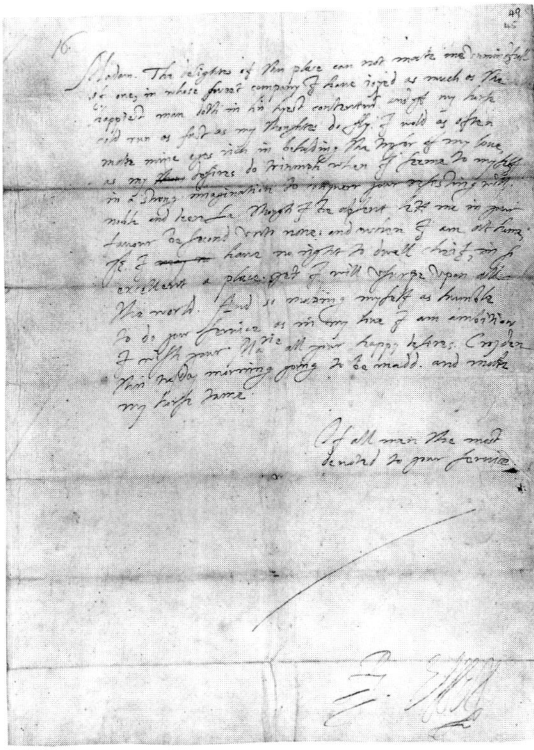
16.
Madam. The delights of this place can not make me vnmindfull of one in whose sweet company I haue ioyed as much as the happiest man doth in his hyest contentment. and yf my horse could run as fast as my thoughts do fly I wold as often make mine eyes rich in beholding the treasur of my loue as my desires do triumph when I seeme to myself in a strong imagination to conquer your resisting will. [illegible] I be absent [illegible] me in your fauour be found worth none; and when I am [illegible] [illegible] I haue no right to dwell [illegible] [illegible] excellent a place, yet I will [illegible] vpon all the world. And so wearing myself as humble to do your seruice as in my loue I am ambitious I wish your Matie all your happy desires. Croydon this [illegible] morning going to be [illegible]. and make my [illegible] [illegible]

Of all men the most deuoted to your seruice
[illegible]

1 Autograph letter signed by Essex to Queen Elizabeth, from Croydon, [undated], among the Hulton letters (BL, Additional MS 74282, fol. 45r)

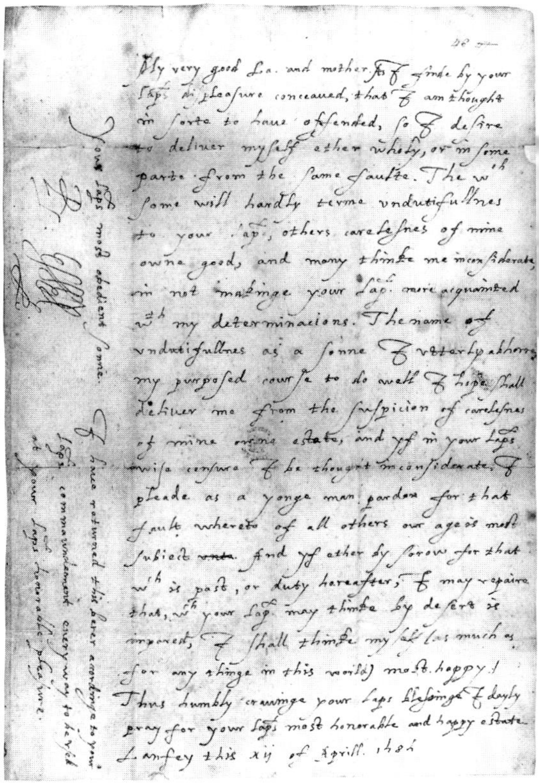
My very good La. and mother for I finde by your Laps displeasure conceaued, that I am thought in sorte to haue offended, so I desire to deliuer myself ether wholy, or in some parte from the same faulte. The wch some will hardly terme vndutifullnes to your lap, others carelesnes of mine owne good, and many thinke me inconsiderate in not makinge your lap. once acquainted wth my determinacions. The name of vndutifullnes as a sonne I vtterly abhorre, my purposed course to do well I hope shall deliuer me from the suspicion of carelesnes of mine owne estate, and yf in your Laps wise censure I be thought inconsiderate, I pleade as a yonge man pardon for that fault whereto of all others our age is most subiect. And yf ether by sorow for that wch is past, or duty hereafter, I may repaire that, wch your lap. may thinke by desert is impaired, I shall thinke my self (as much as for any thinge in this world) most happy. Thus humbly crauinge your Laps blessinge I dayly pray for your Laps most honorable and happy estate. Lanfey this xij of Aprill. 1585

Your Laps most obedient sonne.
[illegible]

I haue returned this bearer accordinge to your Laps commaundement euery way to be ridd at your Laps honorable pleasure.

2 Autograph letter signed by Essex to his mother, Lettice Knollys, 1585 (BL, Additional MS 32092, fol. 48r)

mother's forgiveness. So it is not certain that the later letters from the Hulton archive are *not* fair copies, but they, at least, are not as fairly written as the 1585 letter. The earlier letter demonstrates, nevertheless, that he was capable of using a respectful, deferential calligraphic hand to his mother which he did not employ in writing similar types of letters to Elizabeth, who most certainly should have commanded as much if not more respect as Queen and matriarch. Such behaviour towards the monarch suggests that Essex was confident of her tolerance and indulgence. But I also suspect that, although Elizabeth may have treated Essex at times like the son she should have had with Leicester, he did not treat her as his surrogate mother, or at least with the deference and filial affection that he offered his real mother. This is perhaps not ironic given that Elizabeth was so angered by Leicester's seeming betrayal in marrying Lettice Knollys without permission that she banned Lettice from court for virtually the rest of Elizabeth's life. Perhaps, then, the ways in which Essex expressed his qualified deference to Elizabeth but his complete loyalty to his mother included his handwriting.

Essex was known to have burned some of his letters and papers at various points in his life, most notably before his imminent arrest for treason in 1601, dramatically saying that they '*should tell no tales*'.[24] Nevertheless, after the arrest, Robert Cecil confiscated and kept what could be found of Essex's papers. Indeed, some of Essex's 1599 letters to his friends in which he inveighed against the Queen, after Elizabeth had boxed his ears in 1598 when he had the audacity to turn his back to her,[25] were produced and used in his prosecution in 1601.[26] However, these letters had been circulated in scribal copies, possibly at Essex's instigation. By 1601, Cecil already had a sizeable collection of letters from Essex and other courtiers (and their wives and mothers) directly addressed to Cecil on state business or sent to him to be passed on to the intended recipients, including the Queen or her officials.[27] Judging from the number of autograph or original letters of this latter type at Hatfield House (where they were eventually moved), I assume that Cecil did not always pass on the letters to their intended recipients, including that letter in the hand of Frances Devereux (noted above) addressed to her husband in Ireland and intimately discussing her pregnancy (PLATE 3). Even if Cecil did pass on the majority of letters, he may have kept back some of the most inflammatory or politically useful ones, such as several in which Essex harangued the Queen for punishing him, particularly from 1599, when he became increasingly abusive. If Cecil had sent these letters on to the Queen it would be difficult to understand how they later came back into his possession. Cecil should have taken a particular interest in the Hulton letters, especially as he countersigned one concerning the Lopez conspiracy. The fact that he did not later reclaim the letter and house it among his papers suggests that it may have been out of his reach.

Essex frequently refers in the Hulton letters to the intimate letters he has received from Elizabeth in her own hand. Yet none of these apparently survives. In fact, the very few letters from Elizabeth to Essex that do survive are mostly scribal copies of her formal instructions to Essex or her rebukes or commendations for his service as statesman or soldier. Elizabeth's own autograph personal letters to Essex would have been dangerous matter, especially if they could have been used to support him at his

24 Henry Wotton, *Memoirs of the life of Robert Devereux, Earl of Essex* (London, n.d.), p. 21. Camden records Essex's words slightly differently in noting that he burned the papers 'lest (as he said) they should tell tales' (IV, 177).

25 Essex's behaviour was widely reported. See, for example, Camden who notes that Essex could not persuade Elizabeth at a 1598 meeting with other courtiers that George Carew should be named the new Lieutenant Governor of Ireland, and Essex 'forgetting himselfe, and neglecting his duty, vnciuilly turneth his backe, as it were in contempt, with a scornfull looke. She waxing impatient, gaue him a cuffe on the eare, and bad him be gone with a vengeance. He layed his hand vpon his sword, the Lord Admirall interposing himself, he sware a great oath, that hee neither could nor would swallow so great an indignity, nor would haue borne it at King *Henry* the 8. his hands; and in great discontentment hasted from the Court' (IV, 127).

26 Camden states that evidence against Essex in his 1601 treason trial was produced 'out of his letters written about two yeeres before (wherof copies were lately dispersed by his followers)', including parts of Hayward's history of Richard II, which had been dedicated to Essex (IV, 166).

27 See, for example, this letter in Hatfield House CP 40/67 (*HMC, Salisbury*, VI, 172), which is written by Essex to Cecil: 'In this packett you shall receaue a l*ett*re vnto her Ma*jes*tie w*hi*ch I pray you present from her humble seruant: another from my L*or*d Admirall and me to my L*ord* yo*ur* father, to w*hi*ch, for such little mesur as wee haue, I must referr you and in this to yo*ur* self haue patience if I deale somewhatt freely.'

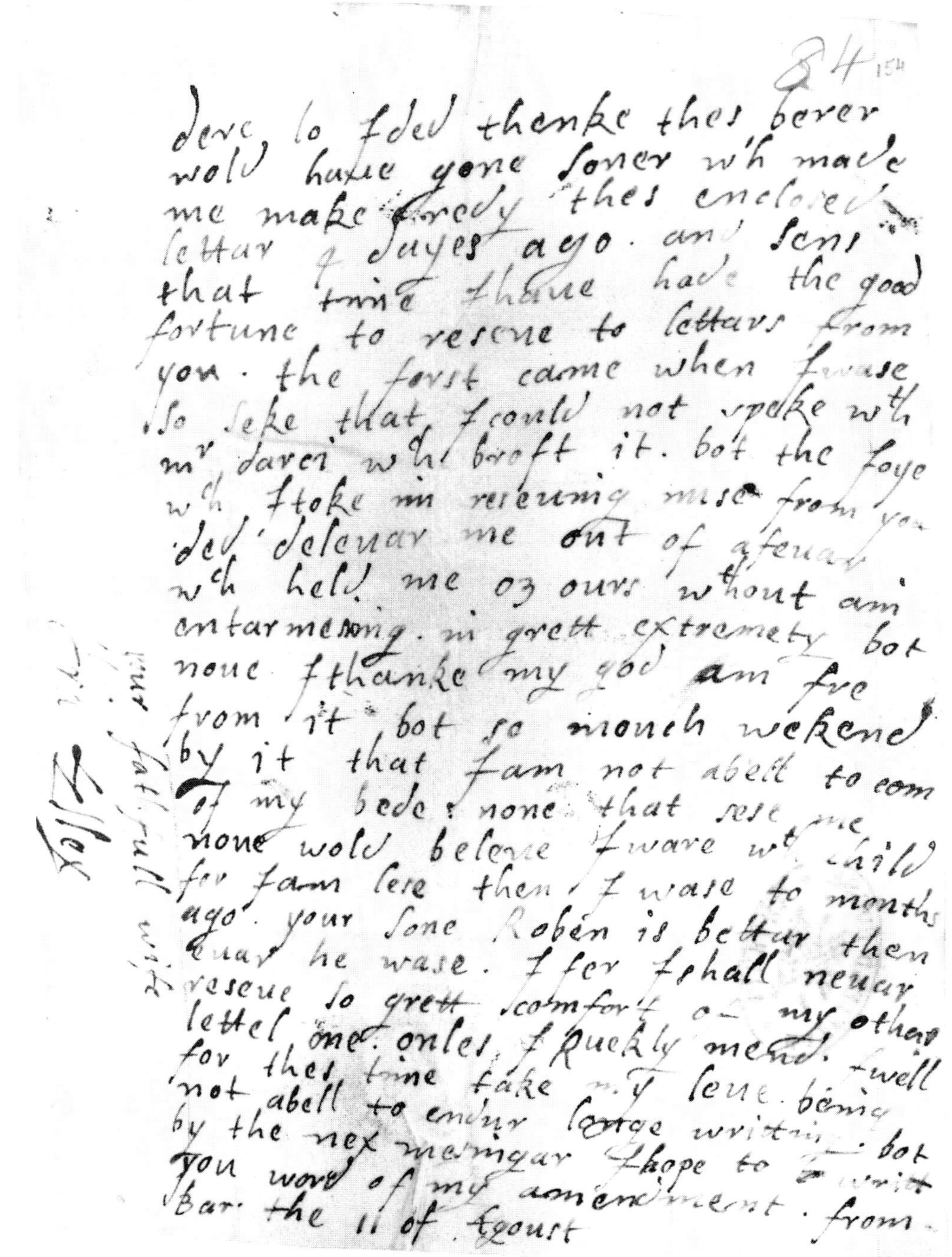
dere, lo I ded thenke thes berer
wold haue gone soner wh made
me make redy thes enclosed
lettar 4 dayes ago and sens
that time I haue had the good
fortune to reseue to lettars from
you. the forst came when I wase
so seke that I could not speke wth
mr davei wch broft it. bot the Ioye
wch I toke in reseuing nuse from you
ded delevar me out of a feuar
wch held me 23 ours whout ani
entarmeting. in grett extremety bot
noue I thanke my god am fre
from it bot so mouch wekened
by it that I am not abell to com
of my bede: none that sese me
none wold beleue I ware wt child
for I am lese then I wase to months
ago. your sone Roben is bettar then
euar he wase. I fer I shall neuar
reseue so grett comfort of my other
lettel one. onles I quekly mend.
for thes time I take my leue. being
not abell to endur large writing. bot
by the nex mesengar I hope to writ
you word of my amendment. from
Bar. the 11 of Agoust

Yor fathfull wif
Essex

3 Autograph letter signed by Frances Devereux (née Walsingham) to her husband, the Earl of Essex, [1599] (Library of the Marquess of Salisbury, Hatfield House, Cecil Papers 63/84)

1601 trial. His prosecutors, including Cecil, may then have deliberately destroyed them. Or perhaps the letters were stolen, as were a set of letters from Essex to his wife. These intimate letters, written before and after their marriage, were taken in September 1599 by John Daniel, the husband of the servant to whom Frances had entrusted them while she was preparing for childbirth. Daniel then paid the scrivener Peter Bales to copy Essex's handwriting in an attempt to forge potentially seditious letters, so that Daniel could blackmail Frances for their return, first demanding £3000 and then settling for the largest amount, less than £2000, that she could gather at short notice. Frances eventually reported the crime, and in June 1601, after Essex had been executed, Daniel was convicted in the Star Chamber of the theft and forgery of the letters. He was jailed for life at the Fleet prison and ordered to be 'sett upon the pillory with his eares thereunto nayled, with a paper on his head inscribed with these words – "For forgery, corrupte cosenages, and other lewde practises" – declaring the nature of his said offences'.[28] The theft of such private property, even that of a recently executed traitor, evidently had its just punishments.

Daniel's lewd practises did not appear to play a role in the descent of Essex's autograph letters to Elizabeth to the private Hulton archive. They seem to have been returned to Essex's son, Robert, the third Earl of Essex, or his grandmother, the Countess of Leicester (*d.*1634), most probably by King James I after his accession in 1603, in recognition of the second Earl's secret support of James's succession to the English throne.[29] This unusual return of State Papers from an executed traitor to his son or mother marks this collection as unique and more than a little mysterious. None of the Hulton letters explicitly concerns the two most politically dangerous episodes in Essex's career: his unauthorised return from Ireland in 1599 and his treason in 1601. This suggests that the Hulton letters are a select set of letters subjected to some scrutiny before they were returned to the Essex family. Or perhaps it suggests that Elizabeth herself held on to only a set of the least incriminating, or hurtful, letters from Essex and either destroyed the rest or sent them to the State Papers Office. She had kept the last letter of her previous favourite, Leicester, who died in 1588, in a casket by her bedside

28 *The Egerton Papers*, ed. J. Payne Collier (London, 1840), pp. 321-7.

29 At the end of the Hulton collection of letters, bound in the nineteenth century into a volume containing facing-page transcriptions of each letter, is a letter from W. D. Macray written on Public Record Office letterhead and dated 6 September 1888, in which he writes: 'it appears from various papers that William Jessop, of Gray's Inn (whose only child Anne married William Hulton who died in 1694) was the lawyer employed [and Clerk to the Houses of Commons and to the Council of State] by the Executor of Robert, the third Earl of Essex (viz. the Earls of Northumberland and Warwick and Oliver St John) in the settlement of the Earl's affairs in 1647-8. It may therefore be possible that the letters of the second Earl to Q. Elizabeth may have come into Jessop's hands amongst other family papers. And if so, it may be that these and the two letters from the Earl of Leicester may have been returned after the Queen's death to the old Countess of Leicester, the mother of the Earl of Essex. That there are letters found here to the third Earl as well, makes the conjecture more probable.' See also Macray's report on the Hulton letters in *HMC, 12th Report, Appendix, Part IV* (1891), pp. 165-78, in which he reiterates these conclusions. As Katherine Duncan-Jones has privately noted to me, Essex's very high rank as a hereditary Earl and his official service as Earl Marshal may have bestowed some continued property rights on his heirs.

where it was found after her death in 1603.[30] She may have had similar sentimental attachments to the letters from Leicester's stepson.

II. 'PRIUATE PLACES FOR VNKINDNES': ESSEX CONSTRUCTS HIMSELF

Most of the Hulton letters deal in some way with affairs of state, including major and minor problems that Essex encountered in Elizabeth's foreign service, ranging from how to manipulate an ally or enemy to how to repair a leaking ship in a naval expedition. More precisely, they narrate Essex's services in France in aid of Henry of Navarre in 1592, his pursuit of the Spanish treasure fleet in 1597, and his campaign against Tyrone in Ireland in 1599. Yet the letters speak most powerfully in Essex's voice when he details his attempts to gain or re-gain Elizabeth's favour, respect, and love, beginning in 1590 and ending around 1599. (Although dated by day and month, the Hulton letters frequently lack the year, which can be established from internal evidence for most but not all of the letters; the order in which they were bound and still remain may not represent their true chronological order.) The letters cover almost all the breadth of Essex's tempestuous relationship with Elizabeth, from their loving familiarity to their petty quarrels, from his intense devotion to his manic anger, from his fervent expressions of love to his harsh recriminations. His early letters are loving, intimate, and familiar in tone, but his later letters are jealous, bitter, and insulting. He contemptuously complains that she draws him near, forcing on him emotional, political, and financial dependence, and then scorns and rejects him. At the same time he passionately yearns for her letters and affection as well as her personal respect, devotion, and approval.

The recent work of Peter Beal, Harold Love, Henry Woudhuysen, Arthur F. Marotti, and David McKitterick, among others, has persuasively demonstrated that the copying and circulation of manuscripts in the early modern period served as an acknowledged form of publication.[31] Although the Hulton letters constitute an unusual case in being so restricted in circulation for so long, copies or originals of some of Essex's other letters, as well as his poems, circulated in manuscript form at court during and after his lifetime. Essex employed a number of secretaries, but as Paul E. J. Hammer has recently argued, only Edward Reynolds appears to have been entrusted with copying out his private correspondence.[32] In fact, in one letter extant at Hatfield House, Essex has Reynolds write in his own hand to Cecil, so that Cecil can recognise the hand and

30 Derek Wilson, *Sweet Robin* (London, 1981), p. 303; Wilson presents the note in Illustration 8c.

31 See, for example, Woudhuysen's claim in *Sir Philip Sidney and the Circulation of Manuscripts*, p. 18, that 'in early modern England there remained some question about whether a single copy taken from a manuscript constituted publication in itself'. See also Harold Love, *Scribal Publication in Seventeenth-Century England* (Oxford, 1993); Arthur F. Marotti, *Manuscript, Print, and the English Renaissance Lyric* (Ithaca, NY, 1995); Peter Beal, *In Praise of Scribes: Manuscripts and their Makers in Seventeenth-Century England* (Oxford, 1998); and David McKitterick, *Print, Manuscript and the Search for Order 1450-1830* (Cambridge, 2003).

32 Hammer, 'The Uses of Scholarship: The Secretariat of Robert Devereux, Second Earl of Essex c.1585-1601, *English Historical Review*, 109 (1994), 32.

assume it carries Essex's authority in future letters.[33] Essex did not appear to have Reynolds make copies of the Hulton letters, however. Thus far, I have found only one Hulton letter that was copied, inaccurately, by contemporary scribes.[34] Copies of Essex's other letters were made by unknown scribes, and these are the copies that appear to have been used most often by seventeenth- and eighteenth-century biographers and historians, including Camden. Some letters purportedly by Essex were in fact counterfeited, not only by servants such as John Daniel, but by friends and allies like Anthony Bacon who assumed they wrote with Essex's permission.[35] Letters extant both in Essex's hand and by scribes show that copyists did not polish, refine, regularise, or even temper Essex's characteristic outbursts of anger or mania, but, perhaps for political reasons, exaggerated and embellished them when making transcripts. More distressingly, contemporary copyists debased his rhetorical style, poetic imagery, and literary turn of phrase in amateurish ways, thus making Essex out to be an incompetent writer and a bad poet.[36]

33 See Essex's letter to Cecil on 26 April 1596 (Hatfield House, CP 40/30; *HMC, Salisbury*, VI, 157) which is in Reynolds's hand with Essex's signature and reads in full: 'S*ir* I do leaue behinde me this bearor my seruant Edward Reynolds to attend my busines: whome I thought good to commend vnto you, & to praye you that you will in my absence favor hym, & afford hym yor best helpe & assistance, in any thing that may concerne my service, as he shall be occasioned to haue recourse unto you. My busines are so manie, as I am forcd to use his hand, whom if it shall please you, on his own particular occasions to countenance, I will with my best thankfulness acknowledge it. And so do committ you to god*es* best p*ro*tection.from ye Court the 26 of Aprill 1596 / yo*ur* most assured frend / Essex.'

34 Hulton Letter 44 (fol. 122), dated 30 August [1599] and beginning 'From a mind delighting in sorow', survives in at least fifteen scribal copies of the early seventeenth century, including Bodleian MSS Ashmole 767, fol. 9r; Ashmole 781, fol. 83; Rawlinson C. 744, fol. 59v; Tanner 82, fol. 27r; Tanner 304, fol. 59v; British Library Add. MS 9828, fol. 7; Add. MS 22587, fol. 40v; Egerton MS 3876, fol. 213v; Royal MS 17 B. L, fol. 17r-v; Cambridge University Library, MS Ee.5.23, p. 429; Folger Shakespeare Library MSS V. a. 239, fols 55-6; V. b. 142, fol. 41r; V. b. 234, fols 41-2; Queen's College, Oxford, MS 121, fol. 444; University College, Oxford, MS 152, fol. 122; as well as in later publications such as *Scrinia Sacra* (London, 1654), pp. 26-7, and *Cabala* (London, 1654), p. 233. These texts show numerous minor variants from Essex's original, including verbal substitutions, omissions, and changes of word order. I assume that other manuscript copies are elsewhere as the letter circulated widely after Essex's execution.

35 See *Hostage to Fortune: The Troubled Life of Francis Bacon* (London, 1999), p. 235, in which Lisa Jardine and Alan Stewart note that Francis Bacon 'drafted an exchange of letters ostensibly between Essex and Anthony [Bacon] (to whom Essex might be expected to write more candidly), designed expressly for the Queen's eyes. ... Bacon always maintained that these letters served no purpose beyond enhancing Essex's standing with Elizabeth, and that Essex not only commissioned them but was instrumental in circulating them. Essex may actually have had no hand in them; at his trial he claimed they had been written to discredit him.'

36 An example of this is the widely copied letter by Essex to Elizabeth, dated in some sources '1600' and beginning 'My dutiful affection to your Majesty', where the considerable number of substantive variants includes such recasted phrases as 'overaymed above' for 'ouerweyed'; 'yet I have deserved' for 'I will not say in'; and 'in regard of my many gracious services both of my selfe and my contrye' for 'but in some gratious estate of service'. This letter, which does not survive in Essex's original, is found copied in Bodleian MSS Ashmole 767, fol. 8r-v; Ashmole 781, fol. 82; Rawlinson C. 744, fol. 61r-v; Rawlinson D. 924, fol. 1r; Tanner 82, fols 25v-26v; BL Add. MS 4166, fol. 72r-v; Egerton MS 3876, fol. 213r-v; Harley MS 1323, fols 246r-7v; Harley MS 3786, fol. 49; Royal MS 17 B. L, fols 14v-17r; Sloane MS 1856, fols 6v-7r; Cambridge University Library, MS Ee.5.23, fol. 417; Folger MSS V. a. 239, fols 50-4; V. a. 321, fols 5v-6r; V. b. 214, fol. 106r-v; V. b. 234, fols 38-41; X. c. 11; Huntington Library, HM 36836, fols 12-15; Inner Temple Library, Petyt MS 538, vol. 18, after fol. 188; Queen's College, Oxford, MS 32, fol. 12; MS 121, fol. 444; University College, Oxford, MS 152, fols 65-7; and printed in *Scrinia Sacra* (1654), pp. 25-6, and in *Cabala* (1654), pp. 232-3.

At times, Essex represents himself in the Hulton letters as remarkably naive, as when he asks Elizabeth to delay her demand for the repayment of a loan, pleading that 'money and land are base thinges butt loue and kindnes are excellent thinges and can nott be measured butt by themselues' (fol. 6). He uses other such simplistic platitudes in the letters, interspersed with strikingly beautiful imagery and politically shrewd advice. Peter Beal has noted the 'series of roles in which [Essex] presents himself ... and by implication, the Queen, as well as the manner of his address, which, paradoxically, has all the carefully contrived artificiality of an elaborate stately dance combined with all the intense drama of a passionately conducted but thwarted love affair'.[37] These letters present courtly love at its most Petrarchan, or, more accurately, its most Elizabethan. Yet, rather than focusing primarily on this 'love affair', I want to examine what the letters tell us about early modern concepts of privacy as Elizabeth and Essex understood them in writing letters to each other.

Essex frequently thanks Elizabeth for writing to him in her own hand, rather than sending a letter in a scribe's hand; in 1597, for example, he speaks of the comfort of 'y*ou*r gracious sending, and honoring and blessing me w*i*th y*ou*r owne hand writing' (fol. 58). Four months later he tells her, 'I will neuer cease to importune y*ou*r Ma*jes*tie thatt I may – by some handwriting from y*ou*r sacred self be assured thatt I do nott decrease in y*ou*r Ma*jes*ties fauor' (fol. 93). Elsewhere he reminds Elizabeth of the extreme conditions under which he sent and received letters. In 1591, Essex defends himself from her charge of 'nott writing oftener to y*ou*r Ma*jes*ties' while laying siege to Rouen in alliance with Henry of Navarre. Essex impatiently chastises her,

> I aunswer before my going to the K*ing*. I wrote 4 tymes in 14 dayes and had written 14 tymes yf I cold haue procured as many passages after my going till I came to Pont de Larch I did dispatch a fr*ench* currer because no English man cold haue passed nott knowing the cuntry and no passage safe butt by night and being ioyned with the footmen I was one day nott like to liue and yett the next I despatched away Mr Darcy though he stayd a day after and saw the spectacle of my misery. (fol. 15v)

Here an angry Essex reminds Elizabeth that sending her letters requires a third party, in this case a courier who must make a perilous journey through enemy territory. To be fair to Essex, he has also just suffered the loss of his younger brother, Walter, in this fruitless campaign against the French Catholics. But Essex may also be responding here to letters from Elizabeth, as Camden records, in which she rebuked him for recklessness.[38] Even in writing in the heat of the moment, Essex recognises that his letters will not remain private, but hopes that they will be made public so that others will see them and recognise his accomplishments. Henry of Navarre was evidently made aware in 1591 of Essex's desire to become a 'public' being, even in the act of dying, for when told in 1601 that Elizabeth had had Essex executed privately at his wish, Henry

37 Beal, Sotheby's catalogue, p. 17.

38 Camden notes of Essex that during the Rouen campaign in 1591, 'The Queene blamed him by her letters, for that without acquainting her hee had gone vnto the King, and had inconsiderately come too neere *Roan*. But hee with a little flattery soone appeased her' (IV, 26).

discounted the report, claiming that Essex 'desired nothing more than to die in public'.[39]

Habermas's virtues of 'excellence, highness, majesty, fame, dignity, and honor', which enable the private man to become a public being, are repeatedly named by Essex in his letters to the Queen as he constantly attempts to establish that he is worthy of representation. He offers these words in private praise of her, but also publicly to construct himself; thus his letters are self-creating and self-institutionalising. Essex also repeatedly tries to make the 'priuate places' she offers him into public spheres in which to receive her honour and that of the court. For example, in a letter written during the Rouen campaign in 1591 (and never printed), Essex bemoans his losses in battle:

> y*ou*r Ma*jes*ties gratious accepting of my humble endevours shall make my danger be thought safety, my labor ease, and the misereis thatt follow the warrs pleasures butt y*our* least unkindess shall make me striue to prouide thatt the most of y*our* men may come safe home butt thatt I, before I returne, may arriue att my last home. ... In this world I repose all my hope and trust in y*our* sacred brest ... other men may haue retyred from y*our* Court into priuate places for vnkindnes. butt I protest when y*our* fauor is gone from me my soule shall retyre from my body. (fol. 12r-v: PLATE 4)

'Unkindness' is a word Essex uses repeatedly in the letters and it serves as a private code for the withdrawal of Elizabeth's favour, public or private, probably with a pun on 'unnaturalness', and perhaps with a further pun on 'unfeminine'. Early in their relationship, he ostensibly lives in fear of receiving her unkindness, and it appears to be the worst punishment that can be inflicted on him. To be 'retyred' from her court into 'priuate places' due to her unkindness, as other men have been, would cost him the loss of his soul. As he knows, the day his relationship with her becomes truly private, he has lost not only his soul, but also his public persona and essential identity. He later learns to weather her unkindness. As their relationship becomes more interdependent he can sign a letter, probably written in 1597, 'y*ou*r Ma*jes*ties seruant wounded but not altered by y*ou*r vnkindnes' (fol. 96).

Yet for all his attempts at playing the devoted lover, Essex constantly reminds her, often contemptuously, that he is her servant. Of course, this was the price of living the public rather than the private life, as Samuel Daniel tells us in *The Prayse of Priuate Life*, sometimes attributed to Sir John Harington, Elizabeth's godson; not ironically both poets were protégés of Essex. Daniel writes:

> I finde this onely difference betwene those that live servantes to meane Masters, and others attendinge great Princes ... the one is tyed in fetters of Iron, the other in gyves of goulde. The one weareth a simple coate, the other a riche Liverie, but theire bondage is like, and he is most to be blamed, whoe doth that by election, which others are constryned unto.

Daniel emphasises that those who serve others abjure the much preferable and more altruistic private life, and

> are governed as others directe, and what they must doe, is to be looked for in an other Mans eyes. They dwell in other Mens Howses, they sleepe not when they woulde, but when they maye and

39 Cited by Robert Lacey, *Robert, Earl of Essex: An Elizabethan Icarus* (London, 1971), p. 2.

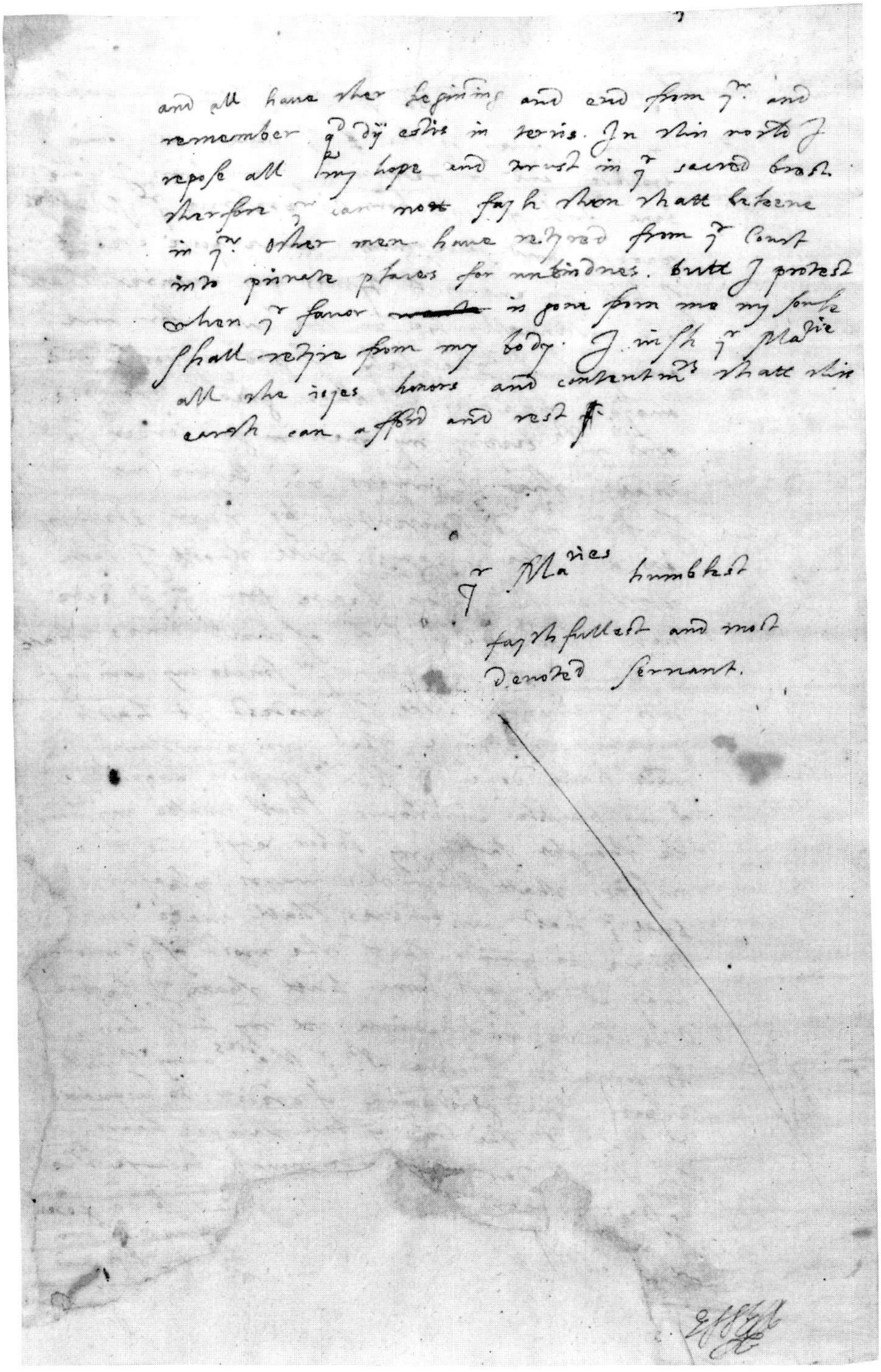

and all haue ther begining and end from yr and
remember quod dii estis in terris. In this world I
repose all my hope and trust in yr sacred brest.
therfore yr can not fayle thou shalt beleeue
in yr other men haue retyred from yr Court
into priuate places for unkindnes. butt I protest
when yr fauor [illegible] is gone from me my soule
shall retire from my body. I wish yr Matie
all the ioyes honors and contentmts that this
earth can afford and rest

Yr Maties humblest
faythfullest and most
deuoted seruant.

Essex

4 Second page of an autograph letter signed by Essex, to Queen Elizabeth, from France, [12 September 1591], among the Hulton letters (BL, Additional MS 74282, fol. 12v)

eate when others doe. Yea that which most is, they sigh or smyle as others shall please to commaunde. They negotiate other Mens affayres and neglecte their owne: they live for others not themselves.[40]

Daniel's description here in fact summarises Essex's frustration, anger, and bitterness in sighing, smiling, and otherwise serving as Elizabeth 'shall please to commaunde' him in these letters.

Essex is determined to live for himself and not for her. For example, in another 1597 letter he pleads:

yf I be too weake an instument to be inspired w.th such a gyft, or thatt wordes be nott able to interprett for me. then to y*ou*r royall deer harte I appeale w*hi*ch w*i*thout my wordes can fully and iustly vunderstand me. Heauons and earth shall wittnes for me I will striue to be worthy of so high a Grace and so blessed a happines. Be pleased therfore most deer Q*ueen* to be euer thus gracious, yf nott for my meritt yett for y*ou*r owne constancy. And so, you shall bestow all those happinesses w*hi*ch in the end of y*ou*r lettre you are pleased to wish. And then yf I may heere y*ou*r Ma*jes*tie is well pleased nothing can be ill w*i*th y*ou*r Ma*jes*ties humblest and most affectionate vassall. (fol. 52)

But his devoted service comes with implied threats, as in a letter two months later, in which he notes that his service far from home has left him open to attack at court by his enemies:

Absent men are subiect to many reports, interpretations and taxations. Butt y*ou*r Ma*jes*tie is iust, and I will proue myself to haue more trew zeale to y*ou*r seruice. perfect obedience to y*ou*r com*m*andm*en*ts, and matchlesse affection to y*ou*r deerest person then all men els thatt haue, do, or shall liue. And If you beleeue, nott this you are nott iust nor do nott right. (fol. 90r-v)

Even more insulting is his complaint in a later letter, probably dating from 1598, in which he rebukes her for giving others an advantage towards his 'ruyne', concluding, 'In holding me as you haue done of late you pleased no body' (fol. 128). This sort of reckless presumption by Essex, who was often rebuked at court, is typical of their long relationship. Yet, privately, she appears to have tolerated Essex's long and repeated harangues; judging from the frequency with which he speaks fatuously, contemptuously, and sometimes abusively to her in these letters, he must have been confident that their private relationship invited such freedom.

He offers her respect as a monarch; he offers her as a woman the type of patronising behaviour in private that is common in aristocratic men of the period. This may have been, then, the secret to their extremely contentious relationship. In public he usually submitted to treating her like a queen; in private she submitted to being treated like a woman. This is the overwhelming sense that these letters suggest: they repeatedly depict the masculine patronisation of, and condescension towards, not simply an ageing, vain monarch, but a person who is submissive and inferior simply because she is a woman. Perhaps this particular type of emotional manipulation is what kept

40 *The Letters and Epigrams of Sir John Harington together with The Prayse of Private Life*, ed. Norman Egbert McClure (Philadelphia, 1930), p. 336. Paul J. Hammer has privately suggested that Francis Bacon makes the same point in his essay 'Of great place'.

Elizabeth bound to Essex. While male historians have claimed that Essex's problem was that he recognised no monarch, particularly Elizabeth, as his equal, I would argue, based on the Hulton letters, that he recognised no woman as his equal. For all his elevated rhetoric and exaggerated sentiments of devotion, he insisted on treating her the way he apparently treated other women, with a kind of wantonness, carelessness, and lack of regard. This sort of treatment may have given her what other women of her time had: a man who expected her submission and surrender in exchange for his care and protection. This may be, then, what, at some level of her private being she craved, and in giving it to her, he created and represented himself as her true patriarch and master.

III. 'WHATT WORDES HAUE I TO OFFER TO SUCH A GODDESSE?': ESSEX AND THE CONSTRUCTION OF ELIZABETH

The Hulton letters are infused with Essex's apparent acceptance of a common belief of his time that 'Mens hearts may be poysoned, and seduced, as well by Manuscripts, and written Bookes and Pamphlets, as those that be Printed, especially after they be once scattered and dispersed abroad into diverse mens hands.'[41] The 'poisoning' and 'seduction' of his muse seem to be the two simultaneous and recurrent aims of the Hulton letters. In constructing himself as either a public or private patriarch, Essex had to construct Elizabeth, and he seems to appropriate the poetic language, tropes, metaphors, and designs of those poets with whom he interacted throughout his life. If at times he appears to poison her, in order to create himself, at others he seduces her into believing that she is his creation. More precisely, in these letters Essex attempts to offer a sonnet sequence to his lady, as if attempting to play Astrophil to Elizabeth's Stella. Or as Peter Beal has put it, Essex offers a 'series of "Lover's Complaints"' in the style of Sidney and Spenser.[42] If Essex's own poems lacked the power, rhetoric, and stylistic beauty of his poet-mentors, his letters did not.

As Sidney noted, a poet 'nothing affirms, and therefore never lieth'.[43] But judging from Essex's words and actions here and elsewhere, he must always brashly affirm something and cannot lie. In life, he was unusually and brutally honest to a fault, at one point recklessly announcing that Elizabeth's conditions were 'no lesse crooked in mind than in body'. He often claimed that he was simply incapable of constructing a persona, poetic or otherwise. Hence the conclusion of a contemporary that, '*In a word, no man was more ambitious of glory by vertue, no man more careless of all things else.*'[44] Essex disingenuously claimed late in his life that he was 'a stranger to all poetical conceits'.[45] But, in fact, he does construct a poetic persona in these letters:

41 Sir Christopher Sibthorp, *A reply to an answere* (Dublin, 1625), cited by David McKitterick, *A History of Cambridge University Press, I: Printing and the Book Trade in Cambridge 1534-1698* (Cambridge, 1992), p. 2.

42 Sotheby's catalogue, p. 18.

43 Sidney, *An Apologie for Poetrie* (London, 1595).

44 Camden, IV, 172.

45 Jardine and Stewart, *Hostage to Fortune*, p. 233.

the disingenuous persona of a man incapable of constructing a persona, hence his simultaneous poisoning and seduction of his beloved. Moreover, he borrows from Sidney to do so. Katherine Duncan-Jones has intriguingly argued that 'of all the women who shaped Sidney's responses to the female sex the most crucial, but also the most enigmatic, is the Queen'. In addition Duncan-Jones claims that Sidney uses poetry, particularly *Astrophil and Stella*, to show 'the speaker's sterile journey into moral and emotional impasse'.[46] It is in these two Sidney-like accomplishments, using Elizabeth to shape his response to women and using a pseudo-sonnet sequence to express sterility and moral impasse, that Essex most succeeds in these Hulton letters.

As noted above, Essex here uses and often abuses both neo-Petrarchan and neo-Platonic imagery – a stratagem, perhaps, he takes to be necessary for constructing Elizabeth. But rather than living in her shadow, she lives in his. As Steven W. May has noted, Elizabeth was known for her 'skill in capitalizing upon public opportunities to identify herself with poetic, fictional entitities'.[47] Essex follows suit. For example, he claims in more than one letter that he has been subject more to her 'naturall bewty' than to her royal power; when he did hope for her favour, he claims, 'I sold my liberty to be a seruant to my loue' (fol. 105). In a late-1591 letter from Rouen, Essex complains of 'the misery of absence' from his 'most deere Lady', noting how 'very vnpleasaunt' his life will be until he can 'once againe enioy the honor, the pleasure, the sweetnes' of her presence. He will claim his 'reward', to 'be soone att home att y*our* Ma*jes*ties feete. whence nothing butt death or (y*our* vnconstancy w*hic*h is nott in rer*um* natura.) can driue me' (fol. 9). In a letter from the same period, he beseeches her, 'geue me leaue once againe ... to tell y*our* Ma*jes*ties thatt no vnkindness from yow, though yt breake my hart, can diminish my affection butt I will end my lyfe complayning of y*our* iniustice and approuing mine owne constancy' (fol. 18). Here and elsewhere in the letters he seems to be using 'heart' to pun on his crest of a stag or hart, the image of which appears in his wax seals on some of the letters (PLATE 5).

However conventional or trite his praise and Petrarchan devotion are here, Essex shows a more deft poetic hand one year later, in a letter from October 1592, before his return from France. He writes:

> In my absence I conceaue an absurd hope to do somthing thatt shall make me worthy of the name of y*our* seruant. Att my returne I will humbly beseach y*our* Ma.tie thatt no cause butt a great action of y*our* owne may draw me out of y*our* sight. For the 2 windowes of your privy chamber shall be the poles of my sphere wher, as long as y*our* Ma*jes*tie will please to haue me, I am fixed and unmoueable: when you thinke that heauen too good for me, I will not fall like a starr, butt be consumed like a vapor by the same sun thatt draw me up to such a height. (fol. 33)

Clearly Elizabeth is not his star but his sun. Essex's metaphor that the two windows of her privy chamber shall be the poles of his sphere around which he shall be fixed and immovable is rather extraordinary, even if derived from early modern poets. His assertion that when she thinks her heaven too good for him he will not fall like a star but be consumed like a vapour by her sun also sounds thrillingly erotic. Although the

46 Katherine Duncan-Jones, *Sir Philip Sidney Courtier Poet* (New Haven & London, 1991), pp. 16, 239.
47 May, *The Elizabethan Courtier Poets* (Columbia, Missouri, 1991), p. 135.

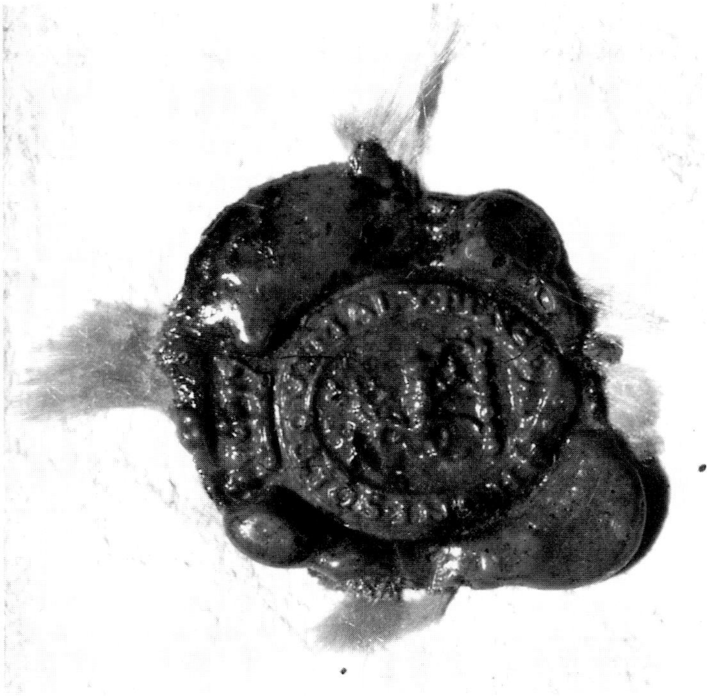

5 One of Essex's 'stag' wax seals on the Hulton letters (slightly enlarged)

sphere he describes here seems provocatively private, it is instead necessarily public and undoubtedly recalls the mythological figure of Icarus, condemned to fall through his own pride in trying to reach the brutal heat of the sun. Sir Francis Bacon later claimed that Essex exploited this self-image as Icarus at other times in his life.[48]

If Essex has over-flown in this metaphor, he comes back to his fixed position in her sphere by continuing with this promise:

> while y*ou*r Ma*ies*tie geues me leaue to say I loue you, my fortune is as my affection, unmatchable. Yf euer you deny me thatt liberty, you may end my lyfe, butt neue[r] shake my constancy, for where the sweetnes of y*our* nature turned into the greatest bitternes thattt cold be, yt is nott in y*our* power, (as greatt a Q[ueen] as you are) to make me loue you less. Therfore for the honor of y*our* sex, show y*our* self constant in kindnes, for all y*our* other vertues are confest to be perfect. (fol. 33)

While such hyperbolic language seems artificial, formal, and rehearsed in these early Hulton letters, in later letters, in which Essex rails and rants against what he perceives to be Elizabeth's injustice and neglect, he seems incapable of containing his emotion or his words. The tempestuous and manic Essex of the later letters cannot use any

48 *Sir Francis Bacon His Apologie, in Certaine imputations concerning the late Earle of Essex* (London, 1604), p. 17.

language that is not honest and real, no matter how cruel and insulting. Like Shakespeare's courtier the Earl of Kent in *King Lear*, 'He cannot flatter, he; / An honest man and plain, he must speak truth'.[49] Nor is Essex a hypocrite; his words are identical to his thoughts and feelings. Essex was exceptionally difficult, rash, reckless, disobedient, impolitic, and naive. He was unable to ingratiate himself with those he felt below his intellectual or social level. Yet Elizabeth constantly forgave him for his blunt words and deeds. She forgave him when he repeatedly ignored her orders in the French, Spanish, and Irish campaigns from the early to late 1590s. She forgave him in 1598 when he tried to draw his sword against her after she boxed his ear at court. She even forgave him in 1590 for marrying Frances Sidney without her permission, although she never appears to have forgiven Frances. The relationship of Essex and Elizabeth is one in which he constantly disobeyed her and she forgave him, until the cooling-off leading to his rebellion in 1601 when he finally fell from her sphere for good. As Camden notes, Essex was 'slow to any wickednesse, of a soft nature to take offence, and hard to lay it downe, and one that could not couer his affections'. The result was that Essex 'carried alwayes his loue and hatred in his forehead and could not conceale it'.[50] Essex cannot dissemble or conceal his love and hatred for Elizabeth in these letters; that is, he is engrossed in the construction of her that he paradoxically both fabricates and believes in. So we should accept his flattery of her in the 1592 letter as genuine praise.

Essex's erratic behaviour may have had a physical cause. In many of the Hulton and other letters he complains of crippling headaches, pains in his face, depression and other illnesses that confine him to bed for long periods. In an extant copy of his horoscope (British Library Sloane MS 1697, fol. 54v) probably cast upon the birth of his son Robert in 1591 (and with later annotations), the astrologer has noted Essex's physical illnesses up until that time (PLATE 6):

> 1585 he fell into a ditch & was almost drow*ne*d
> in going a hunting in September
> 1588 In y[e] end of march a burning Ague
> In y[e] begin*ninge* of June a swelling in y[e] face
> & hurt w[t] a fall on his leg fro*m* a horse.

In an undated letter to his sister Penelope Rich (not part of the Hulton archive) Essex similarly complained: 'I was surprised w*i*th a feuer and this morning I haue such an humor falne downe into one side of my heade as I dare not looke out of my chamb*er*.'[51] So the letter may in fact date from shortly after his 'swelling in the face' in 1588. He had another serious fall in August 1593, and suffered from a number of illnesses over the years including 'a rhewme and a stone'. He was so close to dying in December 1599 while under house arrest that the Queen sent eight of her physicians to treat him. Although tearful about his condition, she eventually declined to see him herself, but was later persuaded by 'his most humble letters' to release him from York House, and from the guardianship of the Lord Keeper, Sir Thomas Egerton, and to return him

49 Shakespeare, *King Lear*, ed. R. A. Foakes (London, 1997), II.ii.96-97.
50 Camden, IV, 189-90.
51 British Library, Additional MS 64081, fol. 1.

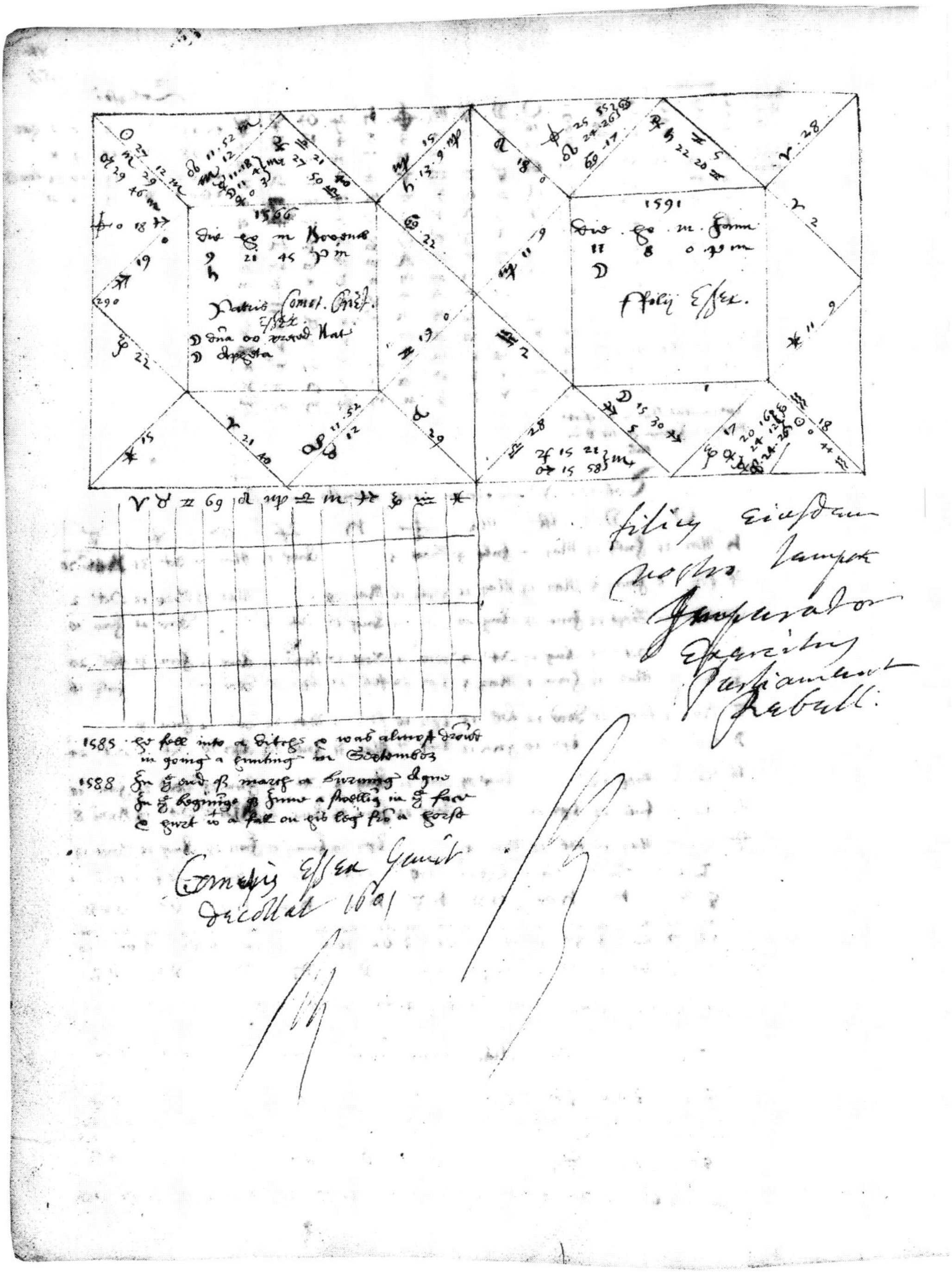

6 Essex's horoscope, c. 1591, in a miscellaneous volume of astrological treatises (BL, Sloane MS 1697, fol. 54v)

to his London home, Essex House.[52] Such physical ailments may not explain the alternating mania and depression expressed in the Hulton letters. Perhaps, then, his increasingly hurtful and insulting private behaviour towards Elizabeth and his impolitic public actions, particularly from 1599 to 1601, were due in part to an increasingly uncontrollable and undiagnosed mental illness.

In the early Hulton letters of 1591 and 1592, Essex expresses genuine affection, concern, and respect for Elizabeth; these are the least tempestuous years of their union. Here he constructs Elizabeth as an unblemished, chaste, and 'perfect' mistress, without the irony required by Sidney for his Stella, Essex's sister Penelope. In letters from 1592, Essex swears that his life 'shall be a continuall performance' and his death 'when soeuer yt comes, a seale' in her service (fol. 36). In a set of Petrarchan conceits, he proffers his impatience to see her: 'Yf my horse cold run as fast as my thoughtes do fly, I wold as often make mine eyes rich in beholding the tresor of my loue, as my desires do triumph when I seeme to myself in a strong imagination to conquerr your resisting will' (fol. 45). Perhaps this last image provocatively and impertinently puns on a contemporary meaning of 'will' as 'genitalia'. But it is not her will but her 'spirit' that he invokes in 1597, as he once again thanks her for her hand-written letters:

> vpon y*ou*r spirite I say I call as only powrefull ouer me, and by his infinite vertu only able to expresse infinite things. Or yf I be too weake ann instument to be inspired w*i*th such a gyft, or thatt wordes be nott able to interprett for me, then to y*ou*r royall deer harte I appeale, w*hi*ch w*i*thout my wordes can fully and iustly vnderstand me. (fol. 52)

His fair words were rewarded with her fair gifts: in 1597 he thanks her for three very 'fyne tokens' she has sent to 'garde' him in battle in the Azores. The first is a 'fayr Angell', which I take to be an 'angel' coin (showing the archangel Michael slaying a dragon) from the period or else a piece of jewellery, probably as a pun on his frequent reference to her as his 'angel'. The second is a watch, possibly that now housed at the British Museum,[53] and the third, a 'thorn' (fol. 64). I suspect that this last gift was a golden replica of a thorn, which punned on Essex's public declaration in 1596 that he wanted to place 'thorns' in the sides of the Spanish.[54] As Jane Lawson demonstrates elsewhere in this volume, gifts to and from Elizabeth could be highly creative and intimate, even when ostensibly presented in public. If we have no example of Elizabeth's intimate words to Essex for his services, we have here the mention of her intimate response in another way. In thankfulness, he can pledge, 'As I am tyed to y*ou*r Ma*ies*tie by more tyes then euer was subiect to a Prince, so I will striue to be worthy of y*ou*r gracious fauor w*i*th more industry then euer did man vpon this erth' (fol. 54).

It is no surprise then that in a slightly later letter he pledges in a marriage metaphor:

52 *HMC, De L'Isle*, II, 144, 407, 423; Camden, IV, 165.

53 The British Museum holds Essex's 'astronomical compendium', which includes a watch and bears his coat of arms. For a digital image, see the BM's 'Compass' archive (www.thebritishmuseum.ac.uk/compass/), using the keywords 'Earl of Essex'.

54 See for example William Camden, who notes on the sacking of Cadiz that 'an agreement was made for restoring of prisoners on both sides. And it was debated whether *Gades* was to be left or holden: *Essex* held opinion that it was to be kept, for that it would be vnto the *Spaniard* as it were thornes in his side' (IV: 94).

to *your*self nott my wordes butt my soule speaketh affectionatest wishes, and faythfull = est vowes yt speakes. Vowes thatt one day *your* Ma*jes*tie shall know you can haue no thing or p*er*son so much *your*s as *your* Ma*jes*ties humblest vassall, Essex. (fol. 81)

But this mock marriage was soon metaphorically annulled, judging from one of the most pathetic and intriguing of the Hulton letters. Although bound as the last in the Hulton volume, it may in fact have predated other letters, and was perhaps written in 1598, after Elizabeth has boxed his ears and exiled him from her presence, or later. Although cited briefly above, it is important to quote it at length here:

This is butt one of the many l*ette*rs w*hi*ch since I saw *your* Ma*jes*tie I wrote, butt neuer sent vnto you. For to write freely to a Lady thatt lyes in weyght for all things thatt I do or say, were too much hazard. To write in a plausible stile when I haue so discontented a hart, were baseness yf nott falshood. To be silent and to putt myself suddenly into a new course if lyfe might be thought lightnes, too much malencholly, and I know nott whatt. By this description *your* Ma*jes*tie seeth the state of my mind, full of confusion and contrariety. I some tymes thinke of running and then remember whatt yt willbe to come in armor triumphing into thatt presence out of w*hi*ch by both by *your* owne voyce I was commaunded and by *your* handes thrust out. Butt god knowes this is no suddayne accident. you may tell those thatt thirst and gape after my ruyne thatt you haue now an aduantage. Thatt being in passion I spake rashly. It is well you haue thatt you looked for and so haue I. In holding me as you haue done of late you pleased no body. (fol. 128)

Certainly his jousting imagery here, of coming in armour triumphant, is meant to recall happier days when she was his champion at tilting. But his last line, 'In holding me as you haue done of late you pleased no body' is particularly nasty, and it recklessly undoes all that he writes before it. He claims that this is one of the letters he has written but never sent, and the letter lacks an address on the reverse side. But the fact that it appears in the Hulton letters at all suggests that it *was* sent to Elizabeth. In an angry letter, apparently in the following year, he mockingly asks her, 'whatt wordes haue I to offer to such a goddesse?' (fol. 119). If by 1599 he has not quite succeeded in constructing Elizabeth as a poetic goddess, he has succeeded in constructing himself as a tragic hero. In one of the earliest Hulton letters, Essex had beseeched Elizabeth to pardon his 'confused rude writing' (fol. 18). In one of the latest, he described himself, perhaps still with a pun on his crest, as 'a hart torne in peeces w*i*th passion' (fol. 122). If he is no longer Icarus whose wings were burnt by the heat of her sun, he is now Actaeon to her Diana. He must recognise, even then, that he would not be saved from being torn to pieces by her followers when he intruded on her most private and intimate world.

IV. 'D'AMOUR' AND ESSEX AND ELIZABETH

Elizabeth's last meeting with Essex took place on 28 September 1599 when he returned to court without leave from the Irish campaign. A contemporary account claimed she saw him three times that day. For the first encounter at 10 a.m., immediately upon his arrival at Nonsuch Palace, Essex

made all hast up to the presence, and soe to the Privy Chamber, and staied not till he came to the Queen's bed chamber, where he found the Queen newly up, the heare about her face; he kneeled unto her, kissed her handes and her faire neck, and had some privat speach with her, which seemed to give hym great contentment. ... 'Tis much wondered at here, that he went so boldly to her Majestie's presence, she not being ready, and he soe full of dirt and mire, that his very face was full of yt.[55]

Like Actaeon disturbing Diana's bath, Essex had clearly violated Elizabeth's privacy again here, both in entering her private chamber and in confronting her before she was dressed. Paul E. J. Hammer has argued that 'the fact that Elizabeth was a female sovereign meant that, during her reign, the status and rewards traditionally to be obtained by physical intimacy with the monarch could not be sought through membership of the privy chamber. Instead, such intimacy was expressed through the conventions of expressing romantic love for the queen.'[56] However, such intimacy in Elizabeth's privy chamber may have been habitual for Essex, as in March 1598, when, angry that Elizabeth had refused to receive his mother, the Countess of Leicester, Essex left his chamber and 'in his night gown went up to the Queen the privy way'.[57] In this later episode in 1599 described above, she was the one in night clothes and he had burst in upon her. Elizabeth still received Essex, most likely in the presence of ladies of her chamber, who must have observed this scene, thus marking the meeting as more public than private, except for Essex's 'private speech' with her. After leaving the chamber, Essex went to his own chamber in the Palace to wash, and returned to Elizabeth for their second meeting from 11 a.m. to 12.30 p.m., during which she was 'very gracious' toward him. He then left to dine with others, after which Elizabeth saw him a third time. But he 'found her much changed in that smal tyme, for she began to call him to question for his return, and was not satisfied in the manner of his coming away and leaving all things at soe great hazard'.[58] She then ordered him to keep to his own chamber. It is significant that this report of the three encounters, made in a letter from Roland White to his master Sir Robert Sidney, was based on Essex's conversation with White the next day. Thus the last meetings of Essex and Elizabeth's were indeed private but made immediately public by Essex, and the Queen herself probably offered her own versions of the meetings, which were similarly reported and gossiped about at court.

Essex and Elizabeth never met again in the seventeen months before his death, most of which time he spent under house arrest and banished from court. Even during this time, he continued to besiege her with letters, perhaps because, as he complained to friends, '*The Queene hath thrust mee downe into a priuate life*',[59] and he was desperate to leave such private places for unkindness and return to his public life. Unfortunately none of these letters appears to survive, nor did Essex truly rebuild himself as a public being. Later, Sir Francis Bacon, determined to distance himself from Essex and perhaps for that reason not to be totally trusted, reported that Elizabeth was distraught to discover that a set of Essex's 'dutifull' letters which had 'moued' her were nothing but

55 *HMC, De L'Isle*, II, 395-6.
56 Hammer, *The Polarisation of Elizabethan Politics*, p. 57.
57 *HMC, De L'Isle*, II, 328.
58 *HMC, De L'Isle*, II, 396.
59 Camden, IV, 172.

a ruse to guarantee his monopoly on the farming of sweet wines.[60] On 29 June 1600 Elizabeth demanded that Essex return a letter that she had sent him the year before, in which she had instructed him not to usurp her power by creating knights without her permission in Ireland. As the story goes, Elizabeth 'sent unto the Earl for her letter, which she writ to command him make none. With a submissive letter he returned answer that he had lost or mislaid it, which displeases her Majesty.'[61] If Essex is to be believed here, the intimate and loving letters that he claims to have had from Elizabeth were not deliberately destroyed by him, his allies, or even his enemies. Instead, Essex, known for being 'careless of all things else', may have simply mislaid, lost, or discarded them. If so, he was more than impolitic and less than calculating, especially if the letters could have been used in his defence at either of his prosecutions in 1599 and 1601. As disturbing as his public treason is this private act of betrayal in destroying correspondence that contained Elizabeth's representations of her true self as well as her intimacy and love.

The Hulton letters carry one last reminder that Elizabeth and Essex lived out a romantic fiction if they believed that the letters would ever truly remain private. Each of the letters is docketed; that is, each bears an annotation below the address written by Essex in his own hand on the outer side of the letter. There appear to be two or more different docketers, each of whose handwriting almost certainly dates from no later than the early seventeenth century (it is not impossible that one of the hands is Elizabeth's, as she docketed Leicester's last letter in a slightly different italic hand). Each letter usually has a single docketer who notes the place from which the letter has been sent, such as 'London', 'Fraunce', 'Ireland', or simply 'at sea', but who often adds some succinct note such as 'malcontent', 'in discontent', 'well pleased', or 'submissive', and once, curiously, 'D'amour'[62] (fols 6v, 18v, 45v, 125v, 99v; see PLATE 7). These annotations appear to refer to Essex, although it is possible that at least 'well pleased' marks Elizabeth's reaction to a particularly flattering letter. If the annotations do refer to Essex, they imply that the docketer has not only catalogued the letter but read it. Such a voyeur would have pleased the self-constructing Essex, but left the self-constructed Elizabeth vulnerable and weak.

This series of letters comprises an epistolary journey, if not an autobiography, through ten years of Essex's relationship with Elizabeth. In his letters to Elizabeth, Essex may be publicising his relationship with her: that is, forcing both his allies and enemies, or even the docketer, to recognise that he holds a private intimacy with her that

60 *Sir Francis Bacon His Apologie*, p. 57.

61 *HMC, De L'Isle*, II, 470.

62 This last annotation appears on the verso of the following (undated) letter: 'Most deere La. y*ou*r kind and often sending is abl ether to preserue a sick man, or rather to rayse a man that were more then half dead to lyfe. since I was first so happy, as to know what loue meant, I was neuer one day nor one howre free from hope and iealousy. and as long as yow do me right, they are the two vnseperable companions of my lyfe. If y*ou*r Ma*jes*tie do in the sweetnes of y*ou*r owne hart nourish the one, and in the iustice of loue free me from the tyranny of the other you shall euer make me happy and increase the worth w*hi*ch is thought to be in yow more by this one meane then by all y*ou*r other excellent perfections. And so wishing y*ou*r Ma*jes*tie to be M*ist*ris of that yow wish most I humble kisse y*ou*r fayre handes. / y*ou*r seruant in loue and duty / before all men / R. Essex' (fol. 99).

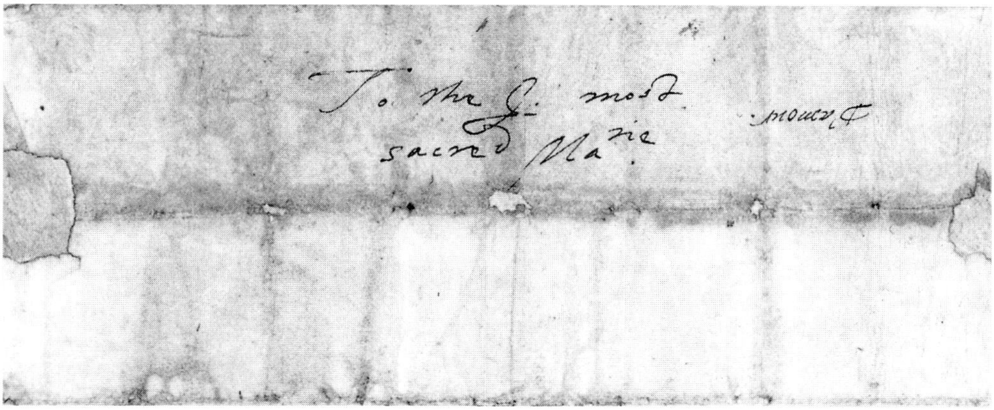

7 The address and endorsement on one of Essex's autograph letters to Queen Elizabeth, [undated, ?1599], among the Hulton letters (BL, Additional MS 74282, fol. 99v)

others cannot fully penetrate or share. Conversely, Essex may be privatising the relationship, in order to convince others that he alone can reclaim as private his relationship to the monarch, while others can only ever accept their relationship to her as public. The Hulton letters demonstrate that he may have used both strategies whenever necessary, thereby showing his relationship with Elizabeth to be infinitely and continually self-constructing. If Essex had lost Elizabeth's letters, she had not lost his, and indeed, in keeping those that descended to the Hulton family she constructed for Essex the poetic legacies he took such great pains in procuring for Sidney and Spenser. Through the British Library's purchase of these letters after nearly four hundred years, Essex finally moved, in theory, from the private sphere to the public. But, alas, in practice, Essex, who lived mostly for the Aristotelian self-publicising virtues that Habermas has outlined and only reluctantly for the privacy that Ariès seeks, has been imprisoned again in a private, or at least a semi-public, sphere. This volume of autograph letters has been catalogued as a 'vault' item and requires special permission for its use in the British Library's Manuscript Room. The original volume is therefore not generally available to readers. In a sense, then, the English establishment is still intent on protecting Essex's privacy, whether he wanted them to or not.

DELIGHTFUL TEACHING

QUEEN ELIZABETH AND SIDNEY'S *ARCADIA*

BLAIR WORDEN

IN 1579 PHILIP SIDNEY wrote the letter to Queen Elizabeth in which he pleaded against her proposed marriage to the Duke of Anjou, the Catholic younger brother and heir of the childless Henry III of France. Though ostensibly composed for the queen's eyes only, the work was widely copied and circulated.[1] Sidney was a young and junior member of the party of his uncle the Earl of Leicester, which had fallen into sharp disfavour. In 1579 its leaders, seeing their influence in the queen's counsels slipping away, appealed to opinion beyond them. They commissioned John Stubbs's sensational tract against the marriage, *The Discovery of a Gaping Gulph*, which echoes Sidney's letter, and they must have been behind the letter itself.[2] The two works, though united by argument and purpose, had different characters and receptions. Stubbs's *Discovery* was condemned by royal proclamation as a 'lewd, seditious book',[3] and his writing-hand was smitten off in a public display of the Queen's fury. Sidney's intended audience was less broad than Stubbs's. Stubbs ventured into print, Sidney only into manuscript. Sidney's text is courtly and mannerly, Stubbs's populist and provocative. Sidney's letter brought no rebuke from the Queen, though the letter did nothing to arrest, and may have hastened, the decline of a political career that had begun so promisingly.

The Anjou match was the most intense and controversial issue to have visited Elizabethan politics. In the eyes of Sidney's party it was the climax of a series of developments which had jeopardised their country and religion, and for which the queen was to blame. Her strength, she failed to grasp, could lie only in the promotion and succour of Protestantism, at home and abroad. At home her regime could acquire roots of public support, and escape the danger of a Catholic coup or rebellion, only through Protestant evangelism and the suppression of Catholic worship and office-holding. Instead the Queen suspended her evangelical Archbishop of Canterbury,

1 For the convenience of both reader and writer I use here the version of the letter which is printed in Katherine Duncan-Jones and Jan van Dorsten, eds, *Miscellaneous Prose of Sir Philip Sidney* (Oxford, 1983: hereafter *MP*). But none of the surviving texts can be regarded as definitive: Peter Beal, *In Praise of Scribes* (Oxford, 1998), ch. 4; Beal, 'Philip Sidney's *Letter to Queen Elizabeth* and that "False Knave" Alexander Dicsone', *English Manuscript Studies*, 11 (2002), 1-51.

2 *MP*, pp. 33-4.

3 Lloyd Berry, ed., *John Stubbs's Gaping Gulph* (Charlottesville, Va., 1968), p. 148.

Edmund Grindal, in 1577, and then presided over an anti-Puritan reaction which coloured the politics of the late 1570s.[4] English Catholicism, its survival winked at by the Queen, achieved a new vitality in the same years, when it seemed that a palace revolution at Whitehall might bring a group of ruthless Catholic politicians on to her council.[5] Overshadowing all Elizabeth's problems was the unresolved succession to the throne. On her death, which Catholic conspirators aimed to hasten, the Catholic Mary Queen of Scots would be next in line. Protestants were ready to challenge Mary's succession, but knew that the cost of their hostility would be civil and religious war of the kind that was devastating France and the Netherlands. Images of the havoc that would follow the Queen's death permeated the politics and the literature of her reign.

Protestants expected a bid for power by English Catholics to be prompted or backed by a Catholic invasion. In the late 1570s it seemed that the mighty Catholic monarchies of France and Spain might join forces to topple Elizabeth. On her survival, believed Sidney and his friends, there depended not only the peace of England but the beleaguered cause of European Protestantism, which England alone had the strength to lead and to whose fate its own was indissolubly tied. Sidney's party bemoaned the Queen's timidity in international affairs, her vacillation, her habit of responding to events instead of shaping them. Rather than passively awaiting an attack which would sooner or later be inevitable, they urged, she must seize the initiative and intervene on the Continent. With a mixture of military and financial commitment she must aid Huguenots in France, Protestant princes in Germany, Protestant advisers to James VI in Scotland, Protestant followers of William of Orange in the Netherlands. Yet she missed her opportunities, and broke her promises, to aid her co-religionists. In the late 1570s she allowed the Dutch cause against Spain to lose half its strength and permitted the control of Scotland to fall into French hands. By 1578-9 England's diplomatic vulnerability had acquired a surpassing gravity.[6]

Why, at that crisis, did Elizabeth contemplate marriage to Anjou, a footloose and unscrupulous adventurer in search of a kingdom, who was half her age? The courtship was, on her side, an intense personal drama, in which her feelings were graphically engaged and displayed. She was told, and perhaps believed, that even in her mid-forties she might still bear an heir. Yet the main purpose of the match lay elsewhere: in diplomatic calculation. She aimed to extract England from the hole into which, as Sidney's party alleged, her failings had cast it. Marriage into the Valois family would end the threat from France. It would also, by raising the prospect of an Anglo-French force under Anjou's leadership in the Netherlands, check the Spanish reconquest there and bring Spain to the negotiating table.[7]

4 Patrick Collinson, *Edmund Grindal 1519-1583* (London, 1979), p. 256.

5 John Bossy, 'English Catholics and the French Marriage, 1577-81', *Recusant History* 5 (1960), 2-18; Patrick Collinson, *The Elizabethan Puritan Movement* (London, 1967), p. 200; Conyers Read, *Sir Francis Walsingham*, 3 vols (Oxford, 1925), ii, 21n.

6 Blair Worden, *The Sound of Virtue: Philip Sidney's 'Arcadia' and Elizabethan Politics* (London & New Haven, 1996), ch. 5.

7 Ibid., ch. 6.

To Sidney's party such thinking was perilously flawed. The match reminded them of the marriage of Elizabeth's sister and predecessor Mary to Philip II of Spain. Now as then, they argued, wedlock with a Catholic foreigner would be catastrophic to the Protestant cause. England would become a satellite of France and be governed by French and Catholic advisers in French and Catholic interests. Sidney's circle thought of Anjou as a demonic figure, as the personification of wickedness, cruelty, persecution. The belief that the marriage would cause 'the overthrow of the [Protestant] religion' was widespread.[8]

What alternative, then, did Sidney's party propose? How was the national predicament which they blamed on the Queen to be met? Their answer was simple. Queen and country must rely not on a sinister foreign alliance but on themselves. They must, as Sidney's letter urges, 'stand alone'.[9] They must mobilise not only the nation's military strength, which Elizabeth had shamefully neglected, but those ethical resources which she had likewise betrayed. The fear and shortsightedness that had governed her policies must yield to the courage, the foresight, the resolution, the faith in God's cause that in Sidney's mind were the inseparable allies of virtue.[10] She must also acquire another ally of virtue, the wisdom of Stoic philosophy. Thus instead of depending on fortune, that infirm foundation of policy, she should rest upon her 'true inward strength', which 'outward accidents' cannot move.[11]

Sidney's letter makes his case delicately. In line with the literary conventions of Renaissance counsel, it credits the Queen with qualities Sidney wishes she had. His restraint and tact become conspicuous when we place the letter beside counsel given to her by her Secretary of State Sir Francis Walsingham, to whom Sidney was bound by every tie of affection and political sympathy. Walsingham, despairing of the royal failings in the period of the Anjou crisis, wrote with a directness that even leading advisers, such as he, normally hesitated to adopt. Sidney, who had no title to counsel her, could not be blunt. Thinking the same as Walsingham, he sometimes has to say the opposite. Where Walsingham lamented the insecure foundations of her reign, Sidney assured her that the foundations were strong, and insisted that they would remain so if she broke off the match. Walsingham urges her to 'look into your own estate' and recognise the discontent and disloyalty that prevail there: Sidney encourages her to 'look in your own estate' and realise how 'devoted' her subjects are to her. Walsingham urges the Queen to remove or prevent 'the contempt of her people': Sidney assures her that her subjects do not hold her in 'contempt'.[12] Walsingham habitually thought in terms of the 'sickness' and 'disease' of the realm and of the sharp 'medicine' needed to cure its 'corruption':[13] Sidney, while inwardly sharing Walsingham's sense of England's

8 *HMC Cecil*, ii. 242; Worden, *Sound*, p. 94.
9 Worden, *Sound*, ch. 7.
10 Ibid., ch. 2.
11 *MP*, pp. 47, 56.
12 Read, *Walsingham*, i. 292, ii. 70; *MP*, p. 54; Beal, 'Philip Sidney's *Letter*', p. 34.
13 Worden, *Sound*, p. 72.

'corruption',[14] tells Elizabeth that so 'healthful a body' as her regime needs no such 'medicine' as marriage to Anjou.[15]

Though the marriage negotiations eventually evaporated, their disappearance owed nothing to Sidney's counsel. Yet his advice to the Queen found another life. It reappears at the start of the first version of the *Arcadia* – the *Old Arcadia* as it has come to be called. We do not know at what point in 1579 Sidney wrote the letter (or first wrote it, for he may have revised it),[16] and we do not know when he composed the beginning of the *Old Arcadia*,[17] but the second exercise probably followed within months of the first and may have been undertaken within weeks of it. Defeated in court politics, Sidney turned to his 'unelected vocation' of poetry and fiction.[18] The writing of the *Arcadia*, however, was no flight from political commitment. On the contrary it afforded him, among his other literary aims, an alternative means of voicing it.

At the outset of the action of the *Old Arcadia*, Duke (or King) Basilius hears a speech of advice by his faithful counsellor Philanax, who tries to dissuade him from his decision, reached after a journey to the oracle at Delphos, to abdicate from his throne for a year (see PLATE 1). Philanax's counsel insistently reproduces, in phrasing and argument, Sidney's letter to Elizabeth. Both advisers are impelled to speak by love and duty, Sidney 'from the deep wellspring of a most loyal affection', Philanax as a 'friend ... in affection' who serves with 'incomparable loyalty'. Sidney's case is made with 'boldness' but also 'with most humble heart', Philanax's 'with humble boldness'.[19]

Philanax's boldness is the sharper, for he speaks with a freedom Sidney's letter cannot emulate. In tone and spirit his speech is much closer to Walsingham's counsel than to Sidney's. Like many other authors in Renaissance England, Sidney found a way of saying in imaginative literature what he could only say less searchingly or critically outside it. Philanax's affection for his ruler is genuine. He would not be impolite. Though he spurns the 'servil[ity]' of other royal advisers, he shuns too the 'obstinate austerity' of counsellors who 'wholly neglect the prince's person'. None the less, living as he does 'in that thrifty world', a 'world, not so far gone in painted vanities', he has no need of the flowers of praise which Sidney hands to 'the excellentest princess in the world'. 'Laying ... myself at your feet,' Sidney speaks for subjects whose 'minds' are 'joyed with the experience of your inward virtues, and our eyes delighted with the sight of you'. His letter ends with the description of Elizabeth as 'the example of princes, the ornament of this age, the comfort of the afflicted, the delight of your posterity'. Philanax's speech ends plainly, with the kernel of his advice.[20] Sidney, so fulsome in his

14 Steuart Pears, ed., *The Correspondence of Sir Philip Sidney and Hubert Languet* (London, 1845), p. 143; John Gouws, ed., *The Prose Works of Fulke Greville, Lord Brooke* (Oxford, 1986), p. 47.
15 *MP*, p. 47.
16 Beal, *In Praise of Scribes*, ch. 4; Beal, 'Philip Sidney's *Letter*', 21-2.
17 Sir Philip Sidney, *The Countess of Pembroke's Arcadia (The Old Arcadia)*, ed. Jean Robertson (Oxford, 1973: hereafter *OA*), pp. xv-xix.
18 Worden, *Sound*, ch. 4.
19 *MP*, pp. 46, 56; *OA*, pp. 5, 7, 286.
20 *OA*, pp. 5-8, 56; *MP*, pp. 53, 55, 57.

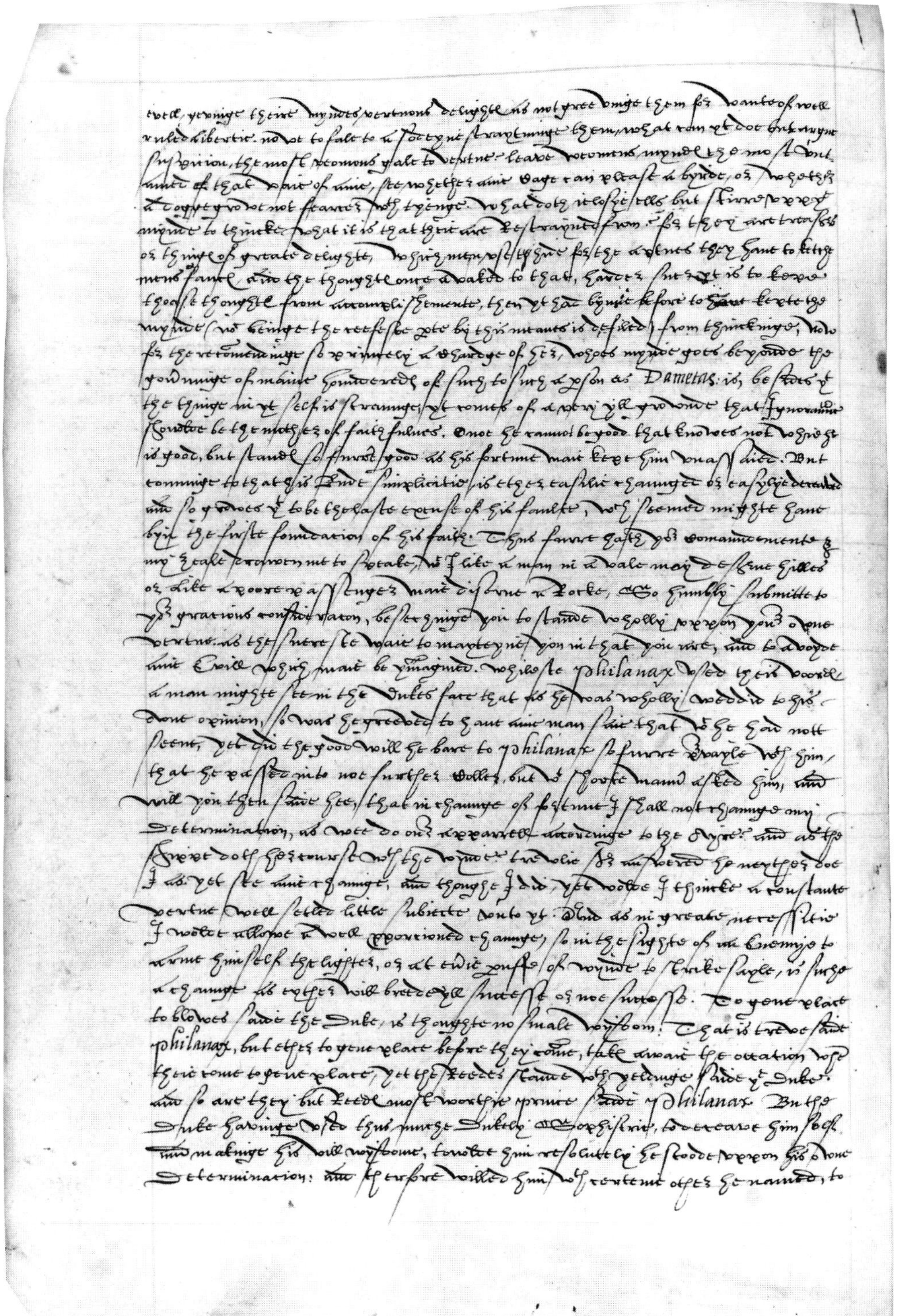

1 Part of Philanax's advice to Basilius in Sidney's *Old Arcadia* as written in a scribal manuscript of the work probably once owned by Sir Lionel Tollemache (1562-1612) of Helmingham Hall, Suffolk (BL, Additional MS 61821, fol. 3v)

letter, wrote strikingly little in praise of the Queen elsewhere, far less than we might expect from a poet at her court. That does not mean that his heart did not enter the loyal sentiments which his letter felicitously expresses. But it is Philanax, not Sidney, whose advice corresponds to the ideal of fearless, manly counsel on which Sidney's party believed the felicity of kingdoms to depend, and which Sidney saw stultified by the artificiality and servility of the Elizabethan court.[21]

The contrast of tone cannot conceal the resemblances of content. Nowhere are they closer than in the advice to the two rulers to remember the inherent strengths of their reigns and to rely upon them. The resources of national support which the two counsellors describe their princes as commanding is in truth scarcely a matter for royal self-congratulation, for in both instances Sidney allows the alert reader to glimpse his conviction that monarchs who have inherited peaceful kingdoms should be able to win their subjects' loyalty easily enough.[22] Both rulers, however, must make the most of that loyalty. Sidney eulogistically urges the Queen to 'let your excellent virtues of piety, justice and liberality daily, if it be possible, more and more shine': Philanax, shedding the eulogy, beseeches the Duke to 'let your subjects have you in their eyes, let them see the benefits of your justice daily more and more'. Elizabeth's subjects, Sidney tells her, would prefer the 'certain good' they have known during her long reign to the 'uncertain good' of the match: Basilius's subjects, Philanax explains, 'must ... needs rather like of present sureties than uncertain changes'.[23] The word 'good' superficially reflects more credit on Elizabeth than 'sureties' and 'changes' can impart to Basilius. Yet in both cases 'change' – the change from national independence under Elizabeth, from attentive rule by Basilius – is the danger. Sidney's question to the Queen, 'What makes you ... to change course?', is Philanax's too: 'Why should you seek new courses?'[24] In both cases the intended change is a 'sudden' breach of 'constancy'[25] – a revealing sign, for constancy is a virtue insistently emphasised in Sidney's fiction, while bad things in it mostly happen suddenly, as the product of false or rootless policy or emotion. Basilius, no less than Elizabeth, is betraying ethical resources. Both monarchs are succumbing to 'fear'.[26] Elizabeth, to overcome her 'fear of standing alone', should 'make that religion upon which you stand to carry the only strength'. Philanax concludes his own advice with the statement that summarises it: 'stand wholly upon your own virtue as the surest way to maintain you in that you are, and to avoid any evil which may be imagined'.[27]

Basilius's rejection of Philanax's advice is as fatal to Arcadia as the Anjou match will be to England. The last of the oracle's prophecies, 'And in thy throne a foreign state shall sit',[28] is also the prospect before Elizabeth, whom Sidney's party warned that the

21 Worden, *Sound*, pp. 146-7, 214-33.
22 Ibid., pp. 262-3.
23 *OA*, pp. 6-8; *MP*, pp. 54-6.
24 *MP*, p. 47; *OA*, p. 7.
25 *MP*, pp. 47, 50, 51; *OA*, pp. 7-9, 358.
26 *MP*, p. 52; *OA*, pp. 7-8
27 *MP*, pp. 51, 56; *OA*, p. 8.
28 *MP*, p. 5.

'foreign prince' Anjou would 'usurp the state'.[29] In the language in which Sidney's circle bemoaned England's crisis, Arcadia is 'brought ... to feel the pangs of uttermost peril', and is likely either to 'run itself upon the rock of self-division or be overthrown by the stormy wind of foreign force'.[30] Arcadia, like England, has an unresolved succession, and it is the succession problem that tears it apart on Basilius's (apparent) death.[31] Sidney's account of the consequent disintegration of the Arcadian commonwealth again reproduces the arguments and language of those who pictured the anarchy awaiting England on Elizabeth's demise. Arcadia is left, as England promises to be, at the mercy of a foreign ruler. As it happens, that ruler, Euarchus, the *deus ex machina*, is benign. Instead of swallowing Arcadia he saves it. But Euarchus is 'unlike most princes' (just as Philanax is 'unlike most men' who advise princes).[32] Such rulers, normally at least, are to be looked for only in fiction, not in the fact of Sidney's Europe. Europe, the antitype to Basilius, is what a monarch should be. Basilius is what Elizabeth is.

Where Basilius's abdication is literal, Elizabeth's will be metaphorical, but no less damaging for that. After Basilius's retreat, Philanax observes 'the pitiful case of the Arcadian people', for they have 'a prince being, and not doing like a prince', who has 'given over all care of government'.[33] Sidney's letter in turn replies to the argument that the marriage would bring 'the easing your majesty of her cares (which is as much to say, as the easing of you of being a Queen and sovereign').[34] For just as Basilius's retreat, which is intended to avoid problems, creates them, the marriage to Anjou would increase, not assuage, the dangers before the Queen. As Book (or Act) Two of the *Old Arcadia* signals, it would intensify the likelihood of rebellion, for the monstrous Phagonian mutiny thrives on grievances which, if Elizabeth marries Anjou, will be levelled at her: the rebels complain of their 'want of a prince' and of the sway of 'foreign hands'.[35]

Basilius reproduces Elizabeth's self-inflicted vulnerability to foreign as well as to domestic peril. Sidney's party stressed that England must 'be always in a readiness for war', that the Queen must have her 'musters kept and continued ... in readiness against all suddens'. Instead, Sidney reminds the Queen, the English have been allowed to become 'generally unexpert in war defence'.[36] Arcadia has the same problem. Whereas Euarchus, the model King of Macedon, has 'put his people in a readiness for war', has 'kept in peacetime a continual discipline of war', has 'prepared' against 'sudden and dangerous invasions', Basilius by contrast has 'unarmed himself', being 'loath to take any matter of arms in hand' and having resolved 'to give place to blows ... before they come' and 'in the sight of the enemy to arm himself the lighter'.[37]

*

29 Northamptonshire Record Office, Fitzwilliam of Milton Papers 111, fols 7v, 11.
30 *OA*, pp. 351, 360.
31 Ibid., pp. 319-22.
32 Ibid., pp. 5-6, 358.
33 Ibid., p. 358; Sir Philip Sidney, *The Countess of Pembroke's Arcadia (The New Arcadia)*, ed. Victor Skretkowicz (Oxford, 1987: hereafter *NA*), p. 325.
34 *MP*, pp. 50, 51.
35 *OA*, p. 127.
36 Worden, *Sound*, pp. 132-3; *MP*, p. 47.
37 *OA*, pp. 9, 356, 358; *NA*, p. 34.

After Basilius has rejected Philanax's advice and withdrawn from politics, politics seem for a time to withdraw from the story too. They make way for a romance and for what seems, at first, a holiday world. Yet there proves to be no escaping them. Their reappearances surprise the characters and surprise us. In Book Two the lovers are in antic pursuit of their desires 'when suddenly the confused rumour of a mutinous multitude' announces the popular rebellion that threatens the Duke's life and the stability of the state. In the Third Eclogues, where the shepherds, free for once from the presence of princes, celebrate a wedding, the mood is abruptly altered by Philisides, who perplexes the company by reciting the beast-fable he learned on Ister Bank about the origins and rise of tyranny. He is rebuked for choosing so cheerless a topic 'when rather some song of love, or matter for joyful melody, was to be brought forth'. No less sudden and unexpected is the information which in Book Four follows Philanax's decision to keep the princes under guard. 'But high time it was for Philanax to do so, for already was the whole multitude fallen into confused and dangerous divisions. There was a notable example how great dissipations monarchal governments are subject unto.'[38] Arcadia subsides into a crisis which exposes the consequences of misrule and from which it will be rescued only at the end of the work.

In reporting those 'dissipations' Sidney moves beyond criticism of Elizabeth to an account of the weaknesses of monarchy as a form of government – or rather of the kind of unlimited monarchy which he took her rule to represent. One of the strands of Sidney's fiction is a meditation on tyranny. It is a theme that can leave Elizabeth and Basilius behind, for neither of them is a bloodthirsty tyrant of the kind depicted in Philisides's beast-fable and recently personified, in the eyes of Sidney's party, by Catholic leaders on the Continent: Catherine de Medici, the Duke of Alva, Philip II. But there is another species of tyrants, the kind classified by Sidney's friend Fulke Greville as 'weak' or 'weak-minded' or 'unactive' ones, who find other ways of abusing their 'power absolute'. They are portrayed in Greville's plays, where the characterisations of 'weak' and 'dotard' rulers derive from Sidney's portrait of Basilius.[39] For Basilius, though to immediate appearances a harmless figure, is 'a mighty duke', with mighty power for good or ill. Being 'corrupted with a prince's fortune', he takes his decisions 'without the advice or allowance of his subjects', 'making his will wisdom', 'being fortified with the authority of a prince whose power might easily satisfy his will'.[40] So did Elizabeth. She overruled her council over the Anjou match, as, during the previous four years, she had vetoed its wishes on at least four occasions when her views clashed with those of Sidney's party.[41] Men of Sidney's persuasion observed how her 'will and pleasure', 'her own will and her own affections', prevailed over 'sound advice of open counsel'.[42]

Subjects whose fates depend on the wills and whims of rulers lose their own political capacities. During the vacancy of the throne upon Basilius's death the Arcadians are like

38 *OA*, pp. 123, 259, 320.
39 Worden, *Sound*, p. 213.
40 *OA*, pp. 4, 6, 9, 45, 358.
41 Worden, *Sound*, p. 97.
42 Thomas Wright, ed., *Queen Elizabeth and Her Times*, 2 vols (London, 1838), ii, 75.

headless chickens. Living as they do in a state where 'public matters had ever been privately governed', they 'had not experience to rule'.[43] That deficiency reveals itself at the successive crises of the Arcadian state, when native resources prove inadequate and the realm has to be saved by a foreigner or foreigners: by Musidorus and Pyrocles when the bear and lion endanger Basilius's daughters and, with them, the succession; by Pyrocles in suppressing, in Book Two, the very rebels who have complained of 'foreign hands'; by Euarchus after the Duke's death.

Arcadia's ruling class is represented, in one of their guises, by the shepherds, who serve the 'great shepherd' Basilius. They 'were not such base shepherds as we commonly make account of, but the very owners of the sheep themselves'. They are supposed to do, and omit to do, 'justice work', the work, among England's landowners, of justices of the peace.[44] Sidney's party believed England's JPs to have been as neglectful of their responsibilities as the Queen had been of hers. They had failed to promote justice and reform, failed to keep effective watch on the Catholic enemy within and to stand up and be counted against it.[45] The Arcadian shepherds, alternately cowardly and neglectful, have parallel faults.[46] Even Basilius is taken aback by their timidity before the lion and bear.[47] Their want of courage and public spirit is still more evident on the Duke's death, when the 'over-tender' shepherds 'yielded themselves over to ... forms of lamentation' and 'ran about his body tearing their beards and garments'. Their real concern is not for the realm but for themselves: they mourn in the manner of men who put 'their own' good first, who 'think the rebound of the evil falls to their own smart'.[48]

If Sidney's letter to the Queen is one guide to the political content of his fiction, his *Defence of Poetry*, which likewise seems to have been written around the same time as the *Old Arcadia*,[49] is another. By winking at each other, passages of the *Defence* and of the *Old Arcadia* alert us to the capacity of particular literary forms – pastoral, and its ally the beast-fable – to communicate political observations underhand. In the *Defence* the use of pastoral to 'show the misery of people' is the province of the 'poor pipe': in the *Arcadia* the 'silly shepherd's poor pipe ... testifies our woes'.[50] Virgil's *Eclogues*, explains the *Defence*, makes its points 'under the pretty tales of wolves and sheep': in Sidney's Eclogues the shepherds 'sometimes ... under hidden forms utter such matters as otherwise were not fit for their delivery' – or, as the passage appears in the *New Arcadia*, 'such matters as otherwise they durst not deal with'.[51] The *Defence* describes the 'pretty allegories' of Aesop's fables as 'stealing under the formal tales of beasts': Sidney labours to remind us that Philisides's fable about tyranny is 'a tale of ... beasts'.

43 *OA*, p. 320.
44 Ibid., pp. 56, 77.
45 Worden, *Sound*, pp. 200-1, 204-5.
46 *OA*, pp. 76-8.
47 Ibid., pp. 45, 56.
48 Worden, *Sound*, p. 203.
49 *MP*, pp. 59-63.
50 Ibid., p. 94 (and p. 121); *OA*, p. 84.
51 *OA*, p. 56; *NA*, p. 24.

It is also, its auditors observe, 'fit to frame a pastoral style'.[52] Pastoral, remarks the *Defence*, 'can include the whole considerations of wrong-doing and patience': Philisides's pregnant concluding couplet exhorts the oppressed beasts to show 'patience' or, by liberating themselves, to 'do well'[53] (the phrase 'doing well' – or more commonly 'well-doing', a more precise reverse of 'wrong-doing' – having an emphatic function in Sidney's fiction).

The political dimension of the *Old Arcadia* points to other writings not only by Sidney but by other Elizabethans. There is Spenser, Sidney's fellow client of Leicester. The first version of Spenser's *Mother Hubberds Tale*, which like the *Old Arcadia* is a response to the Anjou crisis, indicts its sleeping prince in language and imagery that reproduces (or is reproduced in) Sidney's account of the negligence of Basilius. In the *Arcadia* the Duke's conduct is represented as a metaphorical sleep. So, in the observations of Sidney's party, is Elizabeth's.[54] Spenser's *The Shepheardes Calender*, again written around the same time, asks, as the *Arcadia* does, what will happen on the death of Elizabeth (of 'some maiden of great blood'). Arcadia's shepherds resolve on 'endless wailing' now that Basilius is 'absented' and 'is gone': Spenser's shepherds are enjoined to 'waile' in the maiden's 'absence', now that she 'is gone'.[55] Sidney's account of the aftermath of Basilius's death also recalls a work of a different kind, by the radical Protestant Christopher Goodman, to whom Sidney's father and uncle had long given shelter and patronage. Sidney reproduces the language and imagery of Goodman's treatise *How Superior Powers Oght to be Obeyed*, which had been written when Goodman was in exile under Queen Mary, a reign to which the arguments and imaginations of Sidney's party habitually reverted.[56]

Then there are the Elizabethan writers who, with the same perspective on international politics as Sidney's, had anticipated the use the *Arcadia* makes of Greek history to supply analogies to the beleaguered condition of England and of the European Protestant cause. Where Sidney's party pressed Elizabeth to lead and unite Europe's Protestant powers against the threatened conjunction of France and Spain, Euarchus 'saw the Asiatics of the one side, the Latins of the other, gaping for any occasion to devour Greece'. In seeking cooperation among the Greek states, Euarchus makes a point parallel to one made by Sidney's party for the unified action of Protestant ones, 'by many reasons making them see that, though in respect of place some of them might seem further removed from the first violence of the storm, yet being embarked in the same ship the final wrack must be common to them all'. In the retreat of Basilius, who is (after him) 'the mightiest prince of Greece', Euarchus discerns what Sidney's

52 *MP*, p. 87 (and p. 103); *OA*, p. 259.
53 *MP*, p. 94; *OA*, p. 259.
54 Worden, *Sound*, pp. 61-5, 133, 139-40, 163, 201, 300.
55 *OA*, pp. 282, 284, 348; Spenser, 'November Eclogue': 'Argument' and ll. 64-6, 137. See too the excellent discussions of the political dimension of Spenser's verse in Richard A. McCabe, '"Little Book thy selfe present": the politics of presentation in *The Shepheardes Calender*', in Howard Erskine-Hill, ed., *Presenting Poetry: Composition, Publication, Reception* (Cambridge, 1995), pp. 15-39, and in McCabe's *Spenser's Monstrous Regiment: Elizabethan Ireland and the Poetics of Difference* (Oxford, 2004).
56 Worden, *Sound*, pp. 185-90.

party saw in Elizabeth's desertion of her co-religionists: 'he straight considered the universal case of Greece deprived by this means of a principal pillar'.[57] Sidney's Greek analogies are foreshadowed in the translation *The Three Orations of Demosthenes* by Thomas Wilson (who at the time of the Anjou crisis was, alongside Walsingham, one of Elizabeth's two Secretaries of State), published in 1570, and in *Orations, of Arsanes against Philip the Trecherous Kyng of Macedon*, which was written, perhaps around the same time,[58] by the MP Thomas Norton (who would be sent to the Tower for his opposition to the Anjou match). Both works urge the English, as Sidney's party did and as the *Arcadia* does, to withstand a modern Prince Philip. Wilson, who has 'prepared Greek remedies for my unfortunate country', explains that the reader 'should compare the time past with the time present, and ever when he heareth Athens, or the Athenians, should remember England and Englishmen'.[59]

In 1562 Thomas Norton had been the author, with his fellow-MP Thomas Sackville – that leading contributor to the *Mirror for Magistrates*, who would be Burghley's successor as Lord Treasurer – of the play *Gorboduc*, a self-styled 'mirror ... to princes all' which warns them to 'shun' the errors it portrays.[60] Just as the *Arcadia* echoes Sidney's letter to the Queen, so *Gorboduc* was the literary partner of a political document: a petition from the House of Commons which Norton presented to Elizabeth on its behalf and which, in urging her to settle the succession, repeats the reasoning and wording of the play.[61]

Gorboduc, which is set in a mythical ancient Britain, is one of the three works by living English authors to be named in Sidney's *Defence of Poetry*, the others being the *Mirror for Magistrates* and Spenser's *Shepheardes Calender*. Were it not for its defects of form, explains Sidney in the *Defence*, *Gorboduc* would 'remain as an exact model of all tragedies'. The central claim of the *Defence* is that 'the end of poesy' is 'delightful teaching'. So we should pause on his tribute to *Gorboduc*, a work 'full of notable morality, which it doth most delightfully teach, and so obtain the very end of poetry'.[62] The teaching of *Gorboduc*, and the teaching of the *Arcadia*, are as close in content as they are distant in form. In both works an ageing Duke, after a long and peaceful reign, resolves to hand over the governing of his country. In both cases the duke dies at the end of Act Four, after which we watch, in the fragmentation of the state in a succession crisis, the consequences of misrule: in Arcadia, that 'falling steeple', we witness 'the dangerous division of men's minds, the ruinous renting of all estates' and the prospect of 'civil dissension': *Gorboduc* portrays 'civil strife', 'tumults, rebellions, arms'.[63] Like

57 *OA*, pp. 355-9.
58 Worden, *Sound*, p. 162.
59 *OA*, pp. 161-3.
60 William Tydeman, ed., *Two Tudor Tragedies* (Harmondsworth, 1992: hereafter 'Tydeman'), p. 74.
61 Leonard Courtney, 'The Tragedy of "Ferrex and Porrex"', *Notes and Queries* 2nd ser. 10 (1860), 261-2; T. E. Hartley, ed., *Proceedings in the Parliaments of Elizabeth I, 1558-1581* (Leicester, 1981), pp. 90-3; Henry James and Greg Walker, 'The Politics of *Gorboduc*', *English Historical Review* 110 (1995), 109-21.
62 *MP*, pp. 112-13, 116.
63 *OA*, pp. 320, 351; Tydeman, pp. 94, 108.

the *Arcadia* the play warns against what it calls 'foreign thraldom', the 'unnatural thraldom of a stranger's reign'.[64] When Arcadia faces dissolution, the foreigner Euarchus has the chance to seize it as 'prey': in the play the foreigner Albany, who is without Euarchus's scruples, seizes Britain as 'prey'.[65]

Norton's and Sackville's starting-point, like Sidney's, is the defeat, disastrous to the realm, of good counsel. Both Dukes overrule a counsellor with a symbolic Greek name: Eubulus (giver of wise counsel) in *Gorboduc*, Philanax (king-lover) in the *Arcadia*. The 'bold' and 'faithful' counsel of both men is contrasted with the honeyed flattery of advisers who tell princes what they want to hear.[66] In both cases it is thwarted by royal 'will'. Just as Arcadia's problems arise because Basilius 'mak[es] his will wisdom', so in *Gorboduc* the Duke's 'will alone' causes the convulsion of Britain. The play shows what happens 'when kings will not consent/ To grave advice, but follow wilful will'.[67] In *Gorboduc* the Duke's abdication leaves Britain without a 'guide', 'a ship without a stern', with 'empty place of princely governance': once Basilius has 'left the stern of government', his countrymen, having lost their 'guide', have 'a prince ... keeping and not exercising the place'.[68]

The mythical Britain destroyed by the plot of *Gorboduc* was 'whilom in renown'. In the *Arcadia* Philisides's native Samothea – Sidney's mythical Britain – 'whilom stood/ An honour to the world'.[69] Sidney here follows Holinshed, which relates the decline of that honour, and where the Samotheans – like the Elizabethans, like the Arcadians – 'had given over the practice of all warlike and painful exercises' and 'were become now unapt to withstand the force of their enemies'.[70] Philisides makes sure that the equation of Samothea with modern England will not be missed: 'The name of Samothea is so famous that, telling you I am of that, I shall not need to extend myself further in telling you what country that is.' That signal corresponds to a hint supplied by the shepherd Geron in describing the 'miseries' that follow Basilius's death: 'Alas, poor sheep ... which hitherto have enjoyed your fruitful pasture in such quietness as your wool, among other things, hath made this country famous, your best days are now past.'[71] The fame won for England by its wool had been remembered by Sidney in 1577, when he reminded a German audience of his country's 'good and great store of cloths that are made of their wool, and that are so much spoken of among all nations'.[72]

The *Arcadia* is a romance. What are politics doing in it? Fulke Greville, who knew Sidney as well as anyone, was troubled by an opposite question: what is a romance doing in a serious study of politics? To Greville, writing in the restrospect of his gloomy

64 Tydeman, pp. 119, 121.
65 *OA*, p. 358; Tydeman, pp. 119, 120, 122.
66 *OA*, pp. 7, 285; Tydeman, pp. 69, 75.
67 Tydeman, pp. 100, 123.
68 Ibid., pp. 118, 119; *OA*, pp. 320, 349, 358, 360.
69 Tydeman, p. 123; *OA*, p. 336.
70 Ralph Holinshed, *The First and Second Volumes of Chronicles* (London, 1587): 'The History of England', bk I p. 4.
71 *OA*, pp. 327, 334.
72 James Osborn, *Young Philip Sidney 1562-1577* (New Haven & London, 1972), pp. 464-6.

old age, Sidney's love story was a frivolous exercise, unworthy of its author's gifts. That was an ascetic judgement indeed, for Greville was thinking principally of the *New Arcadia*, where, if there is frivolity, there is less of it than in the *Old*.[73] For Greville the essential lessons of Sidney's fictions are political. They relate to the misgovernment of Basilius, to the consequent diminution of majesty, and to the 'map of desolation' to which the Duke reduces his country: failings which Sidney had, by interlinear allusion, compared to Elizabeth's, and which Greville, likewise between the lines, compares to those of her successor James I.[74]

Greville's perspective is radically incomplete. Yet it is no more restricting or misleading than its opposite. Since the seventeenth century most of Sidney's readers have been unaware of or indifferent to his political preoccupations. That deficiency can be traced to the post-Renaissance division of practical politics from the literary imagination and, in modern times, to the distinction between the academic disciplines of literature and history. There is another post-Renaissance separation too, of creativity from thought. The wit and playfulness of the *Arcadia* are the allies, not rivals, of the fertility of the work in analysis and ideas. Jean Robertson, that excellent modern editor of Sidney, who emphasises the 'light-hearted' aspects of his fiction, bids us remember that 'he set out to produce a story rather than a treatise'.[75] Her distinction is anachronistic. If 'delight' is the servant of 'teaching', we must ponder the teaching as well as the delight.

The young princes of the *Arcadia* transgress the teaching which their earnest education, that mirror of the upbringing of Renaissance princes and nobles, has imprinted on them. Brought up for the 'trial' and 'exercise' of their 'virtue', they succumb, like Basilius, to idleness and lust. For them as for him, love is an escape from public concerns but proves inseparable from them. How could it not be, for in Arcadia as in the Renaissance the destiny and stability of monarchies are inseparable from the loves and marriages of their rulers? The princes are ready to abduct the heir to the throne and her sister, to convey them abroad, and to return to Arcadia with armies at their backs. During their trial Philanax calls the princes 'disguisers, falsifiers, adulterers, ravishers, murderers, and traitors'.[76] Of the six charges the first two are incontestable; Pyrocles whets the appetite of the Duke and Duchess for the third crime; Musidorus is foiled in attempting the fourth; Pyrocles, prepared to slay Basilius and his wife, would in doing so commit the fifth; the sixth charge is palpably accurate.

Yet in the conflict between love and duty, love has its own claims to make. The analogies between Sidney's letter and Philanax's counsel soon acquire their own parallel, in the advice given by Musidorus to Pyrocles when Pyrocles is smitten by love. Basilius and Pyrocles alike are urged to stick to the virtuous patterns of conduct which their threatened 'change' of 'course' would ruin. If Basilius's rejection of that counsel is one cause of Arcadia's catastrophe, the other is the failure of Pyrocles, and then of

73 Worden, *Sound*, pp. 362-4.
74 Ibid., pp. 15, 360-1.
75 *OA*, pp. xix, xxv.
76 Ibid., p. 400.

Musidorus himself, to observe Musidorus's precepts. By repetition and emphases of language Sidney presses the resemblance between the two episodes close.[77]

There is, however, a difference. The Duke, being 'wholly wedded to his own opinion', and having solicited Philanax's counsel only 'for fashion's sake', allows merely a token discussion of it, in which he answers Philanax's arguments 'with ... much dukely sophistry'.[78] Philanax is right, Basilius wrong. But Pyrocles, in responding to Musidorus's counsel, gives as good as he gets. The debate between the two cousins gives weight to both sides. The coin of love, disastrous on one of its faces, speaks on the other for youth against age and for humanity and self-discovery against stern and life-denying precept. Musidorus, before love seizes him, is 'high in the pulpit against love', warning Pyrocles against it like a 'schoolmaster'. He soon learns better, grasping that 'all is but lip-wisdom which wants experience'.[79]

If life cannot be contained within ethical prescriptions, no more can the literary imagination. Sidney's didacticism and his invention are often in tension. Yet through the *Arcadia* there runs a philosophy which holds the themes of love and politics – of what he calls 'private and public respects' – together.[80] They merge in the 'skirmish between Reason and Passion' which opens the Eclogues of Book Two. It is occasioned by, and looks back to, the Phagonian rebellion, where the passions of the mutineers escape the government of reason in the state. It is followed by, and points forward to, the anatomy of the conflict between reason and passion in the heart. Passions are the source of disorder in heart and state alike.

Yet 'Reason' makes its own error. For Sidney, as for most writers of the Renaissance, the public and private worlds were both to be interpreted within the ethical system and vocabulary of Aristotle. Aristotle, who explains the difference between kings and tyrants, tells us too that reason rules the passions (or intellect the appetites) as a king not a tyrant: not with a 'despotical' but with a 'constitutional and royal rule'.[81] Musidorus's mistake is to claim for reason, in the sphere of love, the 'absolute commandment' that in politics is claimed by Basilius and Elizabeth. In the 'skirmish', Reason has the same failing. It seeks to impose its 'will' on Passion, whom it scorns as a 'rebel vile'.[82] For passion is healthy when reason respects it: when it guides or steers rather than oppressing it, when it treats it as a servant but not as a slave. The subjects of kings should be governed on the same principle. Throughout the *Arcadia* Sidney applies a common and unifying language to 'private' and 'public respects'.[83] Perhaps no two of his readers will weigh the balance of his sympathies identically, but the coherence of the work will always be missed by readers who divide its political from its amatory themes.

*

77 Worden, *Sound*, pp. 141-5.
78 *OA*, pp. 6-9.
79 Ibid., pp. 42, 168; *NA*, p. 106.
80 Worden, *Sound*, ch. 18.
81 Aristotle, *Politics*, ed. Stephen Everson (Cambridge, 1988), p. 6.
82 *OA*, pp. 19, 135.
83 Worden, *Sound*, pt 5.

Like *Gorboduc*, like the *Mirror for Magistrates*, the *Arcadia* is a mirror for princes, even if it is much else besides. 'The poet,' explains Sidney's *Defence*, 'can ... readily direct a prince.'[84] That was the common aspiration of Renaissance authors whose writings touched on politics. But will the prince listen, or even hear? If Sidney's attempt to sway the Queen by a brief letter failed, he can hardly have expected a long allegorical romance to have converted her, even supposing that she – or her friends or advisers – would have read it. If there was a literary route to influencing Elizabeth it was through the many plays offering political advice, *Gorboduc* among them, that were performed before her.[85] But the *Arcadia*, as far as we can judge, made its impact outside the court, as Sidney's letter against the match, though addressed to the Queen, appears to have done. In any case, by 1580, when most of the *Old Arcadia* seems to have been written, the threat of the Anjou match, that starting-point of Sidney's political allegory, had faded, though the failings of character and policy that had produced it had not diminished.

We cannot tell whom Sidney expected to read the *Arcadia* or how far he expected its political purpose to be grasped. Current critics and historians, surprised, it seems, to discover that texts are read differently by different people, have brought to the subject of Renaissance reading a weight of interpretative ambition which the surviving evidence is too thin to bear. Such late-Elizabethan or Jacobean commentary on the *Arcadia* as survives – none of it, alas, earlier than 1593 – shows that its political dimension was recognised. Apart from Greville's analysis we have, among the Sidney family papers, notes in an unknown late-Elizabethan hand which reveal their author's interest in Sidney's treatment of forms of government and of the corrupting properties of peace. They mingle with observations on topical issues which the *Arcadia* addresses, and with material reproduced from Sidney's letter against the Anjou match.[86] In the Folger Shakespeare Library in Washington DC there are notes on a copy of the *Arcadia* written by one W. Blount, another early reader of the work, who was likewise aware, if apparently less sharply, of Sidney's political themes. Finally, we have the history of the first four years of Elizabeth's reign written around 1611 by Sir John Hayward (whose account of the reign of Henry IV, a transparent use of the past to comment on the present, had caused such a stir, and created so much trouble for its author, near the end of Elizabeth's reign). Hayward's opening paragraph, which describes the dying sickness of Queen Mary and the nation's response to it, is silently lifted from, and mildly paraphrases, Sidney's account of the crisis that follows the death of Basilius, with minor amendments which adjust Sidney's wording from the national predicament of 1579 to that of 1558.[87]

Those three commentators, however, saw the *Arcadia* in a form which Sidney had not sanctioned: the composite version which was printed in 1593, seven years after his

84 *MP*, p. 86.

85 Marie Axton, *The Queen's Two Bodies. Drama and the Elizabethan Succession* (London, 1977); Susan Doran, 'Juno versus Diana: the treatment of Elizabeth I's Marriage in Plays and Entertainments, 1561-1581', *Historical Journal* 38 (1995), 257-74.

86 Kent Archives Office, U1475 (De L'Isle and Dudley Papers), Z1/11.

87 Worden, *Sound*, pp. 205-6, 370-1.

death, and in which the last part of the *Old Arcadia* was tacked on to the uncompleted *New*. Though Philanax's advice to Basilius reappears in the *New Arcadia* (now as a letter rather than a speech), and thus in the composite text, in both version it loses the pivotal function it holds in the *Old Arcadia*. For by the time he wrote the *New Arcadia* Sidney's political concerns, while still prominent in his fiction, had adapted to altered political circumstances.[88] The existence of the *Old Arcadia* as a separate text was concealed and forgotten, to come to light only a century ago. In Sidney's own lifetime the *Arcadia*, in all its forms, was confined (like his letter) to manuscript. To the two obvious explanations of that restriction – the stigma of print, and Sidney's failure to complete a text that satisfied him – there may be a third to be added. The circulation of Sidney's letter to the Queen, as his mentor Hubert Languet remarked to him, was 'by no means a safe proceeding'.[89] 'The chief safety' of the *Old Arcadia*, remarks its dedicatory epistle, 'shall be the not walking abroad'.[90] Where and how far his text 'walked' in his lifetime we have mainly to guess.[91] Perhaps the most he can have hoped is that his images of political virtue and vice, and his account of misrule and of its effects, would impress themselves on the minds of Elizabethan noblemen and intellectuals sympathetic to his outlook, and would help guide their conduct and judgement in the face of present and future dangers.

Beyond a point, however, speculation about literary impulse is always fruitless. If Sidney conforms to the norm of major writers, he writes because he has to, in dialogue with the prompter within him: because there are things he must say, whether or not he is read and however he is read. Yet he also wants his fiction, as the *Defence* testifies, to change the world. The interaction of those two incentives is unlikely to have been a straightforward or constant process or to be tangible by his readers. Whatever his purposes or hopes, the writing of the *Arcadia* shows him summoning all his resources of wit and imagination in the cause of his country's virtue and survival, and creating, out of the gravest of political circumstances, a literary masterpiece.

88 Ibid., ch. 10.
89 Ibid., p. 20.
90 *OA*, p. 3.
91 For what is known see Henry Woudhuysen, *Sir Philip Sidney and the Circulation of Manuscripts* (Oxford, 1996), ch. 10.

THE QUEEN AND THE HERMIT

THE 'TALE OF HEMETES' (1575)

GABRIEL HEATON

IN SEPTEMBER 1575 a tale was related to Queen Elizabeth by the character of a hermit in the park of the royal manor of Woodstock. As with many royal entertainments, the tale the hermit told was written both to entertain the Queen and to write her into its fiction. The 'Tale of Hemetes' (the name of the hermit) was commissioned by Sir Henry Lee, the Lieutenant of Woodstock. After its original performance, it appeared in a number of textual forms.[1] This essay focuses on one of these: the presentation manuscript given to the Queen by George Gascoigne (London, British Library, Royal MS 18 A.XLVIII), even though its author was not Gascoigne, but, probably, a young Oxford fellow named Robert Garrett.

The two presentations of the tale are excellent examples of the complex dynamics of manipulation and dependence that typified writing for Queen Elizabeth. This essay will show how the form it took was determined by Lee's status and ambitions, along with lesser influence from other figures. The manuscript of the 'Tale of Hemetes', perhaps the most carefully worked-out literary manuscript presented to Elizabeth during her long reign, is constructed to give expression to the status and ambitions of Gascoigne. These two ambitious men, Lee and Gascoigne, both saw that writing for the Queen gave them an opportunity to represent their relationship with her in their own terms, but they also recognised that they depended on the Queen's positive reception of their offering. In both cases Elizabeth seems to have accepted the presentation with grace, although the effect of this on their relationships with the Queen is less clear.

I

The month Queen Elizabeth spent at the royal manor of Woodstock in 1575 came at the end of the longest summer progress of her reign, that had taken her as far from

I would like to thank Dr Harriet Knight for careful proof-reading of this piece and much else besides, and also the editorial team of the *John Nichols Project* at the University of Warwick.

1 A pamphlet containing the devices from the Woodstock entertainment was printed by Thomas Cadman in 1585. The only surviving copy of the pamphlet is incomplete, beginning at gathering B, and has been given the title (from the running-title) of *The Queenes Maiesties Entertainment at Woodstocke*. The tale also survives in Alexander Fleming, *A Paradoxe, Prouing by reason and example, that Baldnesse is much better than bushie haire ... Herevnto is annexed the pleasant Tale of Hemetes the Heremite, pronounced before the Queenes Maiestie* (London, 1579), in London, British Library, Add. MS 41499A (Lee's archival copy), and an incomplete copy is in Oxford, Bodleian Library, MS Tanner 169, fol. 179r.

London as Stafford.[2] The 'Tale of Hemetes', which was performed some time between the 10th and 20th of September, was one of a number of devices performed for her entertainment, and had been organised by the Lieutenant of Woodstock, Sir Henry Lee. Woodstock had been a royal manor for many centuries: there are records of tournaments held at Woodstock in the fourteenth century, and King Henry II had kept his mistress 'Fair Rosamond' Clifford in a bower in the park.[3] It was an appropriate location for the sight that Elizabeth came upon when riding in the woods: two knights locked in combat, watched by a maiden and a hermit. On spotting the Queen, Hemetes the hermit stepped forward and ended the combat with the exclamation that the prophecies had now been fulfilled, an announcement he went on to explain to the Queen by telling the tale of how these four exotic characters had found their way to an Oxfordshire wood.

The location of the entertainment in the realm of chivalry not only suited the medieval inheritance of Woodstock, it was also highly appropriate for Sir Henry Lee. During the 1570s Lee emerged as the dominant figure in the Elizabethan tiltyard, a position which he gained especially by his instigation of the annual Accession Day tilts in honour of the Queen.[4] The Accession Day tilts were the most widely accessible form of Elizabethan royal pageantry and their norms were largely established in the 1570s. By the 1580s Lee's eminence in the tiltyard was widely accepted; for example, in early 1582 the Earl of Arundel apparently invited Lee to write his tiltyard speech for the 'Callophisus' tournament, in which Arundel promoted himself at court.[5] His mastery of the tiltyard would have a material benefit for Lee: the normalisation of Accession Day tilts by the early 1580s corresponded with Lee's appointment as Master of the Armoury, one of the responsibilities of which was the provision of equipment for royal tournaments, and it is highly likely that his prominence in the tiltyard was influential in getting him this appointment.

Lee's dominance in the tiltyard depended on his publicly acknowledged relationship with the Queen, whom he served as personal champion, as much as on his prowess. The role of champion was one he created and claimed for himself. It was distinct from that of the official Queen's Champion who was responsible for issuing a challenge at the coronation feast, for this position was inalienably connected to the manor of Scrivelsby in Lincolnshire, and had been held by the Dymocke family since the reign of Richard II. Sir Edward Dymocke had performed the role at Elizabeth's coronation, while his grandson, another Sir Edward, was to officiate at the coronation of James I.[6] Lee was

2 For the Queen's itinerary in 1575 see Mary Hill Cole, *The Portable Queen: Elizabeth I and the Politics of Ceremony* (Amherst, Mass., 1999), pp. 188-9.

3 *Victoria County History: Oxfordshire: Volume 12*, ed. Alan Crosby (Oxford, 1990), pp. 435-9.

4 Lee's first recorded appearance at tilt was in 1571, E. K. Chambers, *Sir Henry Lee: An Elizabethan Portrait* (Oxford, 1936), p. 38. He was appointed Master of the Armoury around 1580, and from 1581 there are annual records of Accession Day tilts. See Alan Young, *Tudor and Jacobean Tournaments* (London, 1987), pp. 35-6.

5 BL, Add. MS 41449A, fol. 6r.

6 For Sir Edward Dymocke at Elizabeth's coronation see Raphael Holinshed, *Chronicles* (London, 1587), III, 1180. For the Dymocke family and their hereditary role as King's Champion, see *DNB*, *sub* Dymocke,

probably able to present himself as an alternative because the incumbent at Scrivelsby in the 1570s, Sir Robert Dymocke, was a recusant who died in Lincoln gaol in 1580.

It is not clear exactly when Lee's status as the Queen's special champion was generally accepted. What *is* clear, however, is that this role is carefully figured in the 'Tale of Hemetes', that the distinct and identifiable role Lee created for himself at court was constructed in large part through pageant fictions, and that the 1575 Woodstock entertainment was the most ambitious entertainment he had presented to that date. He was so successful in constructing this role that when he retired from the tiltyard in 1590 he was even able, through an elaborate ceremonial he himself invented, to bestow his role on a successor: George, Earl of Cumberland.[7]

Lee's self-dramatisation in pageantry and entertainment was therefore central to his success at court. He was himself one of the combatants at Woodstock, who in the tale that followed was named as Loricus. This role provided him with an opportunity to display his highly developed martial skills, and we can be sure that it was only after Lee and his opponent had had a reasonable opportunity to do so that Hemetes stepped forward to stop the combat. Lee's display of his personal skill was a way for him, as an accomplished and well-connected courtier, to promote himself before the Queen as the best man to fight on her behalf. Equally, the very fact that he was able to display himself in this way was itself indicative of favour. His high standing with the Queen is revealed by the fact that Elizabeth had already visited Woodstock twice, in 1572 and 1574, since Lee had taken over there in 1571.[8] The combat of 1575 followed a pattern that had been established in the previous year, when Lee had appeared as an unknown discontented knight. Along with a companion, he 'made an open, and Solempne proclamacion ageynst all nobellmen, and gentyllmen at Armes' who were willing to fight for the sake of Love and Virtue, in order to prove whether the 'farr spred prayse of the noblest yonge gentillmen of theys partes of the worlde, mought be founde as certayne in there warlicke forces, as fame hath throughly publyshed the same'.[9]

With their emphasis on costume, witty *impresa*, fictional personae, and back-stories, Elizabethan tournaments were about much more than martial display; they developed into arenas in which courtiers could dramatise their relationship with the Queen. The chivalric conventions of the 'cult of Elizabeth' were largely developed in the Accession Day tilts with which Lee was so intimately involved.[10] Tournaments were also used to articulate a more personal agenda, and the surviving tiltyard speeches of Lee's (most of which cannot, unfortunately, be dated) show that he exploited his status as a source of patronage, using the access to the royal presence provided by the tiltyard to petition

Sir John. The same family still owns Scrivelsby and a representative served as Queen's Champion at the coronation of Elizabeth II.

7 Lee's retirement entertainment is described in William Segar, *Honor Military, and Ciuill, contained in foure Bookes* (London, 1602), pp. 197-200.

8 Chambers, p. 82. Elizabeth's only other visits to Woodstock during her reign were in 1566 and 1592.

9 London, College of Arms, Tournament Cheques Portfolio, No. 23a.

10 See Frances Yates, *Astraea: The Imperial Theme in the Sixteenth Century* (London, 1975), pp. 88-111; Roy Strong, *The Cult of Elizabeth: Elizabethan Portraiture and Pageantry* (London, 1999), pp. 129-62.

on behalf of suitors.[11] Like these later tiltyard speeches, the 'Tale of Hemetes' was told as an explanation for a combat. The tale has the form of a conventional, if highly condensed, chivalric romance (the entire narrative is crammed into about 2500 words), but its significance cannot be extricated from its function as providing a narrative frame for chivalric display before the Queen. This was a narrative in which all participants, the Queen included, had a specific role to play.

The tale itself can be briefly retold. The princess of Cambaya (roughly corresponding to modern Gujarat), Gaudina, was in love with the base-born but honourable Contarenus. When this was discovered by the Cambaian king Occanon, he hired an enchantress to spirit Contarenus from his kingdom; but when Gaudina heard what her father had done, she promptly quit the country in search of her lover. She eventually reached the grotto of the Sibyl, where she met a knight called Loricus, and they were told that they must travel together until they reached a particularly fortunate land ruled by a most worthy queen, where Gaudina would be contented and Loricus comforted. Loricus had loved a matchless lady but, when she would not even allow him to serve her chastely, he took a curious route to her favour: he pretended to love another woman, one who was 'euery day in her eye'. This only led to his true love disdaining him as inconstant, and Loricus came to the realisation that he was, in fact, unworthy to serve her, so he set off to endeavour to prove his worth with travel and arms.

Contarenus, meanwhile, had been told by the enchantress that he must travel in the company of a blind hermit for seven years, but that, eventually, he would fight the hardiest knight in the world and see the worthiest lady, whereupon he would find contentment and the hermit would regain his sight. The personal history of Hemetes the hermit was no less fraught. He had also loved a lady (fit to be loved of Love himself) but she, unfortunately for Hemetes, was a shape-changer and when she became a ferocious tigress he was deterred from further pursuit. If this was not bad enough, when he went to the temple of Venus to complain, he was struck blind. A jealous Venus was angry that he had always served Apollo in addition to her: books and beauty make no match. Apollo's priest told Hemetes (after explaining that inconstancy was part of women's nature) that he would regain his sight when, in a most peaceful land, two of the most valiant knights fought, two most constant lovers met, and the most virtuous lady in the world looked on. In the end the two groups, Loricus with the Cambaian princess, and her long-lost lover with Hemetes, independently found their way to the promised land, and when Contarenus saw his lady in the company of another man, he did what any self-respecting knight-errant would do – attacked him immediately. So when Queen Elizabeth happened upon the scene (being of course the worthiest queen and most virtuous lady in the world) the prophecies were fulfilled, Hemetes regained his sight, and all was well – or nearly – but that is another story. In any case, Hemetes led the Queen off to his hermitage, where a banquet had been prepared, gifts and verses

11 For example, see BL, Add. MS 41499A, fols 1-2 ('The Supplicacion of thold Knight' and 'The Message of the Damsell of the Q of Fayries').

were given to the Queen and her Maids of Honour, and the Fairy Queen put in an appearance.[12]

As with many entertainments, the fictional world constructed in 'Tale of Hemetes' connects with reality through the figure of the Queen who, as well as being the primary spectator, was drawn into the tale itself. Most entertainments involving armed combat took the form of the challenge, as Lee's display at Woodstock in 1574 had done. In such circumstances, Elizabeth's role was typically that of the mistress for whom the combatants fought, and courtiers' protestations of unmatchable love easily degenerated into acrimonious exchanges, as did that between the Earls of Arundel and Oxford, Lord Windsor, Sir Philip Sidney and Sir William Drury in 1581/2, which began when Arundel challenged all who would dispute that his own love for his mistress was 'for impression so deepe, for continuaunce so lasting, and for passion so extreame, as it is impossible for any other to carry so perfect looue, or to conceaue the like affection'.[13]

The 1575 entertainment is substantially more ambitious. Hemetes's tale elevates the Queen to a different role from that of 'mistress', and configures her presence as fulfilling prophecies and bringing peace, rather than division and competition. The use of a more complex chivalric frame was probably influenced by the 'Princely Pleasures' at Kenilworth in July 1575, which had also given Elizabeth a chivalric role: for example, in freeing the Lady of the Lake, who had been besieged by Sir Bruse sans Pitie. When she first came across the knights locked in combat, given her familiarity with the conventions of chivalric romance, Elizabeth may have assumed that they were fighting over the watching princess, Gaudina. As Hemetes tells his story this is shown to be not quite the case, but Gaudina's role is nevertheless in contrast with that of the Queen herself, who is the source of harmony.

It was the roles chosen by those who were performing for her that determined the part played by Queen Elizabeth in the 'Tale of Hemetes'. The Queen found herself introduced into Hemetes's tale as its culmination, but she was also brought into it at the level of allegory. This was not just a tale told for her entertainment: it was a tale in which the characters are figures for her courtiers. Since Lee is Loricus, who could be the matchless unattainable lady whom Loricus strives to be worthy to serve, but Queen Elizabeth herself? He is casting himself as her knight errant. The fictionalised relationship between Loricus and his lady, which overlays Lee's relationship with Elizabeth, reinforces the importance of his role as her champion, a role which was to be central to his court career for at least the next fifteen years. Loricus is dominated by his desire to be accepted as worthy to serve, but this desire is presented in a highly specific way: his love for her is to be expressed solely through chivalric escapades, for he has already

12 The fairy imagery at Woodstock is discussed in Matthew Woodcock, 'The Fairy Queen Figure in Elizabethan Entertainments', in *Elizabeth I: Always Her Own Free Woman* (Aldershot, 2003), pp. 97-115 (pp. 100-8).

13 *The Challenge of Callophisus* (London, 1582) [STC 4368.5]. The various responses to this challenge are in BL, Lansdowne MS 99, fols 259-64 (printed in *Malone Society Collections*, vol. 1, part 2 (Oxford, 1908), pp. 181-7). See also Katherine Duncan-Jones, *Sir Philip Sidney: Courtier Poet* (London, 1991), p. 203.

scripted her refusal of his courtship, and she – it is hoped – will recognise his worthiness to serve in that capacity.

By making the fictional characters figures for courtiers, the tale suggests itself as an allegory, and it was read as such by contemporaries. When a printed pamphlet appeared describing the events at Woodstock in 1575, the narrator remarked of Hemetes's tale that, 'if you marke the woords with this present world, or were acquainted with the state of the deuices, you shoulde finde no lesse hidden then vttered, and no lesse vttered then shoulde deserue a double reading ouer'.[14] This is one of a number of moments at which the narrator of the pamphlet gestures towards a meaning that is beyond his ken: behind the open, public, and indeed publicised address, it is suggested, lay a private, intimate, even secret, meaning.

An element of the Loricus persona that is particularly important to the 'hidden' meaning of the tale is his feigned love of someone other than his true mistress, which had brought him into disfavour in the first place. The implication of this narrative strand is that Lee's name had recently been connected with someone close to the Queen at court, and this affair was now being represented in such a way as to show that his passion never, in fact, wavered from Elizabeth. The significance of this is indeed hidden since the woman's identity is not known (Lee's wife, Anne née Paget, is unmentioned throughout), but it may well have been an unimportant affair – there is nothing to suggest that Lee was seriously in disgrace with the Queen at the time.[15]

The content of this hidden meaning may well have been less important to Lee than the display of an intimate relationship with the Queen it implied: speaking obliquely of court secrets, however minor, was a means of publicising his ability to talk privately with the Queen. In admitting to transgression, Loricus was also able to present himself as an apologetic suitor. Dedications and petitions throughout the period were suffused with craven apologies: works were inevitably unworthy, petitioners consistently humble and despairing of their capacity to do justice to the worth of their would-be patron. Depicting yourself as unworthy invited a display of clemency and generosity.

Lee must have seen the advantage in apology for he returned to the subject of his own weakness in 1592, when he entertained the Queen at his own manor of Ditchley, just a few miles from Woodstock, and resurrected the persona of Loricus. In an entertainment full of echoes of the 1575 visit, the 'Old Knight' admits that despite having been warned to 'lend not any ladye once an eye', 'vnhappie I was ouertaken/by fortune forcd a straunger ladies thrall'.[16] Although at that time Lee did have a mistress, Anne Vavasour, there is once again no evidence that his behaviour had led to his disgrace with the Queen, and the primary importance of advertising his waywardness and weakness was probably to display his closeness to the Queen by indirectly re-asserting his (doomed) courtship of her.

The 'Tale of Hemetes' was a narrative with multiple strands in which Loricus was

14 *The Queenes Maiesties Entertainment at Woodstocke*, sig. B1ʳ.

15 Chambers suggests that Lady Susan Bourchier may have been the object of Lee's affection in 1575 because she was in attendance at Woodstock and was later remembered in Lee's will (Chambers, p. 91).

16 BL, Add. MS 41499A, fol. 13v.

only one character, but although the other narratives probably also alluded to court events, the identification of Loricus with Lee is the only one that can be made with certainty. The Woodstock entertainment has always been primarily associated with Sir Henry Lee, but it is important to remember that he was the Queen's Lieutenant at a royal manor, not her private host: Lee was not performing in his own dominion. The existence of multiple plots itself suggests that others had an important role at Woodstock that had to be acknowledged also. One figure who played a significant role was the courtier and poet Edward Dyer. Lee ultimately had his rights to the Lieutenantship of Woodstock from Dyer, who had been granted the position of Steward of Woodstock in 1570, but farmed it out. Dyer nevertheless maintained some connection to Woodstock that was evident around the time of the 1575 royal visit. He wrote a poem of Despair that was sung from an oak-tree as Elizabeth returned from her banquet at Hemetes's hermitage, and a letter written by Dyer from Woodstock some weeks after Elizabeth left suggests that he stayed in the area for some time.[17] Considering that Dyer and Lee were both part of Leicester's circle and shared literary interests, it is likely that they collaborated more widely on the entertainment.

E. K. Chambers suggests that the bookish courtier Dyer was figured in Hemetes himself, who had indeed seen fit to flee from a tigerish Elizabeth a few years previously (it has also been suggested that the song of Despair was concerned with Dyer's disgrace).[18] As a stock figure of chivalry, the hermit was a useful persona for courtiers like Dyer or, in later years, Sir Robert Cecil, who had little talent for martial display.[19] Even if Dyer was not meant by Hemetes, Elizabeth was undoubtedly the object of Hemetes's affections, who was 'withoute disdayne to be desiered, but most deynty to be dealt with' (fol. 9r). After all, the allegorical suggestiveness of the tale depends upon its having been told in the presence of the Queen, and in this context all worthy but unattainable women are inevitably associated with Elizabeth.

The one strand of Hemetes's tale that does not have any obvious bearing on the Queen is that of the desperate lovers Gaudina and Contarenus. However, that strand was continued in a play presented later during Elizabeth's stay at Woodstock.[20] In the play, a remorseful Occanon has pursued his daughter from Cambaya to Oxfordshire and, after some debate, the lovers Contarenus and Gaudina find a new respect for place, responsibility, and regal authority, and determine to master their passion and part from each other forever. Gaudina returns with her father while Contarenus seeks out Loricus as a companion for a career in knight-errantry.

Deference to royal opinion on foolish marriage and unruly passion is unmistakable in this unusually level-headed conclusion to a romance, but the play has also been seen

17 The letter, to Burghley, was written on 27 October. HMC, *Salisbury*, II (1888), p. 119.

18 Chambers, p. 91; Ralph M. Sargent, *At the Court of Queen Elizabeth: the Life and Lyrics of Sir Edward Dyer* (Oxford, 1935), pp. 33, 207.

19 On two occasions in the early 1590s Robert Cecil was figured as 'the Hermit of Theobalds'. These were in 1591 (text found in BL, Egerton MS 2623, fols 15-16), and in June 1594 (a number of manuscript copies survive of this oration, all dating from the 1630s: Dublin, Trinity College, MS 802; Bodleian Library, MS Rawl.D. 692; BL, Add MS 72087; London, Lambeth Palace Library, MS 2828).

20 *The Queenes Maiesties Entertainment at Woodstocke*, sigs C3^{v}-G3^{r}.

as alluding to Elizabeth's own relationship with the Earl of Leicester. Since the Woodstock entertainment took place just two months after the Earl of Leicester's 'Princely Pleasures' at Kenilworth, and since Kenilworth has usually been understood as a promotion of Leicester's marriage suit, it has been suggested that the play was a critical response to the earlier entertainment.[21] However, both Lee and Dyer were closely associated with Leicester, and are unlikely to have felt that an intrusion into his relationship with Elizabeth would be in their best interests. Susan Doran has suggested that there are, in fact, important similarities in the agendas of Kenilworth and the Woodstock play: Kenilworth articulated Leicester's ambitions as defender of the Protestant cause in the Low Countries, and the play, which concludes with Contarenus (that is, Leicester) embarking on a career of knight-errantry, can be seen as making a similar plea for Elizabeth to allow Leicester independence and military command.[22] An alternative reading of the allegory can be found in the recent suggestion that the play is alluding to a different potential match, that between Elizabeth and François, Duc d'Alençon.[23] Interpretation of the play does not have to come down to an identification of Contarenus with either Leicester or Alençon, since its general thrust, that the marriage of princes must balance desire with the interests of the state, need not refer to any specific match. Nevertheless, its performance before the Queen made an association between Gaudina and Elizabeth inevitable. In making this connection the play has an agenda distinct from the tale it continues, in which the relationship between Gaudina and Contarenus cannot plausibly be interpreted as referring to any of Elizabeth's courtships.

It was one thing for Sir Henry Lee to represent his idealised relationship with Elizabeth in an allegorical mode, but this was worthless if she chose to ignore the allegory or refused to play the game he wanted her to play. An entertainment that irritated rather than entertained could hardly be said to have served its purpose well; hosts and performers looked, above all, for an acceptance from the Queen of their relationship with her as they depicted it. Entertainments turned on Elizabeth's response, the looked-for smile that would indicate, to the host and the watching court, that she accepted the role she had been given. It is worth emphasising that such a response was not always given, and there is plenty of evidence that Elizabeth was acutely aware of the implications of how she was represented in entertainments. Susan Frye has discussed what she terms this 'competition for representation' in relation to such examples as the coronation pageant and the Kenilworth entertainment.[24] Some entertainments, such as Gascoigne's 'Masque of Zabeta' at Kenilworth, were not

21 J. W. Cunliffe suggested the Woodstock play was a negative response to Kenilworth in 'The Queenes Majesties Entertainment at Woodstocke', *Publications of the Modern Language Association*, 26 (1911), 92-141 (p. 130), and a similar argument was made in Jean Wilson, *Entertainments for Elizabeth I* (Woodbridge, 1980), pp. 120-2. A detailed discussion of Kenilworth and Leicester's wider political agenda is found in Susan Frye, *Elizabeth I: The Competition for Representation* (Oxford, 1993), pp. 56-96.

22 Susan Doran, 'Juno versus Diana: The Treatment of Elizabeth I's Marriage in Plays and Entertainments, 1561-1581', *The Historical Journal*, 38 (1995), 257-74.

23 Woodcock, pp. 106-8.

24 Frye, *The Competition for Representation*.

performed for fear of antagonising the Queen, and she explicitly distanced herself from others. When Sir Philip Sidney set up a figure for Leicester as the most appropriate marriage partner for the Lady of May in 1578, Elizabeth deliberately chose the other candidate.[25] She played along willingly at Theobalds in 1591, but her response made it clear that she refused to countenance the entertainment's central request, that Lord Burghley be allowed to retire.[26]

There were occasions when the producers of an entertainment clearly considered that their underlying message, typically about marriage or religion, was of such importance that it was worth risking disfavour, but these were very much the exception.[27] Uncompromising assertions of that kind disrupted the gracious exchange that was at the heart of entertainments. Entertainments celebrated and developed the hierarchical relationship between monarch and subject. They were also opportunities for gift-giving. The house was symbolically offered to the Queen on her arrival, and during her progresses she was showered with gifts of jewels, books, clothing, and (from civic authorities) money, all accompanied with words of gracious compliment. The entertainments themselves were a form of gift; like other gifts, they attempted to engender a reciprocal response, and this depended on their gracious acceptance.

Elizabeth's response to the tale of Hemetes and the other devices that followed that day was extremely favourable: according to the pamphlet, 'her Maiestie filled with conceites, returneth home, leauing earnest command that the whole in order as it fell, should be brought her in writing'.[28] The Queen's gracious acceptance was itself an important form of reciprocity since it marked an acknowledgement of the status which was claimed by the performers in the entertainment. In this case, she even gave the performance further validation by asking that it be memorialised.

II

The Queen's response to the original telling of the tale, her request for a written copy, ensured that a rich and varied textual life followed from the original performance of the 'Tale of Hemetes'. On 1 January 1576 George Gascoigne took up the opportunity to continue the cycle of gift-giving begun at Woodstock, and presented Queen Elizabeth with a manuscript copy of the 'Tale of Hemetes' (London, British Library, Royal MS 18 A.XLVIII). The tale suited Gascoigne's purposes because the Queen was already written

25 Robert Kimbrough and Philip Murphy, 'The Helmingham Hall Manuscript of Sidney's *The Lady of May*: A Commentary and Transcription', *Renaissance Drama*, NS 1 (1968), 103-19 (pp. 105-6).

26 Elizabeth's response to an entertainment that excused Burghley's retirement on grounds of melancholy was to produce a mock Chancery charter in which she ordered writs 'too abiure desolacon & moourning (the consumers of sweetnes) too the Frozen Seas and deserts of Arabia Petrosa, uppon payn of fyve hundred despights too their terror & contempt of their torment, if they attempt any part of yoour hoous agayn'. This charter is now in the Elizabethan Club of Yale University.

27 For representations of marriage, see Doran. There were a number of anti-episcopal entertainments early in the reign, for example by Cambridge students in 1564, the text of which is found in Cambridge University Library, MS Ff. 5. 14, fol. 141v. See Marion Colthorpe, 'Anti-Catholic Masques Performed Before Queen Elizabeth I', *Notes and Queries*, 231 (1986), 316-18.

28 *The Queenes Maiesties Entertainment at Woodstocke*, sig. C2^{v}.

into it, and the manuscript which he presented to her wrote her into another role, that of his personal saviour.

The original significance of the tale was intimately bound up with its immediate context and occasionality, which in turn depended on its oral performance. The play on the identities of the protagonists, and their relationship with Elizabeth as both character and audience, lost their immediacy in the transition to written form. Gascoigne's manuscript enacted a deliberate and radical re-orientation of the text, compensating for its loss of occasion by overwhelming the tale with paratexts: a frontispiece, a lengthy dedicatory epistle, verses, translations of the tale into Latin, Italian, and French, and an emblem to accompany each translation (see PLATES 1 and 3-5).

Books and other texts were often part of the gift-exchange that characterised entertainments. A well-known symbolic moment at Elizabeth's coronation pageant was the presentation to her of an English bible by Truth, which she ostentatiously clasped to her bosom.[29] Mock letters of state business formed a part of several Elizabethan entertainments, and while she was at Harefield during her last summer progress of 1602, Elizabeth was handed a petition from St Swithin apologising for the terrible weather.[30] Texts were also important as a means of ensuring that the Queen received the message which might have been inaudible or confused in performance. When she was at Bristol in 1574, a prominent citizen had swum the Avon to present her with a velvet-bound copy of Thomas Churchyard's verses explaining the narrative of the ongoing martial entertainment, and verses were also presented both during and after masques at court.[31] Elizabeth had been presented with several texts at Woodstock: commendatory verses by Oxford students were given there in 1566; in 1575 a bible was given to her by Oxford's Vice-Chancellor Laurence Humphrey during his oration to the Queen, and on the same day as she had heard the 'Tale of Hemetes', 'posies' to her and her ladies-in-waiting were offered at Hemetes's hermitage.[32]

Of the examples just cited, the only manuscript given to Elizabeth that survives is the 1566 collection of Oxford verses given at Woodstock. Gascoigne's manuscript of 'Hemetes' is particularly valuable as it is the only surviving example of an entertainment text that was actually presented to Queen Elizabeth. Not only is it a particularly

29 Richard Mulcaster, *The passage of our most drad Soueraigne Lady Quene Elyzabeth through the citie of London to westminster* (London, 1558), sig. C2^{v}.

30 Letters formed part of the Rycote Entertainment (*Speeches Deliuered to Her Maiestie This Last Progresse* (Oxford, 1592), sigs C1^{v}-C4^{r}), the Mitcham entertainment (John Lyly (?), *Queen Elizabeth's Entertainment at Mitcham: Poet, Painter and Musician*, ed. Leslie Hotson (New Haven & London, 1953), pp. 16-17), and a 'Conference Between a Gentleman Usher and a Post' at Cecil House (BL, Harley MS 286, fols 248-9 and Bodleian Library, MS Tanner 79, fols 14-15); for the petition at Harefield, see Robert Krueger, *The Poems of Sir John Davies* (Oxford, 1975), pp. 215-16.

31 Thomas Churchyard, *The First parte of Churchyardes Chippes, contayning twelue seuerall Labours* (London, 1575), sigs. O1^{r}-O2^{v}. References to the production of manuscripts for masques can be found in Albert Feuillerat, *Documents Relating to the Office of the Revels in the Time of Queen Elizabeth* (Louvain, 1908), pp. 209, 239, 286-7, 301, 391.

32 BL, Royal MS 12 A. XLVII was given at Woodstock in 1566. For the 1575 presentation of the bible, see Laurence Humphrey, *Oratio ad sereniss. Angliae, Franciae, & Hyberniae Reginam Elisabetham, in aula Woodstochiensi* (London, 1575), sig. E4^{v}. The 'posies' are in *The Queenes Maiesties Entertainment at Woodstocke*, sigs C1^{v}-C2^{r}.

ingenious piece of self-presentation by Gascoigne, but it is a rare example of a form which was a relatively widespread means of addressing the monarch. The closest comparable examples are John Marston's manuscript of the pageants for the entry of King James and the King of Denmark in 1606, and Ben Jonson's presentation manuscripts of the *Masque of Blacknesse* and the *Masque of Queenes* from the first decade of the seventeenth century.[33]

Before turning to the manuscript itself, it is worth considering the oddity that it was Gascoigne who presented the manuscript. He is quite clear in his preface to the Queen that he did not write the tale, and he claims responsibility only for translating it into Latin, Italian and French for presentation to the Queen. It has been suggested that Lee himself was the tale's author.[34] Lee was commended in his lifetime for his literary skills, for example, in the dedication to Lee of *The Model of Poesy* by his nephew William Scott, which has recently been discussed by Stanley Wells.[35] Scott praises Lee's abilities as a writer of emblems (presumably including tournament *impresa*), abilities which are also referred to in the 1592 'Ditchley' entertainment, which describes how Lee, 'Sometymes ... somoned the witnesses of deepest Conceyts, himmes & songes, and emblems, dedecatinge them to the honor of his heauenly mistres.'[36]

As with many Elizabethan courtier poets, it is easier to find commendations of Lee's skills than a corpus of work that can be identified as his.[37] Although the tale is so attuned to Lee's status and ambitions at court that he must have been closely involved in its production, a manuscript text of part of the tale, unknown to previous commentators on the entertainment, makes possible a fresh ascription of authorship. This manuscript gives the following title: 'The Hermitts tale, made by Garrett master of Arte of my proceedinge.'[38] Stephen Powle, who wrote out this title, was a lawyer and one of the Six Clerks of Chancery; he had proceeded MA from Christ Church, Oxford, on 9 October 1573, some nine months after the man he refers to as the author of the 'Tale of Hemetes', Robert Garrett.[39]

It is possible that Powle's ascription is not correct. The manuscript was written many

33 BL, Royal MS 18 A. XXXI, Royal MS 17 B. XXXI, and Royal MS 18 A. XLV. Other non-royal presentation manuscripts also survive such as a copy of Marston's *Entertainment at Ashby* for Alice Dowager Countess of Derby, for which see James Knowles, 'Marston, Skipwith and *The Entertainment at Ashby*', *English Manuscript Studies,* 3 (1992), 136-92, and Robert White's *Cupid's Banishment* for Lucy Countess of Bedford, for which see C. E. McGee, '*Cupid's Banishment*', *Renaissance Drama*, NS 19 (1988), 227-64.

34 Frances Yates suggested that Lee was the author of 'The Tale of Hemetes' in *Astraea*, p. 97.

35 The manuscript of *The Model of Poesy* is in private possession and not yet accessible to scholars. It is of particular interest as it apparently contains one of the earliest discussions of Shakespeare's work. See Stanley Wells, 'By the placing of his words', *TLS*, 26 September 2003, 14-15. I am very grateful to Professor Wells for discussing the manuscript with me.

36 BL, Add. MS 41499A, fol. 15v.

37 There are three short poems, two of which are connected to his 1590 retirement tilt, that can be assigned with a relatively high level of confidence: see Thomas Clayton, '"Sir Henry Lee's Farewell to the Court": The Texts and Authorship of "His Golden Locks Time Hath to Silver Turned"', *English Literary Renaissance*, 4 (1974), 268-75.

38 Bodleian Library, MS Tanner 169, fol. 179r. The existence of this copy was first noted in H. R. Woudhuysen, *Sir Philip Sidney and the Circulation of Manuscripts, 1558-1640* (Oxford, 1996), p. 72.

39 For Powle, see Virginia F. Stern, *Sir Stephen Powle of Court and Country* (Toronto, 1992).

years after the entertainment took place, probably not before the second decade of the seventeenth century, and there is no evidence to suggest that Stephen Powle had been at Woodstock in September 1575.[40] When he made his copy he dated the performance vaguely, to '1576 or about that time', and he copied only one page of the text. Despite this, there are a number of reasons for taking Powle's ascription seriously. Stephen Powle and Robert Garrett were for seven years contemporaries at Oxford colleges which backed on to each other (Corpus and Christ Church), so they may well have known each other. Another indication of personal knowledge is that Powle was highly interested in the text, copying out the title into the pre-bound manuscript and leaving space before he actually had access to a text – which he must, therefore, have deliberately sought out. Not only was Powle making the ascription on the basis of personal knowledge, but the attributions and notes of sources in Powle's manuscript collection are generally quite careful and detailed; in any case false attributions tend to be made to well-known writers.

In 1575 Robert Garrett was Reader in Rhetoric at St John's College, Oxford. This position is the strongest supporting evidence for his authorship of the tale. Not only does it locate him only a few miles from Woodstock, but St John's was an institution with which Sir Henry Lee had close contacts. His younger brother, Cromwell, may have been a member of the college, and was certainly connected to it in some capacity during the years he lived in Oxford.[41] Sir Henry's personal association with St John's probably began when he first took over at Woodstock manor, when most of the members of St John's were residing at Woodstock. 'Chaucer's House' at the edge of the park (which still stands) was leased to the college from the Crown, and it was used as an alternative residence while plague kept them from Oxford itself, a set-up which ran for over a year until at least Lent 1572.[42] In later years, Lee became closely entangled financially with St John's and continued being a patron to members of the college, taking a personal chaplain from among its members on at least three occasions.[43]

40 Powle wrote the manuscript over an extended period of time. The title of the tale was first written on fol. 177r and then repeated, with the page of text, on fol. 179r. The title on fol. 177 was crossed out and the leaf filled with poems and letters dated November 1617, so the title probably dates from before that. There are many items in the manuscript which, like 'Hemetes', dated from many years before Powle transcribed them. For example at some point after transcribing 'Hemetes', Powle copied into the manuscript a series of letters from the early 1580s (fols 178, 179v-185v). For the identification of the hand responsible for the 'Tale of Hemetes' as Powle's, see Stern, p. 56.

41 Anthony à Wood, *Athenae Oxonienses*, 3rd edition, ed. Philip Bliss (London, 1813-20), I, 715, states he was a member, but the college accounts are not extant for the time when he would have been in attendance, so this cannot be confirmed. However, the library of St John's still possesses an Italian dictionary written by Cromwell Lee. I am very grateful to Mr Michael Riordan, the archivist of St John's College, Oxford, for clarifying the evidence for Cromwell Lee's attendance at St John's.

42 Chambers, p. 28; W. H. Stevenson and H. E. Salter, *The Early History of St. John's College, Oxford*, Oxford Historical Society, NS 1 (Oxford, 1939), pp. 177-9.

43 From at least 1580 Sir Henry also took an active interest in Gloucester Hall, an old university hall that had been incorporated into St John's (Stevenson and Salter, p. 497), and by the 1590s their interests were entangled over the Oxfordshire manor of Charlbury, which Lee leased from St John's, and the advowson of the parish (W. C. Costin, *The History of St John's College Oxford 1598-1860*, Oxford Historical Society, NS 12 (Oxford, 1958), p. 26). The chaplains Lee drew from St John's were Henry Price, John Lee (a distant relative of Sir Henry), and Theophilus Tuer. There is an inconsistency in the record of the dates served by Price: according to the Fleet Marston parish registers he was appointed in 1584, but

So when Sir Henry Lee was looking for someone highly literate whom he could commission to write a tale fit for a queen, the rhetoric reader at St John's would have made an obvious choice. As a young academic whose career depended on the patronage of elders, Garrett would hardly have been in a position to refuse. Garrett, who had been educated at Christ Church, obtained his position at St John's through the influence of the President of St John's, the court-oriented cleric Tobie Matthew (another Christ Church man). It does not seem to have been a particularly happy appointment: in 1574 Garrett was reprimanded for lack of diligence in his readership and ordered to keep the peace, and he was later accused of embezzling college goods.[44] In the summer of 1577 he married and was deprived of his fellowship. The Visitor of the college, Sir William Cordell (Master of the Rolls), commented on this turn of events: 'the College hath no loss in my opinion by the want of such an unnatural branch as he was'.[45] Garrett can probably be identified with the Robert Garrett who, in 1578, was installed as the vicar of Eglingham, Northumberland.[46] If so, this suggests his roots were in the north-east. He does not seem to have been any more successful at Eglingham than he had been at St John's: proceedings were begun against him in 1582 when he was found to have been neglectful of chapels in his parish, and Garrett resigned from his benefice in 1587.[47]

Given his eclipse by Lee and then by Gascoigne, it is entirely plausible that the author of the 'Tale of Hemetes' was relatively young and inexperienced as a court writer: after all, the man who actually wrote this successful piece apparently did not benefit from its success, unlike those who commissioned and translated it. Garrett's role was to fulfil a specific commission, just like the other hirelings on such occasions, such as actors and musicians. This was the typical status of entertainment authors. Entertainments were primarily associated with the commissioning patron in whose name they were performed, and although certain authors like George Gascoigne, who published the Kenilworth entertainment in 1576, and Thomas Churchyard, who signed his name to the Bristol entertainment printed in *Churchyardes Chippes*, were beginning to assert their authorship, it was only in the following century, with the emergence of Ben Jonson as the leading court poet, that the status of entertainment authors really began to change.[48] It is also clear that Lee knew, at least in outline, what he wanted presented. This was the case with many patrons, few of whom had such extensive experience with entertaining royalty.[49] In the rhetorical terms that Lee and

recent unpublished research by Dr Andrew Hegarty shows that he only entered St John's (aged 18) in that year, and re-dates his appointment to 1597. John Lee served Sir Henry from 1601, and Tuer, who was appointed in 1610, was present at his funeral in 1611 (Chambers, p. 298). I am very grateful to Dr Hegarty for allowing me access to his unpublished work.

44 This information is, once again, derived from unpublished work by Dr Andrew Hegarty.

45 Stevenson and Salter, p. 485.

46 *A History of Northumberland: Vol. XIV*, ed. Madeline Hope Dodds (Newcastle, 1935), p. 365.

47 *The Injunctions and other Ecclesiastical Proceedings of Richard Barnes, Bishop of Durham, 1575-87*, ed. J. Raine, Surtees Society 22 (Durham, 1850), pp. 97, 111.

48 George Gascoigne published a pamphlet, *The princelye pleasures at the courte at Kenelworth* (London, 1576). The apparently unique copy of this was destroyed by fire in 1879, but the text was reprinted in *The vvhole woorkes of George Gascoigne Esquire* (London, 1587).

49 The patron whose personal involvement in entertainments has been studied most closely is Robert Cecil, Earl of Salisbury. See James Knowles, '"To raise a house of better frame": Jonson's Cecilian Entertain-

Garrett would have used to understand their respective roles, Garrett was responsible for *dispositio*, but the initial stage of *inventio* was Lee's.

This does not, of course, explain why it was George Gascoigne who presented a manuscript copy of the tale to the Queen. Since he refers to having seen her pleasure in the tale at Woodstock, Gascoigne must have been present there. It is possible that he was employed in some capacity at Woodstock, but the suggestion that he wrote the play, the only other substantial device presented at Woodstock, has been convincingly rebutted; it is more likely that he had tagged along with the court on its progress from Kenilworth in July, where he had been employed by Leicester.[50]

There is nothing other than the manuscript to connect Gascoigne with Hemetes's tale, and her specific request for a copy was undoubtedly the reason he presented Elizabeth with this text rather than, for example, one of his own devices from Kenilworth. It is possible that Gascoigne received a specific commission from Lee to provide the text as a favour to Leicester, Gascoigne's patron at Kenilworth; but since he makes no mention of Lee or of receiving any commission, it is more likely that he took advantage of Elizabeth's invitation on his own initiative.[51]

Gascoigne himself offered an explanation of his presentation of the 'Tale' to the Queen in the manuscript's prefatory epistle. The manuscript was a demonstration of his skill and his willingness to serve:

> I fynd in my self some suffycyency to serue your highnes which causeth me thus presumpteowsly to present you with theis rude lynes/ having turned the eloquent tale of *Hemetes* the *Heremyte* (wherwith I saw your lerned iudgement greatly pleased at Woodstock) into laytne, Italyan and frenche/ nott that I thinke any of the same translacions any waie comparable with the first invencion/ (fol. 5r-v)

The presentation fits into a sustained campaign by Gascoigne to win favour and patronage through his literary labours that began with his return from service in the Netherlands in the summer of 1574, where he had been a Spanish prisoner-of-war for several months.[52] There were two aspects to this campaign: repeated assertions of his reformation of character, and emphais on his links to the royal court. A new edition of his collected poetry appeared early in 1575, revised in an (unsuccessful) attempt to placate the authorities who had been offended with the previous edition of 1572. He adopted a stance of reformed prodigality which was consistently maintained in four

ments', in *Patronage, Culture and Power: The Early Cecils, 1558-1612*, ed. Pauline Croft (New Haven & London, 2002), pp. 181-95; Gabriel Heaton, 'Performing Gifts: the Manuscript Circulation of Elizabethan and early Stuart court Entertainments' (unpub. PhD thesis, University of Cambridge, 2003), pp. 97-130.

50 *The Queen's Majesty's Entertainment at Woodstock 1575*, ed. Alfred Pollard (Oxford, 1910), p. xiii; Cunliffe, pp. 128-9.

51 The two recent discussions of the manuscript both assume it was commissioned. They are: Wendy Wall, *The Imprint of Gender: Authorship and Publication in the English Renaissance* (Ithaca, NY, 1993); and Richard C. McCoy, 'Gascoigne's "Poemata Castrata": The Wages of Courtly Success', *Criticism*, 27 (1985), 29-55.

52 See the biographical introduction to *A Hundreth Sundrie Flowres*, ed. G. W. Pigman III (Oxford, 2000), pp. xxvii-xxxviii. The most extended biography of Gascoigne remains C. T. Prouty, *George Gascoigne: Elizabethan Courtier, Soldier, and Poet* (New York, 1942).

strongly moralistic works that appeared over the following eighteen months, written, he claimed, 'too make amendes for the lost time which I misbestowed in wryting so wantonlie'.[53] Along with announcing his reformed prodigality, Gascoigne also promulgated the idea of himself as a courtly writer. *The Noble Arte of Venerie or Hunting* (London, [1575]), although published anonymously, included woodcuts of Elizabeth with Gascoigne himself in attendance, and in 1576 he produced the *Princelye pleasures at the courte at Kenelworth*.[54]

Although it was the manuscript of 'Hemetes' that brought Gascoigne closest to the court, he is unlikely to have presented the manuscript to the Queen in person. Gascoigne oriented himself towards the court in a number of works, but he did not have any official post, nor did he have the social status, wealth, or connections to be a courtier: he was what Steven May has termed a 'court poet' rather than a courtier poet.[55]

The manuscript was presented at the traditional time for gift-giving, New Year, which, because of the sheer volume of gifts exchanged, was not a time for personal interaction in gift-giving. Non-courtiers who wished to present a manuscript to the Queen in person found other occasions to do so, such as on progress, when the temporary arrangement of the court made the conventions of access more difficult to maintain, or on routine occasions such as when she passed to chapel.[56] A letter describing in detail the process of New Year gift-giving at court reveals it as an impersonal and bureaucratic system. It dates from the early years of James I's reign, but the process was probably much the same in the 1570s:

> You must buy a new purse of about $v^{s.}$ price, and put therinto xx peeces of new gold of $xx^{s.}$ a piece, and go to the Presence-chamber, where the Court is, upon New-yere's day, in the morninge about 8 o'clocke, and deliver the purse and gold unto my Lord Chamberlin, then you must go down to the Jewell-House for a ticket to receive $xviii^{s.}$ $vi^{d.}$ as a gift to your paines, and give $vi^{d.}$ there to the box for your ticket; then go to Sir William Veall's office, and shew your ticket, and receive your $xviii^{s.}$ $vi^{d.}$. Then go to the Jewell house again, and make choice of a peece of plate of xxx ounces waight, and marke it, and then in the afternoone you may go and fetch it away, and then give the gentleman who delivers it you $xl^{s.}$ in gold, and give to the box $ii^{s.}$ and to the porter $vi^{d.}$.[57]

53 *A delicate diet, for daintiemouthde droonkardes* (London, 1576), sig. A2^{v}. The other publications were: *The glasse of gouernement* (London, 1575); *The steele glas A satyre ... Togither with The complainte of Phylomene* (London, 1576); *The droomme of Doomes day* (London, 1576). Gascoigne's use of the prodigal narrative has been noted by many critics, including Richard Helgerson, *Elizabethan Prodigals* (Berkeley, 1976), pp. 44-58, and McCoy.

54 The evidence for Gascoigne's responsibility for *Venerie* is in George Whetstone, *A Remembraunce of the wel imployed life, and godly end, of George Gaskoigne* (London, [1577]), as was noted in Jean Robertson, 'George Gascoigne and *The Noble Arte of Venerie or Hunting*', *Modern Language Review*, 37 (1942), 484-5.

55 Steven W. May, *The Elizabethan Courtier Poets: The Poems and their Contexts* (Columbia, 1991), p. 40.

56 Richard Robinson describes making such a presentation in BL, Royal MS 18 A. LXVI, fol. 8r. For Robinson, see Woudhuysen, pp. 195-203.

57 Letter by the Earl of Huntingdon, 1604/5, in John Nichols, *The Progresses of James I*, 4 vols (London, 1828), I, 471.

But if unmediated personal address was not the privilege of the poet, it was the privilege of the work. The respective roles Gascoigne imagines for himself and the Queen are made clear in the manuscript's frontispiece which, in a late example of a medieval tradition, shows Gascoigne kneeling before Queen Elizabeth offering her a book (PLATE 1).[58] This image is the best known aspect of Gascoigne's manuscript: it has been reproduced several times and discussed by a number of critics.[59] As Wendy Wall has noted, there is an undercurrent of aggression in this image. Gascoigne might be kneeling, but he is at the centre of the picture while the Queen has been pushed towards the margin, his foot resting on the edge of her train. Although in reality he is unlikely to have been able to put the manuscript into her hands himself, in his representation of the act of presentation Elizabeth has no attendants, there are no servants or courtiers in the room, and even the corridor behind is empty: Gascoigne has been granted unmediated and sole access to her person.

Gascoigne's two vocations, soldier and poet, are both represented in the illustration: he holds a lance in his left hand and a book in his right, he has a sword at his belt as well as a pen behind his ear, and a hand descends from the ceiling holding a tablet with his motto, 'Tam Marti quam Mercurio' [as much for Mars as Mercury]. It is, however, the book that has brought Gascoigne into personal attendance on his monarch. The book has not yet reached the Queen's hands, so she cannot have conferred the laurel upon him on the basis of her reading of it: instead, the picture suggests that by accepting Gascoigne's gift Elizabeth will be acknowledging the poetic status he has already achieved.

Although Gascoigne was not unique in using the gift of a manuscript as a means of self-promotion, his manuscript is distinctive and imaginative.[60] The image on its frontispiece that brings together monarch and poet is highly unusual. The closest parallel is a manuscript copy of Beauchesne's *A Booke Contaning Divers Sortes of hands*, with additions and illustrations, prepared by William Teshe in 1580, which depicts Teshe offering the book when kneeling before the Queen, who sits in Fame's Chariot.[61] Most of the formal manuscripts presented to Elizabeth were given by people wishing to demonstrate their penmanship: calligraphers (Teshe was a calligrapher),

58 Ruth Mortimer, *A Portrait of the Author in Sixteenth-Century France* (Chapel Hill, NC, 1980); Cynthia J. Brown, 'Text, Image, and Authorial Self-Consciousness in Late Medieval Paris', in *Printing and the Written Word: The Social History of Books, circa 1450-1525*, ed. Sandra L. Hindman (Ithaca, NY, 1991), pp. 103-42.

59 Wendy Wall provides an acute analysis of the frontispiece (which she incorrectly describes as an engraving) as part of a discussion of Gascoigne's pageant texts in *The Imprint of Gender*, pp. 127-40, seeing in it a mixture of deference and aggression that she finds typical of Gascoigne. Both Wall and McCoy, in 'Gascoigne's "Poemata Castrata"', pp. 46-7, see sexual undertones in the frontispiece with its phallic tokens (sword, pen, lance). The frontispiece is discussed by Catherine Bates as emblematic of the dynamics of Elizabethan courtiership in the prologue to *The Rhetoric of Courtship in Elizabethan Language and Literature* (Cambridge, 1992), pp. 1-4. Carlo M. Bajetta begins his article 'The Manuscripts of Verse Presented to Elizabeth I', *The Ben Jonson Journal*, 8 (2001), 147-205, with this image, commenting that it is 'one of the best known visual images of a poet presenting his work to the Queen' (p. 147).

60 For presentation manuscripts, see Woudhuysen, pp. 88-103, and Bajetta.

61 BL, Sloane MS 1832, fols 7v-8r.

1 Frontispiece to the presentation copy of 'The Tale of Hemetes the Heremyte' (BL, Royal MS 18 A. XLVIII, fol. 1r)

scholars, and heralds. Courtier poets, who had relatively easy access to the Queen, and whose primary interests lay elsewhere, almost exclusively gave her verses in more informal circumstances.[62] Such presentations are unlikely to have been prepared with the attention to detail of Gascoigne's manuscript. For example, Carlo Bajetta argues that the manuscript of Ralegh's *Ocean to Scinthia* at Hatfield House, which is usually assumed to be a working copy, may have been intended for the Queen; a less formal copy serving his purpose better than a more finished one, because it better evoked the distressed mind and feverish penitential writing of the disgraced courtier.[63]

Poets without access to the royal presence who aimed at royal patronage, such as Spenser, tended to pursue their aims through print. One of the closest comparisons to Gascoigne's manuscript is *A rebuke to Rebellion*, by his friend Thomas Churchyard, which was presented to the Queen at an unspecified New Year.[64] However, in his dedicatory epistle to that work, Churchyard comments that it was penned 'vnder the protection of your highnes' (fol. 1r), suggesting that it was presented as the fruits of existing patronage, rather than demonstrating his worthiness of patronage. Neither was it written with the Queen herself as its ideal imagined reader, but rather offered to her as a work 'proffitable for good people, and a pinching rebuke to badd Subiects', ahead of being printed for general readership.[65]

There are few presentation manuscripts by poets of similar status to Gascoigne, and his manuscript is perhaps unique in the careful and coherent way in which his relationship with the Queen was constructed. He used the privileged space of address to the Queen in order to portray himself as an isolated and repentant figure who recognizes that his life has been full of mistakes, but who is surrounded by many detractors who restrict his ability to act out his reformation. This is an authorial position in which Gascoigne placed himself repeatedly in the texts he produced in the last years of his life. At New Year 1577 Gascoigne sent an emblem and letter to the Lord Keeper Nicholas Bacon.[66] That emblem (PLATE 2) illustrates two horses, one being ridden, the other beaten, with a motto explaining that some men are like colts, resistant to service, 'Yett (onse well broke) suche men proue not the worste.' In the accompanying letter Gascoigne explains the emblem's relevance to his own life: although he has now been broken in, his 'koltish trickes' have left him so weak that he is 'enforcede to neye and braye vnto your good Lord and all other which haue the keye of Her Maiesties storehowse'.

Not only does Gascoigne represent himself as desperately in need of patronage, but also as hopelessly indebted to his existing patrons. When dedicating the *Droomme of Doomes day* to the Earl of Bedford, he described the book as a 'pawne of thankfulnesse'

62 Bajetta, pp. 177-82

63 Ibid., pp. 183-4.

64 BL, Royal MS 17 B. VII.

65 *A Rebuke for Rebellion* is listed among Churchyard's works in *Churchyards Challenge* (London, 1593), sig. 1*^{v}, where it is recorded as being dedicated to the Earl of Bedford. The poem appears in the same volume reworked under the title 'A Warning to Wanderers Abroad' (sigs K3^{r}-L4^{v}).

66 The letter is now in the possession of Marquess Townshend of Raynham, on deposit at Norfolk Record Office, RAY 25. It has been misdated to 1 January 1577/8 (after Gascoigne's death).

2 Emblem included with a letter sent from George Gascoigne to Sir Nicholas Bacon, New Year 1577 (Norwich, Norfolk Record Office, RAY 25 (Raynham Loan Box 1))

(sig. **3^{v}) given to serve until an opportunity arose for Gascoigne to repay the true debt of gratitude that he owed to Bedford. Claiming indebtedness is a common part of the rhetoric of clientage, since it asserts a relationship with the putative patron, implying that the writer should be employed so he can display his gratitude.

Gascoigne does not have a great deal to say about the tale itself, which was just a convenient vehicle for his authorial self-presentation, but he is unusually explicit about his desire for patronage:

> Then peereles prince, employe this willinge man
> In your affayres to do the beste he cann/ (fol. 2r)

He does not claim that he should receive her patronage on the basis of the value of his gift. Should Elizabeth compare his translations to the original text, 'you shall fynde my sentences as much disordered, as arrowes shott owt of ploughes / and my theames as vnaptly prosecuted, as hares hunted with oxen' (fol. 5v). To present the monarch with a gift was to engage in a courtly game which was especially tricky for those with limited resources, and asserting the worthlessness of the gift, as Gascoigne does, was a common rhetorical move. Offering a gift to a monarch was not only a fairly extreme example of that timeless problem of what to give someone who has everything, but also required particular care since the donor did not necessarily wish for his or her gift to imply a lack on the part of the recipient. The Renaissance model for gift-giving was provided above all by Seneca's *De Beneficiis*, which emphasises gratitude and asserts that, in the translation of Thomas Lodge, 'that which is offered to the eye, is not the good workes or benefit, but onely a lustre and signe of the same'.[67] What matters is not the material object given but the act of giving: the physical gift is just the trace of goodwill and can be safely denigrated. This is a useful model for exchange between radically unequal transactors such as monarch and subject because it levels the value of the exchange, since the objects themselves are merely signifiers of the true gift – love.

Gascoigne uses the privileged space he has constructed for personal address to Elizabeth in order to assert his abject dependence on her bounty: 'fyndyng my youth myspent, my substannce ympayred, my credytt accrased, my tallent hydden, my follyes laughed att, my rewyne vnpyttyed, and my trewth vnemployed ... I presume ... to knock att the gates of your gracyous goodnes' (fols 4v-5r). The manuscript also includes three emblems that precede the three translations of the tale into Latin, Italian, and French. Their subject is Gascoigne's current status and dependence on favour to allow the fruition of his potential. In the first, a serpent that has been trodden underfoot refuses to die: even those that are trodden underfoot (as Gascoigne has been by fortune), asserts the motto, will rise again. In the Italian emblem (PLATE 3) Gascoigne is himself depicted trying to hold on to a great bundle of sticks while the motto dwells on ambition, as he considers that the man who grasps at too much is often able to hold on to nothing. This was an image he picked up again with reference to himself in his poem *The Grief of Ioye* (1577).[68] The French emblem returns to the theme of Gascoigne's age (to which he had alluded in his preface): just as a walnut tree will be more fertile if it is left to mature before being harvested, so his service will be more fruitful for coming in his middle age.

Features in these emblems, such as the stocky dimensions of the human figures and the decorative borders, are unmistakably the work of the same artist who was responsible for the emblem sent to Nicholas Bacon. Although it has been suggested, initially by B. M. Ward in 1926, that Gascoigne himself drew these illustrations, they

67 *The Workes of Lucius Annaeus Seneca, Both Morrall and Naturall*, (London, 1614), p. 7. The original reads, 'Sic non est beneficium id, quod sub oculos venit, sed beneficii vestigium et nota' (*De Beneficiis*, I.5.vi).

68 In the opening stanzas of the fourth song he compares himself to a boy over-ambitiously gathering wood from a pile, who pulls the entire pile down on his own head (BL, Royal MS 18 A. LXI, fols 30v-31r).

3 Italian emblem in the presentation copy of 'The Tale of Hemetes the Heremyte'
(BL, Royal MS 18 A. XLVIII, fol. 21r)

are more likely to be the work of a professional scribe, since the same scribal hands are also found in both the manuscript and the letter.[69]

The Hemetes manuscript is a display of Gascoigne's personal labour on behalf of his prince. He is also physically present in the manuscript through the illustrations: it is a recognisable likeness that presents the manuscript in the frontispiece, and he re-appears again in the Italian emblem (PLATES 1 and 3). The labour which Gascoigne has spent on providing the multiple translations of the tale, which take up far more of the manuscript than the original tale, display the linguistic abilities that make him suitable for government service. They were also surely calculated to please Elizabeth, who took great pride in her linguistic abilities. A similar emphasis on personal labour is also found in Jonson's presentation copy of *The Masque of Queenes*, in which the original text of the masque is overwhelmed by the citations of scholarly authorities which Jonson has provided, he says, upon express command of Prince Henry, in the hope that it will 'iustefie mee to your owne knowledge'.[70] Both see presentation as an opportunity to display abilities that can find further service in, as Jonson writes, 'some worke as worthy of your fame, as my ambition therin is of your pardon'.

Whereas Jonson wrote out his masque text in his own handwriting with the greatest care, Gascoigne's manuscript is entirely scribal, despite his rhetoric of personal address. The hands bear little resemblance to the hand in Gascoigne's holograph letters to Burghley in 1576.[71] The letters were admittedly written more hurriedly than the Hemetes manuscript, but some similarities should still be expected. The only appearance of Gascoigne's own hand in the manuscript is the signature at the foot of the epistle to Elizabeth (PLATE 4). The occasional corrections in the manuscript also seem to be in the scribal hand, but Gascoigne is likely to have been responsible for the systematic revision of the punctuation in which many parentheses and virgules were added, often as a replacement for commas.

Gascoigne declined to write out the tale himself simply because his handwriting was not fit for a Queen. Nevertheless, he surely collaborated closely with the anonymous scribe and was probably responsible for the overall scheme behind the manuscript's appearance, and its sophisticated use of various visual codes. Ruled red margins demarcate the writing space on each page and leave extensive margins, making the manuscript the equivalent of a large-paper copy (the writing space takes up approximately 55 per cent of the page), an extravagant gesture given that paper was an expensive commodity. The manuscript was written in a variety of scripts. A formal secretary with engrossing capitals was used for the prefatory sonnet and epilogue poem.

69 B. M. Ward, 'George Gascoigne and his Circle', *Review of English Studies*, 2 (1926), 32-41 (pp. 39-41); Peter Beal, *Index of English Literary Manuscripts: Volume I, 1475-1625* (London, 1980), Part 2, p. 99. Beal did not have access to the manuscript, so his comment relied on Ward's article. The Bacon emblem motto is written in the same italic hand as the Hemetes mottoes (note, for example, the long straight ascenders and descenders, the use of serifs, and the tail of *g*), and the text of the letter is in the same distinctive secretary hand as Hemetes.

70 *Ben Jonson*, ed. C. H. Herford, P. and E. Simpson, 11 vols (Oxford, 1925-52), VII, 281.

71 Samples of these letters (in the National Archives, SP 70/139 and 140) are reproduced in W. W. Greg, *English Literary Autographs 1550-1650*, 3 vols (Oxford, 1925-32), II, plate 37.

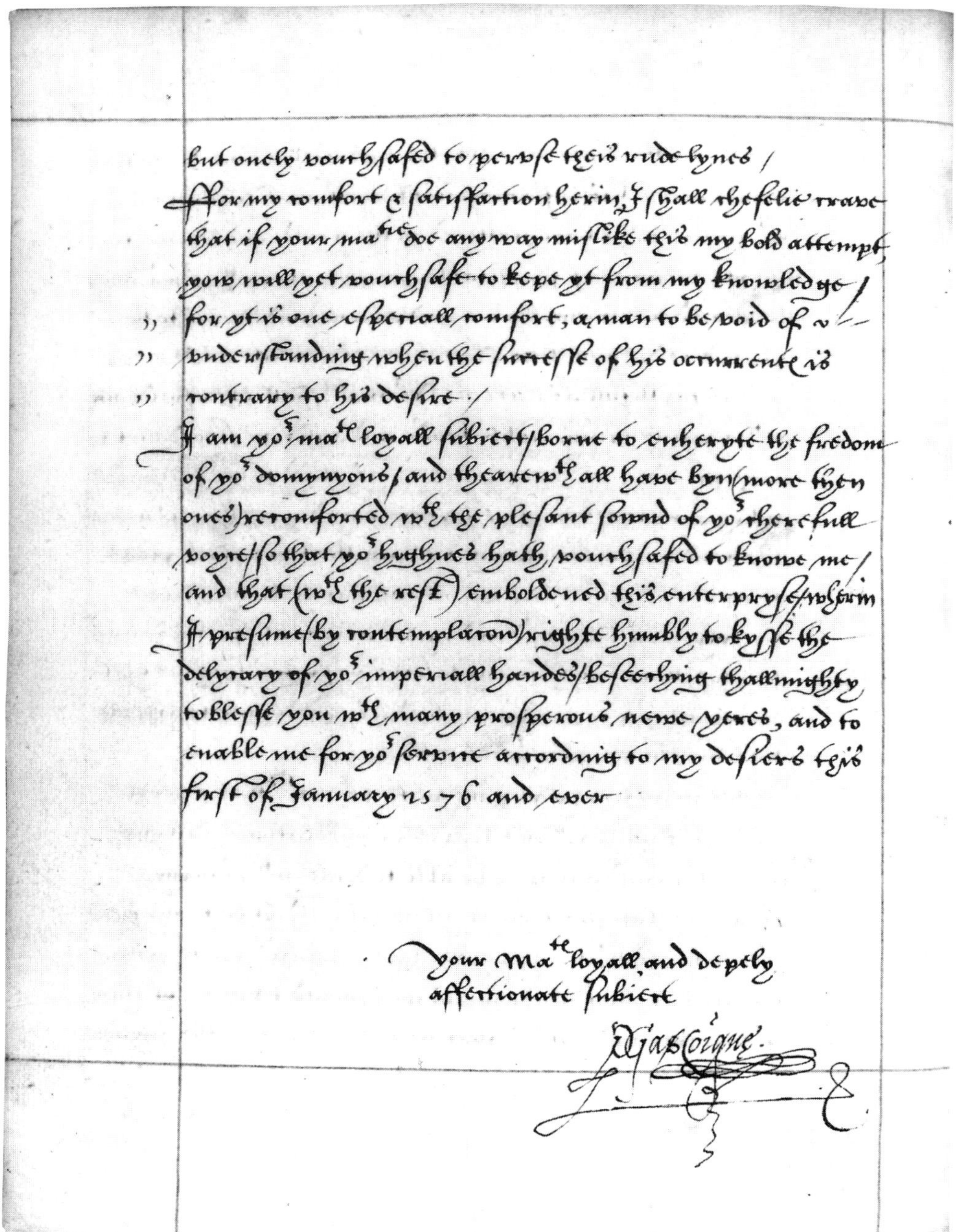
but onely vouchsafed to peruse theis rude lynes /
ffor my comfort & satisfaction herin, I shall therefore crave
that if your matie doe any way mislike this my bold attempt,
you will yet vouchsafe to kepe yt from my knowledge /
for yt is one especiall comfort, a man to be void of
understanding when the succes of his occurrente is
contrary to his desire /
I am yor matis loyall subiect, borne to enheryte the fredom
of yor domynyons, and therewthall have byn (more then
ones) recomforted wth the plesant sownd of yor cherefull
voyce, so that yor hyghnes hath vouchsafed to knowe me /
and that (wth the rest) emboldened this enterpryse, wherin
I presume (by contemplacon) righte humbly to kysse the
delyvery of yor imperiall handes, besechinge thalmighty
to blesse you wth many prosperous newe yeres, and to
enable me for yor service according to my desiers this
first of January 1576 and ever

Your Matie loyall and deeply
affectionate subiect
Gascoigne

4 The end of George Gascoigne's prefatory epistle to the presentation copy of 'The Tale of Hemetes the Heremyte' (BL, Royal MS 18 A. XLVIII, fol. 6v)

The remaining English portions of the text were written in a different secretary script with the conventional use of italic for emphasis and foreign words (PLATE 4). The translations are all in scripts that were deemed appropriate for their language: the Latin translation is in a roman hand, the Italian is in an italic, and the French is in a bastard secretary. The scripts are entirely distinct but the Italian italic (PLATE 5) has some deeper structural differences that result from the scribe's use of space rather than script formation: it is a less compact hand that leaves considerably more space between letters and words, it regularly crosses over the right margin, and it makes no use of line-fillers. This section is therefore probably the work of a different scribe from the rest of the manuscript.

The manuscript is in quarto format, and most of the ten sheets were quired before transcription commenced, suggesting that it was prepared with care and forethought. The paper itself is probably of French origin, and has a watermark of a sword in a shield with the letters 'I C'.[72] However, the second half of the manuscript does not fall into neat gatherings: both the distribution of watermarks and the visible structure of the manuscript suggest that the Italian translation (but not the Italian emblem) was inserted into the centre of an existing gathering, offering further evidence for the possibility that the Italian was farmed out to a different scribe. Since the manuscript now has 39 original leaves, at some point a leaf has been lost; it seems most likely that an earlier version of the Italian emblem was cut out of the manuscript, presumably because a mistake was made in its production.[73]

Gascoigne ensured that he was presenting a very attractive object, but especially at New Year, his gift had considerable competition for royal attention. As George Puttenham complained:

> Gracious Princesse, Where Princes are in place
> To geue you gold, and plate, and perles of price
> It seemeth this day, saue your royall advice
> Paper praesentes, should have but little grace[.][74]

At New Year 1576 the Queen received a golden squirrel from the Lord Strange and a collar of gold in the shape of twin serpents from Secretary Walsingham, along with other fantastic and ornate jewellery and clothing from favoured or ambitious courtiers.[75] A 'paper praesent' would certainly have had difficulty in competing for attention against these, but they were gifts that deliberately deviated from a more mundane norm. Favourites' gifts displayed an excessive desire to please, excessive

72 The watermark is similar to C. M. Briquet, *Les Filigranes* (Amsterdam, 1968), No. 9457, found in documents dating from 1576-78.

73 The first twenty leaves (beginning with an unfoliated original flyleaf) collate I^{10} II^{6} III^{4}. Watermark evidence suggests that fol. 20 is conjugate with fol. 32; fol. 31 with the missing leaf (which therefore falls after the Latin and before the Italian emblem); and fol. 21 with fol. 30. Into the centre of this fourth gathering were placed two additional gatherings (fols 22-5 and 26-9), corresponding exactly with the Italian text. The final six leaves are bifolia, suggesting that the amount of paper needed was at first slightly underestimated.

74 BL, Cotton MS Vespasian E. VIII, fol. 169r.

75 John Nichols, *The Progresses of Queen Elizabeth*, 3 vols (London, 1823), II, 1.

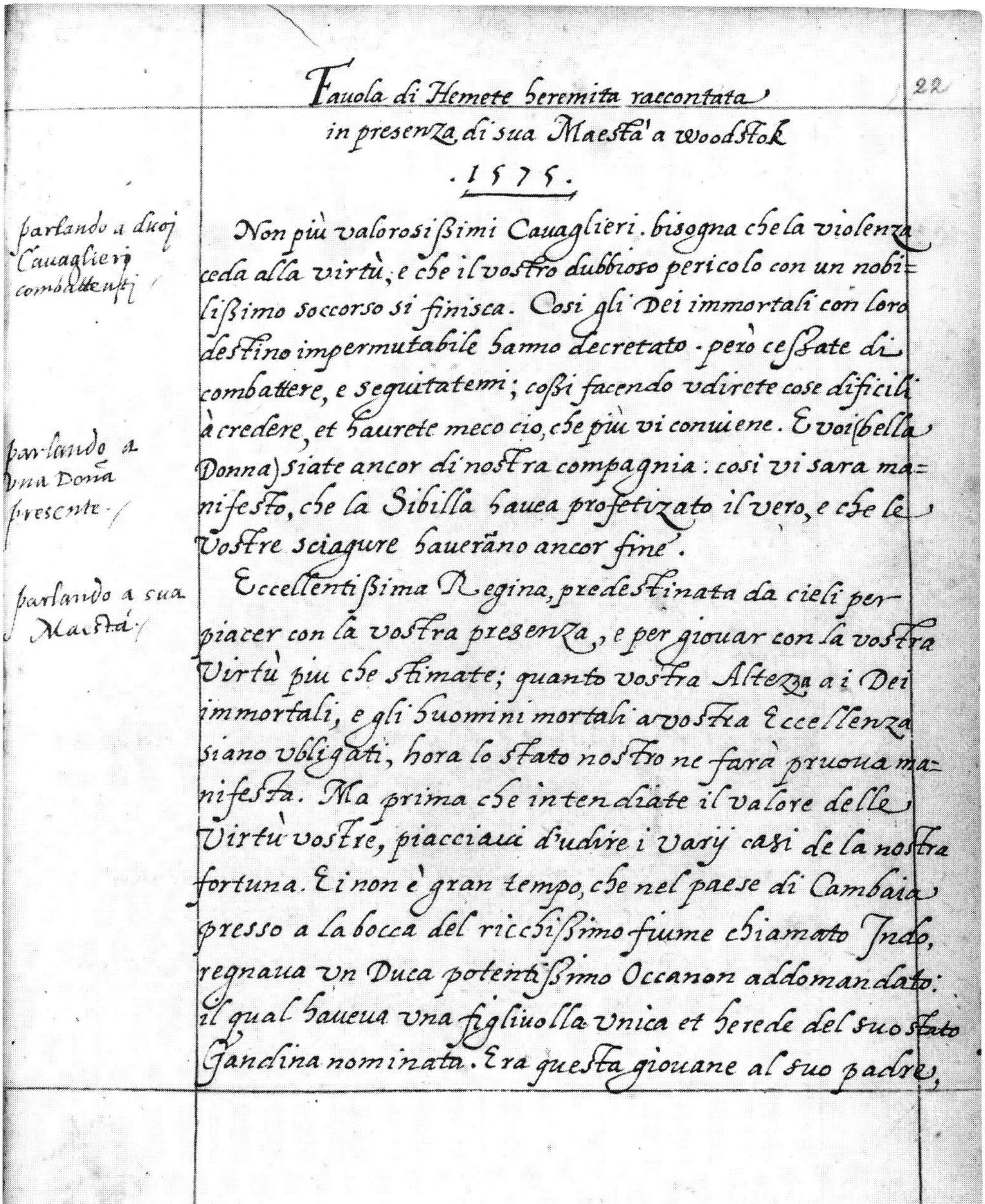

22

Fauola di Hemete heremita raccontata
in presenza di sua Maestà a Woodstok
.1575.

parlando a duoi Cauaglieri combattenti

Non più valorosissimi Cauaglieri. bisogna che la violenza ceda alla virtù, e che il vostro dubbioso pericolo con un nobilissimo soccorso si finisca. Cosi gli Dei immortali con loro destino impermutabile hanno decretato. però cessate di combattere, e seguitatemi; cosi facendo udirete cose dificili à credere, et haurete meco cio, che più vi conuiene. E voi (bella Donna) siate ancor di nostra compagnia: cosi vi sara manifesto, che la Sibilla haueua profetizato il vero, e che le vostre sciagure haueranno ancor fine.

parlando a una Donna presente

parlando a sua Maestà

Eccellentissima Regina, predestinata da cieli per piacer con la vostra presenza, e per giouar con la vostra virtù più che stimate; quanto vostra Altezza a i Dei immortali, e gli huomini mortali a vostra Eccellenza siano ubligati, hora lo stato nostro ne farà pruoua manifesta. Ma prima che intendiate il valore delle virtù vostre, piacciaui d'udire i varij casi de la nostra fortuna. Ei non è gran tempo, che nel paese di Cambaia presso a la bocca del ricchissimo fiume chiamato Indo, regnaua un Duca potentissimo Occanon addomandato: il qual haueua una figliuolla unica et herede del suo stato Gandina nominata. Era questa giouane al suo padre,

5 A page of the Italian translation in the presentation copy of 'The Tale of Hemetes the Heremyte' (BL, Royal MS 18 A. XLVIII, fol. 22r)

because they would never be matched by Elizabeth's return gift, and so suggested a particular dependence on royal favour (either existing or anticipated). Gift exchanges were part of the ritual life of the court and most were no more than tokens recognising an existing service. Many aristocrats simply gave money, and many groups conventionally gave the same things, such as lute-strings from court musicians, or green ginger and orange flowers from apothecaries.

Many manuscripts given to Queen Elizabeth fall into the latter category of tokens of existing service. Few can match the attention to visual detail of Gascoigne's gift. They are usually written in formal hands without messy corrections, but most are fairly plain without any range of hands or illustrations.[76] For example, Pettruccio Ubaldini, who has been described as the Elizabethan court's 'professional Italian', was a highly accomplished scribe, but his frequent gifts of manuscripts to prominent courtiers, including the Queen, were mostly written in his own plain italic hand without extra adornment.[77]

A presentation manuscript would have been first judged on its binding, so it is regrettable that the original binding of Gascoigne's gift has been lost. Like many Royal manuscripts in the British Library, it was rebound in the eighteenth century in red morocco stamped with the arms of George II. Cropping and gilt-edging probably also occurred at that time. The book being presented in the frontispiece to Gascoigne's manuscript may give a clue to the original binding, although it seems to be substantially thicker than the 39 leaves of the actual manuscript. That presentation has a fairly simple finish of two tooled compartments. The original binding probably bore a mark of Elizabeth's ownership, mostly likely the Royal arms, and although velvet is known to have been Queen Elizabeth's favourite binding material, vellum, because of its malleability, is the most likely binding material for a short text like the Hemetes manuscript.[78] Despite the care with which Gascoigne's manuscript was prepared, it is very unlikely that his funds allowed for the sort of binding that would have made any real visual impact; he could not have competed with Sir Henry Lee, the tale's original sponsor, who presented the Queen with a blank manuscript 'booke of golde' on the same occasion.[79]

In 1576 George Gascoigne was employed by the Crown to observe affairs in the Low Countries, where he was unfortunate enough to be caught up in the sack of Antwerp. He must have seen his gift to the Queen as having played a part in his gaining this appointment, because at New Year 1577 Gascoigne presented her with *The Grief of*

76 Carlo Bajetta notes a number of presentation manuscripts with corrections, notably Cambridge University Library MS 8915, and concludes that fine *mis-en-page* is not a universal quality of royal presentation manuscripts (p. 149).

77 BL, Royal MS 14 A. I is Ubaldini's 'examples of writinge very faire', which contrasts with, for example, Royal MSS 14 A. X (to Lord Howard of Effingham, 1588), 14 A. XI (to Sir Christopher Hatton, 1589), and 14 A. XIX (to Queen Elizabeth, 1577); see May, *Elizabethan Courtier Poets*, pp. 38-9.

78 For surviving bindings of Elizabeth, almost all of which have marks of ownership, see William Younger Fletcher, *English Bookbindings in the British Museum* (London, 1895), plates XVIII-XXV; P. J. M. Marks, *The British Library Guide to Bookbinding* (London, 1998), pp. 57-9. I am also grateful to Jan Storm van Leeuwen for comments on bindings.

79 Nichols, *Progresses*, II, 1.

Ioye. This was another scribally produced manuscript (this time Gascoigne does not even seem to have signed his own name), and was once again visually inventive: whenever the word 'Queen' appears it is written in gold – a device that Gascoigne had seen at Kenilworth in 1575.[80]

The poem itself is fully within the mode of reformed prodigality and develops many of the same themes as the Hemetes manuscript, especially in Gascoigne's self-presentation as a grateful, but still needy, recipient of royal bounty. On this occasion the poem was written by Gascoigne himself specifically to be presented to the Queen:

> Not that I thinke my *Poemes* any waie worthie to bee ones redd or beheld of youre heauenly eyes, but that I might make youre Maiestie witnesse, how the *Interims* and vacant howres (of those daies which I spent this sommer in your seruice) have byn bestowed/ (fol. 2v)

Gascoigne continues to denigrate his own abilities whilst constructing for himself a privileged position from which he addresses the Queen directly and alone, and indirectly requests favour through repeated reference to his abject dependence on royal bounty. On this occasion, however, he is able to bring his own voice into the main body of the text. *The Grief of Ioye* is presented incomplete for her judgement, and only if she deems it worthy will he complete the work and put it into print dedicated to her. The Queen, textually privileged in gold, is the only reader for whom he is writing. Throughout the poem, Gascoigne imagines a series of enemies who threaten to bring about an abrupt foreclosure, and it is eventually 'Left unperfect for feare of Horsmen' (fol. 38r) mid-stanza, just as he is about to sing the vanities of equestrian pursuits.[81] The construction of enemies allows him to appeal personally and repeatedly to the Queen for protection, to conjure her into the poem itself as the only point of address with sufficient understanding and power to provide an external authority to legitimate the work. Nevertheless, it was perhaps a genuine anxiety about the Queen's reaction which stalled completion of the poem until the author had received personal encouragement, gratitude for his labour, a reciprocal response to his gift.

Presentations depended on the Queen's response, but such responses are difficult to judge. We do not know whether Gascoigne's employment in royal service had any connection to his presentation of the 'Tale of Hemetes', and Elizabeth's response to Gascoigne's second gift is unknown since the poet was dead before the end of 1577. Equally, it is not clear how Lee's performance as Loricus impacted on his emergence as the Queen's champion. It is not possible to point to specific ways in which these presentations rewrote the presenters' relationships with Elizabeth, and it is unlikely that her smiles of appreciation readily or directly translated into material bounty. The significance of such presentations was that they provided an opportunity for those

80 The hand in this manuscript, BL, Royal MS 18 A. LXI, and the influence of Jean de Beauchesne on it, is discussed in A. Fairbank and B. Dickins, *The Italic Hand in Tudor Cambridge* (London, 1962), pp. 16-17. For the use of gold writing at Kenilworth, see *A letter whearin, part of the entertainment untoo the Queenz maiesty, at Killingwoorth Castl ... is signified* (London, 1575), pp. 13-14.

81 Prouty (p. 97) blamed Spanish cavalry for interrupting Gascoigne's labours, but I do not find this convincing. The courtly horse-lovers follow a succession of enemies, including court beauties who threaten to pull out his muse's tongue when he expounds on the vanity of beauty (fol. 12v).

involved to script their own relationship with the Queen. Beyond the presentation the script was not theirs to write, but the response allowed them to gauge how far the Queen's script of their future relationship coincided with their own.

'FROM A SERUANT OF DIANA' TO THE LIBELLERS OF ROBERT CECIL

THE TRANSMISSION OF SONGS WRITTEN FOR QUEEN ELIZABETH I

JOSHUA ECKHARDT

FOR NEARLY FOUR CENTURIES, Robert Cecil was the most significant 'lost' poet of the court of Queen Elizabeth I. Studious observers of the court, from Gabriel Harvey to Steven May, remained well aware of Cecil's reputation as a courtier poet and lamented that none of his verses had come to light.[1] Especially disappointing was the lack of a song that Cecil wrote for Elizabeth whose context is thoroughly described in a letter that originally accompanied, but had since been separated from, a copy of the song text.[2] So when Katherine Duncan-Jones discovered a lyric in a Bodleian Library manuscript that perfectly fitted the circumstances described in the letter, she not only found a 'lost' poet but also completed an unusually full account of how poetry and music were employed at the late Elizabethan court.[3] The only thing that could have made Duncan-Jones's case stronger would have been an early-seventeenth-century attribution of the poem to Robert Cecil.

One of the primary purposes of this essay is to record such an attribution, specifically to 'R. C.', in another, earlier manuscript copy of Robert Cecil's song (just across the street from the Bodleian at All Souls College Library, Oxford).[4] In addition

1 London, British Library, Add. MS 42518, fol. 422v (Gabriel Harvey's annotated copy of Thomas Speght's 1598 edition of *The workes of ... Geffrey Chaucer*). See also G. C. Moore Smith, *Gabriel Harvey's Marginalia* (Stratford-upon-Avon, 1913); Steven W. May, *The Elizabethan Courtier Poets: The Poems and Their Contexts* (Columbia & London, 1991).

2 London, Lambeth Palace, MS 3203, fols 36r-37v.

3 Oxford, Bodleian Library, MS Don. c. 54, fol. 7v. Katherine Duncan-Jones, '"Preserved Dainties": Late Elizabethan Poems by Sir Robert Cecil and the Earl of Clanricarde', *Bodleian Library Record*, 14, No. 2 (April 1992), 136-44.

4 Oxford, All Souls College Library, MS 155, fol. 128r. I believe that this is the first time that the attribution to 'R. C.' has been recorded in print. In the entry for the poem 'On his Love' (possibly by Sir John Davies) in Peter Beal's *Index of English Literary Manuscripts* (London and New York, 1980), the characters are mistakenly transcribed 'R. S.' (I, i, p. 223: Sir John Davies 158). First of all, this subscription follows not 'On his Love' (which is on fol. 127v) but 'ffrom a servaunt of Diana, as faithfull as the best' (on the facing page, fol. 128r) – which is distinguished from the preceding poem by its line length, metre, and subject-matter. As for the transcription, the primary hand in this manuscript formed the capital letters *C* and *S*

to confirming the authorship of the poem, this manuscript helps to fill out its transmission history. For the two extant copies of Cecil's poem are found in miscellanies that share a dozen texts in common, some of which are rather rare. The only editor to describe both manuscripts at length has therefore suggested that their respective compilers – the judge Sir Christopher Yelverton and Richard Roberts, Justice of the Peace – were part of a social circle of legal professionals who exchanged literature.[5] The texts that appear in both miscellanies are not the only ones that support this hypothesis for, in addition, both Yelverton and Roberts collected poems that the other would have appreciated. For instance, both compilers had six of Sir John Davies's libellous verses on the eminent lawyer Sir Edward Coke; Yelverton also acquired Davies's other five Coke libels, and Roberts found three or four more by other authors.[6] Another poem in both of their miscellanies ridicules the enemies of Robert Devereux, second Earl of Essex – foremost among whom is none other than Robert Cecil.[7] In addition to this text, Roberts collected two other Cecil libels.[8] So the only men to preserve Cecil's long lost court song also collected poetic libels on its author.

As the most successful English politician of the age, Sir Robert Cecil may have been an inevitable target for ridicule. Although he was a younger son and so could not inherit his father's title as Lord Burghley, Robert Cecil was the clear choice to assume his father's position as Elizabeth's most dependable adviser. This role distinguished him from Elizabeth's less predictable and less permanent royal favourites – such as Essex. The contrast between Essex and Cecil was sharp, and evident in their writing. Essex was dashing, hot-headed, quick to war with Catholic Spain; Cecil was short, hunchbacked, and suspiciously soft on Spain. Whereas Essex posed as a Petrarchan lover in lyric poems written for Elizabeth, the only literature that Cecil is known to have written for the Queen before Essex's fall assumed decidedly more modest personae: the 'Hermit's Oration' and perhaps a debate between a gardener and a

by ultimately moving the pen in opposite directions. The main stroke in the capital *C* is counter-clockwise and ends by turning into itself, making a figure somewhat similar to a modern number 6. The capital *S* was made differently: its lower bow was produced in a clockwise fashion and elongated into a tail that continued until it joined the top of the letter. Certain examples of an *S* formed in this way can appear similar to a capital *C* in contemporary hands. Yet each letter was formed by completely different actions of the pen. And the character in question was made in the counter-clockwise manner proper to the capital *C*.

5 Although he did not recognize Cecil's connection to the poem, Robert Krueger recorded both copies of 'ffrom a servaunt of Diana, as faithfull as the best' in the descriptions of manuscripts in his edition of Davies's poems. Describing Roberts's miscellany, he wrote, 'the only known copies of the poem appear here and in *Y*, the manuscript of the judge Sir Christopher Yelverton. Since other material in *Don* [Roberts's miscellany] appears also in *Che* [Manchester, Chetham's Library MS 8012], *Y*, and *Ro* [Philadelphia, Rosenbach Library MS 1083/15], it is evident that Roberts was in a circle of legal acquaintances that exchanged verses with one another': *The Poems of Sir John Davies*, ed. Robert Krueger (Oxford, 1975), p. 438. For the full descriptions of Roberts's and Yelverton's manuscripts, see pp. 438-9, 445-6.

6 All Souls MS 155, fols 262v-3v, 272v-3v; Bodleian MS Don. c. 54, fols 6v-7r; Krueger, pp. 171-6 (NHA 1-11).

7 All Souls MS 155, fol. 59r-v; Bodleian MS Don. c. 54, fol. 7r.

8 Bodleian MS Don. c. 54, fols 19r-20r.

molecatcher.[9] After Essex's fall, though, Cecil wrote a lyric poem for Elizabeth, and anonymous poets wrote the earliest Cecil libels.

The entire manuscript bibliography related to Cecil's song amounts to just three sources: Sir William Browne's letter to the Earl of Shrewsbury at Lambeth Palace, London, which once enclosed a copy of the poem that is now lost;[10] the miscellany of verse and prose transcribed from the papers of the judge Sir Christopher Yelverton, at All Souls College;[11] and the verse miscellany of Richard Roberts, Justice of the Peace, in the Bodleian.[12] This essay considers these three manuscripts first as witnesses, however distant, of the court of Queen Elizabeth I and then as evidence of a transmission history that may have begun, and certainly ended, against Cecil's wishes. That is, they show 'very secrett' texts migrating beyond Elizabeth's court and into a culture of writing that facilitated irreverent criticism of her courtiers.

ROBERT CECIL'S SONG AT COURT

On 18 September 1602 Sir William Browne wrote to the Earl of Shrewsbury with news, and 'som verses', from court. He explained that the verses had been 'compounded by M^r^. Secretary', Robert Cecil. Cecil then 'gott Hales', Elizabeth's favourite musician Robert Hales, to set his poem to music and perform it first in Cecil's chamber and then before the Queen:

9 John Nichols printed 'The Hermit's Oration at Theobald's, 1593-4' as 'Penned by Sir Robert Cecil.': *Progresses, and Public Processions, of Queen Elizabeth* (3 vols, London, 1788), III, 241-5. Marion Colthorpe considered Cecil, Sir John Davies, and John Lyly possible authors of the 1591 Theobald's debate between the gardener and the molecatcher: see 'The Theobalds Entertainment for Elizabeth I in 1591', *Records of Early English Drama Newsletter*, 12 (1987), 2-9. Other compositions of Robert Cecil's include those in 'A Collection of Several Speeches and Treatises of the Late Lord Treasurer Cecil', ed. Pauline Croft, *Camden Miscellany* 29 (Camden Fourth Series, vol. 34, 1987), 245-317; Robert Cecil, Earl of Salisbury, *The state and dignitie of a secretarie of estates place, with care and perill thereof written by the Right Honourable Robert late Earle of Salisbvry* (London, 1642).

10 Lambeth Palace MS 3203, fols 36r-37v are bound into a composite volume of the Earl of Shrewsbury's papers as a bifolium – a single sheet of paper folded once. After he had written the letter on the front of the bifolium, Browne folded the sheet several more times to be sent and endorsed it on the outside. Browne's name was added under the endorsement in another hand, perhaps upon receipt. Cecil's poem, and perhaps the other letter and verses that Browne mentions, must have been originally enclosed within the two leaves and then separated. I thank Matti Watton for checking this manuscript for me.

11 All Souls MS 155 is a thick quarto, almost entirely in a single hand, transcribed from papers collected by Sir Christopher Yelverton throughout his long legal and political career, which culminated in his service as Justice of the King's Bench and Speaker of the House of Commons (in the 1597-98 Parliament). The manuscript was later owned, and annotated, by Nicholas Luttrell (1657-1732), whose descendant Luttrell Wynne (1740-1814) presented it to All Souls College in 1786: see Paul Morgan, *Oxford Libraries Outside the Bodleian: A Guide* (Oxford, 1973), p. 5. The book was then bound in blue cloth-covered boards and its spine and corners wrapped in smooth tan-coloured leather decorated with simple gilt tooling. I thank Dr Norma Aubertin-Potter and Ms Gaye Morgan for granting me access to this manuscript.

12 Bodleian MS Don. c. 54 is an attractive, slender folio written primarily in Richard Roberts's own hand and bound in contemporary parchment. Roberts reserved the manuscript's first two gatherings of sixteen leaves for English and Latin poetry (with some prose) and its other two gatherings of sixteen for Welsh poems (although English verse overflows on to the first leaf of the Welsh gatherings and reappears on the last of the blank pages at the end of the volume). Especially for identifying the twentieth-century hands in the manuscript, I owe thanks to Dr Martin Kauffmann and the extremely hospitable Jean-Pierre Mialon.

I send yo^{ur} Lo: herein enclosed som verses compounded by M^{r}. Secretary who gott Hales to frame a ditty vnto itt, the occasion was as I hear y^{t} the young Lady of Darby wearing about her neck in her bosom a picture wch was in a dainty tablet, the Queen espying itt asked what fyne iewell that was the Lady Darby was curious to excuse the shewing of itt butt the Queen wold haue itt and opening itt and fynding itt to be M^{r}. Secretaryes, snatcht itt away and tyed itt vppon her shoe, and walked long wth it there, then she tooke itt thence and pinned itt on her elbow and wore itt somtymes there also, wch M^{r}. Secre=tary being told of, made these verses, and had Hales to sing them in his chamber, itt was told her ma.$^{ty.}$ y^{t} M^{r}. Secretary had rare musick and songs she wold needes hear them and so this ditty was soung, wch y^{u} see first written.[13]

'Lady Darby' was the countess of Derby, Robert Cecil's niece. The 'dainty tablet' or 'iewell' that she wore around her neck enclosed the 'picture' of her uncle – a miniature portrait, probably the one of Cecil that is known to have been painted by the renowned miniaturist Nicholas Hilliard.[14] Inspecting the locket and recognising the portrait of her courtier, Elizabeth 'snatcht it away' and playfully, even flirtatiously, walked about court with it tied first to her shoe, and then at her elbow.

Browne drew this scene within the last year of Elizabeth's long life. Despite her advanced age, it shows Elizabeth spirited, teasing, and playfully jealous of the affections of a courtier. For his part, Cecil responded by playing one of the games that had come to be expected of Elizabeth's favourite courtiers: writing lyric poetry. The earliest available copy of Cecil's song (from the Yelverton manuscript at All Souls) reads:

ffrom a servaunt of Diana, as faithfull as the best
a lady got a picture, and ware it at her breste
his pereles mistres tooke it, it pleasd her soe to doe
and ware it at her elbowe, though first tyde at her shoo

What meant that Angellike queene to weare that picture so?
meant she to skorne her servaunt, and to disgrace him? no.
She at her elbowe ware it, to signifie that hee
to serve her at her elbowe doth ever love to bee

And at her foote she plac'ed it, where he would prostrat lye
to shewe where he resolved, even at her foote to dye
And at her foot &c.
R. C.[15]

Cecil narrated and interpreted the Queen's actions in a metre that Robert Hales would have had little trouble setting to music. Once Hales had done so, Cecil needed only to have him sing the song in the secretary's chambers and to see to it that word of his 'rare musick and songs' reached Elizabeth. When the Queen heard this, she 'wold needes hear them and so this ditty was soung'. Before Elizabeth and anyone in attendance at court, then, Cecil fashioned himself as worthy of the Queen's show of favour toward him. According to Cecil, Elizabeth wore his picture at her elbow to 'signifie' that Cecil 'doth ever love' to serve her there. And she tied it to her shoe to 'shew where he

13 Lambeth Palace MS 3203, fol. 36r.

14 Duncan-Jones, '"Preserved Dainties"', 138, cites Mary Edmond, *Hilliard and Oliver: the Lives and Works of Two Great Miniaturists* (London, 1983), p. 144.

15 All Souls MS 155, fol. 128r.

resolved, even at her foote to dye'. In a construction of harmony and mutual trust, Cecil claimed Elizabeth as his own spokesperson, and offered to operate as hers. The Queen silently registered the courtier's devotion, and the courtier's verses explicated her actions accordingly.

There may be reason to question Cecil's professed devotion, and to suspect that Elizabeth did so as well. Shortly following the early 1601 coup and execution of the Earl of Essex, who had for at least three years carried on an effectively treasonous correspondence with King James VI of Scotland, Cecil took over as James's most important English contact. In Pauline Croft's judgement, it is 'likely that Elizabeth understood that Cecil was negotiating with James'.[16] In the context of Cecil's risky correspondence with Scotland, the loyalty proclaimed in Cecil's song ceases to look as facile as it might otherwise. Successfully managing James's accession to the English throne was one of Cecil's greatest feats, and it directly led to the enormous benefits that he enjoyed under James. By representing Cecil as a prostrate servant when he could have been charged as a traitor, his only known English poem must have contributed in some small part to that success.

Yet the political gesture of Cecil's song may have more to do with literary than with political history. As Steven May has shown, when Ralegh and Essex wrote their love lyrics for Elizabeth, they were raising the political stakes of a tradition of courtier poetry initiated by Edward de Vere, seventeenth Earl of Oxford. Only a few of the love poems by Elizabethan courtiers had anything explicit to do with the Queen. But some of them were actually addressed to Elizabeth, and several more merged the vocabularies of Petrarchan love poetry and courtly service. If most courtiers were cautious in employing love lyrics at court, Ralegh and Essex abandoned any such prudence. They made full use of love poetry in their competition for the Queen's favour, by casting her as their mistress and one another as a rival for her affections. With his song, Cecil engaged not only the political moment but also this tradition of courtiers writing poems for Elizabeth, and expressing a lover's devotion to her, to promote their careers at court. After the falls of Ralegh and Essex, Cecil's song demonstrated that, in addition to mastering the arts of the courtier, he had outlasted all, or perhaps nearly all, of Elizabeth's other favourites.

For even during the performance of his song at court, Cecil may not have been the only courtier professing his love to Elizabeth. After introducing Cecil's poem in his letter to Shrewsbury, Browne mentioned another, in a construction that suggests that both poems were performed on the same occasion: 'more verses there be lykewyse whereof som or all were lykewyse soung'. Without going into the detail with which he contextualised Cecil's song, Browne briefly described these additional verses: 'some of ye verses argew that he repynes not thoghe her ma^{ty} please to grace others, and contents himself wth th[e fa]vour he hath'. Browne's gloss could refer to the poem that

16 Pauline Croft, 'Foreword: "The translation of a monarchy": The Accession of James VI and I, 1601-1603', *History in Focus: Elizabeth I and James VI and I* (London, 2003) <http://www.history.ac.uk/ihr/Focus/Elizabeth/index.html>. See also Pauline Croft, *King James* (Basingstoke, 2003), 48-9.

immediately precedes Cecil's in both Yelverton's and Roberts's miscellanies: 'My love doth flye wth winges of feare.'

In total, 'My love doth flye wth winges of feare' can be found in three early modern manuscripts and three modern printed sources. In the Burley manuscript at Leicestershire Record Office, it appears without Cecil's song and with a final stanza absent from the other copies.[17] Herbert J. C. Grierson printed the poem from this manuscript among those 'which frequently accompany poems by John Donne in manuscript collections'.[18] Robert Krueger included the poem among those 'possibly by [Sir John] Davies', and used the Yelverton manuscript as his copy-text (supplemented by the Burley manuscript's unique last stanza).[19] Finally, Duncan-Jones copied the version in Richard Roberts's miscellany and followed Roberts's lead in attributing the poem to Richard Bourke, fourth Earl of Clanricarde.[20] On the matter of authorship, which will not be settled here, it is worth pointing out that the Burley and Yelverton copies are unascribed. So it was on the basis of the only seventeenth-century ascription that Duncan-Jones attributed the poem to Clanricarde and suggested that it was performed at the same time that Cecil's was – following the return, in the summer of 1602, of Clanricarde and some of the other victors from suppressing the rebellion of the Earl of Tyrone in Ireland.

As Duncan-Jones argued, Bourke had both reason and occasion to express a courtier's devotion to his beloved Queen. In 1576 his grandfather led a rebellion that was suppressed by Sir Henry Sidney (and perhaps Philip).[21] The 1601 rebellion in Ireland was an opportunity for Bourke to repair the damage that his grandfather had done to the family name. And Bourke made the best of it: on 24 December 1601, at the battle of Kinsale, he was knighted; and within weeks of Elizabeth's death in the spring of 1603 he married Frances, née Walsingham, the widow first of Sir Philip Sidney and then of Essex.[22] This marriage put Clanricarde in the association of the most highly esteemed Elizabethan courtier poets. If Clanricarde was responsible for the poem, 'My love doth flye with winges of feare' must have been part of this effort.

Clanricarde's successful début at the English court adds a suggestive element to the context of Cecil's song. Cecil had watched Ralegh and Essex spar in love lyrics for years while he played the role of the more steadfast, if more prosaic, minister. And the only occasion on which Cecil is known to have turned to such poetry himself corresponded

17 Leicester, Leicestershire Record Office, MS DG7/Lit. 2, fol. 280v. The Burley manuscript is a composite volume of loose papers collected by William Parkhurst (*fl.*1604-74), among the papers of the Finch family of Burley-on-the-Hill, Rutland. In Beal's *Index* (I, i, p. 224), this copy is recorded as Sir John Davies 160.

18 *The Poems of John Donne*, ed. Herbert J. C. Grierson (2 vols, London, 1912), I, 437-8.

19 Krueger, *Poems of Davies*, pp. 306-7 (transcription), 424 (attribution), 438-39 (manuscript description). Krueger supplied the title 'On his Love', under which heading Beal listed the three known copies of the poem (*Index*, I, i, p. 223, Sir John Davies, 158). Krueger recorded Roberts's ascription of the poem to Clanricarde, conceded that if it is not by Davies it is probably by Clanricarde, and gave reasons for doubting Roberts's annotations.

20 Duncan-Jones, '"Preserved Dainties"', 139-40; Beal, *Index*, I, i, p. 223: DaJ 159.

21 Duncan-Jones, '"Preserved Dainties"', 140.

22 Duncan-Jones, '"Preserved Dainties"', 141, quotes John Bruce, ed., *The Diary of John Manningham*, Camden Old Series (vol. 99), London, 1868: 59, 165.

with the emergence of a courtier who may have styled himself a poet. In a diary entry dated 10 October 1602 (less than one month after Browne's letter), John Manningham judged that Clanricarde was 'well esteemed of by hir Majestie, and in speciall grace at this tyme'. With this comment Manningham ascribed to Clanricarde the royal attention proper to a favourite. Of course Cecil would have been in a unique position to witness, and to respond to, the emergence of a new favourite. Could Clanricarde's success at court have provoked Cecil to turn to the sort of love poetry that characterized the Ralegh–Essex rivalry? Any such question is admittedly speculative, especially given a couple of equally likely possibilities. For one, Cecil and Clanricarde could have cooperated to have their songs performed at court together, which could explain how they circulated together. On the other hand, though, the available evidence does not rule out Sir John Davies as author of 'My loue doth flye with winges of feare', which he could have written for a court performance and even for Cecil, as he made several other contributions to courtly entertainments at this time.[23]

Even after acknowledging what is uncertain about their composition and performance, these lyrics offer a unique perspective on the Elizabethan court in its final year or two – in the case of Cecil's song, particularly on the way in which poetry and music were employed by courtiers and enjoyed by the Queen. Yet, of the available evidence of Cecil's song, only Browne's letter was written during Elizabeth's reign; and Browne was not an eye-witness to its performance (he told the story 'as I hear'). The copy in Yelverton's manuscript was made a few years into the reign of James I, and Roberts must have transcribed the poem into his miscellany in the 1620s.[24] While these sources must be treated with caution as evidence of the court of Elizabeth, they confirm that the text's limited transmission put Cecil's song in contact with libels on its author. The concluding section of this essay surveys the three Cecil libels that accompany 'From a seruant of Diana, as faithfull as the best' in manuscript.

23 As Krueger makes clear, Davies was in close contact with Cecil and was quite active in writing verses and entertainments for the court at this time. Perhaps in 1601 Davies was involved in writing a court entertainment for the secretary, and Cecil in turn was a major force in reconciling Davies to Richard Martin, and eventually to the Middle Temple, from which Davies had been expelled after beating Martin in the Temple Hall with 'a stick, which is commonly called 'a Bastinado ... till it broke': Krueger, *Poems of Davies*, pp. xxxiv-xliv, 424, citing Charles Henry Hopwood, ed., *Middle Temple Records*, London, 1904, I, 379-80.

24 The Yelverton manuscript contains texts composed and presumably collected throughout Yelverton's long sixteenth-century career, including Ben Jonson's Theobalds entertainment, performed on 22 July of the year Yelverton died, 1607 (fols 319r-21r). Although Roberts's miscellany has been dated variously between 1602 and 1621, 1622, and 1630, a few of the dates that he recorded suggest that he transcribed at least the majority of the English and Latin section between 1624 and 1628, and that he made a correction during or following 1630: on fol. 9r he referred to 'this paste Moneth / of April 1624' and on fol. 29r he recorded the date '23. Iune. 1628'. Then, on fol. 23r, he made an amendment after 'a° 1630': see Krueger, pp. 438-9; Duncan-Jones, '"Preserved Dainties"', 141-2; Pauline Croft, 'The Reputation of Robert Cecil: Libels, Political Opinion and Popular Awareness in the Early Seventeenth Century', *Transactions of the Royal Historical Society*, 6th ser., 1 (1991), 43-69, 45; Beal, *Index* 1, i, p. 506 (DnJ 3329); II, i, p. 177 (CoR 257).

CECIL'S SONG WITH CECIL LIBELS

Browne told Shrewsbury that he would not share Cecil's verses with anyone else, 'for I hear they are very secrett'. Nevertheless, Cecil's poem found its way into two miscellanies with a variety of texts in common. One of the poems that appears in both Yelverton's and Roberts's manuscripts is of particular interest in regards to Cecil, for it is a libellous poem that reserves most of its censure for him. '(Admire all) weaknes wrongeth right' satirizes the enemies of Essex and, with a pun on the word *secretary* ('(Secret are)'), first includes Cecil among opponents of Essex (who is here figured as 'true honor').

(Secret are) ever their designes
through whose desertes true honor pynes
(A ward) in worth wch is esteemed
by vertues wracke must be redeemed [25]

Briefly considering yet another manuscript copy of this libel will help to establish Cecil's starring role in it. In a Bodleian miscellany of political poetry and prose, this poem is marginally annotated with explicit references to the political figures suggested in the text of the poem. Cecil is the only enemy of Essex to appear more than once in the marginalia of this annotated copy; in total, he appears five times.[26] Beside the first line quoted above, for instance, the gloss 'Secretary Cecill' appears. And the note two lines down indicates what was at issue between Cecil and Essex: 'ye Court of wardes / promised to Essex / giuen to S.^r^ Ro: Cecill'. Moreover, the marginalia for a line farther down that complains of the 'crookd waies' of Essex's enemies registers the hunchback that was to become requisite in Cecil libels: 'S.^r^ Ro: Cecill Crooked'.

One need not conflate the libeller's politics with those of the manuscript makers to recognise that only verse collectors comfortable with irreverent representations of Cecil could have reproduced this libel. It is significant that this can be said of the only two men to preserve Cecil's song. In transcribing both Cecil's song and this Cecil libel in the same miscellany, or at least gathering both among the same set of papers, Yelverton and Roberts each demonstrated that their interest in Elizabeth's principal secretary was not limited to his self-presentation, and that their taste for literature on the court was not restricted to the sorts that could be openly countenanced there.

Richard Roberts transcribed his copy of 'Admire = all weaknes, wronge the right' right before the lyrics 'My loue doth flye with winges of feare' and 'From a seruant of Diana, as faithfull as the best' (on the preceding recto and among a group of texts that also appear in Yelverton's manuscript). Farther on in his miscellany, Roberts collected a couple of libels with similar sentiments regarding Cecil. One of these is another poem

25 All Souls MS 155, fol. 59r-v.

26 All annotations for this libel are quoted from Bodleian MS Eng. Hist. c. 272, p. 41. In addition to All Souls MS 155, fol. 59r-v, and Bodleian MS Don. c. 54, fol. 7r, other copies of the poem include Bodleian MS Rawl. Poet. 26, fol. 20v; British Library Add. MS 5956, fol. 23r; and London, Victoria & Albert Museum, MS D.25.F.39, fol. 81r.

on Essex's enemies, like 'Admire = all weaknes, wronge the right'.[27] This libel is constructed as 'A dreame • alludinge to my L. of Essex and his adversaries'; yet marginal notes make its allusions clear. After the 'Earle of Essex' is figured as a 'HART' and 'The Queene' as a 'LION', the familiar cast of evil councillors appears, led by 'Sr Rob: Cecill / crookbackt', who is correspondingly represented as 'a CAMMELS uglie broode'.[28] The poem proceeds to tell how the camel turned the lion against the hart, or how Cecil convinced Elizabeth to send Essex on the ill-fated Irish expedition. As in 'Admire = all weaknes, wronge the right', this allegorical poem charges Cecil with leading the opposition to the honourable Essex.

In the very next poem that Roberts transcribed, headed 'Libell against s^r^ / Robert Cecill', Cecil is mocked as a 'Dissemblinge smothfac'd dwarfe'. Since the only known copy of the poem that isolates Cecil is in Roberts's 1620s miscellany, and given the rise of libels on Cecil later at the time of his death, these verses cannot be confidently given an Elizabethan date.[29] Nevertheless, the pun on Cecil's Elizabethan position ('Secreat-are') and the subscription 'God saue the Queene' evoke an Elizabethan frame of reference – as do the other Cecil libels considered above. For Roberts, these libels must have complemented and, in an openly biased way, contextualised Cecil's song. They oppose Cecil to a seminal courtier poet who fell from favour before Cecil wrote his own lyric to Elizabeth. And, along with the Cecil libel that also appears in Yelverton's miscellany, they made sure that, beyond court, Robert Cecil was allowed to fashion himself only where he was also libelled.

27 Bodleian MS Don. c. 54, fols 18v-20r. These two libels are followed by another 'Against the Lord / Cobham', who also appears in 'Admire = all weaknes, wronges the right' ('Come to the black friers, and enquire for my Lord Cobham, at his': fol. 20r). Roberts's copy of 'Admire = all weaknes, wronges the right' is on fol. 7r.

28 The only other copy of this poem is in British Library Add. MS 58215, fol. 46v. In part, I am quoting from Andrew McRae's transcription, in Alastair Bellany and Andrew McRae, eds, in 'Early Stuart Libels: An edition of poetry from manuscript sources', *Early Modern Literary Studies*, Text Series I (2005) <http://purl.oclc.org/emls/texts/libels/>. Another complete transcript is found in Arthur F. Marotti, *Manuscript, Print, and the English Renaissance Lyric* (Ithaca, NY, & London, 1995), pp. 95-7.

29 See Croft, 'Reputation of Sir Robert Cecil'.

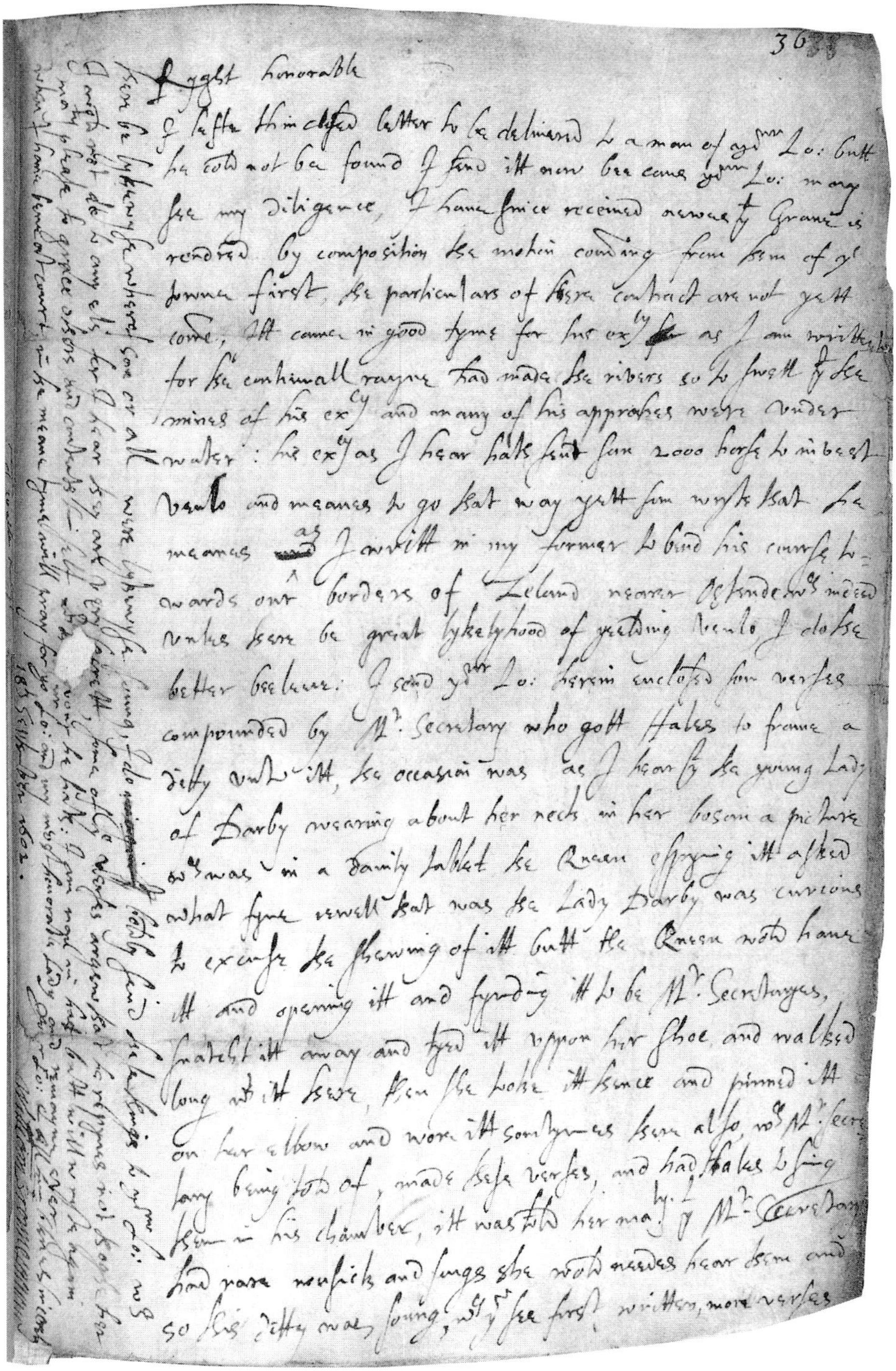

36

Right honorable

I lefte thinclosed letter to be delivered to a man of yor Lo: butt
he cold not be found I send itt now bee cause yor Lo: may
see my diligence, I have since receaved newes yt Grave is
rendred by composition the motion comming from them of ye
towne first, the particulars of there contract are not yett
come, itt came in good tyme for his exty as I am written
for the continuall rayne had made the rivers so to swell yt the
mines of his exty and many of his approches were under
water: his exty as I hear hath sent som 2000 horse to invest
Venlo and meanes to go that way yett som wryte that he
meanes as I writt in my former to bend his course to-
wards our borders of Zeland neerer Ostende wch indeed
unles there be great lykelyhood of yelding Venlo I do the
better beleeve: I send yor Lo: herein enclosed som verses
compounded by Mr Secretary who gott Hales to frame a
ditty unto itt, the occasion was as I hear yt the young Lady
of Darby wearing about her neck in her bosom a picture
wch was in a dainty tablet the Queen espying itt asked
what fyne jewell that was the Lady Darby was curious
to excuse the shewing of itt butt the Queen wold have
itt and opening itt and fynding itt to be Mr Secretaryes,
snatcht itt away and tyed itt uppon her shoe and walked
long wt itt there, then she toke itt thence and pinned itt
on her elbow and wore itt somtymes there also, wch Mr Secre
tary being told of, made these verses, and had Hales to sing
them in his chamber, itt was told her maty yt Mr Secretary
had rare musick and songs she wold needes hear them and
so this ditty was songe, wch ys the first written, more verses

[illegible]

1 Sir William Browne's letter to the Earl of Shrewsbury, 18 September 1602
(London, Lambeth Palace Library, MS 3203, fol. 36r)

I. Sir William Browne to the Earl of Shrewsbury, 18 September 1602

Ryght honorable –
I lefte thinclosed letter to be deliuered to a man of yo^{ur} Lo: butt
he cold not be found I send itt now beecaus yo^{ur} Lo: may
see my diligence, I haue since receiued newes y^{t} Graue is
rendred by composition the motion com[m]ing from them of y^{e}
towne first, the particulars of there contract are not yett
com[m]e, Itt came in good tyme for his ex^{cy} ~~for~~ as I am written t[o]
for the continuall rayne had made the rivers so to swell y^{t} the
mines of his ex^{cy} and many of his approches were vnder
water: his ex^{cy} as I hear hath sent som 2000 horse to invest
venlo and meanes to go that way yett som wryte that he
meanes ~~and~~^{as} I writt in my former to bend his course to =
wards our borders of Zeland nearer Ostende wch indeed
vnles there be great lykelyhood of yeelding venlo, I do the
better beeleeue: I send yo^{ur} Lo: herein enclosed som verses
compounded by M^{r}. Secretary who gott Hales to frame a
ditty vnto itt, the occasion was as I hear y^{t} the young Lady
of Darby wearing about her neck in her bosom a picture
wch was in a dainty tablet, the Queen espying itt asked
what fyne iewell that was the Lady Darby was curious
to excuse the shewing of itt butt the Queen wold haue
itt and opening itt and fynding itt to be M^{r}. Secretaryes,
snatcht itt away and tyed itt vppon her shoe, and walked
long wth it there, then she tooke itt thence and pinned itt
on her elbow and wore itt somtymes there also, wch M^{r}. Secre =
tary being told of, made these verses, and had Hales to sing
them in his chamber, itt was told her ma^{ty}. y^{t} M^{r}. Secretary
had rare musick and songs she wold needes hear them and
so this ditty was soung, wch y^{u} see first written, more verses

[*continued down the left margin*:]

there be lykewyse whereof som or all were lykewyse soung, I do ~~imagin y^{t}~~ boldly send
these things to yo^{ur} Lo: w^{ch}
I wold not do to any els for I hear they are very secrett, some of ye verses argew that he
repynes not thoghe her
ma^{ty} please to grace others, and contents himself wth th[e fa]vour he hath: I am now in
hast butt will wryte again
when I haue bene at court, in the meane tyme will pray for yo^{ur} Lo: and my most
honorable Lady and remayne ever

Your Lo: in All humblenes sincerely
William Broune//////////

18th September 1602.

[*Page break*]

To the ryght honorable my
most singular good Lord the
Earle of Shrewbury knyght
of y^{e} garter and one of her
ma^{ties} most honorable priuy
Counsell giue these wth
speed

S:^{r} W^{m}: Browne.

[London, Lambeth Palace, MS 3203, fols 36r, 37v. Italics indicate script in another ink and probably another hand.]

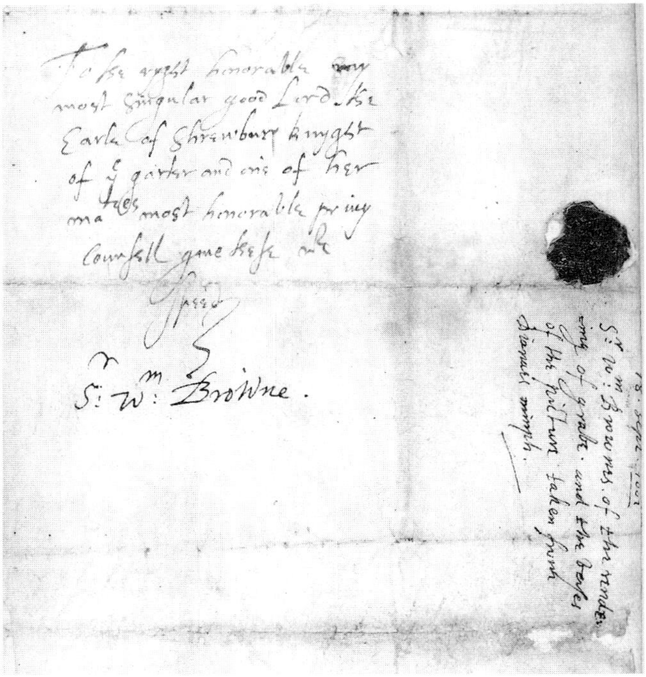
To the right honorable my most singular good Lord the Earle of Shrewsbury knight of the garter and one of her ma^{ties} most honorable privy Counsell give these

Sr W^{m}: Browne.

2 The endorsement on Sir William Browne's letter to the Earl of Shrewsbury, 18 September 1602, with Browne's name added in another hand (London, Lambeth Palace Library, MS 3203, fol. 37v)

II. Sir Christopher Yelverton's miscellany

| *On one Loveing his M$^{rs.}$* |

My love doth flye wth winges of feare
and doth a flame of fyer resemble
w^{ch} ~~burntinge~~ mounting high and burning cleare
yet evermore doth waue and tremble

My love doth see, and doth admire
admiring breedeth humblenes
blinde love is bold, but my desire
the more it loues presume the lesse

my love seekes not reward, no^{r} glorie
but wth it selfe it selfe contentinge
is never sullen, never sorry
never repyning no^{r} repentinge
~~But whoe the sun beames can behold~~

But who the sunne beames can behold
but hath some passion, feeles some heate?
for though the sunne himselfe be cold,
his beames reflecting fire beget

O that myne eye, ô that myne hart
were both enlarged to contayne
the beames and ioyes she doth impart
while she this love doth not disdaine

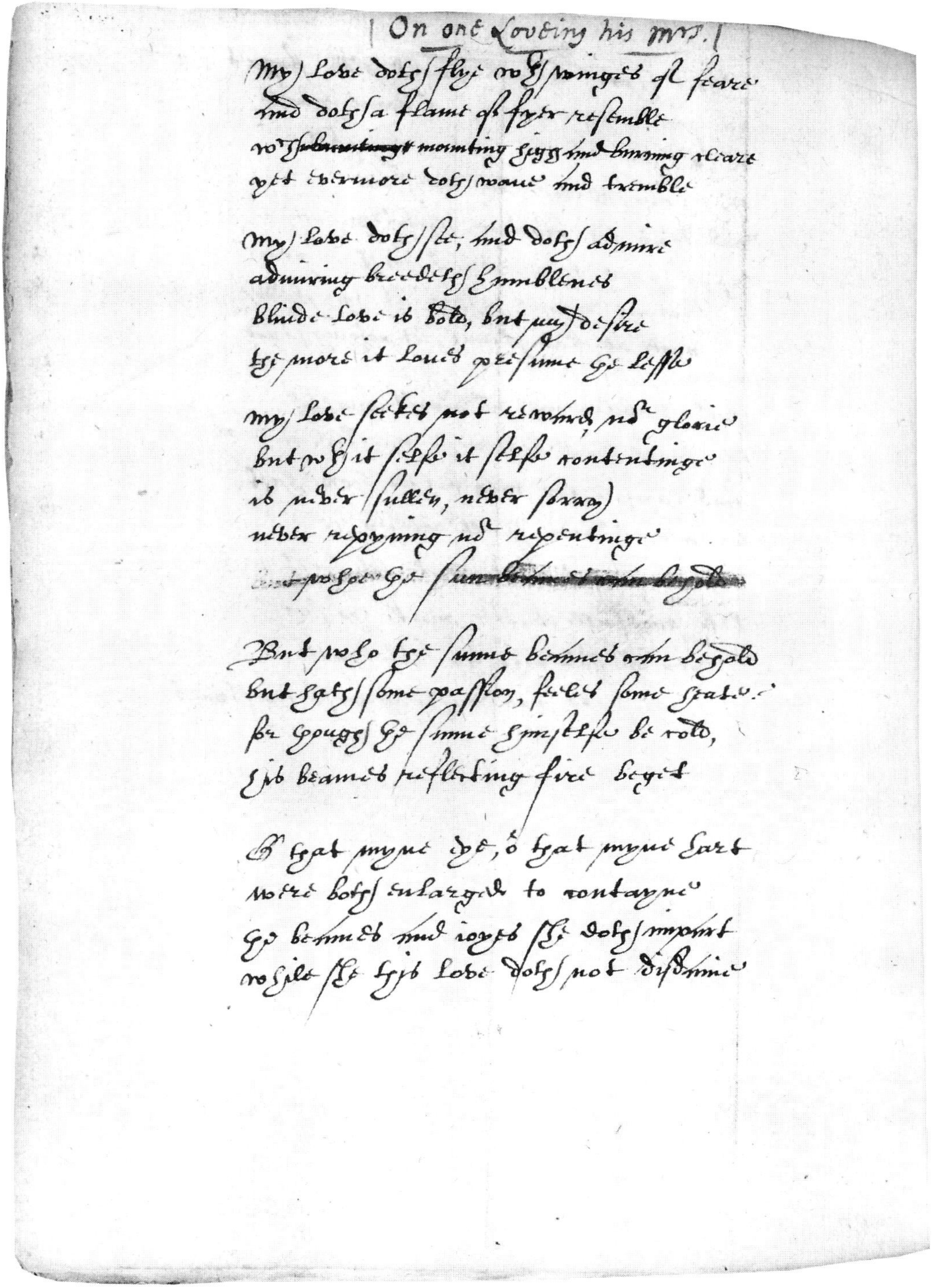

[On one Loving his Mrs.]

My love doth flye wth winges of feare
And doth a flame of fyer resemble
wch ~~[illegible]~~ mounting highe and burning cleare
yet evermore doth wave and tremble

My love doth see, and doth admire
admiring breedeth humblenes
Blinde love is bold, but myne desire
the more it loves presume the lesse

my love seekes not rewarde, nor glorie
but wth it selfe it selfe contentinge
is never sullen, never sorry
never repyning nor repentinge
~~but who the sunne beames can beholde~~

But who the sunne beames can beholde
but hath some passion, feeles some heate
for though the sunne himselfe be cold,
his beames reflecting fire begett

O that myne eye, o that myne hart
were both enlarged to contayne
the beames and ioyes she doth impart
while she this love doth not disdaine

3 Copy of 'My love doth flye wth winges of feare', unattributed, in Sir Christopher Yelverton's miscellany, the heading in the hand of Narcissus Luttrell (Oxford, All Souls College Library, MS 155, fol. 127v)

[*Page break*]

ffrom a servaunt of Diana, as faithfull as the best
a lady got a picture, and ware it at her breste
his pereles mistres tooke it, it pleasd her soe to doe
and ware it at her elbowe, though first tyde at her shoo

What meant that Angellike queene to weare that picture so?
meant she to skorne her servaunt, and to disgrace him? no.
She at her elbowe ware it, to signifie that hee
to serve her at her elbowe doth ever love to bee

And at her foote she plac'~~e~~d it, where he would prostrat lye
to shewe where he resolved, even at her foote to dye
And at her foot &c.

R. C.

[Oxford, All Souls College Library, MS 155, fols 127v-128r. Italics in the heading indicate amendments in the hand of Narcissus Luttrell (1657-1732).]

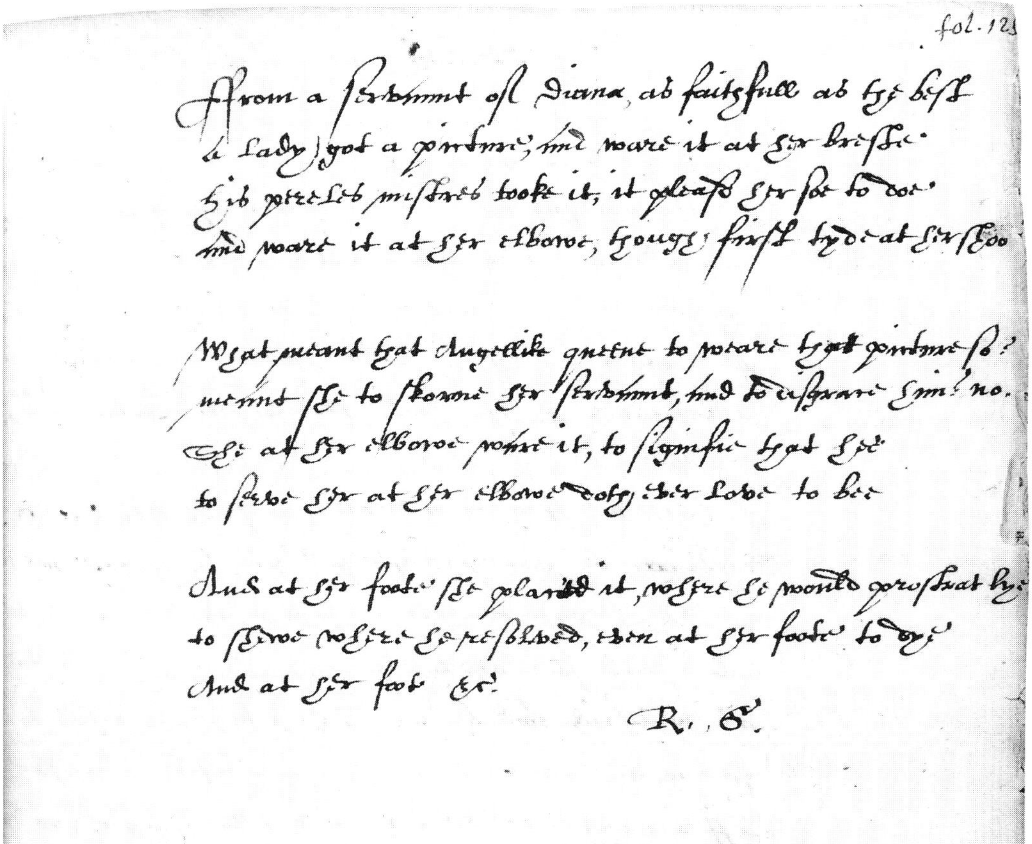

fol. 128

ffrom a servaunt of Diana, as faithfull as the best
a Lady got a picture, and ware it at her breste
his peereles mistres tooke it, it pleasd her so to doe
and ware it at her elbowe, though first tyde at her shoe

What meant that Angellike queene to weare that picture so?
meant she to skorne her servaunt, and to disgrace him? no.
She at her elbowe wore it, to signifie that hee
to serve her at her elbowe doth ever love to bee

And at her foote she placed it, where he would prostrat lye
to serve where he resolved, even at her foote to dye
And at her foot &c.

R. C.

4 Copy of Robert Cecil's 'ffrom a servaunt of Diana, as faithfull as the best', attributed to 'R. C.', in Sir Christopher Yelverton's miscellany (Oxford, All Souls College Library, MS 155, fol. 128r)

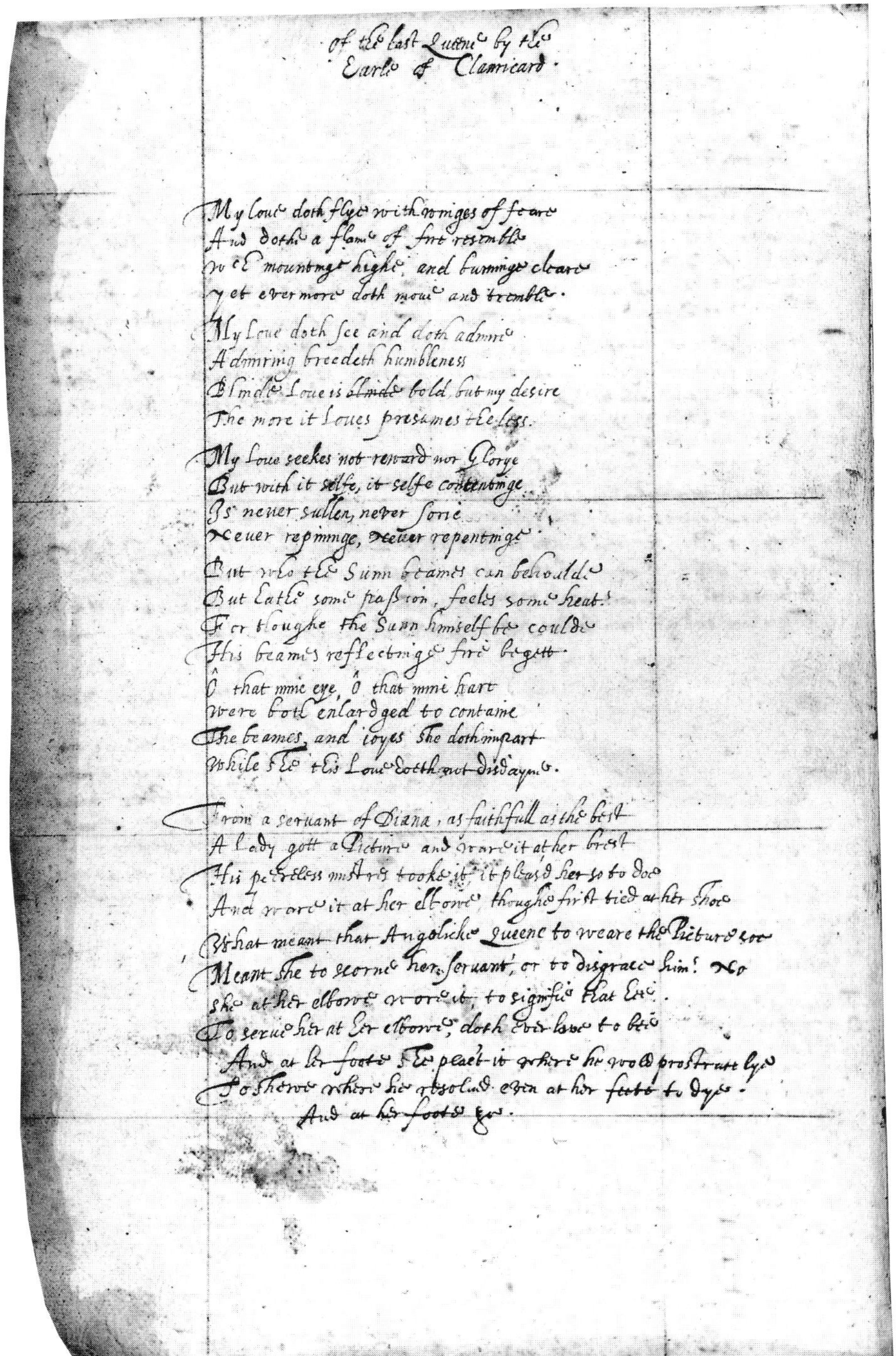

of the last Queene by the
Earle of Clanricard.

My loue doth flye with winges of feare
And doth a flame of fire resemble
wch mountinge highe and burninge cleare
yet evermore doth moue and tremble.

My loue doth see and doth admire
Admiring breedeth humbleness
Blinde loue is blinde bold but my desire
The more it loues presumes the less.

My loue seekes not reward nor Glorye
But with it selfe, it selfe contentinge
Is never sullen, never sorie
Never repininge, never repentinge.

But who the Sunn beames can beholde
But feeles some passion, feeles some heat.
For thoughe the Sunn himself be coulde
His beames reflectinge fire begett.

O that mine eye, O that mine hart
were both enlardged to containe
The beames, and ioyes she doth impart
While she this loue doth not disdayne.

From a seruant of Diana, as faithfull as the best
A lady gott a Picture and wore it at her brest
His peerless mistres tooke it, it pleasd her so to doe
And wore it at her elbowe, thoughe first tied at her shoe
What meant that Angelicke Queene to weare the Picture soe
Meant she to scorne her seruant, or to disgrace him? No
She at her elbowe wore it, to signifie that hee
To serue her at her elbowe, doth euer loue to bee
And at her foote she placet it where he would prostrate lye
To showe where hee resolued even at her feete to dye.
And at her foote &c.

5 Copy of 'My loue doth flye with winges of feare', attributed to Richard Bourke, Earl of Clanricarde, and of Robert Cecil's 'From a seruant of Diana, as faithfull as the best', unattributed, in Richard Roberts's hand, with alternating colours of ink (Oxford, Bodleian Library, MS Don. c. 54, fol. 7v)

III. Richard Roberts's Miscellany

Of the last Queene by the
Earle of Clanricard.

My loue doth flye with winges of feare
And dothe a flame of fire resemble
wch mountinge highe, and burninge cleare
yet evermore doth moue and tremble.

My loue doth see and doth admire
Admiring breedeth humbleness
Blinde loue is ~~blinde~~ bold but my desire
The more it loues presumes the less.

My loue seekes not reward nor Glorye
But with it selfe, it selfe contentinge
Is ne**u**er sullen, never sorie
Neuer repininge, Neuer repentinge.

But who the Sunn beames can behoulde
But hathe some passion, feeles some heat?
For thoughe the Sunn himself be coulde
His beames reflectinge fire begett.

Ô that mine eye, Ô that mine hart
Were both enlardged to containe
The beames, and ioyes she doth impart
While she this loue doeth not disdayne.

From a seruant of Diana, as faithfull as the best
A lady gott a Picture and ware it at her brest
His peereless mistres tooke it, it pleas'd her so to doe
And ware it at her elbowe, thoughe first tied at her shoe
What meant that Angelicke Queene to weare the Picture soe
Meant she to scorne her seruant', or to disgrace him? No
she at her elbowe wore it, to signifie that hee
To serue her at her elbowe, doth ever love to bee
And at her foote she plac't it where he wold prostrate lye
To shewe where he resolued even at her feete to dye.
And at her foote &c.

[Oxford, Bodleian Library, MS Don. c. 54, fol. 7v. The second and fourth stanzas of 'My love doth fly' and the first four lines of 'From a servant of Diana' are in red or brown ink; everything else is in black ink.]

THIS REMEMBRANCE OF THE NEW YEAR

BOOKS GIVEN TO QUEEN ELIZABETH AS NEW YEAR'S GIFTS

JANE A. LAWSON

BOOKS, BOTH PRINTED AND MANUSCRIPT, were frequent gifts to Tudor sovereigns in the New Year's gift exchanges, which were a major annual Court celebration. The exchange protocol was already well established by 1494 under Henry VII, as described in London, British Library Sloane MS 4712.[1] The donors' servants presented the sovereign with gifts in the order of their social rank and official status, and this order is preserved in all later accounts of the New Year's gift exchanges. The gift rolls are the primary sources of information about the gift exchanges because they record what types of gifts, including books, were given and by whom, providing a valuable insight into the operation of the Court. The lists begin with relatives of the sovereign followed by peers of the realm in order (Dukes and Duchesses, Bishops, Earls and Countesses, Lords and Baronesses), then Ladies and Knights, ending with the Gentlewomen and Gentlemen.[2] One side of the roll records the gifts given by the donors ('By' list) while the reverse side records the gifts given to those participants ('To' list) by the sovereign. Books form a small but steady component of gifts presented to Queen Elizabeth I and other Tudor sovereigns. A precursor of the types of books given to Elizabeth can be found in the records of New Year's gifts of books given to her father, Henry VIII, and her half-siblings, Edward and Mary.

While the New Year's gift rolls were prepared every year of Elizabeth's reign, only twenty-four have survived to this day. These rolls provide a wealth of information about the Court and the Queen.[3] They record a varied collection of over one hundred and fifty written and printed books given to the Queen for over half of the New Year's exchanges of her reign. The number of book gifts listed in the surviving rolls suggests that perhaps another one hundred such items would have appeared on the missing gift rolls. Givers carefully considered the New Year's gifts they gave the Queen, and

1 *A Collection of Ordinances and Regulations for the Government of the Royal Household, made in Divers Reigns* (London, 1970), p. 120.

2 In the order of the gift rolls, Ladies and Gentlewomen precede their male counterparts of Knights and Gentlemen.

3 See Appendix IV for a list of the extant gifts rolls including their present locations. I am grateful to Lucas Erne for informing me of the location of the 1600 roll in Geneva, Switzerland.

discussions of what to give the sovereign circulated among the donors in contemporary letters.[4] Over Elizabeth's forty-five year reign, the subject-matter of these gift volumes changed very little. Early in the reign, donors were more likely to provide the Queen with instructional and devotional works. In later years the printed materials often highlighted the achievements of the giver and became, perhaps, somewhat routine as the Queen's preferences became well known. Fourteen donors gave Elizabeth a total of fifty-two books and manuscripts in the first year of her reign, more than in any other year. This number is rivalled in the extant Tudor gift exchanges only by the twenty-six gifts of books Queen Mary received from fifteen donors in 1557. While some donors gave single volumes, others assembled several volumes as a package gift, such as the six French books given to Mary by the Secretary to the French Ambassador in 1557. Similarly, in 1559 Edward Atkinson presented Elizabeth with twenty-four books in English by a variety of authors. After Elizabeth's first year the number of books presented as New Year's gifts declined. Elizabeth received eight such gifts in 1563, six gifts of books in 1584 (see PLATES 1-3), five gifts of books in 1579 and 1581, and four gifts each in 1562, 1564, 1568, and 1577. For all other years to the end of her reign Elizabeth received no more than three gifts of books in any one year.

The New Year's rolls identify the physical location of the Court during each celebration by including the palace name in the header of the 'To' and 'By' sides of most rolls.[5] While one palace may have been preferred over another for comfort or convenience of access, no one palace seems to have held particular significance as a special place to celebrate New Year's day. The sixteenth-century court did not reside in any one location continually and did not move from one palace to another in any scheduled pattern. Henry VIII celebrated more than half of his New Year's days at Greenwich, but he also spent that day at Eltham, Hampton Court, Windsor, Richmond, and Westminster.[6] Elizabeth seemed to favour residing at Westminster for the New Year's day celebration, but she also celebrated the day at Hampton Court, Richmond, Windsor, and Greenwich. Elizabeth celebrated the first and last New Year's days of her reign at Westminster;[7] however, she did not receive her New Year's gifts at Greenwich, the palace of her birth, until the twenty-seventh year of her reign in 1585.

The British Library catalogue of the Royal Library lists numerous titles which possibly entered the collection during Elizabeth's reign, but this catalogue does not provide complete provenance for all the titles. In his Panizzi lecture, T. A. Birrell briefly

4 M. St Clare Byrne, *The Lisle Letters* (Chicago, 1981); Elizabeth, Countess of Shrewsbury, *Letters to and from herself and various members of her family,* in the Cavendish-Talbot Manuscripts at the Folger Shakespeare Library, MS X. d. 428.

5 Locations of the Court for the New Year's celebration are also drawn from the Court calendar compiled by E. K. Chambers, *The Elizabethan Stage* (4 vols, Oxford, 1923), IV, 75-116.

6 J. P. Carley, *The Libraries of King Henry VIII* (London, 2000), p. xlvi, n.86. For a discussion of books given to King Henry VIII as New Year's gifts, see J. P. Carley, *The Books of King Henry VIII and his Wives* (London, 2004), pp. 53-72.

7 For purpose of place locations, I have followed Janet Backhouse: 'in the present context Westminster and Whitehall are synonymous'. The compilers of the inventory of Henry VIII also listed under Westminster Palace 'all rooms situated in what we would now call Whitehall'. See J. Backhouse, 'Sir Robert Cotton's Record of a Royal Bookshelf', *British Library Journal*, 18 (1992), 44-51.

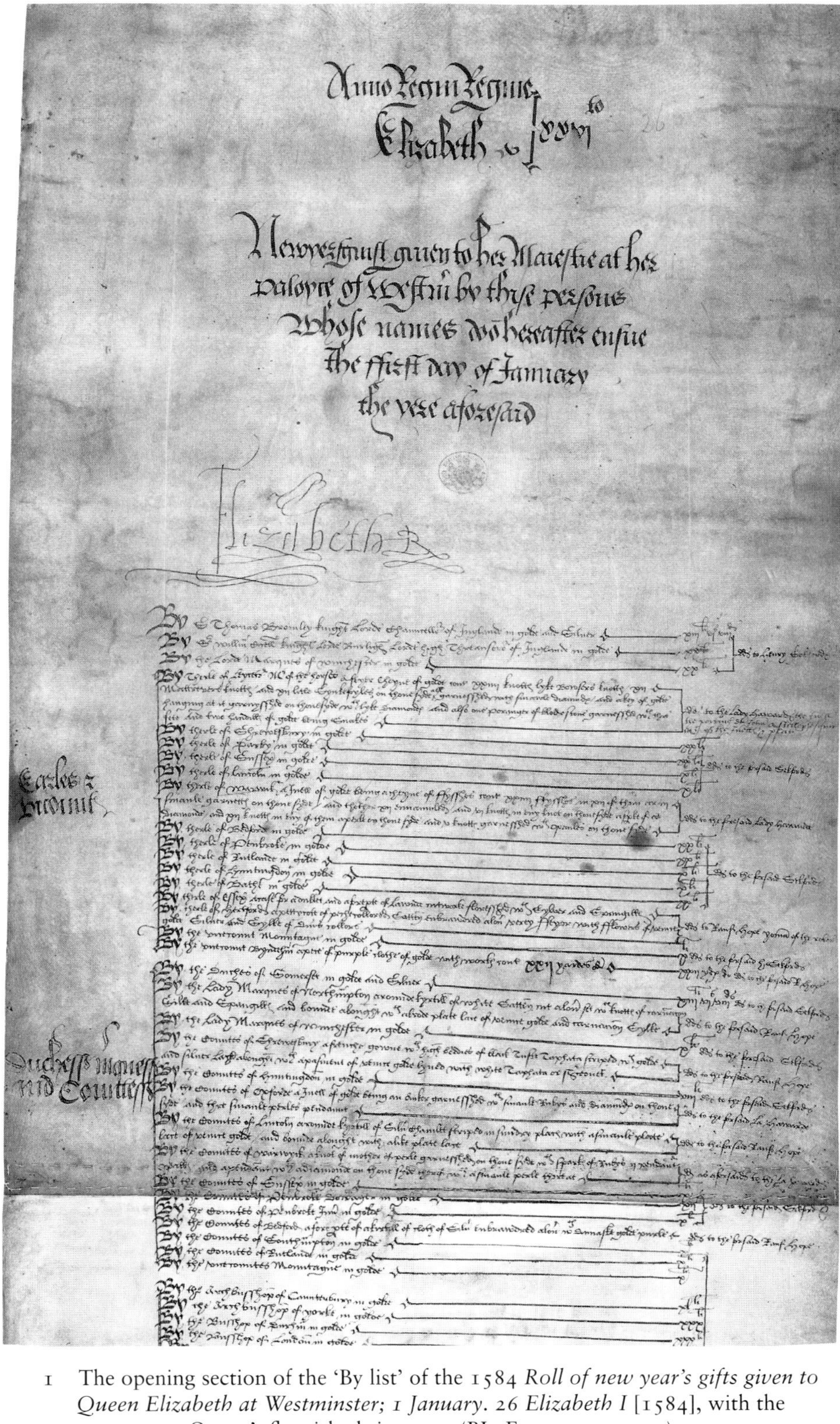

1 The opening section of the 'By list' of the 1584 *Roll of new year's gifts given to Queen Elizabeth at Westminster; 1 January. 26 Elizabeth I* [1584], with the Queen's flourished signature (BL, Egerton MS 3052)

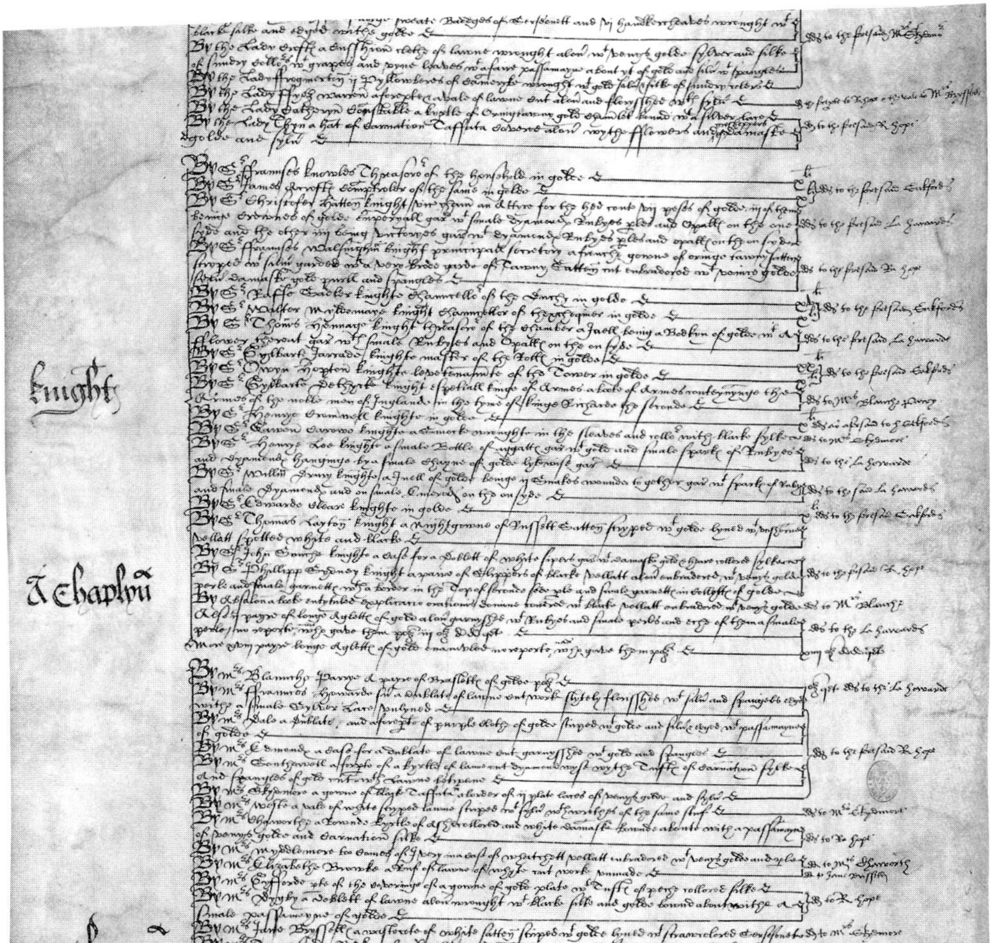

2 A section of the 'By list' of the 1584 Roll detailing the gifts given to Queen Elizabeth by some of the Knights and Gentlewomen (including Hatton, Walsingham, Sir Henry Lee, Sir Philip Sidney, and William Absolon) (BL, Egerton MS 3052)

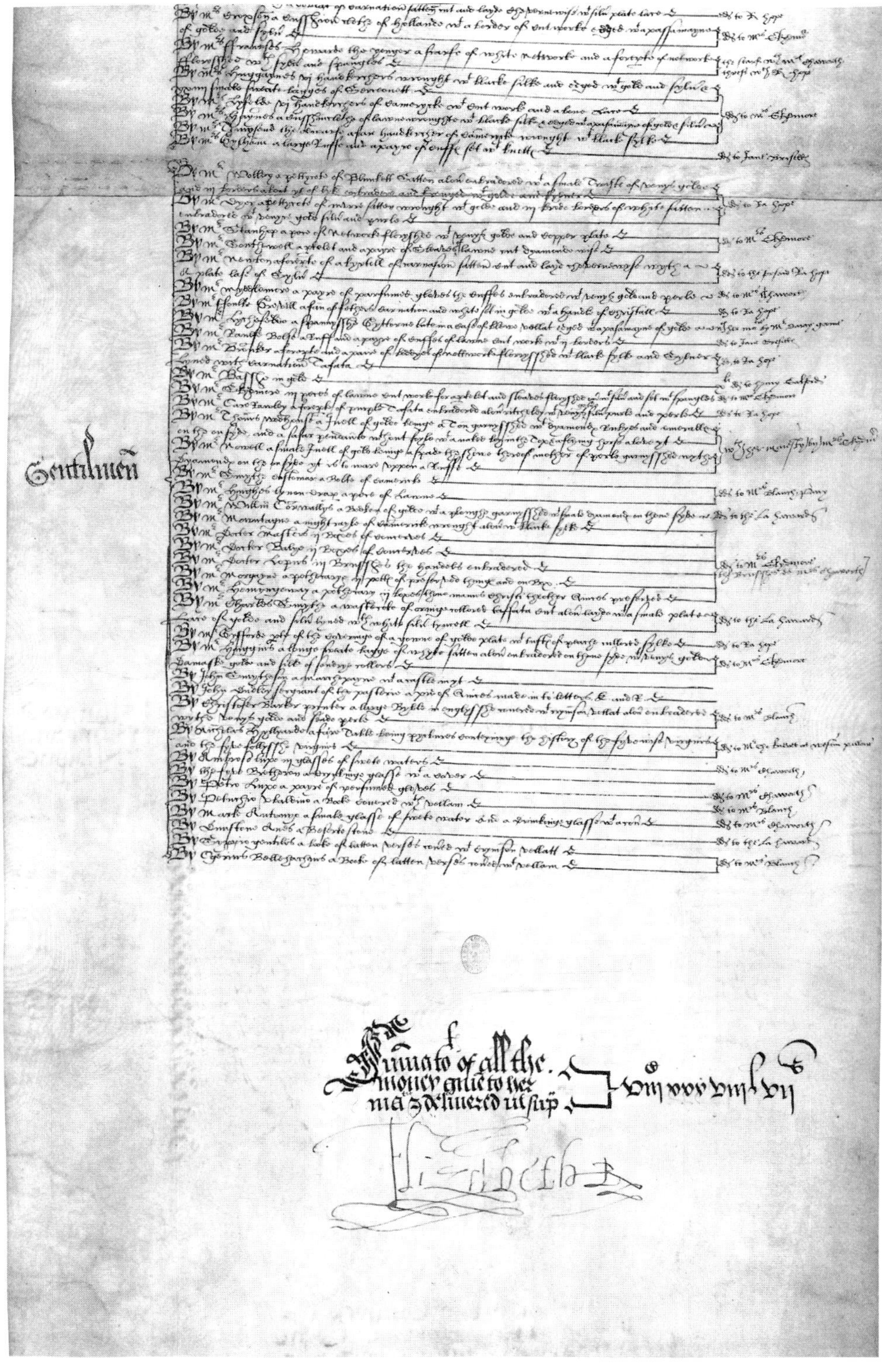

3 The closing section of the 'By list' of the 1584 Roll detailing the gifts given to Queen Elizabeth by some of the Gentlemen (including Fulke Greville, Nicholas Hilliard, and the printer Christopher Barker), with the Queen's flourished signature (BL, Egerton MS 3052)

describes Elizabeth's library and compares it to the library of her sister Mary, but he does not mention the New Year's exchanges as sources of the books given to either Queen or to other sovereigns.[8] A. J. Collins notes a small number of books given to Elizabeth as New Year's gifts in the context of their jewelled bindings, and John Nichols refers to several volumes garnished with silver gilt.[9] The inventory of Henry VIII[10] records more than two hundred books, along with where they were located in his palaces, but there is no indication of which were New Year's gifts. No similar inventory of Elizabeth's possessions lists her books, but five books with jeweled covers appear in the inventory of Queen Elizabeth's jewels in the custody of Lady Katherine Howard, while none are included in the later inventory of Mistress Mary Radcliffe.[11]

The choice of books as New Year's gifts for Elizabeth may reflect the givers' knowledge of her own fondness for such presents. From her early childhood, Elizabeth produced New Year's gifts designed for her nearest relatives. She was eleven when she selected and prepared the 1544 New Year's gift to be given to her stepmother, Catherine Parr. She translated the *Mirror or Glass of the Sinful Soul* from French into English and wrote a letter to accompany this gift.[12] She embroidered a canvas cover for her manuscript in blue and silver silk, with pansies and heartsease in violet, yellow, and green silk. Catherine's initials are in the middle of the cover (Oxford, Bodleian Library, MS Cherry 36).[13] The next year Elizabeth prepared another volume, a translation of Catherine Parr's *Prayers or Meditations*, in Latin, French, and Italian. She gave this volume to her father as a New Year's gift, prefaced by her only extant letter to Henry. This book, now British Library Royal MS 7 D. X, was bound in canvas cloth embroidered in red and silver silk with heartsease in gold in each corner and all the letters of both 'Katherin' and 'Henry' worked in a monogram in blue and silver silk.[14] In Edinburgh, National Archives of Scotland, RH 13/78, is another volume prepared by Elizabeth, entitled *How we ought to know God*, a translation of Calvin's *Institution de La Religion Chrestienne* from French to English with the dedication in French to Queen Catherine Parr, dated 1545, the same date as the volume to Henry. Based on their dates and on the similarity of the same monogram on their covers, these two translations with embroidered covers were prepared for presentation to Henry VIII and Catherine Parr as a pair.[15] The cover of the book for Henry is red with a blue and silver

8 T. A. Birrell, *English Monarchs and their Books: from Henry VII to Charles II* (London, 1987).

9 A. J. Collins, *Jewels and Plate of Queen Elizabeth: The Inventory of 1574* (London, 1955).

10 D. Starkey, *The Inventory of King Henry VIII* (London, 1998).

11 Lady Howard's accounts (BL Harley MS 4698 and Sloane MS 814) cover the years from 1572 to 1587, the year of Mary Radcliff's appointment. Mary Radcliffe's accounts (BL Royal MS Appendix 68 and Add. MS 5751A, fols 231-85) cover 1587 to 1603, when a new inventory of personal jewellery was prepared for her successor, the Countess of Suffolk (Calendar of State Papers Domestic, 1603-10, pp. 35, 66).

12 *Queen Elizabeth I: Selected Works*, ed. S. W. May (New York, 2004), pp. 94-7; M. Shell, *Elizabeth's Glass* (Lincoln, Nebr., 1993).

13 This volume remained with Catherine after Henry's death; it was later acquired by Francis Cherry, whose widow presented it to the Bodleian Library.

14 M. Perry, *The Word of a Prince: A Life of Elizabeth I from Contemporary Documents* (Woodbridge, Suffolk, 1990), p. 34; L. M. Klein, 'Your Humble Handmaid: Elizabethan Gifts of Needlework', *Renaissance Quarterly*, 50 (1997), 476-7.

15 M. H. Swain, 'A New Year's Gift from the Princess Elizabeth', *Connoisseur*, 183 (1973), 262.

monogram while the cover presented to Catherine is blue with a red and silver monogram, the same colour scheme used in the *Glass of the Sinful Soul*. The same kind of silk is used, the volume sizes are similar, and heartsease are embroidered in the corners. These paired books reveal the Princess Elizabeth designing carefully coordinated gifts to present to both her parents for the 1544 New Year's day celebration.

One other work composed by Elizabeth did not survive the fire at Whitehall in 1698. Sir Robert Cotton included this volume in a list of books 'In the privy closet at Whitthall' (BL, Cotton MS Vespasian B. IV), describing it as 'A treatis in french to king H 8 wrighten with the Lady Eliz his daughter hand'. This is probably the book shown to Paul Hentzner in 1598 as one of the treasures of the palace. Hentzner described the French dedication on parchment in Elizabeth's handwriting, but he did not describe the binding in detail.[16] Margaret Swain proposes that this volume was a companion to the 1544 blue-bound gift to Catherine, bound in red for Henry.[17] This brings the total to four extant manuscript books prepared by Elizabeth as coordinated New Year's gifts to Henry and Catherine.

Elizabeth continued giving her translations and hand-embroidered covers with the translation of Bernardino Ochino's *De Christo Sermo* (Bodleian MS Bodl.1/6) which she prepared for Edward in 1547, his first year as King. Edward rewarded the Lady Elizabeth's servant with 54*s* 4*d* for the delivery of this gift,[18] the same amount given to servants of Princess Mary and Anne of Cleves for their gifts. In 1548, Elizabeth apologized to Edward for not sending him her usual translation work as a New Year's gift, explaining that she had been ill. Another reason for the lack of a gift was the Lord Protector Somerset's ban on the giving of New Year's gifts, on grounds that they were part of the superstitions of the Catholic Church. However, gift rolls, now lost, are recorded for 1552 and 1553, meaning that this ban was short-lived, although no details of further translations by Elizabeth have come to light.[19]

The practice of presenting a piece translated and written specifically as an example of one's scholarly accomplishment was not unique to Elizabeth. It was an acceptable practice for educated young women of the mid-sixteenth century, and the gift was often packaged, as was Elizabeth's, with a further example of the young lady's skill with the embroidery needle. The gift thereby highlighted some of the skills an aristocratic Tudor lady should possess. Mary Fitzalan, for example, prepared four such volumes as New Year's gifts for 1554-1557 for her father, Henry, Earl of Arundel (BL Royal MS 12 A. I-IV). She prepared two of these volumes prior to her marriage to Thomas Howard, Duke of Norfolk, in 1555; the other two afterwards. These little volumes consist of Latin exercises studiously written out in an italic hand, probably with assistance from her tutor.[20]

16 Backhouse, p. 46.
17 Swain, p. 265.
18 *Literary Remains of King Edward the Sixth*, ed. John G. Nichols (London, 1857), pp. cccxi-cccxviii.
19 Collins, p. 246; D. Starkey, *Elizabeth: Apprenticeship* (London, 2000), p. 85.
20 There is no mention of embroidered covers as part of this gift, and the volumes have been rebound in contemporary bindings. They were part of the collection of John, Lord Lumley, and were listed in the catalogue of 1661 as stored in the 'third press against the chimney'.

The procedure of the New Year's gift ceremony remained remarkably stable from one Tudor sovereign to another. The 1538 Greenwich celebration of the New Year is described by John Hussey as he presented Lord Lisle's gift to Henry VIII.[21] In 1542, Princess Mary presented Prince Edward with a 'Boke lymned in gold' and received a gilt standing cup in return,[22] but no further details have been discovered regarding this book. The only extant roll from Mary's reign records the 1557 exchange in her court and offers a preview of the exchanges under Elizabeth.[23] Of the 266 New Year's gifts Mary received in 1557, fifteen were books, which is essentially the same ratio as the fourteen such gifts out of 221 that Elizabeth received two years later. The books Mary received in 1557 fall into three broad categories: the first, Scripture and Devotional Literature; the second, Classics and Instruction; the third, Poetry and Music. Mary received a primer or book of hours along with a prayer book and psalter in this gift exchange. The Jewel House inventory of 1559 lists two gospels, two primers, and one copy of the Epistles among Mary's possessions; these items were listed here because of the precious metal and jewel content of their covers. While their descriptions are consistent with New Year's gifts and it is possible that they were gifts to Mary, no surviving gift roll records the presentation of these exact items.

The primer given to Mary in 1557 by her chaplain, William Knight, and the book of prayers given by Sir John Alley were Catholic editions, published after Mary came to the throne. John Wayland published the first Marian edition of *An vniforme and catholyke prymer in Latin and Englishe* in 1555 (STC 16060), with multiple editions following in the next three years by Wayland, John Day, and other printers. The 'book of passion' is a manuscript presented by Giles 'Beraldus', a giver not yet identified. Francis Mallet, Royal Almoner, gave a psalter in 1557, probably the edition printed by Thomas Berthelet about 1553 (STC 3006) or 1556 (STC 3006.5) with a prayer for Queen Mary printed at the end. Another possible candidate for this gift is Franciscus Titelman's *Psalterium Davidicum paraphrasibus et argumentis illustratum* in the Lumley catalogue, printed at Antwerp in 1553. This volume, bound originally in purple velvet with silver and gilt, but presently bound in leather with the initials 'M.R.' on the spine is now BL 689. a. 5.[24]

The procedure of the gift exchange allowed a dean of a cathedral or a chaplain of the Queen's Chapel to give a gift, often a bible or devotional book, instead of the money expected from a bishop. John Christopherson, Bishop elect of Chichester, was not confirmed in his bishopric until November 1557. His gift of a 'book written' was most likely a copy of his *An exhortation to all menne to take hede and beware of rebellion* (STC 5207) published in 1554, which contains a folding genealogical table of Philip and Mary.

The second group of books Mary received in 1557 were popular titles of the day in classics and instruction. The wide variety of subject-matter among these titles provides

21 Byrne, V, 10.
22 F. Madden, *Privy Purse Expenses of the Princess Mary* (London, 1831), pp. xcvii, 99, 108.
23 Appendix III contains the transcription from the 1557 gift roll of these book gifts.
24 *The Lumley Library: The catalogue of 1609*, ed. Jayne Sears and Francis R. Johnson (London, 1956), p. 69.

an insight into the intellectual climate and international atmosphere of the mid-sixteenth-century court, ranging from moral justification to history to practical technology. Walter Earle, a Gentleman of the Privy Chamber, gave *The comentaries of Don Lewes de Auela ... which treateth of the great wars in Germany*, translated out of Spanish into English (STC 987). John Cawood and Reginald Wolfe, printers, appear on both the 1557 Marian and the 1559 Elizabethan gift exchanges; the books they gave to Mary are discussed below with their gifts to Elizabeth. In 1557 William Babington gave Mary a green velvet book in French instructing 'howe a king shulde chose his Counsorte'. William Babington served Mary as an Esquire for the Queen's Body and Elizabeth, his wife, was a Gentlewoman of her Privy Chamber.

Gifts of poetry and music comprise the third category of books Mary received in 1557. Miles Huggard was a poet and an opponent of the reformation who most likely gave the Queen one of his own works. Two manuscripts in his hand are promising candidates for his gift in 1557, or are, possibly, his New Year's gifts in other years. The original manuscript of his work, *A Mirroure of myserie*, now San Marino, California, Huntington Library, HM 121, is dedicated to Mary and appears to be a presentation copy. Huggard also wrote BL Harley MS 3444, a poem he addressed 'To the most highe & myghtie prynces Mary, by the grace of God Quene of England, France, and Ireland, etc. the compiler heroff wisheth longe healthe and prosperitie with moche honour'. The dedication is signed 'youre highnesse humble Servant Myles Huggard', and the volume is bound with the Royal Arms and the initials 'M.R.' on the covers.

The vague descriptions provided in the 1557 gift roll make it difficult to identify the givers and the extant manuscripts of the remaining book gifts: six French volumes, plus three rolls of songs, 'a book of ditties', and a book of 'certayne verses'. The French books were a gift of Durand, the French Ambassador's secretary, but further details of the secretary and his books are not known. John Shepherd, Chaplain, and Richard Edwards of the Chapel gave her the verses and rolls of songs. Sebastian Westcott presented Mary with a book of ditties, perhaps from one of the entertainments he produced at St Paul's. He held the post of Schoolmaster of St Paul's Cathedral school through the reigns of four sovereigns, although his refusal to subscribe to the Thirty-nine Articles caused him to be deprived of his place as a vicar about 1563. He retained his favoured status with Elizabeth, however, working with the St Paul's boys and producing plays with music for various entertainments until his death in 1582, but he did not appear on any Elizabethan New Year's gift roll.

Only five individual book donors who participated in the Elizabethan New Year's gift exchange also participated in the exchanges with other Tudor sovereigns. John Cawood and Reginald Wolf appeared on the 1557 Marian and 1559 Elizabethan gift rolls, presenting books to both queens. The names of Sir John Alley and Armigal Waad also appear on those two gift rolls, but Alley's gift to Elizabeth was a carved and painted wooden coffer instead of the book he gave to Mary, and Waad's gift to Mary was 'a glasse of Aqua compossata'. Sir John Mason participated in gift exchanges with three Tudor sovereigns – Edward, Mary, and Elizabeth – giving gifts of books, a map, hourglasses, and jewelry, as well as gifts of money. The other book donors on the Marian gift roll did not reappear on any Elizabethan gift roll, which is consistent with the changing climate of the Court, as Elizabeth dismissed Mary's followers and surrounded herself with her own supporters.

Among the more than 1100 different participants on the twenty-four extant Elizabethan New Year's gift rolls, only forty-nine individuals presented her with books, accounting for only 150 of more than 4500 New Year's gifts she is known to have received during her reign. To clarify my account of the types of books given to Elizabeth as New Year's gifts, as with the discussion of Mary's books, I have sorted the books into broad subject categories: (1) Scripture and Devotional Literature, (2) Classics and Instruction, (3) Heraldry, and (4) Poetry, Music, and Other. In Appendix I, I include the transcriptions from the gift rolls for all printed and manuscript items, listed chronologically within these subject headings. In Appendix II, I list alphabetically the individuals who presented these gifts with the number of items given, the years of their participation, and the subject categories of their books. Of these forty-nine individuals, seven presented books in multiple years, while a group of fifteen donors presented gifts other than books in one or more other years. Eighteen donors participated in only one gift exchange, each presenting a single volume as their New Year's gift. They apparently hoped to gain some favour from Elizabeth through their selection of a particular book for her.

SCRIPTURE AND DEVOTIONAL LITERATURE

The Elizabethan New Year's gift rolls record seven editions of the Bible presented to the Queen between 1559 and 1603. The printer Reginald Wolfe presented the first bible listed as a New Year's gift for Elizabeth in 1559, probably a copy of the Geneva Bible published by Richard Hall in Geneva (STC 2093). This version was dedicated to the 'noble Elisabet, Quene of England Ireland France &c'. The bible Christopher Barker gave Elizabeth in 1584 is now in the Bodleian Library (Douce Bib. Eng. 1583 b.1). The gift roll describes it as having seed pearls sewn into the embroidery. The crimson cover has faded and the pearls are no longer attached, but the embroidery in metal thread with its Tudor roses can still be seen.[25] The woodcuts, borders, and capitals of this bible are delicately hand-coloured or gilded, and the fine embroidery on the covers portrays Tudor roses in an arbor embroidered in gold, silver and coloured silk threads; the edges are gilt and tooled. The text has been described as 'one of the most decorative and in many ways the finest of all the remaining embroidered books of the time'.[26] Barker was granted the patent in 1577 to print the Queen's books in Latin, Hebrew, and Greek, all bibles, the Book of Common Prayer, statutes of the realm and royal proclamations. At his death in 1599, his son, Robert, acquired this patent. In 1603 he followed his father's example by giving the Queen a printed bible, probably the Geneva version, one of the editions printed in 1602 or 1603 (STC 2186-2191). STC 2192 shows the transition in sovereigns as the Old Testament title-page shows 'R. Barker, printer to the Queenes maiestie, 1603', but the New Testament title-page

25 *Elizabeth: The Exhibition at the National Maritime Museum*, ed. S. Doran (London, 2003), pp. 108-9.
26 G. Barber, *Textile and Embroidered Bindings* (Oxford, 1971), p. 5.

specifies the 'Kings maiestie'. In 1597, another printer, George Bishop presented Elizabeth with a Latin Vulgate translation of the Bible, probably a copy of the *Biblia Sacra Vulgatae Editionis*.

William Absolon presented the Queen with bibles as New Year's gifts in 1578 and 1581 and with books of prayers or devotions in 1579, 1584, and 1585. He served as chaplain to Elizabeth, and also as Master of the Savoy and Clerk of the Closet. After studying at Oxford during the reign of Queen Mary, Absolon served as pastor of several churches and was a supporter of the Princess Elizabeth, who remembered and rewarded him when she came to the throne. The bibles Absolon gave were richly bound in cloth of gold and crimson velvet, bindings that pleased the Queen. The gift rolls fail to specify that these were either printed or manuscript volumes, but they were meant for use in the Queen's chapel. The Geneva Bible published in 1577 by Richard Jugge (STC 2121) and the version printed by Christopher Barker in 1578 (STC 2123) are likely candidates for either Absolon's or Barker's gifts to the Queen. The bible Absolon gave in 1578 has two plates of the Queen's arms and was placed in the Privy Closet by John Thornborough. In 1581 Absolon presented Elizabeth with a four-volume Latin bible, possibly similar to the *Testamenti veteris Biblia siue libri canonici* published by Henry Middleton in six parts in 1580 and 1581 (STC 2056, 2057). In 1579 Absolon's gift to Elizabeth was a 'boke covered with Cloth of Tyssue garnesshed with Siluer and guilte', which could be BL Stowe MS 30, *Prayers in various languages* – Greek, Latin, English, French, Italian, Spanish, German, Dutch, and Hebrew – described in the British Library manuscript catalogue as 'beautifully written in inks of various colours, with illuminated titles and initials' prepared for presentation to the Queen. This work is attributed to Petruccio Ubaldini in the *DNB* and is recorded by Maria Ricci in her unpublished study of Ubaldini,[27] although its Latin dedication and mixture of languages does not resemble Ubaldini's normal practice. In 1584, Absolon chose an explication of the Lord's Prayer, possibly the volume published by Lambert Daneau at Geneva in 1584 (see PLATE 4). The BL copy of this edition with its binding of embroidered velvet is noted as 'from the library of Queen Elizabeth' (BL shelf mark C.24.a.34). Absolon selected a book of Christian exercises for his gift to Elizabeth in 1585. A volume of a similar title, *The Exercise of a Christian Life*, was written in Italian by Gaspar de Loarte, translated by James Sancer, the alias of Stephen Brinkley, and published at Rheims in 1584. John Brydges, Chaplain and Dean of Salisbury, presented 'a Testament in Ingelissh of old wrytten hand couered with purple vellat and gold' to Elizabeth in 1581 (PLATE 5). This manuscript, listed on the inventory found in the closet at Whitehall and now BL Royal MS 1 A. XII, retains its presentation binding of faded blue velvet, with impressions of the original bosses and clasps in the form of roses and fleur-de-lis.[28]

The donors of books to the Queen included only two women. They presented their books early in the reign (1559 and 1563), and in both cases their gifts are described more fully for their jeweled and embroidered covers than for their texts. The very first

27 M. Ricci, *Petruccio Ubaldini* (unpub. thesis, Università degli Studi di Firenze, 1940), p. 102.
28 Backhouse, p. 46.

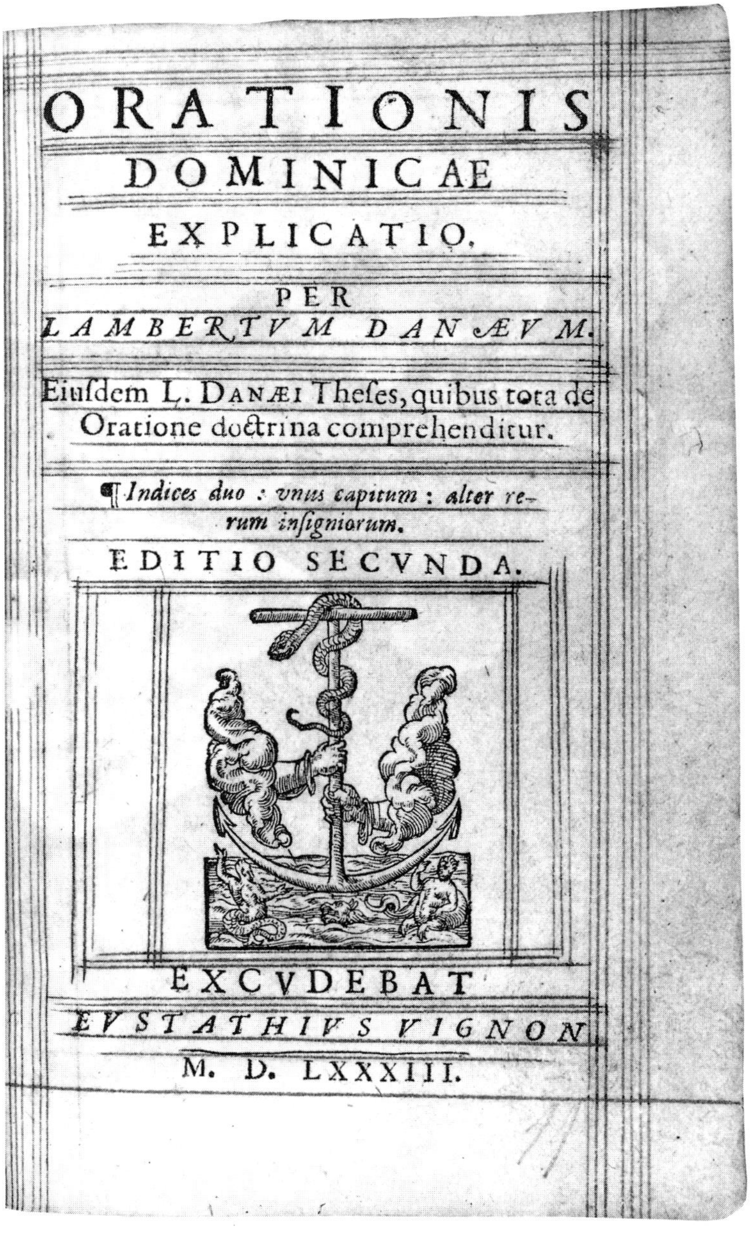

ORATIONIS
DOMINICAE
EXPLICATIO.
PER
LAMBERTVM DANÆVM.

Eiuſdem L. DANÆI Theſes, quibus tota de Oratione doctrina comprehenditur.

¶ *Indices duo : vnus capitum : alter rerum inſigniorum.*

EDITIO SECVNDA.

EXCVDEBAT
EVSTATHIVS VIGNON
M. D. LXXXIII.

4 Title-page of the British Library copy of Lambert Daneau's *Orationis Dominicæ explicatio*, 1583, from the library of Queen Elizabeth, bound in embroidered velvet resembling the description of Absolon's New Year's gift to her in 1584 (BL, C.24.a.34.)

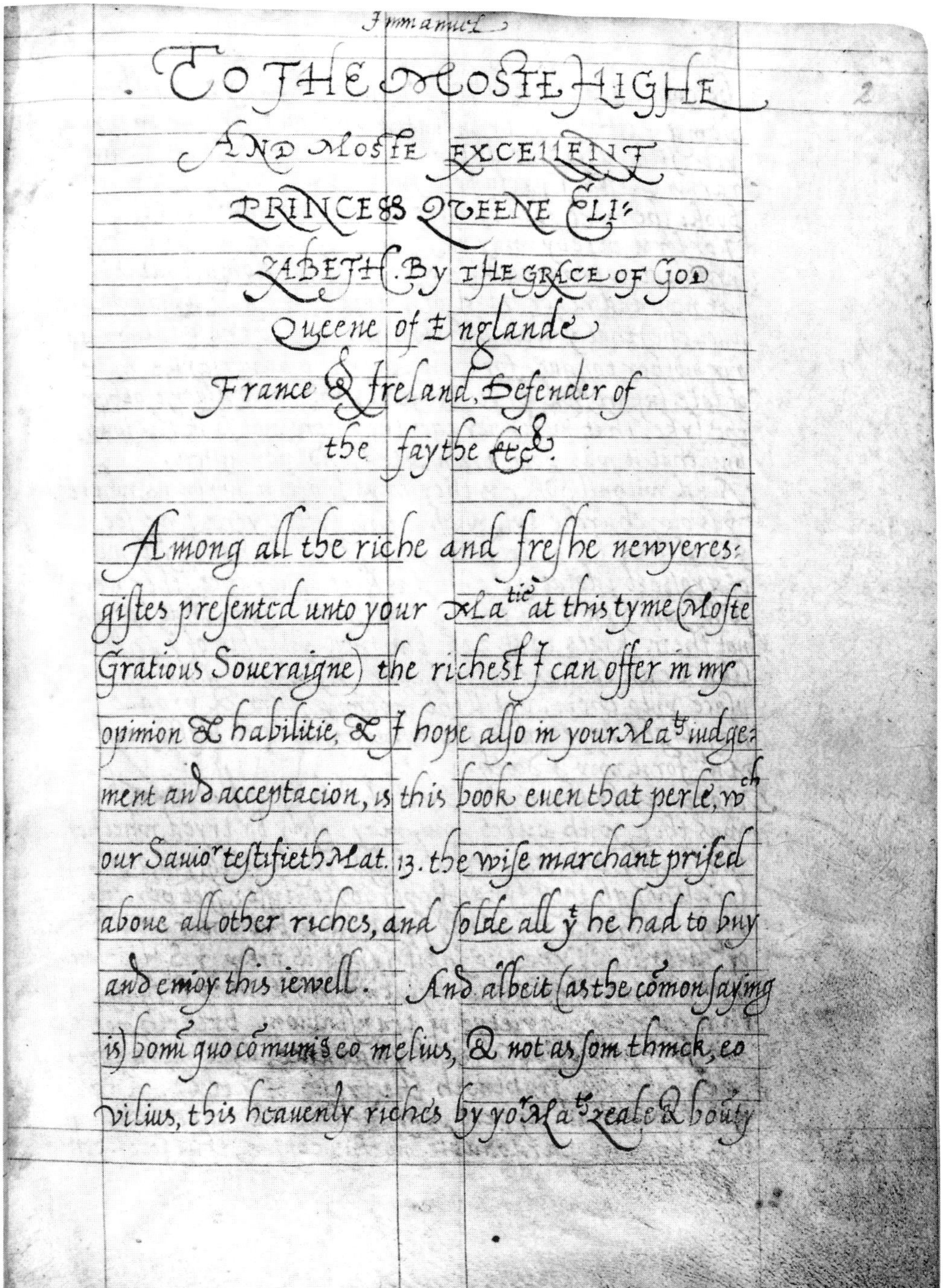

Immanuel

TO THE MOSTE HIGHE AND MOSTE EXCELLENT PRINCESS QUEENE ELIZABETH. By THE GRACE OF GOD Queene of Englande France & Ireland, Defender of the faythe etc.

Among all the riche and freshe newyeres gistes presented unto your Matie at this tyme (Moste Gratious Soueraigne) the richest I can offer in my opinion & habilitie, & I hope also in your Mats iudgement and acceptacion, is this book even that perle, wch our Savior testifieth Mat. 13. the wise marchant prised above all other riches, and solde all yt he had to buy and enioy this iewell. And albeit (as the comon saying is) boni quo comunis eo melius, & not as som thinck, eo vilius, this heavenly riches by yor Mats zeale & bouty

5 Letter by Dr John Brydges, Royal Chaplain, presenting to Queen Elizabeth his 1581 New Year's gift, the *New Testament* in English in the revised Wycliffite translation (BL, Royal MS 1 A. XII, fol. 2r)

gift listed on the first New Year's gift roll of Elizabeth's reign was a copy of Ecclesiastes from her first cousin, Frances, daughter of the French Queen Mary Tudor (1496-1533) and Charles Brandon, Duke of Suffolk, and thus, like Elizabeth, a granddaughter of Henry VII. Frances appeared in this primary position on the gift roll as Elizabeth's nearest royal relative.The book was bound in purple velvet and trimmed with silver. Although the gift roll does not specify if this was a printed or manuscript copy, it may be *Ecclesiastes and the Song of Solomon*, now BL Royal MS 2 D. III. It is likely that Mistress Elizabeth Wingfield personally embroidered the cover for the Latin psalter she gave in 1563, just as the Princess Elizabeth had embroidered covers for her own New Year's gift books. This volume may have been the psalter published by William Seres in 1563 (STC 2384.5) which she covered 'with nedleworke of golde Siluer and blewe silke'. As Mother of the Maids, Wingfield presumably had expertise in needlework that she shared with the maids of honour in her charge. It is quite probable that she consulted with her brother, Sir William Cecil, in preparing their gifts for the Queen and perhaps intended that her psalter should complement the book of prayers he gave Elizabeth in the same year. In later years, the New Year's gifts from the women in Elizabeth's court continued to focus on jewels and embroidery, but did not include books.

The manuscript Latin psalter given by John Lord Lumley in 1587 was placed in the charge of Lady Howard by virtue of its jewelled cover. At some later date the cover was probably removed and disassembled for its gold. Considering Lumley's interest in books and libraries, it is interesting to note that, while he participated in every extant Elizabethan New Year's exchange, he gave the Queen only this one book. Through his marriage to Jane Fitzalan, Lumley was a brother-in-law to Mary Fitzalan, who had prepared four books as New Year's gifts for her father, the Earl of Arundel. Lady Jane Lumley's English translations from Greek literary texts are also in the British Library (Royal MSS 15 A. I, II, and IX), although there is no indication that they were royal New Year's gifts. Lord Arundel bestowed his library, part of which came from the collection of Thomas Cromwell in 1539, to his son-in-law, Lumley, about 1557. Both Arundel and Lumley continued adding to the collection, which numbered more than three thousand books and manuscripts by 1609. After Lumley's death, this library seems to have reverted to the crown where portions of it were merged into the Royal Library and duplicates were removed.[29] Royal MS 1 E. III is one of several manuscript copies of the Psalms which entered the Royal Library through the Lumley collection, and may be similar to the manuscript Lumley gave Elizabeth in 1587.

Several of the New Year's gifts Elizabeth received in the early years of her reign were designed to discover or direct her religious inclination, as it was unclear what type of Protestantism would emerge from the Elizabeth Settlement. It is possible, though undeterminable, that the 'Twentie and foure Englishe bookes of Sondrey writers vpon the Scripture' given by Edward Atkinson in 1559 was a collection of homilies and religious instruction. Elizabeth issued injunctions in 1559 concerning the use of official homilies as an instrument in restoring English Protestantism. With these instructions in

29 *The Lumley Library*, ed. Sears and Johnson (1956), p.13.

mind, the Queen's printers, Richard Jugge and John Cawood, issued the official books of homilies for the Church of England in 1559, 1560, 1562, and 1563.[30] The homilies were designed to be read from the pulpit of every parish church in the realm; they explained the articles of belief, justified them from the Bible and the Fathers of the Church, and set doctrine on many public issues. The leather-covered volume of Homilies given in 1559 by Edward Whitchurch, another printer, was probably the edition printed by Jugge and Cawood in 1559 (STC 13648.5). Whitchurch probably combined this with a copy of the 1559 edition of the Book of Common Prayer (STC 16292) also published by Jugge and Cawood.

Prayer books were appropriate and personal gifts that appeared on the gift rolls throughout Elizabeth's reign. The prayer book Sir William Cecil gave Elizabeth in 1563 included the personal touch of her own coat of arms and that of her mother 'on both sides of golde garnisshed and clasped with golde sett with Garnettes and Turquisses'. The arms were designed to bring special recognition to Anne Boleyn, the Queen's mother, as did the mother-of-pearl and ruby ring with the enamel portraits of Elizabeth and Anne likewise given to the Queen about 1575.[31] Cecil's prayer book publicly acknowledges the Queen's mother a dozen years earlier than this ring, an indication that Anne Boleyn was held in high esteem very early in Elizabeth's reign. The Queen probably received another prayer book at New Year's, 1582, when Robert Dudley, Earl of Leicester, gave her a 'litle boke of golde', which was encased in an enamelled cover garnished with rubies and diamonds, 'with a ring of golde to hang it by'. The description parallels that of another prayer book owned by Elizabeth and passed along to Queen Anne, wife of James I. Anne's inventory of her personal jewelry includes 'A book of gold with claspes all garnished ouer with small Diamonds & Rubies, hauing the Picture of Queen Elizabeth & of Mounsieur in it, with a booke of Praiers written in parchment'.[32] Dudley's gift is not specifically described as a prayer book, nor is there any mention of the portraits of Elizabeth and the Duke of Anjou, which would have appeared in the later inventory description, but the content of a small jewelled book meant to hang from a gold chain at the waist was probably devotional in nature. A girdle prayer book, a gift from Elizabeth to her cousin Henry Lord Hunsdon, was included in the Elizabeth I exhibition at the National Maritime Museum and is illustrated in that catalogue.[33]

As Bishop of Rochester, Edmund Gheast would have been expected to give the Queen a New Year's gift of £10 or £20 in half sovereigns, angels or other gold and silver coins, usually in an embroidered silk or satin purse. As the Queen's almoner in

30 I. Lancashire, *A Brief History of the Homilies* (Toronto, 1997); http://www.library.utoronto.ca/utel/ret/homilies/elizhom3.html

31 This ring was on display at the National Maritime Museum in 2003; it is described and illustrated in the catalogue of this exhibition, ed. S. Doran, pp. 12-13. Mary Hill Cole described the ring as illustrative of the respect awarded to Anne as Elizabeth's mother in 'Elizabeth I and her family', a paper presented at the Queen Elizabeth I Society Meeting, New Orleans, 6-8 March, 2003.

32 D. Scarisbrick, 'Anne of Denmark's Jewellery Inventory', *Archaeologia*, 109 (1991), 220.

33 This prayer book, with the prayers of Edward VI inside and its covers of a roundel of translucent green and red enamel and of a shell cameo bust of a young warrior, was part of the 2003 exhibition at the National Maritime Museum; it is described and illustrated in the catalogue, ed. S. Doran, p. 62, No. 57.

1564, however, Gheast was apparently entitled to present a non-monetary gift to the Queen. His choice of 'a Boke of thexposition of the newe Testament in latten' reflects his role as one of the first Protestant bishops of Elizabeth's reign, and he chose a Latin text with assurance of Elizabeth's competence in that language. In 1588 John Thornborough, William Absolon's successor as Clerk of the Closet and Master of the Savoy, gave Elizabeth 'a small Booke covered with Carnation vellat being Intituled Speculum virtutis', most probably a manuscript, now presumed lost. The terms *speculum* (mirror) and *virtutum* (virtue) were popular in devotional literature, but I have found no pairing of these two terms in a manuscript title.

CLASSICS AND INSTRUCTION

In 1563, Sir John Mason presented 'two Bookes of Augustynes worke' and 'a Case of siluer guilt with three hower glasses' which was listed as 'being broken in pieces and sent to the Mint in 1600'.[34] The Augustine is perhaps *Two bokes of the noble doctor and B. S. Augustine* (STC 921), translated by John Scory. Mason gave Elizabeth 'a smale collog of serpentyne garnesshid with siluer guilt and two bookes' in 1562 and 'a Booke in Greek' in 1564. He was a diplomat by profession who began his service to Tudor sovereigns in 1529, serving as Henry's French language secretary and envoy to France, Spain, and Germany. Through his marriage to Richard Hill's widow, Elizabeth Isley, Mason was related to William Cecil, Lord Burghley, and to Sir John Cheke. He continued at Court as Ambassador to France and Privy Counsellor under Edward, Ambassador to the Emperor under Mary, and Treasurer of the Household under Elizabeth. He is listed as one of the richest officials in the Queen's household in the 1559 subsidy assessment.

Jean Belmain, 'late schole Mr to King Edward', participated in the 1559 gift exchange with his gift of 'a booke finly printed De la Vie de la Morte couerid with Crimsen Satten allouer enbrauderid with golde'. This work is *Dialogue de la vie et de la Mort* by Innocenzio Ringhieri, translated from Italian into French by Jean Louveau and published at Lyon in 1557. Belmain tutored both Edward and Elizabeth in French, and in 1552 had given the Princess Elizabeth a French translation out of Greek, an epistle on the *Virtues of the Single Life* by St Basil (BL Royal MS 16 E. I).[35] Retiring from court some time after the 1559 gift exchange, he became a nephew by marriage to John Cheke and William Cecil with his marriage to Jane Allington.[36] Belmain was a Calvinist with strong Protestant beliefs.

In 1568 two young Frenchmen presented New Year's gifts to the Queen which were recorded on the 'By' list of the gift rolls, although the donors were not listed on the 'To' list as receiving plate from her. Their arrival in England may have been associated with the flight of other Huguenot refugees to England in 1567. Jacques Bellot presented Elizabeth with 'a Booke conteignyge certeyne wordes and rules of the Frenche Tonge',

34 Collins, p. 350.
35 Starkey, *Elizabeth: Apprenticeship*, p. 86.
36 A. R. Maddison and A. S. Larken, *Lincolnshire Pedigrees* (London, 1902), vol. 50, p. 6.

probably a manuscript copy of his work *The French grammar* printed in London in 1578 (STC 1852). BL Sloane MS 3316 is not a presentation copy suitable for a royal New Year's gift, although its text is perhaps similar to the one the Queen received. The 'litell Booke written in Frenche coverid with parchement' that Jacques Grévin, a French poet, playwright and physician, gave Elizabeth was probably a manuscript of his French verse. He was a Huguenot whose plays were directed toward a college audience, and who served as personal physician to the Duke of Cleves and Margaret of Savoy. He studied in Paris, lived in Germany and Austria, and died in Italy in 1570.

In 1559, John Cawood, printer and stationer, gave Elizabeth a Greek edition of Josephus, possibly *Flavii Iosephi opera,* the 1544 Greek edition printed at Basel by Jerome Froben. In 1557 Cawood had given Mary two books published during the reign of Henry VIII: *Vita Christi* by Ludolf von Sachsen, printed either at Cologne 1534, or Paris 1534 or 1539, and a copy of Thomas Lupset's *An Exhortation to yonge men, perswadinge them to walke in the pathe way that leadeth to honeste and goodnes* (STC 16938), probably the 1544 edition of Thomas Berthelet. No editions of these titles were published between 1544 and 1557. Cawood replaced Richard Grafton as the Queen's Printer to Mary in 1553, and was granted a patent to print all statute books, acts, proclamations, injunctions, and other volumes in English, a position which was granted to Richard Jugge in 1558 and then was held jointly by Cawood and Jugge from 1559. Richard Jugge presented to Elizabeth 'oone Mappe Ptholomeis Tables in Italion' in 1559. This map was probably based on Ptolemy's *Geography* (STC 20481.3), which provided instructions on how to project a sphere on to a flat piece of paper using a system of gridlines, and may be similar to BL Maps 1.d.2.[37] Cawood was also granted a patent in reversion of Reginald Wolfe's patent for printing Latin, Greek, and Hebrew books; however, he never enjoyed this reversion, for he died a year before Wolfe. Reginald Wolfe, printer and stationer, presented to Mary a copy of *De metallicis rebus*, the leading textbook for miners and metallurgists for almost two centuries, translated from German into Latin (1556) and into Italian (1563) within ten years of its publication.[38] Wolfe's gift to Elizabeth in 1559 was a Geneva Bible (STC 2093).

George Bishop was admitted a freeman to the Stationers' Company in 1577, served as stationer and deputy printer to the Queen, and was a son-in-law of John Cawood. He participated in several gift exchanges from 1597 to 1600, always presenting books in either French or Latin. The Latin vulgate bible he gave in 1597 was probably the edition printed in Rome in 1592. The 'booke of Eclesiasticall histories in Frenche' Bishop gave in 1598 might be the *Histoire des martyrs persécutéz et mis à mort pour la vérité de l'Évangile* of 1597 by Jean Crespin.[39] For his gift in 1599, Bishop presented 'twoe Bookes of Plynnies workes in Frenche', which could have been an edition of *L'histoire du monde* by Pliny the Elder. His final gift to Elizabeth in 1600 was 'two bookes of Titus Lyvius in Frenche'.

37 Ptolemy's map and others were displayed in 1997 in a British Library exhibition on maps and map-making: see http://193.55.96.69/genet/aut2.html

38 The English translation of the work was completed by Herbert and Lou Hoover in 1912.

39 In 1579, Crespin's *Lexicon Graecolatinum* (STC 6037) was entered into the Stationers' Register by J. Harrison, G. Bishop, and Wm Norton.

Italian works in manuscript were favoured as gifts to Elizabeth from the artisans, physicians, and musicians of her Court, many of whom came from the towns of Venice, Bologna, Florence, and Padua. Petruccio Ubaldini appeared on eighteen New Year's gift rolls from his first appearance in 1563 up to the time of his death in 1600. For twelve or more of these years he displayed his calligraphic talents by giving the Queen illuminated manuscripts and presentation copies of his own literary works. A Florentine, he served Henry VIII as early as 1545, left England in 1551 to work in Venice and Florence, then returned to England in 1563, when Elizabeth appointed him Schoolmaster to the Henchmen, a sinecure. Although he never attained courtier status, he was regularly at court 'as a professional Italian' who sought patronage from other courtiers.[40] The rolls describe Ubaldini's gifts during the 1560s and 1570s by their titles, such as 'the seremonyes of the Coronation of Themperors' and a book of 'the seven psalmes in latten'. By the 1580s and 1590s the descriptions of his gifts are abbreviated to simply 'a book in Italian' or 'an Italian Booke', indicating that Elizabeth and her Court had become quite familiar with Ubaldini's work. But these later, generic descriptions also make it difficult to match with certainty his surviving manuscripts with the years when they were given. In 1563, Ubaldini participated in his first Elizabethan gift exchange with an illuminated manuscript, *La Vera Forma e regola dell' eleggere e coronare in imperadori,* now BL Royal MS 14 A. VIII. *Septem psalmi penitentiales*, the psalter he gave in 1565, is presently in Cambridge, Mass., Houghton Library, MS Typ 75.[41] He dedicated another psalter, *Salmo di David* (BL Royal 2 B. IX), to Henry Fitzalan, Lord Arundel, not to Elizabeth. I have not yet identified the 'certayne verses' which Ubaldini gave in 1571 on 'a table painted with a picture of a woman', but these could be similar to the calligraphic manuscript he presented to Lord Arundel *c.*1550-53 (BL Royal MS 14 A. I). Ubaldini's 1576 gift of 'viij Englishe ladies', an Italian manuscript, is presumably lost, but his manuscript gift of 1577, the 'book wrytten in Italian fayre' is *Le Vite e i Fatti di sei Donne Illustri*, now BL Royal MS 14 A. XIX. The six ladies in the 1577 manuscript are mythical or historical princesses, not the eight English ladies of the 1576 manuscript. Ubaldini's 1579 gift of an Italian book with pictures, 'the lyfe & metomerpheses of Oved', appears to be lost, and I have not been able to identify his 1581 gift of 'an Italian Booke of a phisition towching man's complextion and physike'.

A comparison of Ubaldini's New Year's gifts with his manuscripts listed in chronological order allows a possible reconstruction of the titles of the works he presented to the Queen as such gifts in later years. Ubaldini's servant received a reward of 6*s* 8*d* for delivering the 1582 gift, perhaps a copy of his *La vita di Carlo Magne imperadore*, the first book printed in Italian in London and dedicated to the Queen (John Wolfe, 1581, STC 24486). Ubaldini's gift for 1584 was 'a Booke couered with vellam', possibly a copy of *Lasino doro di Nicolo Macchiauelli, con tutte laltre sue operette* (STC 17158), a work printed by John Wolfe. It is possible that Ubaldini

40 S. W. May, *The Elizabethan Courtier Poets: The Poems and their Contexts* (Asheville, 1999), pp. 38-9.

41 This psalter was part of an exhibition held in 1968 and is described in David Sandler Berkowitz, *In Remembrance of Creation: Evolution of Art and Scholarship in the Medieval and Renaissance Bible* (Waltham, 1968), p. 50.

assisted with the London publication of this Italian work on the life of Machiavelli.[42] In 1585 Ubaldini gave Elizabeth a 'pettygrye', the only mention of a work of this type being prepared by Ubaldini, but it is probably similar to the pedigrees given by Robert Cooke. One of Ubaldini's 'two books of Italian' (1588) may be his *Descrittione del regno di Scotia, et delle isole sve adiacenti di Petruccio Vbaldini cittadin fiorentino* (STC 24480), printed by John Wolfe 'Il di primo di gennaio' 1588, according to its title-page, and dedicated to Christopher Hatton, Robert Dudley, and Francis Walsingham. The other book he presented to the Queen in 1588 could be his *Historie (di Firenze) ... nuovamente ammendate*, also printed by Wolfe (STC 17161). The major event of 1588 was the defeat of the Spanish Armada, and Ubaldini's gift for 1589 was 'a book Couered with vellum of Italian'. Ubaldini's Italian works, *Commentario del successo dell'armata spagnola dell'assalir l'Enghilterra l'anno 1588* (BL Royal MS 14 A. X) and *Commentario dell'impresa fatta contro il regno d'Inghilterra dal re Cattolico l'anno 1588* (BL Royal MS 14 A. XI) are candidates for the 1589 offering, although Ubaldini did not dedicate these manuscripts to Elizabeth. The *Memoriale di Petruccio Ubaldini, fiorentino, alla serenissima Elisabetta felicissima regina d'Inghilterra*, now BL Lansdowne MS 98, No. 22, is probably his New Year's gift for 1594, a year for which the roll has not survived. In the same Lansdowne volume is another Italian composition, a 'Description of the State of England'. This may be one of Ubaldini's gifts to Lord Burghley; if so, it is interesting to note that his lordship described it as the work of 'some ignorant Italian' (BL Lansdowne MS 98, No. 45). Ubaldini's gifts of 1595, 1597, 1598, and 1599 were all books in Italian, congruent with the works he published in those years: *Scelta di alcune attioni ... occorsi tra alcune nationi differenti del mondo*, 1595 (STC 24484), *Rime*, 1597 (STC 24483), *Militia del gran duca di Tuscana*, 1598 (STC 24482), and *La vita di Carlo Magno Imperadore*, 1599 (STC 24487). Ubaldini did present a few gifts other than manuscripts to Elizabeth, including 'a Glasse of swete water with certeigne other Instrumentes for Teethe parts' in 1567 and 'a peire of writing Tables the claspes and corners garnesshid with siluer' in 1568. Ubaldini's manuscripts seem, however, to have been gifts which Elizabeth found appropriate throughout her reign.

Guilio Borgarucci, familiarly known as 'Doctor Julio', usually followed the practice of court physicians in presenting Elizabeth with sweets and candies at New Year's, but his first New Year's gift to her, in 1575, was 'Six bookes of Italian prynted'. Dr Julio had become physician to Robert Dudley, Earl of Leicester in 1563 and was known for his successful treatment for the plague.[43] He was made physician to the royal household for life in 1573 and participated in every extant gift exchange from 1575 until his death in 1581. Borgarucci's two brothers, Borgaruccio and Prospero, wrote or edited several volumes on the history of science and anatomy, printed in Italian, which are perhaps the titles Guilio gave to Elizabeth. Prospero's *Secreti diversi* (1565), a work on alchemy, was followed by Borgaruccio's *Le rime burlesche* (1570), *Sententiae insigniores* (1573),

42 Ricci, p. 98; J.-P. Genet, *Le Dictionnaire des auteurs actifs dans les champs de l'histoire et de la politique en Angleterre de 1300 à 1600*; http://193.55.96.69/genet/refus003.htm

43 Borgarucci treated the plague by bleeding and using a ball (*pomo*) compounded of balsamic substances (ODNB).

and *La fabrica del mondo* (1575). Dr Julio contributed a short commendatory epistle in Latin to John Banister's *The Historie of Man* (1578).

HERALDRY AND ARMOURY

Books of arms were another type of manuscript gift that seemed to please the Queen, and which also appeared on the New Year's rolls during the reigns of Elizabeth's successors. Those presented by Gilbert and William Dethick, father and son, comprise the largest component of such volumes, but Sir George Howard, Sir Ambrose Cave, William Monge, and Robert Cooke presented four such manuscripts, along with eight maps and one printed book of heraldic material among them between 1562 and 1567. The early years of Elizabeth's reign sparked a renewed interest in coats of arms and crests and an interest in armoury as seen in the tilt and tourney held at the Inner Temple during this Christmas season 1561/62 and repeated at Whitehall in January 1562. In 1563 William Monge gave Elizabeth a 'Booke callid the Acidente of Armes', a copy of Gerard Legh's *Accedens of Armoury* (STC 15388). This popular book of heraldry, in which Legh describes the tilt and tourney of 1562, saw six editions between 1563 and 1612. In 1562 Sir George Howard gave Elizabeth 'a Booke conte thoffice of the Armery covered with blak vellat and bounde with passamayne of siluer with two plates of silver'.[44] The manuscript, which survives with its original cover under the title 'Inventory of the Armouries', includes a portrait entitled 'Ser George Howarde Knight Master of the Qwenes Maiesties Armory Anno Domini 1561'.[45] Howard, a brother of Catherine, fifth wife of Henry VIII and a cousin to Elizabeth, was appointed Master of the Armoury in 1561 and Gentleman Usher of the Privy Chamber in 1576. He gave Elizabeth £9 'in a lether purse' in 1559, 'oone Strainer for Orainges of siluer and guilt with two Christalles in the handle' in 1575, and continued to appear on the gift rolls from 1576 until 1579, but only on the 'To' list, receiving 'Free Gifts' from the Queen. In 1563 Sir Ambrose Cave, Chancellor of the Duchy of Lancaster, presented Elizabeth with eight small maps 'of Castelles within the said Duchey', a departure from his usual monetary gift, but representative of his position as Chancellor. Similar items may be the pen and ink maps in BL Royal MS 18 D. III, which are catalogued by the British Library as showing 'plans of the county with the names of gentry and houses filled in'.

Robert Cooke was appointed Chester Herald in 1562, a post he held until 1567 when he succeeded as Clarenceux. His gifts to the Queen take the same form as those of his fellow herald, Sir Gilbert Dethick. A 'Booke containing the Armes of all the Gentilmen in Lyncolneshire couerid with purple vellat', his first manuscript gift of 1563, is possibly BL Harley MS 810, No. 9, a *Callendar to the Arms of the Lincolnshire Gentlemen*. Cooke's 1565 gift to Elizabeth is another pedigree: 'one petygree of the Quenes Matie from William Conquerer'. The location of this manuscript is unknown, but it was probably similar to the manuscript, *Armourial bearings of the kings and*

44 Alan Nelson, *Monstrous Adversary: The Life of Edward de Vere, 17th Earl of Oxford* (Liverpool, 2003), fig. 4, following p. 236. Figure 4 is an equestrian illustration from this manuscript, which is on long term loan to the Tower of London from the Earl of Dartmouth.

45 Nelson, pp. 58-9.

noble families of Great Britain from the reign of William the Conqueror to that of James I, now in Chicago, Newberry Library, Case MS F 0745.1915. His 1567 gift, 'A Booke of Armes of the Quenis maties progonitors Tytle to the Crowne of Englande and Fraunce', is BL King's MS 396, a *Genealogical Tree, showing the descent of Queen Elizabeth.*[46]

Between 1562 and 1584, Sir Gilbert Dethick presented at least twenty-three illuminated books of arms to Elizabeth; fourteen of these have survived to this time. He entered the College of Arms in 1536, became Garter King at Arms in 1550 upon the death of Sir Christopher Barker, uncle of the printer of the same name, and was knighted in 1551. In 1547 and 1548, Edward VI rewarded Dethick and the other heralds on New Year's Day with £6 to be divided among them; the record of what, if anything, they gave the King has not survived. In 1562, the first year he appeared on the Elizabethan gift rolls, Dethick began the tradition of presenting the Queen with an illuminated heraldic manuscript, 'a booke of the Armes of the Knightes of the Garter now', present location unknown. In the same year, Gilbert Dethick (mistakenly listed as William) also received a christening gift for his son Robert, for whom Elizabeth served as godmother. In each year subsequently he prepared a different book of arms, usually picturing the arms of the Knights of the Garter for a specific reign from Edward III to Elizabeth. His last gift to Elizabeth, in 1584, was a book of arms 'of the noble men of Inglande in the tyme of King Richarde the seconde'. I have located five of his manuscripts and found references to nine more. His gift of 1563, 'a Book of Armes of all the Lordes as they sytt in perliament', is now BL Stowe MS 684, *Armes, Creastes and Supporters of all the noblemen withein the realme of Englande in ordre as they sitte in the Parliament Howsse.* The book of arms he gave to Elizabeth in 1565, 'a book of all tharmes of the knyghtes made from the beginnyng of her highness reyne', is now in New Haven, Yale University, Beinecke Library MS 97, and the gift of 1574, 'a book of all the Knightes of the most noble order of the Garter made in the shorte raigne of Richarde III' is now at Yale, Lewis Walpole Library, Hazen MS 2551. The books of arms that Dethick gave the Queen in 1575 and 1576 are now in the Royal Library at Windsor (Royal Collection MS RCIN 1047442 and MS RCIN 1047443). Gilbert Dethick retained the position of Garter King at Arms until his death on 3 October 1584. Heraldic offices were not hereditary, yet three of Sir Gilbert's sons, Nicholas, Henry, and William, also served as heralds.

William Dethick continued the tradition established by his father of presenting illuminated books of arms to Elizabeth. He first appeared on the gift roll as York Herald in the year following his father's death, 1585, when he presented his first heraldic volume to Elizabeth, 'a boke of Armes of the knyghtes of the Garter made sence her Maiestyes Reignne'. His gift to Elizabeth in 1589, 'a booke of Armes of the noble men in Henry the Fiftes tyme', is now BL Harley MS 1864. Harvard University Houghton Library has the 1593 book of arms 'of the knights of the garter in the time of Henry VII' (MS Typ 96). Dethick's gift to Elizabeth in 1603 was 'One Booke couered

46 This volume was part of the 2003 exhibition at the National Maritime Museum; it is described and illustrated in the catalogue, ed. S. Doran, pp. 105-6, no. 100.

with purple vellett of the knightes of the garter this present yere', now BL King's MS 417. Elizabeth apparently found these books of arms pleasing and appropriate as New Year's gifts. William Dethick continued this tradition into the reign of James I, who knighted him in 1603. The popularity and continuity of books of arms as New Year's gifts is confirmed by John Dugdale's 1685 account of his presentation of a book of arms to Charles II: 'I presented a Roll of the Nobilite (as they now stand) yesterday to his Majestie, who toke it well, I thought, saying "Ho! Ho! I know what it is!".' The books of arms presented by the Dethicks remained in the Royal Library until the reign of Charles I, but were dispersed during the Commonwealth Sale of 1649/51. The present day locations of most are not known, but it is possible that they have survived in private collections, as did the set of nine sold by Sotheby's in 1986 (PLATE 6).[47] These volumes, dated 1568, 1569, 1570, 1571, 1572, 1577, 1578, 1579, and 1580, were purchased by 'Owen', having belonged to the Keppel collection for more than two centuries; their current owner is unknown.

POETRY AND MUSIC

In 1559, Thomas Phaer (or Phayer) presented Elizabeth with 'a booke written of Aeneados in Englesh verses', certainly a manuscript of his own English translation from Latin of the *Aeneid*. This manuscript, presumably lost, perhaps continued his translation, incomplete at his death in 1560. Phaer published *The seuen first bookes of the Eneidos* in 1558 (STC 24799), with a dedication to Queen Mary; William Wightman edited the edition published in 1562 as *The nyne fyrste bookes* (STC 27800). Phaer was a physician, lawyer, classical scholar, and an associate of William Baldwin and George Ferrers, who wrote his epitaph. He apparently contributed the 'Tragedy of Owen Glendover' to *A Mirror for Magistrates*. He wrote *A Book of Children*, the first English work on children's diseases, and two legal handbooks of municipal laws, *Natura Brevium* and *Newe Boke of Presidentes*, which were published by Edward Whitchurch, Baldwin's associate and the publisher of the *Mirror for Magistrates*.

In 1559, 1562, and 1563, John Young gave Elizabeth three gifts of poetry that may have derived from the Phaer–Baldwin–Ferrers circle. Young gave Elizabeth a 'book of Devises for the avauncement of the state of a realm' in 1559, followed by 'certeyne verses' about money in 1562 and 'a story of poetry' in 1563. Elizabeth knighted him during her progress to Bristol in 1574 when she visited his house, and he repaid her for the honour with a jewel 'conteyning divers rubyes and dyamondes, wherein is a phenex and a salamaundre of agathe'.[48] Young served as a Member of Parliament for five terms, representing four different boroughs, probably through his service to William

47 Sotheby's sale catalogue, 18 December 1986, lot 203. I am grateful to Emma Stuart, Assistant Bibliographer at the Royal Library for identifying the 1575 and 1576 gifts presented by Sir Gilbert Dethick and for ascertaining that no other Books of Arms prepared by either Sir Gilbert or Sir William Dethick are preserved in the Royal Collection.

48 J. Nichols, *The Progresses and Public Processions of Queen Elizabeth* (London, 1823), Vol. 1, 379.

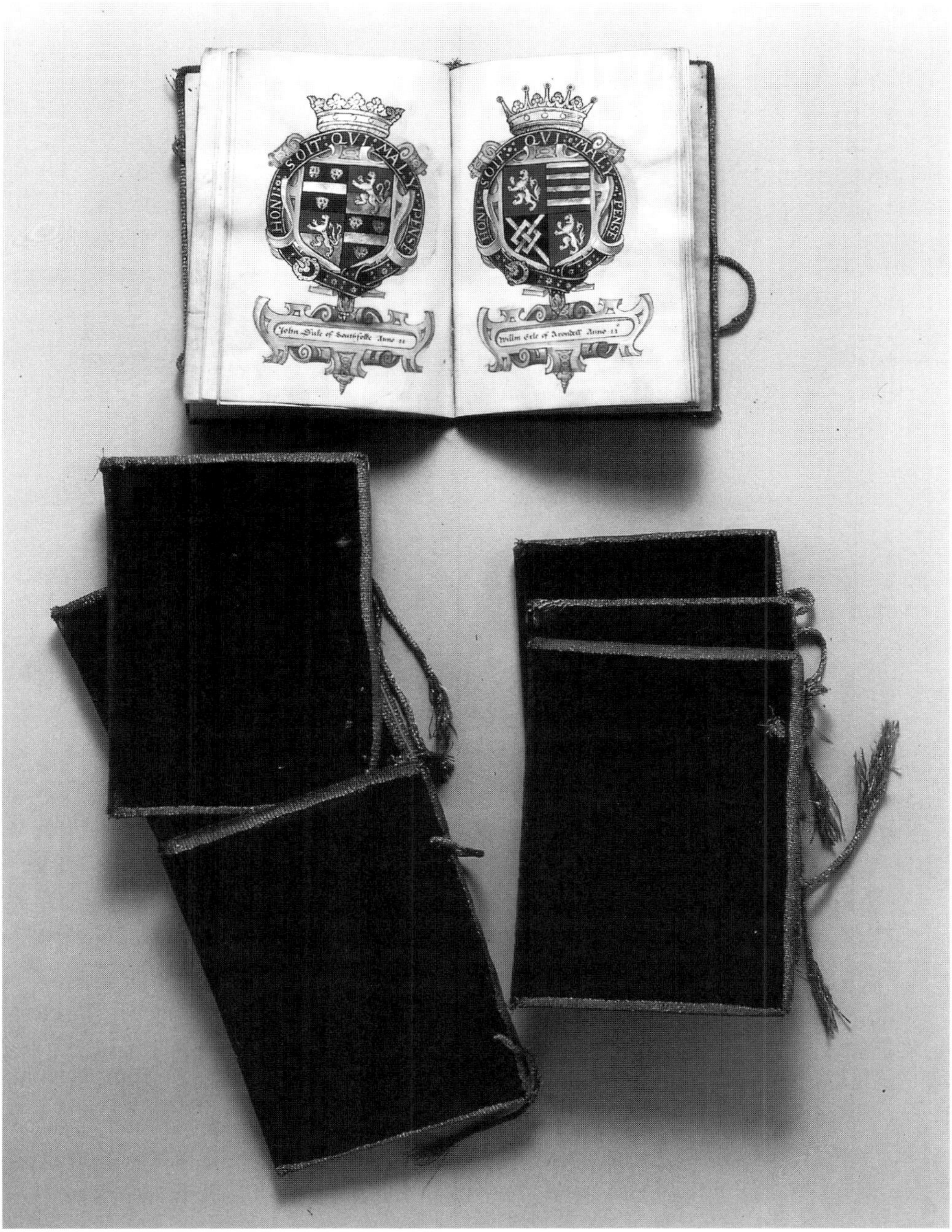

6 A collection of nine illuminated volumes presented as New Year's gifts to Queen Elizabeth by Sir Gilbert Dethick, Garter King of Arms

Herbert, Earl of Pembroke.[49] Young is not among the collaborators of the *Mirror for Magistrates*, and was probably not himself a poet, but both Young and his relative, George Ferrers, were friends with William Baldwin and Thomas Phaer. In 1570, Baldwin dedicated *Beware the Cat* (STC 1244), the first English novel, to Young.[50] In the same year that Young first appeared on the New Year's rolls, he was returned to Parliament for the Wiltshire borough of Devizes. Young's 1559 gift to the Queen, described as 'the avauncement of the state of a realm', is now Bodleian Library MS Laud 683, 'A discourse of John Yonge, gentleman, for a Banke of money to be established for the releef of the common necessitie'. The poetry painted on the two gifts of tables given by Young were also verses possibly written by Baldwin or another contributor to the *Mirror for Magistrates*.

Beginning with the first New Year's celebration in 1559 and continuing throughout her reign, Elizabeth received gifts of poetry, sometimes incorporated into painted tables and described as 'certain verses'. In 1559 Armigal Waad presented Elizabeth with 'Certaine Verses' and a looking-glass in an ebony table, and William Bayard gave her a painted table of a king with 'certain Scriptures belonging to the same'; the tables were both delivered to Westminster Palace by George Bridgeman. Waad, known as the 'English Columbus' because of his voyages to America in 1536, appeared on every extant gift roll from 1557 to 1565, usually offering a gift of glasses. His last gift to Elizabeth in 1565 was a 'half picture of mettall of Sigismend king of polo sett in wood'. Bayard, a French painter, probably painted King David or Solomon with selected Psalms or Proverbs on his table. In 1568, Anthony Maria Alberti, a Venetian musician, gave Elizabeth an Italian manuscript book, *Caualarie della citta de ferrara*. The present location of this manuscript is unknown; however, the duchal court of Ferrara operated as a centre for financial growth, a patron of musicians, and a haven for immigrants fleeing the Inquisition. Alberti, known as Anthony Maria in English documents, was a sackbut player who came to England in 1539 and served four Tudor sovereigns. Alfonso Ferrabosco, a musician from Bologna, also chose an Italian manuscript for Elizabeth as his gift in 1577, certainly an attempt to gain the Queen's favour after he had suffered unknown difficulties with her in 1576, which resulted in his sudden move to Rome in 1578.[51] The manuscript he gave may be the text of a masque for the court, now lost, that he wrote in collaboration with Petruccio Ubaldini about 1572.[52]

In 1577 Henry Gyrtens presented Elizabeth with 'an Englisshe boke in verse beinge a Story translated', but nothing further is known about the giver, the title, or the original language of the story. Anthony Finet's gift of 'a smale booke in Italian meter' in 1579 was probably a manuscript and appears not to have survived. Finet was most likely related to the John Finet who came to England in 1519 with Cardinal Campeggio

49 S. T. Bindoff, *The House of Commons, 1509-1558* (London, 1982), III, 684.

50 William Baldwin, *Beware the Cat: The first English Novel*, ed. William A. Ringler and M. Flachmann (San Marino, 1988). Norman Jones identifies Young's 1559 gift in *The Birth of the Elizabethan Age: England in the 1560s* (Oxford, 1993), pp. 7, 14.

51 David Lasocki and Andrew Ashbee, *A Biographical Dictionary of English Court Musicians, 1485-1714* (Aldershot, 1998), I, 408.

52 Genet: http://193.55.96.69/genet/aut2.html

and settled in Dover, marrying one of Catherine of Aragon's maids of honour. Later another John Finet, great-grandson of this John Finet, became Master of Ceremonies to the Court of James I. The younger John Finet wrote *The Court Ceremonies of Charles I*, which describes rites and ceremonies of the seventeenth-century English court. The 1584 gift exchange includes two gifts in Latin verse. The book of Latin verses by Ogerius Bellehachius is a verse paraphrase of the Song of Solomon published in 1583, as *Ogerii Bellehachii Sacrosancta bucolica Elizabeth Britanniae, Franciae, et Hiberniae reginae dicata* (STC 1846). Bellehachius must have been known to his printer, Henry Middleton, and bookseller, William Ponsonby, for both of their names appear in the printed volume; but I have not been able to identify him. Scipione Gentili gave the second book of Latin verses that year, Tasso's 'Jerusalem Liberated', fully entitled *Plutonis concilium Ex initio quarti libri Solymeidos Gerusalemme liberata*, translated into Latin by Gentili and published in London in 1584 by John Wolfe (STC 23700, 23701, 23702). Gentili, an Italian, taught Roman law. In the early 1580s he came to Oxford where his brother, Alberico Gentili, taught international law. Scipione became a protégé successively of Robert Dudley, Earl of Leicester, Sir Francis Walsingham, and Robert Devereux, Earl of Essex. Gentili and Bellehachius appear successively on the gift roll as the last two donors of 1584; their positions in the gift exchange and the similarity of their gifts indicate that they were quite possibly acquainted.

Some gifts from the missing years for the New Year's gift rolls can be identified from the inventories kept by those in charge of Elizabeth's gold and jewels. The accounts kept by Lady Howard and Mrs Radcliffe were designed to keep track of the many pieces of jewellery for the Queen's use. Five of Elizabeth's courtiers gave her five books of gold. The psalter 'inclosed all over on the outeside with golde enamuled cut-worke, with divers colours, and one little claspe' given by Lord Lumley in 1587 is recorded in Lady Howard's account, as is the little book, probably a prayer book, with gold, diamonds and rubies on the cover given by Robert Dudley in 1582. In the 1572 gift exchange, Sir Owen Hopton, Lieutenant of the Tower, gave Elizabeth a 'booke of golde enamuled and glased over with two clasps'. In 1576 Sir Henry Lee, successor to Sir George Howard as Master of the Armoury, gave a book of blank pages with an elaborate cover of gold, silver, and enamel. Lee was Elizabeth's champion at tilt from 1559 to 1590 and regularly appeared on the gift rolls, usually presenting an ornate jewel as his gift. Sir John Pakington came into favour with the Queen during the progress of 1572, living in great splendour and outspending his wealth. He acquired the nickname, 'Lusty Pakington', and he favoured amethysts as the gemstones in his gifts, as on the cover of his book in 1582 and in the pair of bracelets he gave in 1580.

Music-related gifts were a minor component of the gift rolls, even though musicians are numerous in the category of Gentlemen among gift roll participants. Their recurring, favourite gifts to Elizabeth were perfumed gloves, but they also gave other music-related New Year's gifts to the Queen including a bandore, a cornet, gitterns, lutes, and a pair of virginals, along with lute strings. George Comy, a Venetian musician, presented to Elizabeth in 1559 'two rounde Globes of Asia and Europa', most likely of Italian origin and probably made of papier mâché, plaster, or printed paper. Globes of these materials were first printed in England in the late 1580s.[53] In 1557 Queen Mary had received one gift of three rolls of music at New Year's. Elizabeth received two gifts of songbooks in 1559 and one more gift of fivesong books in 1579, but there is no other mention of music or songbooks in the gift rolls from the middle to the end of her reign. I have been unable to trace these songbooks because the rolls provide no actual titles or names of composers, while only a few details about the givers have come to light. Thomas Kent, who gave Elizabeth 'a Songe booke' in 1559, came to court as a page in 1543. He sang at the funerals of Henry VIII and Edward VI and continued to serve both Mary and Elizabeth as a singer and viol player. He seems to have retired from court after 1567, living in Lingfield, Surrey, until his death in 1590.[54] John Colley, who gave the Queen 'Thyrtene Songe bookes couerid with lether of diuers makings', appears only on the 1559 New Year's gift list and nothing more is known about him. Peter Lupo, who gave Elizabeth five songbooks in 1579, appeared on the gift roll under his anglicized name Peter Wolf. The Lupos, a Venetian musical family, served as court musicians from the 1540s to the 1600s, beginning with Peter's father, Ambrose, and continuing with his son, Thomas.[55]

William Byrd, a gentleman of the Chapel Royal, compiled *My Ladye Nevell's Booke,* a collection of keyboard music, described as the best of his virginal music,[56] written down by John Baldwin, completed in 1591 and presented to the Queen. A note in the manuscript, written in a seventeenth-century hand, relays its history as recalled by a member of the family: 'This Book was presented to Queene Elizabeth by my Lord Edward Abergevenny called the Deafe.'[57] The manuscript, recently acquired by the British Library, does not appear on any extant gift roll, nor does Byrd participate in any extant gift exchange, partly because of his lack of courtier status and partly because of his strong Catholic leanings. Edward Neville does not appear on the extant gift rolls, but his cousin, Henry Neville, son of George, exchanged gifts with Elizabeth from 1559 until his death in 1587. The identity of the Lady Neville has been assigned to several candidates, including Frances Manners, Rachel Lennard, Jane Howard, Anne Killigrew, Elizabeth Gresham, and Elizabeth Bacon. Of this group, the most promising candidate is Elizabeth Bacon, daughter of Sir Nicholas Bacon and second wife of another Henry Neville, Edward's nephew, Henry's first cousin and son of another Edward. Deafness affected at least two Neville men: Edward, Lord Abergavenny, and Sir Henry, son of Henry Neville and Elizabeth Gresham.[58]

Some identifiable manuscripts and books were New Year's gifts for Elizabeth, but are not found on surviving gift rolls. It is probable that the manuscripts given by Anthony Cooke, Thomas Wilson, and Thomas Butler would appear if the rolls for those years had survived. A probable gift from a missing gift roll came from Sir Anthony Cooke,

53 *Elizabeth: The exhibition at the NMM*, ed. S. Doran, p. 134.
54 Lasocki and Ashbee, II, 647.
55 Ibid., II, 748.
56 Davitt Moroney, 'William Byrd', *Grove Music Online,* ed. L. Macy: http://www.grovemusic.com
57 William Byrd, *My Ladye Nevells Booke of Virginal Music*, ed. Hilda Andrews (New York, 1969), p. xvi.
58 J. Harley, *William Byrd: Gentleman of the Chapel Royal* (Aldershot, 1997), pp. 402-7.

the father of the Cooke sisters.[59] Sir Anthony's gift of the translation from Gregory Nazianzen (BL Royal MS 5 E. XVII), dated 1562, would have qualified as an appropriate gift to the Queen given his interest in education as a former tutor to both Prince Edward and Elizabeth. Cooke dedicated his translation to Elizabeth, to whom he sent 'this remembrance of the newe yere not of golde or siluer'. As Master of Requests, 1571, and Principal Secretary, 1577, Thomas Wilson participated regularly in the gift exchanges from 1575 until his death in 1581, but his 1567 gift to Elizabeth of the *New Year Address* in Latin (BL Royal MS 12 A. L) does not appear on an existing roll. Thomas Butler, son of Thomas Earl of Ormond, dedicated his *Rhetorical Exercises* to Elizabeth as a New Year's gift. This manuscript (BL Royal MS A. LI) has been dated possibly 1603, but it does not appear on the 1603 gift exchange roll, and more likely dates from the exchanges of 1601 or 1602, for which the rolls have not survived.

A gift given to the Queen at the New Year's celebration was not, however, necessarily listed on the gift roll for that year. While the gift may have been acceptable, the giver may not have held the proper status to be included on the gift rolls. This status was determined partly by office or rank in the peerage and partly by personal acquaintance with and recognition by the Queen.[60] Mathew Parker, as Archbishop of Canterbury, participated in gift exchanges from the time of his appointment, 1562, until his death in 1575, giving the expected Bishop's gift of £40 in gold in an embroidered purse. But if the ornately decorated bible he gave the Queen, *De antiquitate Britannicae Ecclesiae* (BL c.24.b.8), with its embroidered cover,[61] was a New Year's gift, it is not recorded on any extant roll. Neither the manuscript given by Petrus Perusinus, *De principe* (1561), nor the embroidered book given by Esther Inglis (1599), appear on any extant roll. Thomas Churchyard and George Gascoigne, both professional poets associated with the court, composed and presented manuscript books of poetry to Elizabeth that are also preserved among the Royal manuscripts, but none of their gifts was ever listed on the New Year's rolls, nor did Elizabeth offer them gifts in return.

A clue to where the books were kept after they were received as New Year's gifts is found in Sir Robert Cotton's description of some books 'in the privy closet at Whitthall' (BL Cotton MS Vespasian B. IV). The Privy Closet was a room in the Queen's suite just off the corridor between the Presence Chamber and the Privy Chamber. The Queen's chaplain held private religious services for the sovereign in the Privy Closet. It would be a logical location for keeping books of scripture and devotional literature. The inventory of Henry VIII records items based on their locations in the palace, with books usually in closets. Records of other presents given to the Queen survive in other documents, most familiarly the inventories of the Jewel House (BL Harley MS 1650 and Stowe MS 555) and the wardrobe (Stowe MS 577; Washington, Folger Shakespeare Library, MS V. b. 72; and London, National Archives, LR 2/121). No similar inventory

59 Mildred Cooke, Lady Burghley, married Sir William Cecil, Anne Cooke married Sir Henry Killigrew, Katherine Cooke married Sir Nicholas Bacon, and Elizabeth Cooke married first Sir Thomas Hoby, then John Lord Russell: Sheriden Harvey, *The Cooke Sisters* (unpub. Ph.D. thesis, Indiana University, 1981).

60 May, *Courtier Poets*, p. 18.

61 Klein, pp. 472-4; *The British Library Souvenir Guide* (London, 1998).

of all the books given to Elizabeth has been located, partly because of the multiple persons into whose custody the books were placed.

As Appendix I below shows, the New Year's gifts were distributed to various members of the Queen's Privy Chamber or Household for safe-keeping. The type of gift was one factor in where it went, although the Queen's pleasure assured that some items remained with her. The greater number of books was placed in the care of Grooms and Gentlewomen of the Privy Chamber. The gift rolls record books placed in the custody of Blanche Parry, Lady Katherine Howard, and Mary Radcliffe, as Gentlewomen of the Privy Chamber and Keepers of the Jewels, who were responsible for the bindings with jewels and precious metals. Among the Grooms of the Privy Chamber who received books were Edward Carey, John Baptist Castellion, Ralph Hope, Henry Killegrew, Thomas Knevet, Thomas Lichfield, Henry Seckford, and John Tamworth. Other individuals receiving the charge of books were George Bridgeman, Keeper of Westminster Palace; Sir Charles Howard, Lord Admiral; John Asteley, Master of the Jewel House; John Thornborough of the Chapel; and Sir William Cecil, Principal Secretary. Books were described as sent 'to the Chapel', deposited 'in the Privy Chamber', or 'with the Queen'. Maps were usually delivered to George Bridgeman for keeping in the palace of Westminster. Table 1 shows the distribution of books and other printed matter by decade with number of donors and number of persons to whom they were entrusted.

Table 1

years	*gifts*	*donors*	*custody of*
1557 4 Mary	22 books, 1 map, 3 rolls	15	4
1559 1 Eliz	47 books, 1 map, 2 tables, 2 globes	12	5
1560-1569	24 books, 8 maps, and 2 tables	13	8
1570-1579	27 books, 1 table	10	8
1580-1589	20 books	10	6
1590-1603	15 books, 1 table	4	5

Books and manuscripts form a small but steady component of gifts presented to Queen Elizabeth and other Tudor sovereigns. The New Year's gift rolls provide a unique catalogue of the titles chosen for Elizabeth as New Year's gifts. The rolls also provide information about the givers, the custody of the gifts and the locations of the court at the times the exchanges took place. The subject-matter of these gift manuscripts changed very little throughout the reigns of Elizabeth and other Tudor sovereigns, although the quantity of books given did fluctuate. The subjects were chosen to please the sovereign and usually avoided topics of technical, scientific, and medical material. The books presented to Elizabeth were written and printed in languages readily accessible to a Queen fluent in Latin, Greek, French, and English, with a high percentage of Italian works. Some of the gift books were displayed as treasures of the royal palaces because of their elaborate illuminations or ornamental bindings, as they are displayed today or enjoyed in private collections. The majority of the givers of books tended to be poets, printers, artisans, and booksellers, all from the 'Gentlemen' category of the gift roll protocol. The Elizabethan Court placed value on the written and printed materials, considering them gifts as precious as gold, silver, and jewels and appropriate gifts to a sovereign. Each gift of a book for Elizabeth was chosen with the goal expressed by John Brydges in his letter to Elizabeth accompanying his New Year's gift in 1581: 'Among all the riche and freshe newyeres giftes presented unto your Maiestie at this tyme the richest I can offer in my opinion and habilitie; and I hope also in your Maiesties iudgement and acceptacion, is this book' (BL Royal MS 1 A. XII, fol. 2) (see PLATE 5).

APPENDIX I. BOOKS GIVEN TO ELIZABETH

(transcribed from the surviving Gift Rolls)

Scripture and Devotional Literature

By the Duches of Suffolk oone booke couerid with purple vellat garnisshid and clasped with Siluer and guilt of Ecclesiastes. The book with the Quene. 1559

By Rayne Wolfe Prenter one bible couerid with Crymsen vellat. Deliuered to the said Mrs Blaunche. 1559

By Whitchurche thre bokes one of the commen preier couerid with Crimsen vellat another of the Homilyes couered with Lether the thirde of a letter couerid with Lether. Delyvered to the said Mrs Blaunche Appare. 1559

By Edwarde Atkensone yeoman purvier of wine Twentie and foure Engleshe bookes of Sondrey writers vpon the Scripture. Deliuered to the said Mrs Blaunche. 1559

By Syr William Cicell Secretary a large Booke of Prayers and many other things in it couerid with siluer enamuled with the Quenes and her Maties Mothers Armes on both sides of golde garnesshed and clasped with golde sett with Garnettes and Turquisses. With her Matie. 1563

By Mrs Winkefilde a Booke of the Psalter in latten couerid with nedleworke of golde Siluer and blewe silke. With her Matie. 1563

By the Busshop of Rochester Amner ... a Booke of thexposition of the newe Testament in latten. Deluyered to Blaunche Apparrey. 1564

By Petruchio baldini an Italion a booke of the seven Psalmes in latten coverid with blewe Satten. Delivered to the said Blaunche. 1565

By Absolon Master of the Savoy a Bible covered with cloth of golde garnesshed with Siluer & gilte & ij plates with the queenes armes. Delivered to John of the Closet. 1578

By Absolyn Clerc of the closet a boke covered with cloth of Tyssue garnesshed with Siluer and guilte. With her Majestie by Mr Sackford. 1579

By Absolon Clerk of the closet the Byble in iiij Tomes being in latten couerid in crymson vellat. Delivered to Mr Knevett. 1581

By Brydges Deane of Salisbury a Testament in Ingelissh of old wrytten hand couered with purple vellate and gar and clapsed with golde. Delivered to Mr Knevett. 1581

By Christofer Barker the Quenes prynter a Byble in Inglishe couered with Crymson vellate enbradored. Delivered to Mr knevet. 1581

Item paid to Mr Absolon servunt - vj s viij d. 1582

Item, a litle boke of golde enamuled, garnished and furnished with smale diamondes and rubyes, bothe claspes, and all hanging at a chayne of golde, viz. six peces of golde enamuled, two of them garnished with raged staves of smale sparcks of diamondes, and four of them in eche, two smale diamonds and two smale sparcks of rubyes, 16 lesser peeces of golde, in every of them a smale diamonde, and also 24 peeces of golde, in every of them four perles with a ring of golde to hang it by. All geven by therle of Leycetor, Master of the Horse. 1582

By Absalon a booke entytuled explicacio orationis dominie couered with blacke vellatt enbradered with venys golde. Delivered to Mrs Blanche Parry. 1584

By Christofer Barker prynter a large Byble in englysshe couered with crymson vellat alouer enbradered wythe venys golde and seade perle. Delivered to Mrs Blanche. 1584

By Master Absolon Clerke of the Clossett A boke of Cristian exersyes covered with Crymsonn vellatt embraudered with venis golde and Sylver. Deliuered Mrs Blanch Parry. 1585

Item, a booke, wherein are divers Psalmes in Lattine written, the bourds greate, inclosed all over on the outeside with golde enamuled cut-worke, with divers colours, and one litle claspe. Geven by the Lorde Lomley. 1587

By John Thorneborowe Clerke of the Closset a small Booke covered with Carnation vellat being Intituled Speculum virtutis. 1588

By Mr Bushop a Stationer one faire Bible in latine of the Vulgare Translation. Delivered to Mr Knevett ut supra. 1597

By Mr Barker her Maties Prynter one bible of a large volume faier bounde. Delivered into the privie chamber. 1603

Classics and Instruction

By Mr Belmaine late schole Mr to King Edward a booke finly printed De la Vie de la Morte coverid with Crimsen Satten allouer enbrauderid with golde. Delyvered to the said Mrs Blaunche Apparye. 1559

By Cawodde printer Josephus in Greeke. Delivered to Mrs Blanche Apparry. 1559

By Jugge printer oone Mappe Ptholomeis Tables in Italion. The mappe delyvered to the said George Brideman. 1559

By Thomas Phaire a booke written of Aeneados in Englesh verses. With the Quene. 1559

By Sir John Mason Threasourer of the Chamber a smale Collog of serpentyne garnesshid with siluer guilt And two Bookes. Dylivered to the said John Astley. 1562

By Syr John Mason Threasourer of the Chamber ... two Bookes of St Augustynes worke. Delivered to Mrs Blaunche Parry. 1563

By Sir John Mason Threasourer of the Chamber ... a Booke in Greek. Delivered to the saide Blaunch Apparry. 1564

By Petrus Vbaldinus florentinus a Booke conteigninge the seremonyes of the Coronation of Themperors. Delivered to the said Blaunche Apparrye. 1564

By Petricio Ubaldino a peire of writing Tables the claspes and corners garnesshid with siluer. Deliverid to the said Blaunch Pary. 1568

By Anthony Marye a booke in Italian called *Caualarie della citta de ferrara* coverid with parchement paynted & gilt. Deliverid to the said Blaunch Pary. 1568

By James Bellott a Booke conteignyge certeyne wordes and rules of the Frenche Tonge. Deliverid to the said John Tamworth. 1568

By Petricio Ubaldino a table painted with a picture of a woman and certayne verses. 1571

Item, a booke of golde enamuled and glased over with two claspes. 5 oz. qa. dim. Geven by Sir Owen Hopton, Knight. Given to the charge of Katherine Howard. 1572

By Doctor Iulyo Six bookes of Italian prynted. 1575

By Sir Henry Lee a boke of golde enamelled full of leaves of paper and parchment garnished with silver poz together – viij oz. Delyvered to the saide Lady Hawarde. 1576

By Petrucho Ubaldino A booke of Italian written of viij Englishe ladies. Delivered to Mr Baptest. 1576

By Petricio a book wrytten in Italian fayre. Deliverd to Mr Bapteste. 1577

By Mr Alfonsus an Italian booke wrytten. With Kylligrew. 1577

By Petricho a boke of Italian with pictures of the lyfe & metomerpheses of Oved. Delivered to Mr Baptest. 1579

By Petrucio Vbaldino an Italian Booke of a phisition towching mans Complextion and phisike. Delivered to Mr Bapteste. 1581

Item, a booke of golde enamuled garnished with eight amatestes. Geven by Mr Packington. 1582

By Petuchio Vbaldino a Booke couered with vellam. Delivered to the Mrs Blanch Parry. 1584

By Petruchio Vbaldino a Pettygrye. Delivered to Mrs Blanch Parry. 1585

By Mr Petruchio two Bookes of Italian. Delivered to Mr Babtest. 1588

By Petruchio Vbaldino a book Covered with vellam of Italian. Delivered to Mr Baptiste. 1589

By Mr Petruchio Vbaldino one Booke of Italian Couered with vellam of the forentine melet[ing?] (text illegible). Delivered to Mr Knevett. 1597

By Mr Peter Vbaldino one Booke of Italian couered with vellam. 1598

By Mr Bushop a Stationer one booke of Eclesiasticall histories in Frenche. Delivered to the Chappell. 1598

By Mr Byshop A Stacyoner twoe Bookes of Plynnies workes in Frenche. Delivered to Mr Knevett. 1599

By Mr Petruchio Vbaldyno A Table with a picture and a Booke in Italian. Delivered to Mr Knevett. 1599

By Mr Byshop a statyoner two bookes of Titus Lyvius in Frenche. Delivered to Mr Thomas Knevett. 1600

Heraldry and Armoury

By Mr Belmaine late schole Mr to King Edward a booke finly printed De la Vie de la Morte coverid with Crimsen Satten allouer enbrauderid with golde. Delyvered to the said Mrs Blaunche Apparye. 1559

By Cawodde printer Josephus in Greeke. Delivered to Mrs Blanche Apparry. 1559

By Jugge printer oone Mappe Ptholomeis Tables in Italion. The mappe delyvered to the said George Brideman. 1559

By Thomas Phaire a booke written of Aeneados in Englesh verses. With the Quene. 1559

By Sir John Mason Threasourer of the Chamber a smale Collog of serpentyne garnesshid with siluer guilt And two Bookes. Dylivered to the said John Astley. 1562

By Syr John Mason Threasourer of the Chamber ... two Bookes of St Augustynes worke. Delivered to Mrs Blaunche Parry. 1563

By Sir John Mason Threasourer of the Chamber ... a Booke in Greek. Delivered to the saide Blaunch Apparry. 1564

By Petrus Vbaldinus florentinus a Booke conteigninge the seremonyes of the Coronation of Themperors. Delivered to the said Blaunche Apparrye. 1564

By Petricio Ubaldino a peire of writing Tables the claspes and corners garnesshid with siluer. Deliverid to the said Blaunch Pary. 1568

By Anthony Marye a booke in Italian called *Caualarie della citta de ferrara* coverid with parchement paynted & gilt. Deliverid to the said Blaunch Pary. 1568

By James Bellott a Booke conteignyge certeyne wordes and rules of the Frenche Tonge. Deliverid to the said John Tamworth. 1568

By Petricio Ubaldino a table painted with a picture of a woman and certayne verses. 1571

Item, a booke of golde enamuled and glased over with two claspes. 5 oz. qa. dim. Geven by Sir Owen Hopton, Knight. Given to the charge of Katherine Howard. 1572

By Doctor Iulyo Six bookes of Italian prynted. 1575
By Sir Henry Lee a boke of golde enamelled full of leaves of paper and parchment garnished with silver poz together – viij oz. Delyvered to the saide Lady Hawarde. 1576
By Petrucho Ubaldino A booke of Italian written of viij Englishe ladies. Delivered to Mr Baptest. 1576
By Petricio a book wrytten in Italian fayre. Deliverd to Mr Bapteste. 1577
By Mr Alfonsus an Italian booke wrytten. With Kylligrew. 1577
By Petricho a boke of Italian with pictures of the lyfe & metomerpheses of Oved. Delivered to Mr Baptest. 1579
By Petrucio Vbaldino an Italian Booke of a phisition towching mans Complextion and phisike. Delivered to Mr Bapteste. 1581
Item, a booke of golde enamuled garnished with eight amatestes. Geven by Mr Packington. 1582
By Petuchio Vbaldino a Booke couered with vellam. Delivered to the Mrs Blanch Parry. 1584
By Petruchio Vbaldino a Pettygrye. Delivered to Mrs Blanch Parry. 1585
By Mr Petruchio two Bookes of Italian. Delivered to Mr Babtest. 1588
By Petruchio Vbaldino a book Covered with vellam of Italian. Delivered to Mr Baptiste. 1589
By Mr Petruchio Vbaldino one Booke of Italian Couered with vellam of the forentine melet[ing?] (text illegible). Delivered to Mr Knevett. 1597
By Mr Peter Vbaldino one Booke of Italian couered with vellam. 1598
By Mr Bushop a Stationer one booke of Eclesiasticall histories in Frenche. Delivered to the Chappell. 1598
By Mr Byshop A Stacyoner twoe Bookes of Plynnies workes in Frenche. Delivered to Mr Knevett. 1599
By Mr Petruchio Vbaldyno A Table with a picture and a Booke in Italian. Delivered to Mr Knevett. 1599
By Mr Byshop a statyoner two bookes of Titus Lyvius in Frenche. Delivered to Mr Thomas Knevett. 1600

Poetry, Music and Other

By John Younge a book of certeigne Deuises for the Avauncement of the state of a Realme couerid with blake vellat edged with siluer passamayne. With the Quene. 1559
By Armygell Wade one Table of Ebonet wherin is a loking glasse and Certeine Verses. Delyvered to the said George Bredeman. 1559
By William Bayarde a Table painted of a king with certeigne Scriptures belonging to the same. Deliuered to the said George Brideman. 1559
By Thomas Kentt a Songe booke. Delyvered to Mr Lichefelde. 1559
By John Cavely Thyrtene Songe bookes couerid with lether of diuers makings. Delyvered to the said Mrs Blaunche Apparey. 1559
By George Comy musitian two rounde Globes of Asia and Europa. With the Quene by Baptest. 1559
By Mr John Younge a Table paynted in a frame of walnuttre, and certeyne verses about it of money, And a round piece of siluer. The table delyvered in charge to George Bredeman keper of the pallace at Westminster the piece of siluer with the Quene. 1562
By John Younge A feire Table paynted of a Story of Poetry. In the pryvy chamber. 1563
By Jaques Greuen a litell Booke written in Frenche coverid with parchement. Deliverid to the said Blaunch Pary. 1568
By Henry Gyrtens an Englisshe boke in verse beinge a Story translated. Delivered to Rauf Hoope. 1577
By Peter Wolfe v songe books. With her Majestie by Mr Knevet. 1579
By Anthonias Phenotus a smale booke in Italian meter. Delivered to Mr Baptest. 1579

By Ogerius Bellehachius a Booke of latten verses couered with vellam. Delivered to Mrs Blanch Parry. 1584

By Syppio gentilis a booke of latten verses couered with crymsen vellatt. Delivered to Mrs Blanch Parry. 1584

New Year's Gifts from Other Sources

By Sir Anthony Cooke, 'Gregorii Nazianzeni in Theophania siue de Natali Seruatoris oratio' 1561. BL Royal MS 5 E. XVII

By Sir Thomas Wilson, New Year Address, 1567. BL Royal MS 12 A. L

By Sir Gilbert Dethyck, (a book of arms of the Knights of the Garter made in the reign of) Henry the fourth. 1569

By Sir Gilbert Dethyck, (a book of arms of the Knights of the Garter made in the reign of) Henry the fifth. 1570

By Sir Gilbert Dethyck, (a book of arms of the Knights of the Garter made in the reign of) king Henry the sixth. 1572

By Robert Cooke, Armourial bearings of the kings and noble familes of Great Britain from the reign of William the Conqueror to that of James I. 1572

By Sir Gilbert Dethick king at armes, a book of all the Knightes of the most garter made in the shorte raigne of Richarde III. 1573

By Sir Gilbert Dethyck, a book of arms of the ...made in the reign of Henry II and Richard I. 1580

By Mr William Dethick, (a book of) Arms of the Knights of the Garter in the time of Henry VII. 1593

By Petruccio Ubaldini, Memoriale di Petruccio Ubaldini, fiorentino, alla serenissima Elisabetta felicissima regina d'Inghilterra, 1594. BL Lansdowne MS 98, No. 22

By Mr William Dethick, The Progenie of the Monarchs of the Englishmen, conteyning the Titles & Reynes of them. 1595

By Thomas Butler, Rhetorical Exercises, in *Latin*, on the judgement of Solomon ca.1603. BL Royal MS 12 A. LI

APPENDIX II. INDIVIDUALS WHO PRESENTED BOOKS TO ELIZABETH AS NEW YEAR'S GIFTS

giver	*books/MS/other*	*participation years*	*subject*
Absolon, William	6 books	1578, 1579, 1581, 1582, 1584, 1585	Scripture/DevLiterature
Alberti, Anthony Maria	1 MS	1568	Classics/Instruction
Atkinson, Edward	24 books	1559	Scripture/DevLiterature
Barker, Christopher	2 books	1581, 1584	Scripture/DevLiterature
Barker, Robert	1 book	1603	Scripture/DevLiterature
Bayard, William	1 table	1559	Poetry/Music
Bellehachius, Ogerius	1 book	1584	Poetry/Music
Bellot, Jacques	1 MS	1568	Classics/Instruction
Belmaine, Jean	1 book	1559	Classics/Instruction
Bishop, George	6 books	1597, 1598, 1599, 1600	Scripture/DevLiterature, Classics/Instruction

APPENDIX II – *continued*

giver	*books/MS/other*	*participation years*	*subject*
Borgarucci, Guilio	6 books	1575	Classics/Instruction
Brandon, Frances, Duchess of Suffolk, alias Grey	1 book	1559	Scripture/DevLiterature
Brydges, John	1 ms	1581	Scripture/DevLiterature
Butler, Thomas	1 ms	1603?	Classics/Instruction
Cave, Sir Ambrose	8 maps	1563	Heraldry
Cawood, John	1 book	1559	Classics/Instruction
Cecil, Elizabeth, alias Wingfield	1 book	1563	Scripture/DevLiterature
Cecil, William, Lord Burleigh	1 book	1563	Scripture/DevLiterature
Clerk of the Closet		see Absolon	
Colley, John	13 books	1559	Poetry/Music
Comy, George	2 globes	1559	Poetry/Music
Cooke, Anthony	1 ms	1561	Classics/Instruction
Cooke, Robert	3 mss	1563, 1565, 1567	Heraldry
Dethick, Sir Gilbert	19 mss	1562, 1563, 1564, 1565, 1567, 1568, 1569, 1571, 1572, 1573, 1574, 1575, 1576, 1577, 1578, 1579, 1580, 1581, 1584	Heraldry
Dethick, William	8 mss	1585, 1588, 1589, 1593, 1597, 1598, 1599, 1600, 1603	Heraldry
Dudley, Robert, Earl of Leicester	1 book	1582	Scripture/DevLiterature
Ferrabosco, Alphonso	1 ms	1577	Classics/Instruction
Finet, Anthony	1 book	1579	Poetry/Music
Garter King at Arms		see Dethick, William & Gilbert	
Gentili, Scipione	1 book	1584	Poetry/Music
Gheast, Edmund, alias Bp of Rochester	1 book	1564	Scripture/DevLiterature
Gittens, Henry	1 ms	1577	Poetry/Music
Grévin, Jacques	1 ms	1568	Poetry/Music
Grey, Frances		see Brandon	

APPENDIX II – *continued*

giver	*books/MS/other*	*participation years*	*subject*
Hopton, Sir Owen	1 book	1572	Classics/Instruction
Howard, Sir George	1 ms	1562	Heraldry
Jugge, Richard	1 map	1559	Classics/Instruction
Julio, Doctor		see Borgarucci	
Kent, Thomas	1 book	1559	Poetry/Music
Lee, Sir Henry	1 book	1576	Classics/Instruction
Leicester, Earl of		see Dudley, Robert	
Lumley, John, Lord	1 book	1587	Scripture/DevLiterature
Lupo, Peter	5 books	1579	Poetry/Music
Mary, Anthony		see Alberti	
Mason, Sir John	3 books	1562, 1563, 1564	Classics/Instruction
Master of the Horse		see Dudley, Robert	
Monge, William	1 book	1563	Heraldry
Pakington, Sir John	1 book	1582	Classics/Instruction
Phaer, Thomas	1 book	1559	Classics/Instruction
Rochester, Bishop of		see Gheast	
Suffolk, Duchess of		see Brandon	
Thornborough, John	1 ms	1588	Scripture/DevLiterature
Ubaldini, Petruchio	16 mss, 2 tables	1564, 1565, 1571, 1576, 1577, 1579, 1581, 1584, 1585, 1588, 1589, 1592, 1597, 1598, 1599	Classics/Instruction (Scripture/DevLiterature), (Poetry/Music)
Waad, Armigal	1 ms	1559	Poetry/Music
Whitchurch, Edward	2 books, 1 ms	1559	Scripture/DevLiterature
Wilson, Thomas	1 ms	1567	Classics/Instruction
Wingfield, Mrs		see Cecil, Elizabeth	
Wolfe, Peter		see Lupo, Peter	
Wolfe, Reginald	1 book	1559	Scripture/DevLiterature
York Herald		see Dethick, William	
Young, John	1 book, 2 tables	1559, 1562, 1563	Poetry/Music

APPENDIX III. BOOKS GIVEN TO QUEEN MARY, NEW YEAR 1557

Scripture and Devotional Literature

By Doctor Mallet Amner a faire Salter couerid with purple vellat and garnisshed with siluer and guilt. Delyverid to the said Rycardes.

By the Busshop of Chichester elect Christopherson a booke written couerid with crymsen vellat. With the Quenis matie.

By Sir John Alee a prymer couerid with purple vellat and garnisshed with Damaskynwork. Delyvered in chardge to Edmund Sheffelde keper of the howse at Grenewich.

By Knight a booke of prayers couerid with crymsen vellat and garnisshed with siluer and guilt. With the Quene her matie.

By Egidius Beraldus a booke of the passion written. With the Quene her matie.

Classics and Instruction

By Sir John Mason a mappe of Englande stayned vpon cloth of siluer in a frame of wodde having a Drawing couer painted with the kinges and Quenis Armes / And a booke of Spanish couerid with blake vellat. With the Quenis matie.

By Mr Walter Earle a booke couerid with blake vellat [of the] of the comentary of warr in Englishe. With the Quene.

By Cawodde Printer a Booke in laten entitelid vita christi de ludolphus carthagienses and a litell booke of an exhortacion to yonge men. The exhortacon with the Quene. Thother booke delyvered to the said shefilde.

By Reyne Wolf a booke called Georgius Agricola de re metellaca. Delyvered to the said Shefilde.

Poetry and Music

By Myles Huggard a booke written. With the Quene her matie.

By Mr Babington a boke in french couerid with grene vellat wrytten howe a king shulde chose his Counsaile. With the Quene her matie.

By The Secretary to the frenche Ambassador four frenche bookes bounde in parchement and two bookes couerid with red lether in french. Delyverid to the said Edwarde Sheffilde.

By Sabastian Scolemaster of Powles a booke of Dities written. With the Quenes matie.

By Sheparde of the Chapell thre Rolles of Songes. Delyvered into the Chapell.

By Richarde Edwardes of the Chapell certeigne verses.

APPENDIX IV. THE EXTANT NEW YEAR'S GIFT ROLLS

year	*regnal*	*location*	*manuscript shelf mark*
1557	4 Mary	British Library	Add. MS 62525 (MS RP 294, vol.2)
1559	1 Eliz	John Rylands Library, Manchester	MS Eng 117
1562	4 Eliz	British Library	Harleian Roll V.18
1563	5 Eliz	National Archives	C 47/3/38
1564	6 Eliz	Folger Shakespeare Library	MS Z. d. 12
1565	7 Eliz	Folger Shakespeare Library	MS Z. d. 13
1567	9 Eliz	British Library	Add. MS 9772
1568	10 Eliz	Society of Antiquaries, London	MS 538
1571	13 Eliz	Duke of Buccleuch & Queensbury	private collection
1575	17 Eliz	Folger Shakespeare Library	MS Z. d. 14
1576	18 Eliz	British Library	Add. MS 4827
1577	19 Eliz	National Archives	C 47/3/39
1578	20 Eliz	Society of Antiquaries	MS 537
1579	21 Eliz	Folger Shakespeare Library	MS Z. d. 15
1581	23 Eliz	Eton College	MS 192
1582	24 Eliz	British Library	Harley MS 1644
1584	26 Eliz	British Library	Egerton MS 3052
1585	27 Eliz	Folger Shakespeare Library	MS Z. d. 16
1588	30 Eliz	British Library	Add. MS 8159
1589	31 Eliz	British Library	Lansdowne Roll 17
1597	39 Eliz	Pierpont Morgan Library, New York	MA 3199 (BL MS Facs 672, vol.1)
1598	40 Eliz	National Archives	C 47/3/40
1599	41 Eliz	Folger Shakespeare Library	MS Z. d. 17
1600	42 Eliz	Musée Fondation Martin Bodmer, Geneva	(BL, MS RP 294, vol.1)
1603	45 Eliz	National Archives	C 47/3/41

Appendix V.1. Manuscripts Identified as Gifts, Listed by Year of Appearance on Gift Roll

year	*location*	*manuscript shelf mark*	*donor*
1545	Bodleian Library	MS Cherry 36	*Elizabeth*
1545	British Library	Royal MS 7 D. X	*Elizabeth*
1546	National Archives of Scotland	MS RH 13/78	*Elizabeth*
1547	Bodleian Library	MS Bodl. 1/6	*Elizabeth*
1557	Huntington Library	HM 121	*Huggard*
1557	British Library	Harley MS 3444	*Huggard*
1557	British Library	Stowe MS 955	*Babington*
1559	British Library	Royal MS 2 D. III	*Brandon*
1559	Bodleian Library	MS Laud 683	*Young*
1561	British Library	Royal MS 5 E. XVII	*Cooke*
1562	Tower of London, on loan from Earl of Dartmouth	shelfmark unknown	*Howard*
1562	British Library	Royal MS 18 D. III	*Cave*
1563	British Library	Stowe MS 684	*Dethick*
1563	British Library	Harley MS 810	*Cooke*
1564	British Library	Royal MS 14 A. VIII	*Ubaldini*
1565	Yale, Beinecke Library	MS 97	*Dethick*
1565	Harvard, Houghton Library	MS Typ 75	*Ubaldini*
1567	British Library	Royal MS 12 A. I	*Wilson*
1567	British Library	King's MS 396	*Cooke*
1571	British Library	Royal MS 14 A. I	*Ubaldini*
1573	Yale, Lewis Walpole Library	Hazen MS 2551	*Dethick*
1575	Royal Library	MS RCIN 1047442	*Dethick*
1576	Royal Library	MS RCIN 1047443	*Dethick*
1577	British Library	Royal MS 14 A. XIX	*Ubaldini*
1579	British Library	Stowe MS 30	*Ubaldini*
1581	British Library	Royal MS 1 A. XII	*Brydges*
1584	British Library	Sloane MS 536	*Ubaldini*
1584	Bodleian Library	Douce Bibl Eng 1583 b.1	*Barker*
1587	British Library	Royal MS 1 E. III	*Lumley*
1588	British Library	Royal MSS 14 A. X-XI	*Ubaldini*
1589	British Library	Harley MS 1864	*Dethick*
1593	Harvard, Houghton Library	MS Typ 96	*Dethick*
1594	British Library	Lansdowne MS 98, Nos. 22, 45	*Ubaldini*
1595	British Library	Harley MS 1416	*Dethick*
1603	British Library	Royal MS 12 A. LI	Butler

APPENDIX V.2. STC BOOKS IDENTIFIED AS GIFTS, LISTED BY YEAR OF APPEARANCE ON GIFT ROLL

year	*STC number*	*author : title*
1557	987	*Avila* : The comentaries of don Lewes de Auela
1557	3006, 3006.5	*Bible. Selections* : Psalmes or prayers
1557	5207	*Christopherson* : An exhortation to all menne to take hede
1557	16060	*Liturgies. Latin Rite* : An uniform and catholike prymer
1557	16938	*Lupset* : An Exhortation to yonge men
1559	2093	*Bible. English* : The bible and holy scriptures
1559	2678	*Bible. OT.* : The whole book of psalmes
1559	13648.5	*Homilies:* Certain sermons or homilies
1559	16292	*Liturgies. Church of England* : Boke of common praier
1559	20480-20481.3	*Ptolemy* : The compost of Ptholomeus
1559	24800	*Virgilius Maro* : The nyne fyrste bookes of Eneados ... Phaer
1563	921	*Augustine* : Two bokes of the noble doctor
1563	2384.5	*Bible. OT.* : The whole book of psalmes
1563	15388	*Legh* : The accidens of armory
1568	1852	*Bellot* : French grammar
1578	2121, 2123	*Bible. English* : The holy byble
1581	2056, 2057	*Bible. Latin* : Testamenti vetera biblia sacra
1581	24486	*Ubaldini* : La vita di Carlo Magno imperadore
1584	1846	*Bellehachius* : Ogerii Bellehachii Sacrosancta
1584	17158	*Macchiavelli* : Lasino do di Nicolo Macchiauelli
1584	23700-23702	*Tasso* : Torquati Tassi Solymeidos
1588	24480	*Ubaldini* : Descrittione del regno di Scotia
1589	24481	*Ubaldini* : A discourse concerning the Spanishe fleete
1595	24484	*Ubaldini* : Scelta di attioni
1597	24483	*Ubaldini* : Rime
1598	24482	*Ubaldini* : Militia del gran duca di Toscana
1599	2190	*Bible. English* : The bible
1599	24487.5	*Ubaldini* : Le vite della donne illustri

ELIZABETH'S EXECUTION WARRANTS

PETER BEAL

IN SHAKESPEARE'S *Measure for Measure* (IV, ii) the Provost tells the imprisoned Claudio 'Look, here's the warrant, Claudio, for thy death', and in the very next scene the executioner tells the condemned Barnardino 'Truly, sir, I would desire you to clap into your prayers; for, look you, the warrant's come.' Not that it is particularly unusual in Elizabethan or early Stuart drama to find references to executions and to the documents authorising them. In Massinger's *The Roman Actor* of 1626, for instance, we have an antithesis drawn between, on the one hand, the good emperor Titus Vespasian, who is referred to as having 'A readie teare when he was forc'd to signe / The death of an offender', and, on the other hand, his son, the sadistic emperor Domitian, who carries about him what is referred to as a 'fatall booke' or 'bloudie scrole' with the names of those marked for execution.[1] Being a tyrant, who is effectively *outside* the law, Domitian (unlike his father) has no need of signed warrants – his command alone is sufficient to condemn those named in his 'booke'. Both Domitian's 'booke' and the 'warrants' for Claudio and Barnardino do, as it happens, appear as stage props – as a 'Table booke' and documents of some kind: pieces of paper or parchment flourished on the stage. Their exact form would hardly have mattered in the theatre. *Any* representation of a death warrant would have served as a potent dramatic symbol. Few spectators are likely to have known what a real execution warrant looked like in any case.

By contrast, I propose to discuss briefly three actual examples: warrants for arguably the three most important executions authorised by Queen Elizabeth. Each is historically a milestone in its own way. Each is shrouded in a context far more dramatic than anything I can begin to delineate here. Each represented an agonising decision by the Queen; and each was revoked or delayed before being finally put into effect. My general question is this. What significance do the form and wording of these warrants have in relation to the historical events?

My first example (PLATE 1) is the surviving warrant for the execution in 1572 of Thomas Howard, Duke of Norfolk (see Appendix I for full text). Norfolk was

A version of this paper was delivered at the 31st Annual Meeting of the Shakespeare Association of America, in Victoria, BC, Canada, on 12 April 2003.

1 Quotations from *The Roman Actor* are I.i.87-89, V.i.99, and V.i.160: see *The Plays and Poems of Philip Massinger*, ed. Philip Edwards and Colin Gibson (Oxford, 1976), III, pp. 24, 83, and 85.

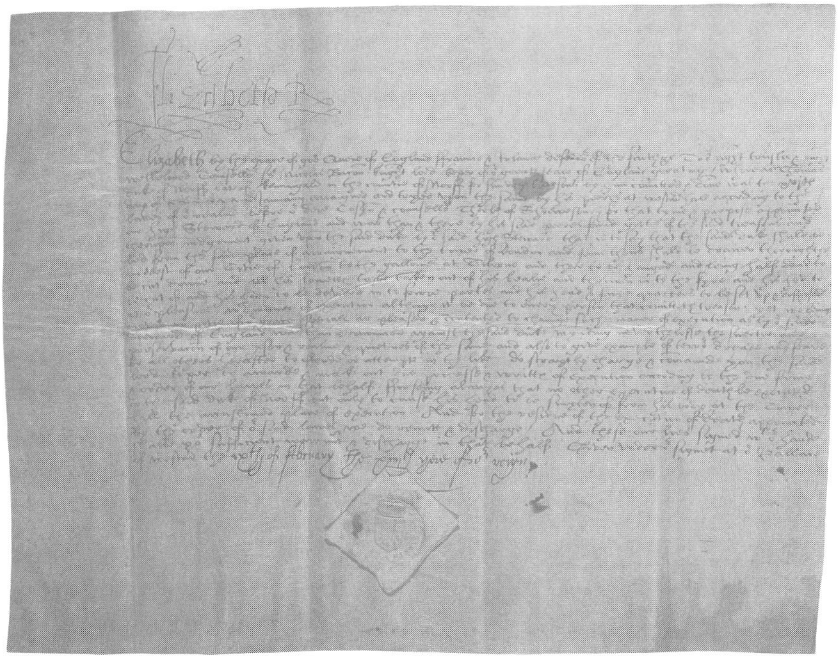

1 Execution warrant of Thomas Howard, fourth Duke of Norfolk, signed by Queen Elizabeth, 9 February 1571/2 (Library of the Duke of Norfolk, Arundel Castle, G.1/22)

arraigned and convicted of treasonous intrigue with Mary, Queen of Scots, on 16 January 1571/2. The execution was initially set for five days later, but deferred by the Queen. Elizabeth then signed a formal warrant for his execution on February 9th, a Saturday, and the execution was set for the following Monday morning. On the Sunday night, at about eleven o'clock, even though all the preparations had been made, she changed her mind and cancelled it. During the next two months, while Howard languished in the Tower not sure whether he would live from one week to the next, several further dates were set and again cancelled. She issued another order for execution on February 27th only to revoke it the next morning two hours before daybreak. Yet another was apparently issued and revoked, before a further one was drawn up, dated April 9th. The draft for this in Lord Burghley's hand survives at Hatfield House (see Appendix II). Characteristically Elizabeth changed her mind yet again. She wrote a hastily penned letter to Burghley deferring the execution – saying 'the causes that move me to this ar not now to be expressed lest an irreuocable dede be in mene while com*m*itted'. An eloquent testimony to the confused state of Elizabeth's mind, this lettter, now in the Bodleian Library (see Appendix III), is endorsed by Burghley as having been received at 2 o'clock in the morning of April 11th. Finally, in May, after repeated pleas by Burghley and her Parliament, the Queen gave way, and the long-suffering Norfolk was led out and executed at Tower Hill (instead of the common public scaffold at Tyburn) on the morning of Monday 2 June 1572.[2] Even then, according to William Davison later, 'the imputation of [Norfolk's] death she laied heavily vpon my l*ord* Tre*asure*r [Burghley] for dyvers yeares together'.[3] The precedent of a nominal scapegoat was already established.

What makes this execution so special – and the reason the Queen was so fearful about it – is that Norfolk was by far the most eminent nobleman in the realm, as well as being well respected by the people at large. He was at that time the *only* Duke in England – the highest rank of the nobility – and indeed he was the very first nobleman of any rank to be executed in her reign.

We may see in PLATE I the formal extant warrant signed by Elizabeth on 9 February 1571/2, now preserved at Arundel Castle. The physical document itself is a single oblong-shaped membrane of parchment, or vellum, 11 inches deep and 14 inches wide. The text is entered in a scribal hand, in a professional secretary script, as a single block of writing ranged to the right, and was evidently written some days before it was signed, for another secretary hand has added the date on the last line. The warrant is invested with royal authority by virtue of the royal papered (or wafer) seal affixed to the lower border and, of course, by the Queen's unmistakable flourished signature – or sign manual – occupying more than two-and-a-half inches of the upper border. It has the look, to all appearances, of any routine royal warrant. Unlike certain kinds of elaborate Royal Letters Patent, there is no sense of conspicuous display embodied in this document: no physical or 'patent' (open) manifestation of any special status or significance. Given the extraordinary nature of its function, the document is conspicuous only by looking so ordinary.

The text itself conforms to a traditional formula. The Queen – whose titles are briefly recited – addresses the warrant to her Lord Keeper of the Great Seal (here Sir Nicholas Bacon). There follows a brief recital of the arraignment and conviction of the guilty party – the Duke of Norfolk's conviction on January 16th last for 'sundry treasons' – and the sentence itself (here expounded in gruesome detail): that the traitor should be hanged, drawn, and quartered at Tyburn. Then the Queen steps in, as it were, to moderate the sentence. Although the extreme penalty is a fitting sentence 'due to every person that committeth treason' in order to 'give example of terror dread and fear' to others, she gives order that Norfolk should only have his head cut off, the rest of the sentence being remitted. As per normal, the Lord Keeper is also ordered to 'make out due processe & writtes of execution' himself to carry out the execution. This warrant is, as it were, the first step in the process – the first link in a paper- (or

2 For the history of Norfolk's post-trial imprisonment and eventual execution, see the Calendar of State Papers for 1571-2; Neville Williams, *Thomas Howard Fourth Duke of Norfolk* (London, 1964), last chapter; and Francis Edwards, S. J., *The Marvellous Chance: Thomas Howard, Fourth Duke of Norfolk, and the Ridolphi Plot, 1570-1572* (London, 1968), chapter 6.

3 William Davison's 'true relation of that which passed betwixt her majestie and me in the cause of the late Scottish Queene', dated 20 February 1586/7: London, British Library, Harley MS 290, fols 222r-3r (fol. 222v quoted). Edited versions of this relation are printed in Nicholas Harris Nicolas, *Life of William Davison, Secretary of State* (London, 1823), Appendix B, pp. 256-69 (p. 264), and in *Calendar of the State Papers relating to Scotland and Mary, Queen of Scots, 1547-1603*, ed. William K. Boyd, IX (1915), 296-300 (p. 298).

parchment-)chain of command, as more orders and warrants are drawn up – at least one presumably bearing the Great Seal (which is not attached to this warrant) – for the various people involved in the actual performing of the execution.[4]

So this formula is designed to balance carefully the responsibility for the execution. Judgement on Norfolk is made not by the Queen but by his 'peeres' in a lawful trial; the sentence is pronounced by the judge, the Earl of Shrewsbury, in accordance with the legally prescribed penalty for treason. The verdict and sentence are duly accepted by the Queen, as necessary for the preservation of her person, the safety of the realm, and as an example to other would-be traitors. But she intervenes personally to exert her prerogative, her 'grace especiale', to apply mercy: to remit the harsh, if appropriate, penalty of hanging, drawing, and quartering in favour of beheading alone. No reason for this mercy is given (though in fact it *is* because of Norfolk's rank), and the Lord Keeper is entrusted with all the practical arrangements for the execution. Thus the whole process is a legal one, all in accordance with the due forms of 'our lawes'; it is a communal one, involving a host of government counsellors, peers, and dignitaries, with the Queen herself appearing in a thoroughly positive light as bringer of mercy; and it is all sanctioned by precedent and tradition.

If we skip nearly three decades to our second warrant, that of Robert Devereux, second Earl of Essex, we find this formula – this careful verbal balancing act – more or less still in place.

It is hardly necessary to be reminded of the importance and sheer drama of Essex's relationship with Elizabeth – his ill-judged and ill-fated rebellion against her on 8 February 1600/1 and his arraignment and conviction at Westminster Hall on February 19th. Elizabeth's feelings about her old favourite and the breakdown of their relationship can only be imagined. She signed the warrant for his execution the day after his trial, on February 20th, had characteristic second thoughts about it, but then allowed it to be delivered to the Lord Keeper three days later. On the 24th, the Privy Council (Robert Cecil, Thomas Egerton, and others) sent to the Constable of the Tower, Thomas Howard, their instructions for the arrangements for the execution the next day ('Her M*ajesty* having now sent you the writs of execution of the late E*arl* of Ess*ex*').[5] On February 25th (Ash Wednesday, the first day of Lent, day of Atonement), it was put into effect and the thoroughly penitent Essex was executed within the precincts of the Tower.

The physical form of the document (PLATE 2) is not all that different from the Norfolk warrant twenty-nine years earlier. It is on a membrane of vellum 13¼ inches deep by 16¾ inches wide; written in a professional secretary script as a single block of text, and with a similar royal papered seal attached to the lower border. The flourished signature of Elizabeth herself in the upper border has grown over the years even bolder and more elaborate – it now stretches to nearly 5 and a half inches. However, the scribe

4 That a properly engrossed warrant was drawn up, in Latin, for the application by the Lord Keeper of the Great Seal is suggested by the text of this warrant in Latin later copied by Sir Stephen Powle: see Appendix I.

5 National Archives, SP 12/278/111; Calendar of State Papers Domestic 1598-1601 (1869), p. 591.

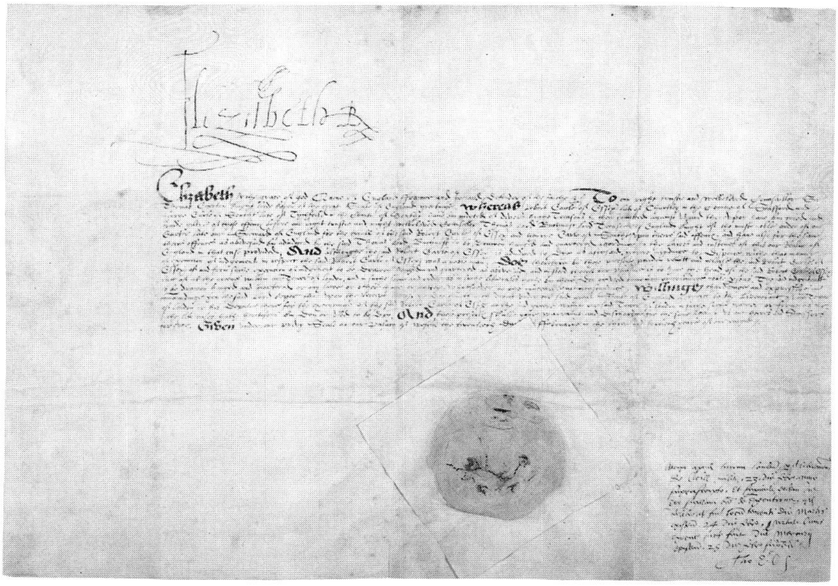

2 Execution warrant of Robert Devereux, second Earl of Essex, signed by Queen Elizabeth, 20 February 1600/1 (BL, Loan MS 34)

now makes the warrant look even more like a conventional legal indenture by engrossing, or enlarging in bold, occasional words in the text to define logical divisions – at 'Elizabeth', 'To', 'whereas', 'And', 'Doe', and so on.

As for the text (see Appendix IV): like the Norfolk warrant, it is addressed to the Lord Keeper of the Great Seal (this time Sir Thomas Egerton); it briefly recites the arraignment and conviction for high treason of the guilty party (this time by a court before Thomas Sackville, Lord Buckhurst, and incidentally mentioning Essex's conviction along with the Earl of Southampton, who was subsequently pardoned), as well as the court's sentence of death. Again it presents the Queen as mitigating the extreme penalty to beheading alone; and again it entrusts the Lord Keeper with all the practical arrangements. There are just one or two notable differences. This time the Queen specifies why the sentence is being mitigated: because 'the said Robert Earle of Essex was a noble man' and such mitigation is customary 'concerninge noble persons'. This concession is the sole but telling hint here as to just how important a man this particular traitor was. (No such reason is given for the similar remission of the extreme penalty in the warrant for the execution of two of Essex's fellow-conspirators, Sir Christopher Blount and Sir Charles Danvers).[6] The warrant also omits some of the gory details of the extreme penalty specified in the Norfolk warrant – an omission made, perhaps, because the execution of the popular Essex was controversial enough without stressing the customary severity of the law unduly.

6 BL Loan MS 83.

Otherwise the striking difference is the docketing at the bottom in the hand of the Lord Keeper himself, Sir Thomas Egerton (later Baron Ellesmere). He has carefully recorded, in Latin, the exact history of the warrant so far as he was concerned: its delivery to him by Sir Robert Cecil three days after the Queen signed it; and his immediate signing of a further warrant (presumably bearing the Great Seal), in the next stage of the process, for the Lieutenant of the Tower (Sir John Peyton), which was delivered the next day, leading to the actual execution at the Tower the day after.[7] This does not, on the face of it, seem to be a particularly unusual piece of record-keeping. But a sense of irregularity was recorded shortly afterwards by Sir Stephen Powle, acting Clerk of the Crown in Chancery, whose job was to engross and deliver official warrants. The 'warrant signed', he says, 'was sealed by the priuy Seale and then deliuered the L*ord* Keeper who kept the same secretly for his dischardge: neauer [never] enrowling the same'.[8]

The wisdom of Egerton's doing this, of keeping a precise account of his own role in the chain of command, as well as carefully and 'secretly' preserving the original signed warrant himself, may become a little more evident in the light of my third example.

This is for the execution of Mary, Queen of Scots, fourteen years earlier, in 1587. Mary was arraigned and convicted in an elaborate trial at Fotheringay Castle on 14 and 15 October 1586. After having already formally instructed Burghley on October 12th that if the court found her guilty, they should forbear proclaiming any sentence against her until the commissioners had returned and reported to her in person,[9] there followed weeks of indecision on Elizabeth's part. Parliament presented her with a petition (a draft of which, revised and corrected by Burghley, is now among the Ellesmere Manuscripts in the Huntington)[10] beseeching her – for the sake of saving 'this whoale state & com*m*en Weale' from 'forray*n* subiection and vtter ruyne & confusion' and for 'the p*re*servac*io*n & defence of vs yo*ur* moost lovinge, dutyfull & faythfull Subiecte*s*' – to publish by proclamation the commissioners' sentence against Mary and put it into effect.[11] This itself was an innovation; not even the Norfolk execution had required a public proclamation. Receiving the petition on November 12th, and as a delaying step in the painful process leading to the most controversial decision she would ever have

7 For the translation of Egerton's Latin note (given in Appendix IV) I am grateful to Hilton Kelliher.

8 Oxford, Bodleian Library, MS Tanner 168, fol. 110r.

9 Transcript in BL Harley MS 290, fol. 193r.

10 San Marino, California, Huntington Library, EL 1191. This draft, occupying the rectos of five large double-folio sheets, is written in a professional secretary hand, with numerous deletions and revisions in two other hands, the predominant one that of Burghley, the other that of Egerton (then Solicitor-General). It is endorsed 'The Copye of the Petic*io*n del | ded [delivered] to both the houses of Parlem*en*t. Penned by the L*ord* Tre*asure*r Burghley.' In Robert Beale's papers is a scribal transcript of this draft, or a version of it, annotated in Beale's hand at the end: 'Memorandu*m* that the enterlininges in the Roman letter were of the hand of ye l*ord* Thres*ore*r [Burghley]' (BL Add. MS 48027, fols 651r-653r).

11 Huntington, EL 1191. For an account of the Parliamentary pressure on Elizabeth to publish a proclamation and put it into effect, see especially J. E. Neale, *Elizabeth I and Her Parliament: 1584-1601* (London, 1957), pp. 103-44. See also Conyers Read, *Lord Burghley and Queen Elizabeth* (New York, 1960), p. 574 ('... One gets the impression that Burghley was regarded as an expert in selecting words likely to influence Elizabeth ...').

to make, Elizabeth made the famous speech – a partly autograph version of which survives among the Lansdowne manuscripts (also probably derived from Burghley's papers) – in which she explained to Parliament her deep misgivings about this matter, so 'rare, weighty, and of great consequence' as it was. 'We Princes,' she said, 'are set on stages, in the sight and veiw of al the worlde duly observed' and 'It behoveth vs therefore to be carefull that our proceedings be Just and honorable.'[12]

After yet further parliamentary pressure, on December 1st she gave consent for a proclamation about the sentence passed on Mary to be published. Burghley was very much involved in the drafting of this proclamation ('the sente*n*ce is allredy more than a full mo*n*th and iiij dayes old', he wrote to her new secretary William Davison in the early hours 'afor day light' of November 24th; 'It were full tyme it shold also speak');[13] and evidently he expected the Queen to make changes to his draft too: on November 30th he sent Davison what he calls 'the proclama*cio*n ingrossd in parchement, w*hi*ch will require sum*e* more time for the altering thereof accordinge to hir Ma*jes*ties pleasure'.[14] Within four days it was finalised, on Sunday December 4th, and published as a broadside in London on Tuesday December 6th (PLATES 3 and 4).[15] Incorporating much of what Burghley had written earlier in his draft parliamentary petition, the proclamation expounds the 'unnatural and monstrous' crimes of which Mary has been found guilty, the proof of which Elizabeth has reluctantly and grievously been obliged to accept; Mary's danger to the realm of England; the lawfulness and justice of her trial and sentence – in accordance with the Statute of 27 Elizabeth (*i.e.* the Act concerning the Queen's safety passed in 1584-5, authorising, among other things, the execution of anyone of any degree who plotted against the Queen's life) – and the 'earnest requests' of her subjects, both nobles and commons, fearful of their own safety, which obliged her to 'yield' and to publish this proclamation so that they might have 'full understanding and knowledge' of the judgement and sentence. Nowhere, incidentally, in this 1700-odd-word proclamation is the sentence of death actually specified, or if, where, and when the sentence will be carried out. The Queen still effectively retained her prerogative of making the final decision.

By contrast, the sentence *is* made clear in a draft for an execution warrant already drawn up by Burghley and Sir Francis Walsingham. This draft, or a contemporary copy of it, was once preserved among the Cecil Papers at Hatfield House, but is now known only from what would seem to be a careful transcript of it made in the eighteenth

12 BL Lansdowne MS 94, fols 84r-85r. Robert Cecil's published version of this speech (1586) is edited in *Elizabeth I: Collected Works*, ed. Leah S. Marcus, Janel Mueller, and Mary Beth Rose (Chicago & London, 2000), pp. 190-6 (including a facsimile of fol. 84r of the manuscript), and the manuscript is printed, in original spelling, in their companion volume, *Elizabeth I: Autograph Compositions and Foreign Language Originals* (Chicago & London, 2003), pp. 67-72. A colour facsimile of fol. 85r appears in Felix Pryor, *Elizabeth I: Her Life in Letters* (British Library, 2003), pp. 88-9 (No. 37).

13 NA, SP 12/195/22.

14 NA, SP 12/195/28; CSPD, Elizabeth 1581-1590 (1865), 368-9. For the history of this proclamation see, *inter alia*, Read, esp. p. 362 *et seq.*

15 STC 8160. The full text is printed, in modernised spelling, in *Tudor Royal Proclamations: Volume II: The Later Tudors (1553-1587)*, ed. Paul L. Hughes and James F. Larkin (New Haven & London, 1969), pp. 528-32 (No. 685).

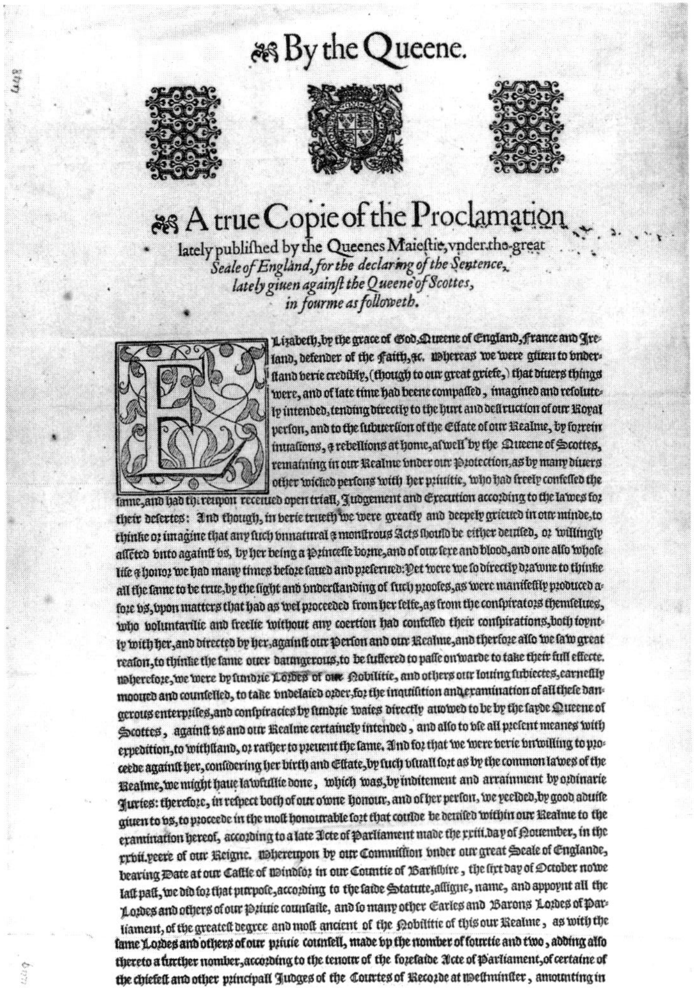
By the Queene.

A true Copie of the Proclamation lately published by the Queenes Maiestie, vnder the great *Seale of England, for the declaring of the Sentence, lately giuen against the Queene of Scottes, in fourme as followeth.*

Elizabeth, by the grace of God, Queene of England, France and Ireland, defender of the Faith, &c. Whereas we were giuen to vnderstand verie credibly, (though to our great griefe,) that diuers things were, and of late time had beene compassed, imagined and resolutely intended, tending directly to the hurt and destruction of our Royal person, and to the subuersion of the Estate of our Realme, by forrein inuasions, & rebellions at home, aswell by the Queene of Scottes, remaining in our Realme vnder our Protection, as by many diuers other wicked persons with her priuitie, who had freely confessed the same, and had thereupon receiued open triall, Judgement and Execution according to the lawes for their desertes: And though, in verie trueth we were greatly and deepely grieued in our minde, to thinke or imagine that any such vnnatural & monstrous Acts should be either deuised, or willingly assented vnto against vs, by her being a Princesse borne, and of our sexe and blood, and one also whose life & honor we had many times before saued and preserued: Yet were we so directly drawne to thinke all the same to be true, by the sight and vnderstanding of such proofes, as were manifestly produced afore vs, vpon matters that had as wel proceeded from her selfe, as from the conspirators themselues, who voluntarilie and freelie without any coertion had confessed their conspirations, both ioyntly with her, and directed by her, against our Person and our Realme, and therfore also we saw great reason, to thinke the same ouer daungerous, to be suffered to passe onwarde to take their full effecte. Wherefore, we were by sundrie Lordes of our Nobilitie, and others our louing subiectes, earnestly mooued and counselled, to take vndelaied order, for the inquisition and examination of all these daungerous enterprises, and conspiracies by sundrie waies directly auowed to be by the sayde Queene of Scottes, against vs and our Realme certainely intended, and also to vse all present meanes with expedition, to withstand, or rather to preuent the same. And for that we were verie vnwilling to proceede against her, considering her birth and Estate, by such vsuall sort as by the common lawes of the Realme, we might haue lawfullie done, which was, by inditement and arrainment by ordinarie Juries: therefore, in respect both of our owne honour, and of her person, we yeelded, by good aduise giuen to vs, to procede in the most honourable sort that coulde be deuised within our Realme to the examination hereof, according to a late Acte of Parliament made the xxiii. day of Nouember, in the xxvii. yeere of our Reigne. Whereupon by our Commission vnder our great Seale of Englande, bearing Date at our Castle of Windsor in our Countie of Barkshire, the first day of October nowe last past, we did for that purpose, according to the saide Statute, assigne, name, and appoynt all the Lordes and others of our Priuie counsaile, and so many other Earles and Barons Lordes of Parliament, of the greatest degree and most ancient of the Nobilitie of this our Realme, as with the same Lordes and others of our priuie counsell, made vp the nomber of fourtie and two, adding also thereto a further nomber, according to the tenour of the foresaide Acte of Parliament, of certaine of the chiefest and other principall Judges of the Courtes of Recorde at Westminster, amounting in

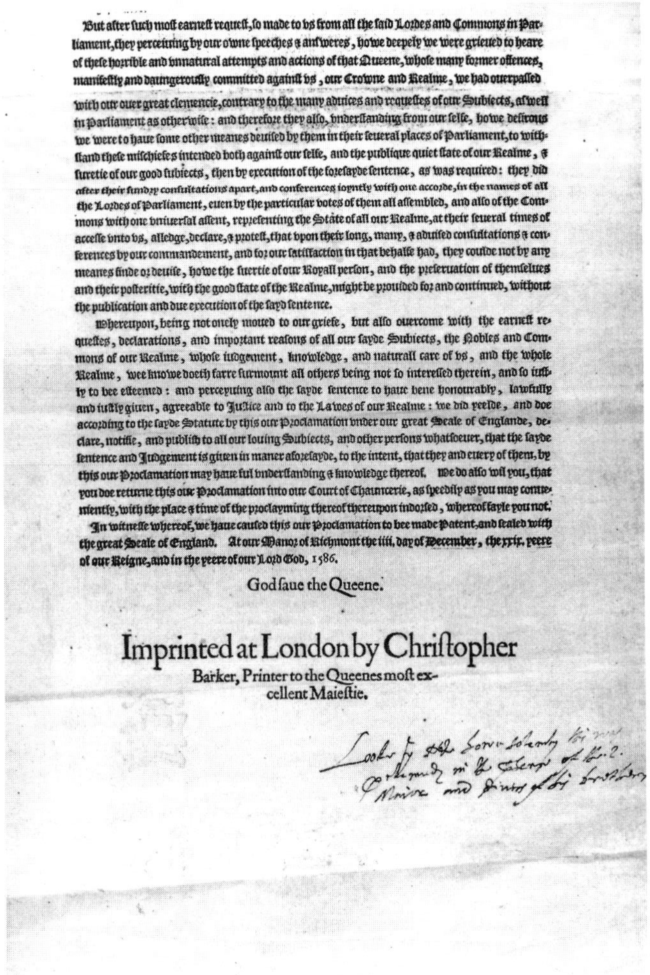
But after such most earnest request, so made to vs from all the said Lordes and Commons in Parliament, they perceiuing by our owne speeches & answeres, howe deepely we were grieued to heare of these horrible and vnnatural attempts and actions of that Queene, whose many former offences, manifestly and daungerously committed against vs, our Crowne and Realme, we had ouerpassed with our ouer great clemencie, contrary to the many aduices and requestes of our Subiects, aswell in Parliament as otherwise: and therefore they also, vnderstanding from our selfe, howe desirous we were to haue some other meanes deuised by them in their seueral places of Parliament, to withstand these mischiefes intended both against our selfe, and the publique quiet state of our Realme, & suretie of our good subiects, then by execution of the foresayde sentence, as was required: they did after their sundry consultations apart, and conferences ioyntly with one accorde, in the names of all the Lordes of Parliament, euen by the particular votes of them all assembled, and also of the Commons with one vniuersal assent, representing the State of all our Realme, at their seueral times of accesse vnto vs, alledge, declare, & protest, that vpon their long, many, & aduised consultations & conferences by our commandement, and for our satisfaction in that behalfe had, they coulde not by any meanes finde or deuise, howe the suertie of our Royall person, and the preseruation of themselues and their posteritie, with the good state of the Realme, might be prouided for and continued, without the publication and due execution of the sayd sentence.

Whereupon, being not onely moued to our griefe, but also ouercome with the earnest requestes, declarations, and important reasons of all our sayde Subiects, the Nobles and Commons of our Realme, whose iudgement, knowledge, and naturall care of vs, and the whole Realme, wee knowe doeth farre surmount all others being not so interessed therein, and so iustly to bee esteemed: and perceyuing also the sayde sentence to haue bene honourably, lawfully and iustly giuen, agreeable to Justice and to the Lawes of our Realme: we did yeelde, and doe according to the sayde Statute by this our Proclamation vnder our great Seale of Englande, declare, notifie, and publish to all our louing Subiects, and other persons whatsoeuer, that the sayde sentence and Judgement is giuen in maner aforesayde, to the intent, that they and euery of them, by this our Proclamation may haue ful vnderstanding & knowledge thereof. We do also wil you, that you doe returne this our Proclamation into our Court of Chauncerie, as speedily as you may conueniently, with the place & time of the proclayming thereof thereupon indorsed, whereof fayle you not.

In witnesse whereof, we haue caused this our Proclamation to bee made Patent, and sealed with the great Seale of England. At our Manor of Richmont the iiii. day of December, the xxix. yeere of our Reigne, and in the yeere of our Lord God, 1586.

God saue the Queene.

Imprinted at London by Christopher Barker, Printer to the Queenes most excellent Maiestie.

3 and 4 First and last pages of the printed proclamation declaring the sentence against Mary Queen of Scots, 4 December 1586 (STC 8160), Robert Beale's copy (BL, Additional MS 48027, fols 448r and 450r)

century (see Appendix V). The original was docketed: 'Note. that this must Beare date the day after the Proclamation made' and also 'Endors'd by Ld Burg[hley]. the latter part writ by Sec[retary]. Walsingham.' This thousand-word warrant recites at length the judgement against Mary made according to legal statute, cites the attempts against the Queen's life made by Mary and her confederates, including Anthony Babington, and orders that Mary's head should be 'Cutt off' at Fotheringay Castle.

On 10 December 1586 Burghley even drafted an order by the Queen for Mary's custodian at Fotheringay, Sir Amias Paulet, to deliver Mary into the hands of the Sheriff of Northampton for the execution to be carried out – one written, as usual, in Burghley's distinctive, cursive, elongated italic (see Appendix VI and PLATE 5). Again, this warrant cites the reason for the execution – for 'ye suerty of our p*er*son' and 'for ye pr*eser*vatio*n*' of her subjects and 'their posterite, and state of ye realm', and stresses the necessity of the execution though 'ageynst our own na*tur*all dispositio*n*' (this phrase initially crossed out, but reintroduced in the penultimate line written down the margin).

Both these draft warrants proved to be premature. They were not used because Elizabeth still procrastinated, in a turmoil of indecision over the enormity of this step. Executing the conspirator Babington was one thing – she turned a deaf ear to his pleas for clemency.[16] But the execution of a lawful, anointed monarch was another, establishing, besides all else, an extremely dangerous precedent. It was, Burghley wrote later, a thing 'utterly repugnant to her mind'.[17]

Nevertheless, a fresh execution warrant was drawn up, certainly again by Burghley,[18] possibly again in collaboration with Walsingham (see below) – and it was left with the Queen's new secretary William Davison. After long delays, 'some 5. or 6. weekes at the least', according to Davison,[19] she did finally sign this warrant (in circumstances that would be forever hotly debated) on 1 February 1586/7. Following, according to Davison's account, a series of circumspect steps by him, including showing the signed warrant to, and effectively getting assurances about it from, the Earl of Leicester, Walsingham, Sir Walter Mildmay, Sir Christopher Hatton, and Lord Burghley before it was carried 'to the great seale', Davison delivered the warrant to Burghley at his request ('... his lo*rdshi*p, having some vse of the war*ran*t, praied me to leave it w*i*th him w*hi*ch in pr*esen*ce of Mr Viecchamberlen [Hatton] I d*elivere*d into his lo*rdshi*ps owne hand*e*s, who from thenceforth kept it till it was sent away ...');[20]

16 Babington wrote to the Queen on 19 September 1586 imploring a 'miracle of mercy' from her, which she refused, and the next day he and four co-conspirators were subjected to the full rigours of hanging, drawing while still alive, and quartering. Hearing the details of their brutal execution, however, Elizabeth did order that the remaining conspirators should be hanged the next day until they were dead before their bodies were mutilated.

17 Burghley to Sir Robert Carey, 3 April 1587: CSP Scotland, IX, 394.

18 According to an account 'Touching the Com*m*ission for th'execution of the Scotish Queene' among Robert Beale's papers (in a scribal hand with Beale's autograph insertions), Davison testified that the commission 'was drawen by the L*ord* Threa*sur*er [Burghley] and wrytten by him selfe' (BL Add. MS 48027, fols 636r-639v). According to Davison's testimony, the Queen 'did at length giue order to the lo*rd* Treasurer to drawe the warr*ent* for her execution' (Davison, 'relation', BL Harley MS 290, fol. 222r; Nicolas, p. 257; CSP Scotland, IX, 296).

19 Davison, 'relation', BL Harley MS 290, fol. 222r; Nicolas, p.257; CSP Scotland, IX, 296.

20 Davison, 'relation', BL Harley MS 290, fol. 223r; Nicolas, p.264; CSP Scotland, IX, 299.

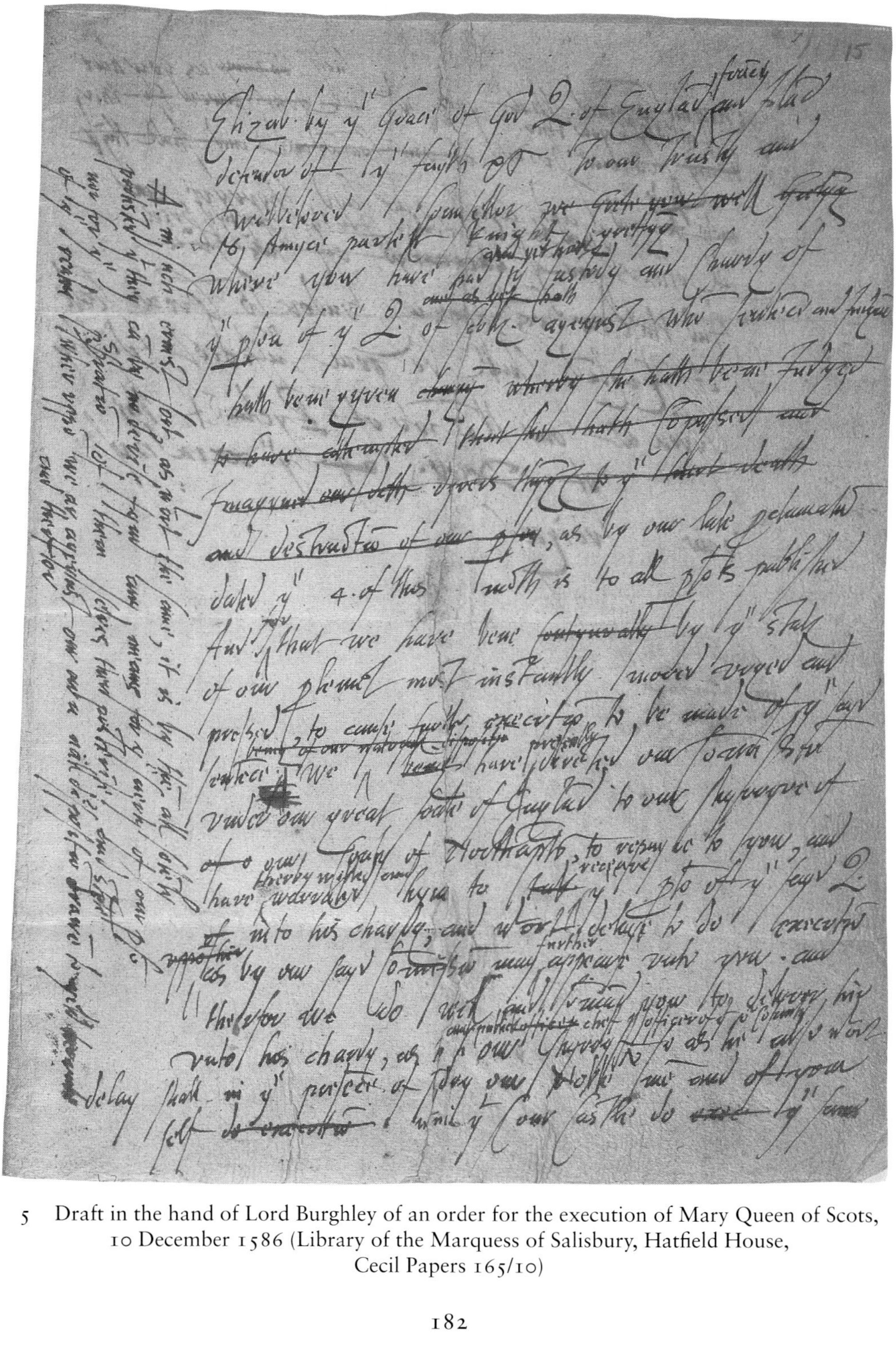

5 Draft in the hand of Lord Burghley of an order for the execution of Mary Queen of Scots, 10 December 1586 (Library of the Marquess of Salisbury, Hatfield House, Cecil Papers 165/10)

the Council approved of its enactment; Burghley wrote the formal letters to the commissioners of the execution to put the warrant into effect (see PLATE 6 for an extant example of these letters);[21] the warrant, by now under the Great Seal,[22] was delivered to Robert Beale for delivery; and it *was* duly enacted.

So far as we know the original warrant no longer exists. However, a few contemporary transcripts of it do survive. In particular, two scribal copies were made for, and annotated by, Robert Beale, Clerk of the Privy Council, the man who actually delivered the warrant (or 'commission', as he called it) to Fotheringay; who was present when it was read out to Mary on the evening of February 7th, and who attended the execution itself the next morning. One of his transcripts (PLATE 7) is among Beale's papers in the Yelverton Manuscripts now in the British Library. As can be seen from the full text (Appendix VII), both structure and wording differ to a remarkable degree from the 'normal' formula exemplified by the Norfolk and later Essex warrants. Although retaining in modified form some of the basic statements and even occasional phrasing of its predecessors (including Burghley's draft petition to the Queen, the printed proclamation, and Burghley's brief draft warrant to Paulet), this final version differs greatly from that first lengthy draft warrant made by Burghley and Walsingham some weeks earlier (Appendix V). That version, couched in ponderous and repetitive legalistic terms, had stressed repeatedly the Statute of 27 Elizabeth concerning the Queen's safety which effectively sanctioned the court's death sentence against Mary. By the time the final warrant was drawn up, it seems that Burghley had realised that this legalistic approach would not serve – things had moved beyond that (and, in fact, in the final version there is not even a mention of the Statute of 27 Elizabeth at all).[23]

The warrant is addressed not to the Lord Keeper or Lord Chancellor (at this time Sir Thomas Bromley), but to five specified commissioners – Lords Shrewsbury, Kent, Derby, Cumberland, and Pembroke – who were all members of the Council that had tried and sentenced Mary. Instead of simply referring to the trial and sentence given, it

21 These letters, directed for the Queen's 'speciall s*er*uice tending to the safety of her royall person and vniversall quietnes of her whole Realme', were signed on 3 February 1586/7 by the whole Council. PLATE 6 shows the original of the one sent to the Earl of Kent; formerly among the Fairhurst Papers, it was sold at Sotheby's on 16 December 1996, lot 40 (illustrated in the catalogue), and is now at Lambeth Palace, MS 4267, fols 19r-20v. The letter, informing Kent of the delivery of the execution 'Commission' by Robert Beale ('a person of great trust and experience'), is signed by Burghley, Derby, Leicester, Howard, Hunsdon, Cobham, Knollys, Hatton, Walsingham, and the Queen's secretary William Davison himself. The version of this letter in BL Cotton MS Caligula C. IX, fol. 156r (reproduced in an engraved facsimile in Strickland, II, facing p. 241) is a scribal copy. The similar letter sent to the Earl of Shrewsbury (copies in BL Harley MS 290, fol. 194, and Sloane MS 650, fol. 139) is printed in *Original Letters, Illustrative of English History*, ed. Sir Harry Ellis [Second Series], 3 vols (London, 1827), III, 111-12.

22 It 'had the greate Seale of England putt to it' (BL Add. MS 48027, fols 636r-639v). If these words are meant literally, it means that no separate engrossed version on parchment was prepared for the Great Seal – another sign of the Council's haste in the warrant's dispatch. Robert Beale, for his part, was assured by Hatton 'that I neaded not to doubte therof, seinge I had her Ma*jesties* hande and the Greate Seale' (Beale to Burghley, 24 April 1595: BL Lansdowne MS 79, fols 192r-195v (fol. 193v)). For references to Beale's letters in the Lansdowne manuscripts, I am grateful to Patricia Brewerton.

23 The importance of this statute was remembered, nevertheless, as is shown by Robert Beale's citing it as a major 'authoritie' under which he and others 'must shrowde' themselves for their part in the execution (Beale to Burghley, 17 March 1592/3: BL Lansdowne MS 73, fols 4r-13r (fols 5v-6r)).

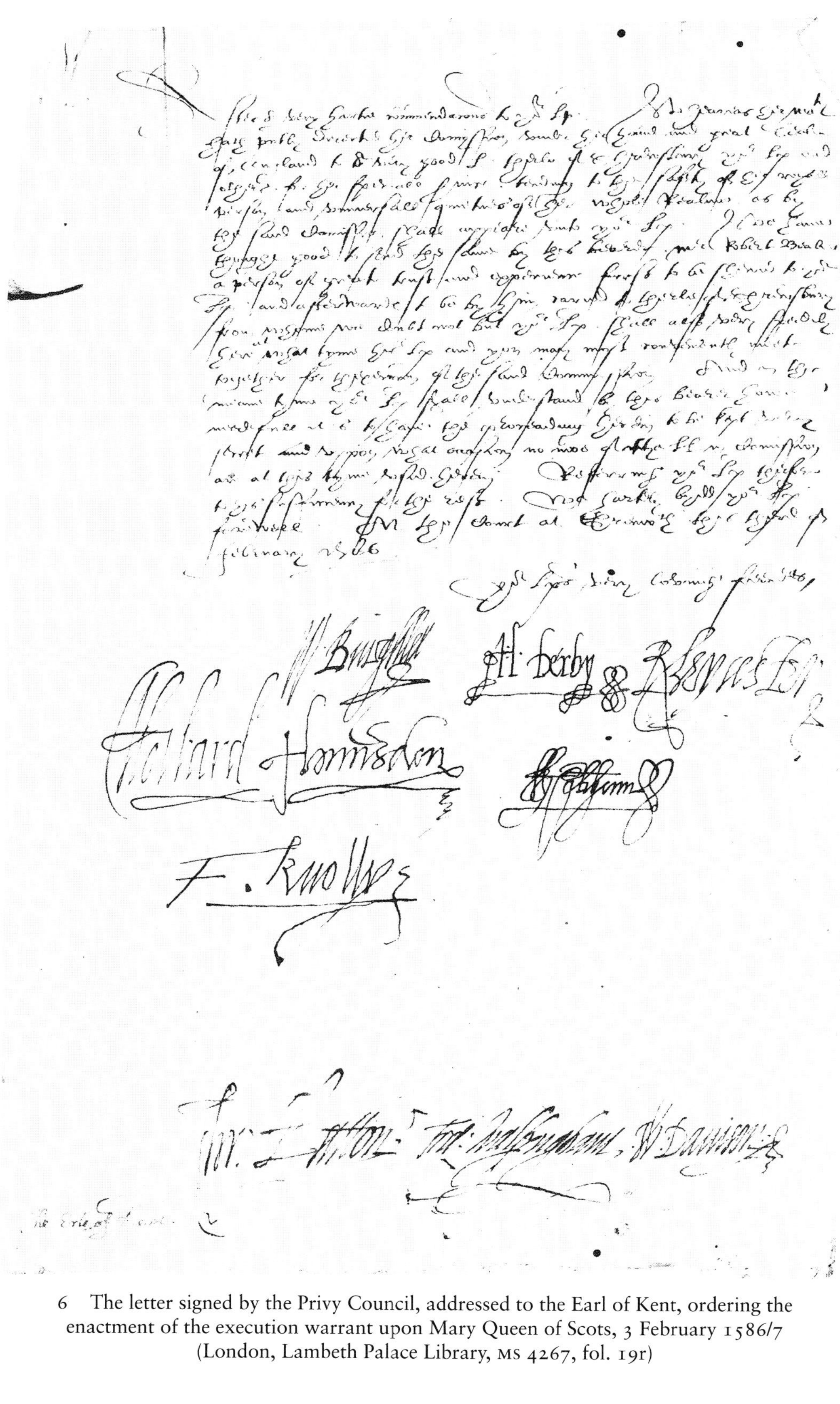

6 The letter signed by the Privy Council, addressed to the Earl of Kent, ordering the enactment of the execution warrant upon Mary Queen of Scots, 3 February 1586/7 (London, Lambeth Palace Library, MS 4267, fol. 19r)

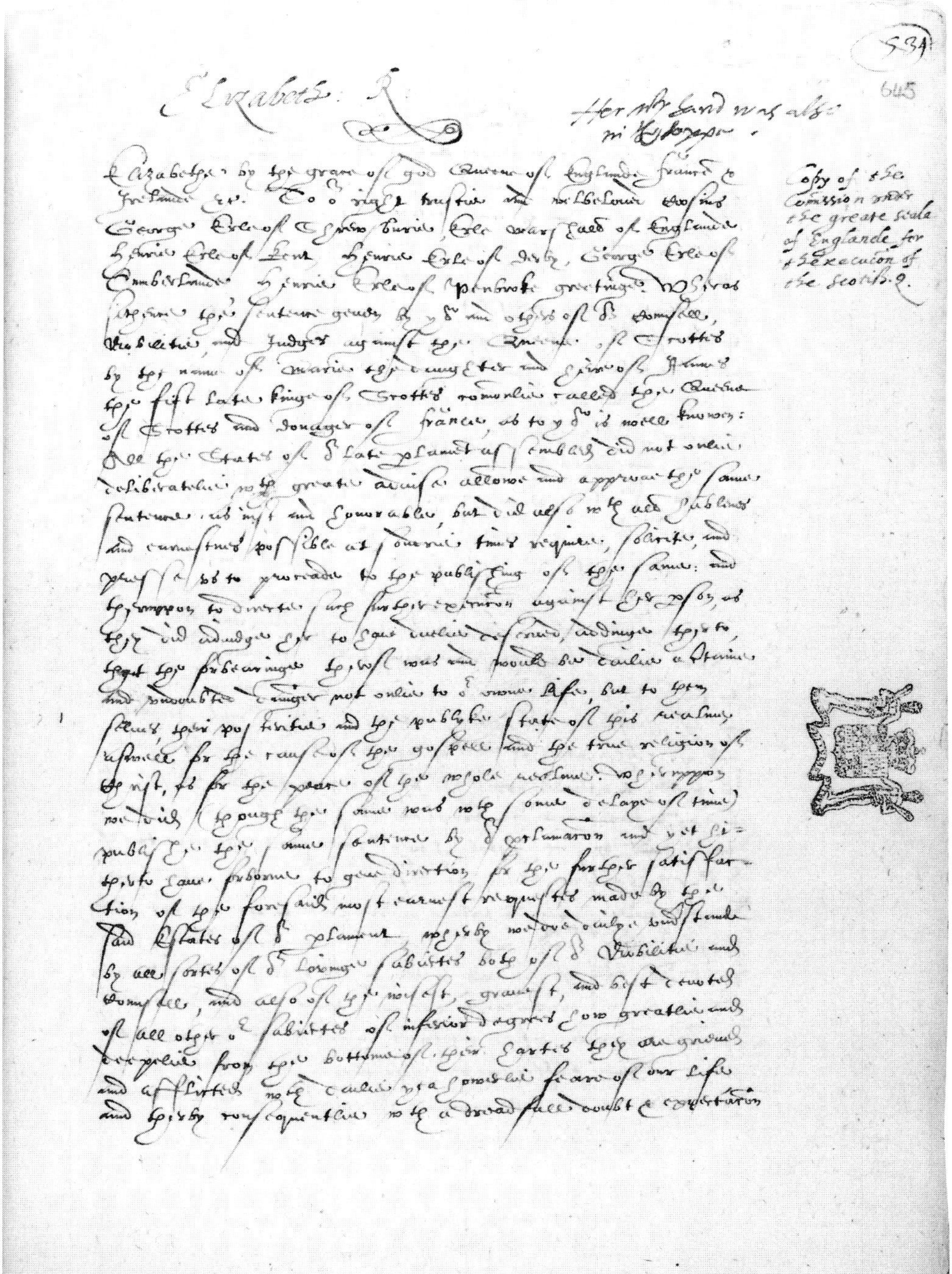
Elizabeth R

Her Ma[jesty's] hand was also in the paper.

534

645

Copy of the comission under the greate seale of Englande for the execucion of the Scottish Q.

Elizabeth by the grace of god Queene of Englande Fraunce & Irelande &c. To o[u]r right trustie and welbeloved Cosins George Erle of Shrewsburie, Erle Marshall of Englande, Henrie Erle of Kent, Henrie Erle of Derby, George Erle of Cumberlande, Henrie Erle of Pembroke greetinge. Whereas sithence the sentence geven by yo[u] and others of o[u]r Counsell, Nobilitie, and Judges against the Queene of Scottes by the name of Marie the daughter and heire of James the fift late Kinge of Scottes commonlie called the Queene of Scottes and Dowager of Fraunce, as to yo[u] is well knowen: All the States of o[u]r late parliament assembled did not onlie deliberatelie with great advise allowe and approve the same sentence as iust and honorable, but did also with all humblenes and earnestnes possible at sundrie times require, solicite, and perswade us to proceade to the publishing of the same: and thereupon to direct such further execution against her person, as they did adiudge her to have iustlie deserved, addinge therto, that the forbearinge thereof was and would be daylie a certaine and undoubted danger not onlie to o[u]r owne life, but to them selves, their posteritie and the publique state of this realme, aswell for the cause of the gospell and the true religion of Christ, as for the peace of the whole realme. Whereupon wee did (though the same was with some delaye of time) publishe the same sentence by o[u]r proclamation and yet hitherto have forborne to geve direction for the further satisfaction of the foresaid most earnest requestes made by the said Estates of o[u]r parliament, whereby we doe dailie understande by all sortes of o[u]r lovinge subiectes both of o[u]r Nobilitie and Counsell, and also of the wisest, gravest, and best counseled of all other o[u]r subiectes of inferior degrees how greatlie and deeplie from the bottome of their hartes they are greived and afflicted with a daylie yea hourelie feare of our life and thereby consequentlie with a dreadfull doubt & expectation

7 First page of a scribal copy of the final version of Queen Elizabeth's warrant for the execution of Mary Queen of Scots, 1 February 1586/7, owned and annotated by Robert Beale (BL, Additional MS 48027, fol. 645r)

embarks upon a lengthy summary, elaborating on the printed proclamation some weeks earlier – explaining the lawfulness of the procedure, the broad base of support for its justness and honourableness, support by 'All the States of our late parliament', by her nobility and council, and by all ranks of her loving subjects, even those 'of inferior degres' and explicating the necessity of the speedy enactment of the sentence: namely, for the common good, 'for the peace of the whole realme', for the support of religion, and to avert the imminent national danger that Mary posed. Overwhelmed by the prayers and beseeching of her loving subjects, who are in fear of their lives so long as Mary lives, Elizabeth has no option, even though it is contrary to her own natural disposition, but to allow the execution to proceed. She also takes the practical step of ordering a duplicate of the warrant to go to each of the commissioners responsible for the necessary arrangements for its enactment (a step which, incidentally, helps to explain why contemporary transcripts of this warrant exist).

Thus the responsibility for the execution becomes about as broad-based as it could possibly be. Trial judges, Privy Council, nobility, all her loyal and loving subjects, of both high and low rank, support the verdict and beseech the Queen to enact it. It becomes a kind of communal, indeed national matter. Elizabeth herself is reluctant to endorse a sentence so much against her nature, but is obliged to accept the will of her people. She herself is thereby, ostensibly, exonerated from personal blame in the matter. Above all, the warrant stresses the justification of the sentence – its essential lawfulness and its necessity for the good of the realm.

Even if we knew nothing about the circumstances of the trial and execution of Mary, Queen of Scots – subjects which, as it happens, are well documented – the text of this warrant alone would tell us how extraordinary were the events to which it relates. This would be true even if we were ignorant of the degree of desperation that led Elizabeth into seriously contemplating having Mary quietly assassinated to avoid the odium of public responsibility for her death.[24] Far from its being an instrument of finality – of decision and closure on the fate of a traitor – it is as if this warrant is simply another step in the process of debate: as if that debate is still raging, the attempt still under way to bring it to a decisive conclusion. What does it tell us about the Queen's power except to highlight the dilemma, if not insoluble paradox, of her position? She is at once the

24 The incriminating letter signed by Walsingham and Davison on 1 February 1586/7, conveying to Paulet the Queen's displeasure that he had not yet 'found out some way to shorten the life of that Queen' without casting 'the burthen upon her', is known only from copies. It is printed, with the indignant refusal by Paulet and Sir Drue Drury, in, *inter alia*, Nicolas's *Life of Davison*, pp. 86-7, 100-2; William Tytler's partisan *An Inquiry Historical and Critical, into the Evidence against Mary, Queen of Scots* (4th edn, 2 vols, London, 1790), II, 321-4 ('What a cruel snare is here laid for this faithful servant!', declares Tytler; 'He is tempted to commit a murder, and at the same time has orders from his Sovereign to destroy the warrant for doing it. ...'); and the no less partisan *Letters of Mary, Queen of Scots*, ed. Agnes Strickland (2 vols, London, 1844), II, 235-8. For Davison's account of the sending of this letter and of how the Queen received their reply, with her cynical remarks about the 'daintiness' and 'niceness of those precise fellows (as she termed them), who in words would do great things for her surety, but in deed perform nothing', see Nicolas, pp. 236, 244-6. While reflecting on the moral consciences of Paulet and Drury, she was presumably also equating them with the 'Lawiers ... so nice and so precise in sifting and scanning euery word and letter' that 'stand more vpon forme, then matter, vpon syllabs, then the sense of the lawe', that she condemned in her speech to Parliament on 12 November 1586 (see note 12 above).

ultimate authority for the execution while at the same time only the reluctant instrument of the will of the *nation* in the matter.

It is as if we can read two agendas in this warrant. One, the predominant one, is that of Burghley, and with him the Queen's Council and her Parliament, fervently pleading, still trying to persuade her to do what is necessary. It is as if they know that they must still exhort her, remind her of all the reasons for the execution, even up to the very moment that she lifts her pen to sign it, in order to make her go ahead with it. The other is that of Elizabeth herself, crying out that she has to do it, but that this is *not what she wants*. On many other occasions Elizabeth could invoke the will of her loving subjects and her duty towards them. But this is different. Elizabeth was hardly democratic in practice – one of her proclamations condemns the very act of lowly common people ('every most meanest person of judgment') daring to discuss 'in every blind corner at their several wills' the 'affairs of public estate, a thing most pernicious in any estate'.[25] So, among the various personal, emotional, and political reasons why she afterwards reacted so violently to this warrant is that she perceived not only the personal stigma it represented but perhaps even also the frightful prospect of democracy confronting her. Not only was Elizabeth denied her customary positive role as bringer of mercy – in Mary's case there was no question of an extreme penalty (of hanging, drawing, and quartering) for her to remit – but the carefully worded distribution of responsibility for the execution – to the judges, Council, and people high and low – was also looking ominously like a distribution of *power*. The people – even those 'of inferior degres' – were coercing her into doing something against her will. It may have occurred to her that, besides all else, she was in danger of becoming not the master of her people, but their servant.

There is one final coda to all this. As is well known, the aftermath of the execution was a series of bitter recriminations and heated disputes as to who was responsible for it. Despite all his detailed account of the circumstances in which the Queen signed the warrant and entrusted it to him for expedition ('... she finally willed me to take vp the said war*ran*t & to cary it im*m*ediatly to the great seale comaunding me expressely to dispatch & send it awaie vnto the com*missione*rs w*i*th all the expedici*o*n I might ...'),[26] her secretary William Davison was tried and imprisoned for delivering the signed warrant to the Council without her express command. Lord Burghley – undoubtedly the chief player involved – was ferociously upbraided by Elizabeth, nominally dismissed from office, and banished from court for some four months.[27] Despite Elizabeth's pledge to Mary's son, James VI of Scotland, that, if she had meant the execution to take place, she would never lay blame for it 'on others' shoulders',[28] the lives, reputations, and careers of virtually everyone who had had anything to do with the execution were in some degree blighted – not least those of Robert Beale, who, for

25 The Queen's proclamation against John Stubbs's *Gaping Gulf*, 27 September 1579, reprinted in *Tudor Royal Proclamations: Volume II* (1969), pp. 445-9 (No. 642).

26 Davison, 'relation', BL Harley MS 290, fol. 222r; Nicolas, p.260; CSP Scotland, IX, 297.

27 See, *inter alia*, Read, esp. pp. 369-79.

28 Elizabeth to James, 14 February 1586/7 (BL Cotton MS Caligula C. IX, fol. 212r; *Elizabeth I: Collected Works*, p. 296).

carrying 'downe the Commission' as he was commanded, got, he lamented, 'as much displeasure at home as anie of the rest, and abroade diffamed ... and my selfe and my posteritie threatned w*i*th all reue*n*ges'.[29]

We might even wonder whether the loss of the original warrant was accidental. We have already noted Stephen Powle's observation of government irregularities when it came to execution warrants. Not only does he record several cases (including that of Essex) when execution warrants were kept 'privat' or 'secretly' by the Lord Keeper 'for hes owne discharge', but he also notes (in connection with the warrant for Blount and Danvers in 1601) that it had 'bin never inrolled noe more then any other hath bin heretofore of *tha*t nature'.[30] In other words, unlike normal warrants and letters patent, it had not, for many years (if ever), been customary to have execution warrants enrolled in official government or Chancery rolls as a matter of public record. They were kept secret. In the case of Mary, Queen of Scots, Robert Beale would later complain to Burghley (the warrant's self-appointed custodian) that 'the copie' (meaning the original) 'of the same Commission vnder the greate Seale ... hathe ben denyed vnto me; co*n*trarye to promise, and the verye wordes of the Com*m*ission'.[31] A sensitive, even dangerous item, whose authority the Queen totally repudiated, the original warrant was, it seems, hidden away by Burghley, who is even recorded as having taken steps to retrieve the drafts of the relevant letters putting the warrant into effect.[32] Since there is no sign of the original warrant among any of Burghley's extant papers (in the Hatfield Cecil or BL Lansdowne papers, or at Burghley House), it might not be altogether surprising to learn that it might at some time have been deliberately destroyed as a thing accursed.

Given all this, it is interesting to note Beale's annotations in his transcripts of the warrant (made, presumably, when it was briefly in his custody). In the Yelverton manuscript (PLATE 7) can be observed Beale's telling comment: 'Her m*aje*stys hand was also in the Copp*ie*' – the 'Coppie' here, again, meaning the original text or actual warrant. Beale's implication is, I would suggest, not only that Elizabeth had signed the warrant, but that – as was her wont – she had changed some of its wording: she was, in a sense, *in* the text, not outside it.

This interpretation would seem to be supported by Beale's second transcript (now in a private collection: see Appendix VII, *copies* i, and PLATE 8). This is a scribal copy owned by one of the commissioners, the Earl of Kent, probably sent to him by Beale at a time when they were both under the general cloud of royal disfavour, having to justify

29 Beale to Burghley, 24 April 1595 (BL Lansdowne MS 79, fols 192r-195v (fol. 193v)). See also Beale's complaints to Burghley, on 16 October 1592, about his being deprived of office after twenty years' service because of the Queen's continuing 'displeasure' and his ill fame as 'a Compagnon of the hangman' (BL Lansdowne MS 72, fols 197r-198v (fol. 197v)).

30 Bodleian MS Tanner 168, fols 110r-129v *passim* (fol. 128r quoted). Other execution warrants copied by or for Powle here include those of Thomas Cromwell (1540) and Philip Howard, Earl of Arundel (1589, though not put into effect).

31 Beale to Burghley, 17 March 1592[/3] (BL Lansdowne MS 73, fols 4r-13r (fol. 5r)).

32 '... the L. Tre*asuro*r vppon the com*m*ittinge of Mr Dauison after gott the originals of the said draughtes co*n*ceyued by him self into his owne hande*s* agayne, and were according to the Copies sett downe before' (BL Add. MS 48027, fol. 637v).

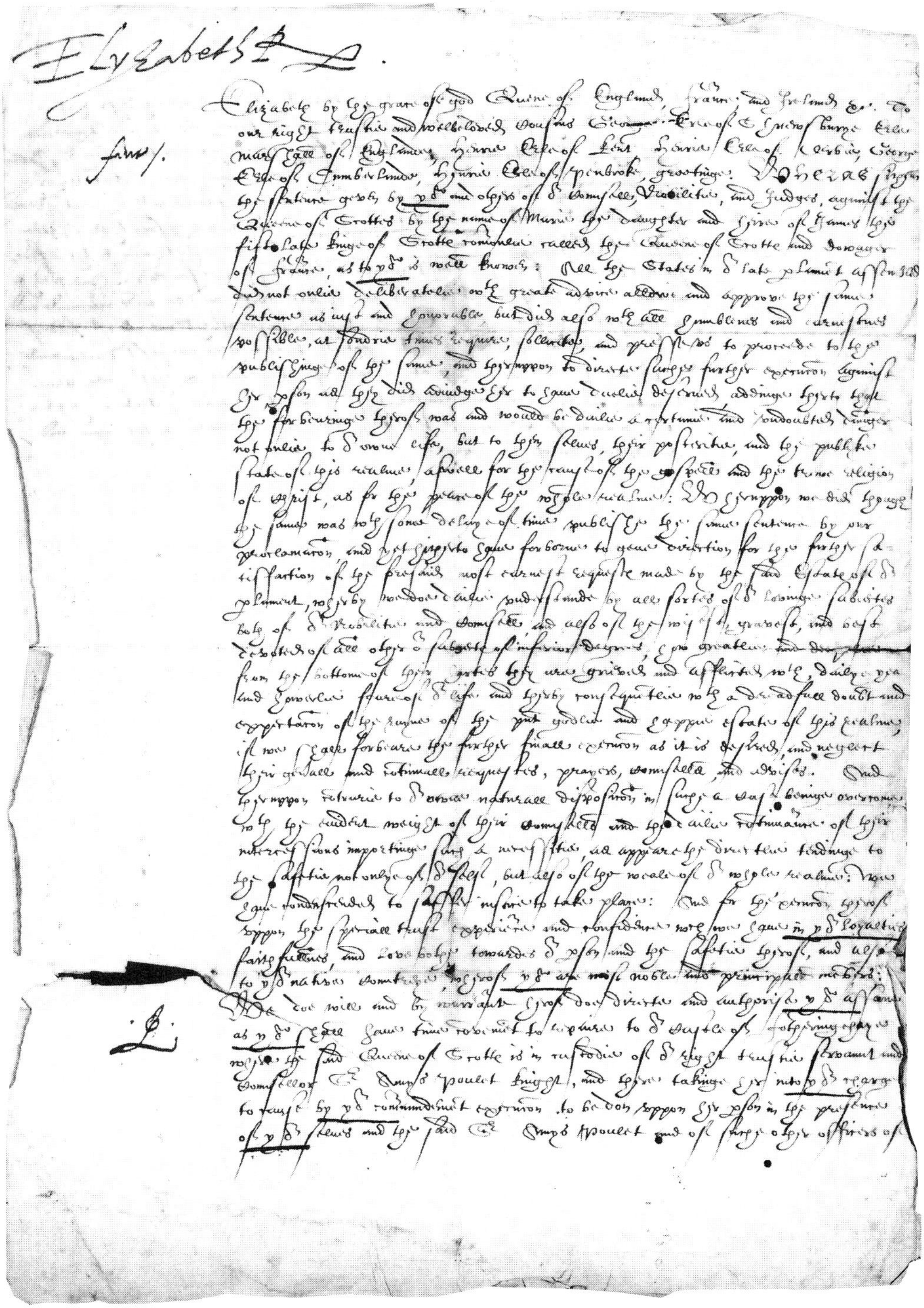

8 First page of a scribal copy of the final version of Queen Elizabeth's warrant for the execution of Mary Queen of Scots, 1 February 1586/7, annotated probably by Robert Beale and sent to the Duke of Kent

their conduct and therefore having to take stock and check their facts.[33] It is Beale, I think, who, as the man once in custody of the original signed warrant, makes various little markings and underlinings, where he draws attention not only to the precise instructions given by the Queen to her commissioners – to '*you*' in each case – but also, perhaps, to the person who wrote them.[34] I suspect that what, in the margin near the top, looks (for all its fumbled minims) like the initials 'F. W.' might refer to Francis Walsingham. But more tellingly, the letter in the margin towards the bottom is certainly a 'Q.', meaning 'The Queen', and this is repeated on the second page against a flurry of further underlinings – indicating, possibly, where the Queen had herself made changes in the text. Although in their formal self-vindications neither Beale nor Kent would have dreamed of saying it directly, there is little doubt who *they* thought bore ultimate responsibility.

So, to conclude: it is in this way that the warrant for Mary's execution – a single piece of material manuscript text, from which derived other manuscript copies – served multiple functions. Although it certainly achieved its ostensible (and fundamentally intended) object – Mary *was* put to death – it ironically became different things to different people. Its verbal formulation was the product of more than one 'author' or sets of interests. Its physical embodiment was as an undemonstrative, legalistic, properly authorised, formal written instrument. The warrant served as an official vindication of judicial homicide for the benefit of the commissioners directly concerned, yet was also a semi-private discourse – it was certainly *not* what it claimed to be, a 'letters patent' (a warrant open to public scrutiny) – and it was one that could even be turned to its own refutation. It was a declaration of resolution and finality which might also prove to be not final at all but only part of an extended and continuing process. And it was the focal point of reference, and basis, for the self-defence of those agents who enacted it ('I had her Ma*jesti*es hande and the Greate Seale,' insisted Beale)[35] – of those who actually conveyed it from one queen to another – but who found that its claim to be for them 'a full suffici*en*t warrau*n*t and discharge for ever' would prove to be bogus. Neither Elizabeth's sign manual nor the Great Seal itself, the very symbols of regal and executive authority, could exonerate those agents who put the warrant into effect or render absolute a mandate that the circumstances of its production and enactment negated in practice. The Queen herself, and she alone, would ultimately exert her supreme power and prerogative in determining what was

33 Kent's retained copy of his letter to the Queen strongly vindicating the commissioners' conduct (once among the Fairhurst Papers and sold at Sotheby's, 16 December 1996, lot 43) is now at Lambeth Palace, MS 4267, fols 33-34. A formal petition to the Queen on the subject, on vellum, signed by Beale, Kent, Paulet, Drury and others, is in Beale's papers: BL Add. MS 48027, fols 700r-701r. The fact that it bears a series of scissor cuts and remains among Beale's papers suggests that the signatories changed their mind and it was never delivered. According to Beale later, Kent did, in fact, suppose 'that I had abused him, and that I was wittinglye vsed as an instrument to bring him into that action, that was so much mislyked' (Beale to Burghley, 16 October 1592: BL Lansdowne MS 72, fols 197r-198v (fol. 197v))

34 Beale's professional acumen in identifying the handwriting of important documents is illustrated by, *inter alia*, his notes on the will of Mary, Queen of Scots, where he carefully distinguishes between text written in her hand and text written by a secretary: see BL Add. MS 48027, fol. 530r.

35 Beale to Burghley, 24 April 1595 (BL Lansdowne MS 79, fols 192r-195v (fol.193v)).

and was not 'authoritative'. Even so, it is not accidental that, in the truly *public* proclamation of December 4th which the Queen allowed to be printed, she did not commit herself to a decision that she would have had difficulty in publicly revoking. With the non-public, non-patent *manuscript* warrant she could do just that, and with impunity.

APPENDICES

The texts printed below are diplomatic transcriptions of the relevant documents with abbreviations generally expanded in italic for the sake of clarity.

APPENDIX I

EXECUTION WARRANT OF THOMAS HOWARD, FOURTH DUKE OF NORFOLK, 9 FEBRUARY 1571/2

The Text

Elizabeth R

Elizabeth by the grace of god Quene of England ffraunce & Irlande defendor of the faith &c To *ou*r right trustie & right welbeloved Counsellor S*ir* Nicolas Bacon knight lord keper of *ou*r great seale of Englande greating. / where as Thomas duke of Norff*olk* late of Kenningale in the countie of Norff*olk* for sundry treasons by him com*m*itted & done was the xvith day of ~ ~ ~ ~ ~ ~ ~ January arraigned and tryed vpon the same by his peeres at westm*inste*r hall according to the lawes of *ou*r realm before *ou*r dere Cosyn & counsellor Theerle of Shrewesbury for that tyme & purpose appointed our High Steward of England and was than & there by his said peeres found giltie of the said treasons and therupon iudgement given vpon the said duke by *ou*r said high Steward, that is to say that the said duke shuld be led from the said place of arraignement to the tower of London and from thens shuld be drawen thorough the middest of our Citie of london to the gallowes at Tiborne and there to be hanged and being half dead to be cut downe and all his bowelle*s* to be taken out of his bealie and throwen in to the fyre and his hed to be cut of and his body to be devided in to fowre partes and his head & fowre quarters to be set vp & disposed at *ou*r pleasure: w*hi*ch manner of execution although it be due to euery person that com*m*itteth treason: yet we being moved to pitie of *ou*r grace especiale are pleased & contented to chaunge such maner of execution as by *ou*r saide Steward of England was than pronounced against the said duke mynding neverthelesse the suertie and preservac*i*on of our p*er*son & realme & quietnes of the same and also to give example of terror dreade and feare for all others herafter to offende or attempte in the like do straigtly charge & com*m*aunde you the saide lord keper to awarde & make out due processe & writte*s* of execution according to the due forme & order of our lawes in that behalf. ffor seing alwayes that no other execution of death be executed to the said duke of norff*olk* but only to cause his head to be smytten of from his body at the Tower hill the accustomed place of execution. And for the residue of the execution of death appointed by the order of *ou*r said lawes we do remitt & discharge / And these our l*ett*res signed w*ith* *ou*r hande shalbe yo*ur* sufficient warraunt & discharge in that behalf Given vnder *ou*r signet at *ou*r Pallace of westm*inste*r the **ixth of february the xiiijth yere of *ou*r reign.**

The Manuscript

Library of the Duke of Norfolk, Arundel House, G.1/22. Written in brownish ink in a professional secretary hand, ranged to the right leaving a wide margin to the left, seven swung dashes on the fourth line filling a 35mm space where a date was erased by the scribe, the last nine words of text added in another secretary hand in darker ink; written on vellum, 280 × 355mm (11 × 14 inches), upper border 65mm deep containing the royal signature which is 65mm long and the initial capital 50mm high, lower border 70mm deep containing a square papered privy seal (40mm wide) with embossed royal arms partly circled by the legend ELIZABETH REGINA; the document endorsed in yet another secretary hand 'The Quenes Warraunt touching the Duke', and now bearing four vertical folds. See PLATE I.

Provenance

Given to Henry Fitzalan-Howard, twentieth Duke of Norfolk (1847-1917), on 14 February 1895, by the Rt Hon. Sir Joseph Cockfield Dimsdale (1849-1912), Sheriff of London (Lord Mayor in 1901-2). In his accompanying letter presenting the warrant, Dimsdale writes that 'It has been in my family for nearly a century'. As Vice-President of the London and Middlesex Society, Sheriff Dimsdale exhibited this warrant at a general meeting at Innholders' Hall on 12 June 1894. It appears in the printed programme as item 18, along with other sixteenth-, seventeenth- and eighteenth-century seals and state documents that he owned (including, as item 21, Elizabeth's signed 'commission for issue of warrant for the arrest and execution of the Earl of Northumberland ... 20th July, 1572').

A later transcript of a Latin version of the Norfolk warrant (presumably the formal Latinised version engrossed to pass the Great Seal) was made in the early 1600s by a scribe for Sir Stephen Powle (*c*.1553-1630), acting Clerk of the Crown in Chancery, in one of his folio compilations (Bodleian Library, Oxford, MS Tanner 168, fol. 118v).

APPENDIX II

DRAFT WARRANT, PARTLY BY LORD BURGHLEY, FOR THE EXECUTION OF THE DUKE OF NORFOLK, 9 APRIL 1572

The Text

By the Queene

Trustie and welbeloved we greete yow well. We will that notw*ith*standing any our formar l*ett*res addressed vnto you, sence the first delivery to yow of our writt vnder our great Seale for execution of Justice vpon the Judgment given against the late Duke of Norfolke, you shall procede according to the tenor of the sayd writt in such maner, as you owght to have doone before the recept of our sayd l*ett*res for the stay therof. Which we did commaund than only for a tyme vpon some resonable respecte*s* w*ith*out any intention to forbeare wholly the execution of Justice.

S*ir*./ Where sence ~~the~~ our wrytt vnd*er* o*u*r gret seale of England delyvered vnto yow to p*ro*cede to the executio*n* of the Judgeme*n*t of the ^late^ Duke of Norfolk, yow have bene at sondry tymes willed ^in o*u*r name^ to stay therin vppo*n* certe*n* good consid*er*atio*n*s nor the tyme than fou*n*d, ^to differ the same^ now vppo*n* ~~other iust~~ ^sundry ~~yet~~ necessary^ consideratio*n*s therto vs moving we will and com*m*au*n*d yow that notw*ith*standing any form*er* ~~stay commaundment~~ ^ordre gyve*n* to yow for the^ stey of the same yow shall vppo*n* the recept of these o*u*r L*ett*res w*ith*out furd*er* stey p*ro*cede to the executio*n* of o*u*r formar writt accord*ing* to the tenor therof, and that yow gyve knolledg*e* of this our determinatio*n* to y̅ᵉ the lievtena*n*t of o*u*r tower of Londo*n* to thinte*n*t yow and he may agree vppo*n* the tyme convenient for that purpose and this shalbe your Warrant in that behalf.

To y[e] shreifs of London
9. Apr*i*ll 1572 **for the**
executio*n* of the D.

The Manuscript

Library of the Marquess of Salisbury, Hatfield House, Cecil Papers 7/24. Edited in William Murdin, *A Collection of State Papers relating to Affairs in the Reign of Queen Elizabeth ... transcribed from Original Papers ... left by William Cecill Lord Burghley ... at Hatfield House* (London, 1759), pp. 177-8. The present transcription is published by permission of the Most Honourable the Marquess of Salisbury.

APPENDIX III

AUTOGRAPH LETTER SIGNED BY QUEEN ELIZABETH TO LORD BURGHLEY REVOKING THE EXECUTION OF THE DUKE OF NORFOLK, 11 APRIL 1572

The Text

My lord me thinkes that I am more beholdinge to the hindar part of my hed than wel dare trust the forwards side of the same and therfor sent to the Levetenant and the S: as you knowe best the ordar to defar this execution till the here furdar and that this may be done I doubte nothinge without – curiocitie of my further warrant for that ther rasche determination upon a very unfit day was countermaunded by your considerat admonition the causes that move me to this ar not now to be expressed lest an irreuocable dede be in mene while com*m*itted. If the wyl nides a Warrant let this suffice all writen with my none hand. Your most lovinge soveraine

Elizabeth R

The Manuscript

Bodleian Library, MS Ashmole 1729, fols 13r-14v. Autograph letter signed by the Queen, hurriedly written, with a papered royal privy seal. Endorsed in Burghley's hand: 'xj Ap[l]. 1572. / The Q. Ma[ty] w[t] hir own / hand. for staying of y[e] / Execvtio*n* of y[e] D. o. / Rc. at .2. in y[e] morni*ng*'.

The text is edited in *Original Letters, Illustrative of English History*, ed. Sir Henry Ellis, [First Series], 3 vols (London, 1824), II, 262-3; and in *Elizabeth I: Collected Works*, ed. Leah S. Marcus, Janel Mueller, and Mary Beth Rose (Chicago & London, 2000), p. 131 (where is also noted an eighteenth-century copy of it in Bodleian, MS Smith 68, art. 54, fol. 54); and a more diplomatic transcription appears in *Elizabeth I: Autograph Compositions and Foreign Language Originals*, ed. Janel Mueller and Leah S. Marcus (Chicago & London, 2003), pp. 42-3. The letter is reproduced in colour facsimile, with near-literal transcription, in Felix Pryor, *Elizabeth I: Her Life in Letters* (British Library, 2003), pp. 64-5 (No. 25), and also reproduced in colour, in smaller format, in *Elizabeth: The Exhibition at the National Maritime Museum*, ed. Susan Doran (London, 2003), p. 219.

APPENDIX IV

EXECUTION WARRANT OF ROBERT DEVEREUX, SECOND EARL OF ESSEX, 20 FEBRUARY 1600/1

The Text

Elizabeth R

Elizabeth by the grace of god Quene of England ffraunce and Ireland Defender of the faithe &c. **To** our right trustie and welbeloved Counsaillor Sir Thomas Egerton knight lorde keper of the great Seale of England greetinge; **whereas** Robert Earle of Essex late of Chartley in the County of Stafford and henrye Earle of South*ampton* late of Tychfeild in the Countie of South*ampton* haue bin indyted of divers highe Treasons by them comitted against vs, and therevpon haue bin tried and founde giltye of those offence*s* before our right trustie and right welbeloved Counsellor Thomas Lord Buchurst lord Treasorer of England knight of the moste noble order of our Garter late our Steward of England for the triall of the said Robert Earle of Essex and henrye Earle of South*ampton* vpon theire said offence*s*, and haue also for the same theire offences as abovesaid bin adiudged by the said Thomas Lord Buchurst to be Drawen hanged and quartered accordinge to the lawes and customes of this our Realme of England in that case provided, **And** althoughe the said Robert Earle of Essex is adiudged to Dye as aforesaid, yet we myndinge to Dispence withe that manner of execucion of iudgement in respect the said Robert Earle of Essex was a noble man, **Doe** therefore by these presente*s* pardon remitt and release the said Robert Earle of Essex of and from suche execucion of iudgement to be Drawen hanged and quartered as abovesaid, and in steed therof our pleasure is to haue the head of the said Robert Earle of Essex cutt of at the greene within our Tower of London, and in suche sorte and order as in suche like cases hathe bin their Don or Vsed touchinge or conc*er*ninge noble p*er*sons. The said iudgement to be drawen hanged and quartered or any lawe or other thinge or matter Whatsoever to the contrarye notwithstandinge, **Willinge** chardginge and expresslye com*m*aundinge you the said lord keper that vpon the receipt hereof yo*u* Doe fourthwith direct vnder our said great Seale of England a writt to the Livetenant of our Tower of london or his Deputie there for the executinge of the said Robert Earle of Essex at the said greene within our said Tower of london in suche sorte manner or forme as in suche like cases hathe heretofore bin Don or Vsed to be Don, **And**, these presente*s* shalbe your warraunt and Dischardge for the same against vs our heires and Successors for ever. **Given** vnder our privy Seale at our Palace of Westm*inster* the twenteeth Day of ffebruarye in the three and fortieth yeare of our raigne /.

The Manuscript

British Library, Loan MS 34. Written in brownish ink in a professional secretary hand, ranged to the right leaving a 90mm margin to the left, on vellum, 337 × 475mm (13¼ × 16¾ inches), upper border 110mm deep containing the royal signature which is 150mm long and 70mm deep including flourishes, the lower border 150mm deep containing a diamond-shaped papered privy seal 120 × 110mm with embossed royal arms partly circled by the legend ELIZABETH REGINA, the document docketed by Sir Thomas Egerton (see below), endorsed in a contemporary secretary hand 'Comiss de Exec .... Essex' and, in a later seventeenth-century hand, '20th Feb^{ry} 43. Eliz Queen Elizabeths Warr^{t} for the Execution of Robert Earl of Essex who was Executed on the 25 ffeb^{ry}. followinge'; the document now bearing three vertical and two horizontal folds.

The lower right hand corner of the warrant (recto side) is inscribed in the hand of Sir Thomas Egerton, Lord Keeper of the Great Seal, as follows:

> Recepi apud turrim Londin*ensem* p*er* deliberac*ion*em, Ro*berti* Cecill militis .23. die febr*uarii* anno suprascripto. Et sup*er*inde, eodem die ego sigillavi bre*vem* de executione, qu*ae* deliberat*a*

fuit locu*m* tenenti die Martis existen*te* .24. die febr*uarii*, virtute Cuius execut*io* fact*a* fuit die Mercurij existen*te* .25. die febr*uarii* sup*radic*ti Tho*mas* Eg*erton* Cust*os* Sig*illi*

[*Translation:* I received this at the Tower of London by delivery of Sir Robert Cecil 23 day of February in the year written above. And thereupon on the same day I signed the warrant of execution, which was delivered to the holder of the post [Lieutenant of the Tower] on the present Tuesday 24 day of February by virtue of which the execution was carried out the present Wednesday 25 day of February above written Thomas Egerton, Keeper of the Seal]

This warrant is reproduced in colour facsimile in Felix Pryor, *Elizabeth I: Her Life in Letters* (British Library, 2003), pp. 124-5 (No. 55), and see also PLATE 2 above.

Provenance

The warrant has remained in the family papers of Sir Thomas Egerton, Baron Ellesmere and Viscount Brackley (1540?-1617), and his descendants, Earls and Dukes of Bridgewater, and is now owned by the Duke of Sutherland, although on permanent deposit in the British Library. A contemporary transcript of the warrant (with a few minor variants and omissions) was made by a scribe for Sir Stephen Powle, acting Clerk of the Crown in Chancery, in one of his folio compilations (Bodleian Library, MS Tanner 168, fols 110v-111r). He dockets it in his own hand: 'Note that this was ingrossed in secretary hande perused by the L^{d}. Chiefe Justice & L^{d}. Keeper afterward, signed and then passed the privy seale, as appeareth by the Teste[36] ouerslipping the privy signet office so that the warrant signed was sealed by the priuy Seale and then deliuered the Ld Keeper who kept the same secretly for his dischardge: neauer enrowling the same.' (A somewhat garbled transcription of this note is printed in Virginia F. Stern, *Sir Stephen Powle of Court and Country* (London & Toronto, 1992), p. 119.)

APPENDIX V

DRAFT BY LORD BURGHLEY AND SIR FRANCIS WALSINGHAM, OF AN EXECUTION WARRANT FOR MARY, QUEEN OF SCOTS, THE BEGINNING OF DECEMBER 1586

The Text

Where we were geven to understand, that after the end of the Session of Parliament begonne and holden at Westminster in our Countey of middlesex the xxiii Day of November in the xxvii yeare of our Raigne, that is to saye, after the first Day of June in the said xxvii yere of our Raigne, Divers things were Compassed and imagined tending to the hurte of our Royall person, as well by marie the Daughter and Heire of James the fifth, late Kinge of Scotland, comonly called the Queene of Scotts and Dowager of ffraunce, pretendinge title to the crowne of this Realme of England, as by diverse other persons with the privetie of the said Marie. And where thereuppon we intendinge and Determyninge that the Statute in that behalf made at the said Session of Parliament holden the said xxiii Daie of November by all things and in everye respecte shold be rightlie and effectuallie executed, according to the tenor of the same statute, and that all the said offences and the circumstances thereof shold be exa*m*ined, and Sentence or Judgement thereuppon geven, accordinge to the tenor and effecte of the same Statute, Dyd for that purpose and accordinge to the forme and effecte of the same Statute in that behalf, and by force thereof

36 The *Teste* (meaning 'in witness') is the final clause naming the person who authorises the affixing of the royal seal.

by our Commission under our greate Seale of England bearinge Date at our Castle of wyndsor in our Countie of Berk*shire* the Sixth Daie of October now last past, assigne and name the Lordes and others of our Privie Counsell, and so many other Lordes of Parliament, as with the same Privie Counsell made upp the number of forty two, and did also thereby accordinge to the same Statute for their assistance in that behalf and for the Purpose in the same Statute mentioned, assigne and appoynte Certayne of the Judges of the Court of Record at Westminster. And furthermore accordinge to the tenor of the same Statute Did in and by the same Comission name and Assigne the same Counsell, Lordes, and Judges, and the more Parte of them accordinge to the tenor of the said Statute, to examyne all and everye thinge and things compassed and imagined, tendinge to the hurte of our Royall Person aswell by the said Marie as by any other Person or Persons with the Privetie of the said Marie, and all the circumstances thereof, And thereuppon, accordinge to the tenor of the said Statute to geve Sentence or Judgement as uppon good prooff the matter unto them shold appere, as in and by the same Comission more fully and at large appeareth. And whereas afterwardes the more parte of the sayd Counsell, Lordes, and Judges in our sayd Comission named Did accordinglie in the Presence of the sayd Marie at divers tymes verie exactlie and with greate Deliberation examyne all the matters and offenses mentioned in our said Comission, and all the Circumstances thereof, and heard at large what the said Marie cold say for her excuse and Defence in that behalf, and thereuppon afterwards, that is to saye, the xxv^th^ Day of october now last past, as uppon good prooff the matter to them Did appere, the more Parte of the sayd Counsell Lordes and Judges in our sayd Comission named Did with one assent and Consent, geve Sentence and Judgement, that after the end of the said Session of Parliament, that is to saye, after the said first Daie of June in the said xxvii^th^ yere of our Raigne, and before the Date of our said Comission, Divers things were Compassed and imagined within this Realme of England by Anthonye Babington, and others with the privetie of the said Marie pretendinge title to the Crowne of this Realme of England, tending to the hurte, Death and Destrucc*i*on of our Royall Person, And lykewyse that after the Same first Daie of June in the xxvii^th^ yere aforesaid, and before the Date of our said Comission, the said Marie, pretending title to the Crowne of this Realme of England had Compassed and imagined within this Realme of England Divers things tendinge to the hurte Death and Destrucc*i*on of our Royall Person Contrarie to the forme of the said Statute, as in and by the Record thereof and the same Sentence more fullye it doth and may appere. And where thereuppon at the humble Petition and instant Sute of the Lordes and Com*m*ons in this present Parliament assembled, unto us in that behalf made, we accordinge to the said Statute by our Proclamac*i*on under our greate Seale of England bearing Date at Rychmont the Daye of this instant moneth of December Have Declared and published the said Sentence and Jugement. and Wher the sayd Lordes and Com*m*ons in this present Parliament assembled Depelye foreseing the continuall Dangers, that we and thys whole Realme Do stand in through the said Dangerous practyses, and Seing withall that by the ancyent Lawes off thys our Realme they do Justlye Deserve Death, and that all the favours and tollerance by us heretofore used towardes the sayde Marye have and do Imbolden her, and her Confederats to Persevere in their myschevous attempts against us, and this our Relme have therfore in lyke manner by their said Petition Instantly moved us that execution off Death which she hath Is [so] Justly deserved myght be Done on the same Marye according to the trew meanying off the sayd Statute; We therefore Do hereby Dyrect in that behalf that the same mary shall and may be persued unto Death according to the sayd Statute, and for the convenyent Doing theroff, we do hereby Direct and Com*m*and you the sayd [*blank*] and any two, or more off you, that at our Castle off ffotheringhay in our Co*u*ntie of Northampton you Do Imedyatly cause the hedd off the same Marye to be Cutt off, whereoff fayl ye not. and these our Letters Patents, or the enrolement therof together with the sayd Statute shalbe to you and to every two or more off you, and to all others to whome it shall aperteyne, a Suffycyent Warrant and Dyscharg in that behalfols In witnes whereoff &c.

The Manuscript

Library of the Marquess of Salisbury, Hatfield House, Cecil Papers 15/56. An eighteenth-century transcript, possibly by William Murdin; headed 'A coppy of the Warrant for the execution of Mary Q. of Scotts' [*sidenote*:] 1586. December. The Direccyon / Note. that this must Beare date the day after the Proclamation made.'; [*Docketed in the left margin near the top*:] Endors'd by Ld Burg. the latter part writ by Sec. Walsingham'; endorsed 'Warr^{t}. for Excut. of Ma: Q. Scotts'/ Printed'. Edited versions, without the cancelled text, are printed in Murdin, *op. cit.*, pp. 576-7, and in *The Last Years of Mary, Queen of Scots: Documents from the Cecil Papers at Hatfield House*, ed. Alan G.R. Smith (London, 1990), pp. [63-4], no. 24. The present transcription is published by permission of the Most Honourable the Marquess of Salisbury.

APPENDIX VI

DRAFT BY LORD BURGHLEY OF AN ORDER FOR THE EXECUTION OF MARY, QUEEN OF SCOTS, 10 DECEMBER 1586

The Text

Elizab. by ye Grace of God Q. of England ^fra*n*ce^ and Irla*n*d defendor of ye fayth &c
To our Trusty and Welbeloved Counsellor ~~we grete yow well Grety*ng*~~ s^{r} Amyas paulett Knight grety*ng* Where yow have had ^and yet hathe^ <~~and as yet hath~~> y^{e} Custody and Chardg of y^{e} p*er*son of y^{e} Q. of Scotte*s* ageynst who*m* sente*n*ce and Iudgme*nt* hath bene gyven [?~~charge~~] ~~wherby she hath bene Judged to have attempted that she hath Co*m*passed and Imagyned our deth dyvers thynges to y$^{\bar{e}}$ hurt death and destructio*n* of our p*er*son~~, as by our late p*ro*clamatio*n* dated y^{e} 4. of this mo*n*th is to all p*er*sons published And ^for^ that we have bene ~~Contynually~~ by y^{e} state*s* of our p*a*rleme*n*t most instantly moved vrged and pressed, to cause furth*e*r executio*n* to be made of ye sayd sente*n*ce [*added in margin:* in such ernest sort, as wit*h*out the same, it is by the*m* all sole*m*ly protested y^{t} they ca*n* by no devise fynd any meanes for ye suerty of our p*er*son nor for ye p*re*s*er*vatio*n* of them selves their posterite, and state of ye realm wher vppo*n* we ar ageynst our own na*tur*all dispositio*n* drawe*n* to yelde hervnto and therfor] We ^~~being of our natural dispositio*n*~~^ ~~being~~ have ^presently^ directed our Co*m*missio*n* vnder our great seale of Engla*n*d to our shyrryve of ~~of~~ our County of Northa*m*pto*n*, to repayre to yow, and have ^thereby willed and^ warra*n*ted hym to ~~tak~~ ^receave^ ye p*er*so*n* of ye sayd Q. ~~of~~ into his chardg, and wit*h*out delaye to do executio*n* ^~~uppo*n* her~~^ as by our sayd Com*m*issio*n* may ^further^ appeare vnto yow. and therfor we do will and Com*man*d yow to delyver hir vnto his chardg, as to ^~~and~~ publick ~~officer~~^ our shyrryf ^chef officer of y^{t} o*u*r County^ so as he also wit*h*out delay shall in ye prese*n*ce of su*n*dry our Noble me*n* and of your self ~~do executio*n*~~ wit*h*in y^{t} (our Castle do ~~exec~~ y^{e} same exequutio*n*, and that yow wit*h* ~~all your power~~ ^such ~~co*m*panys~~ as yow have^ ther ~~being~~ ^atte*n*da*n*t o*n* yow ther^ for our s*er*vice ~~at our Co*mman*dme*nt* and shall thys mch~~ to ^do^ ayd and assist our sayd shyrryve and all others ~~for y$^{\bar{e}}$~~ ^y^{t} shall ther be present^ exequtio*n* ~~off his service~~ ^for the forsayd s*er*vice^ And these our l*et*res patente*s* vnder o*u*r Great Seale of Engla*n*d shall be your sufficie*n*t disch*a*rg Gyven at our Manor of Rychmo*n*t the [*blank*] of Dece*m*b*er* .~~29.~~ y^{e} xxixth of our reign/

The Manuscript

Library of the Marquess of Salisbury, Hatfield House, Cecil Papers 165/10. A draft in the hand of Lord Burghley, on a folio page, endorsed '10 December 1586'. Edited versions, without the cancelled text, are printed in Murdin, pp. 574-5, and in *The Last Years of Mary, Queen of Scots:*

Documents from the Cecil Papers at Hatfield House, ed. Alan G.R. Smith (London, 1990), p. [65], No. 25. A colour facsimile of the manuscript appears in Felix Pryor, *Elizabeth I: Her Life in Letters* (British Library, 2003), pp. 90-1 (No. 38), and see PLATE 5 above. The present transcription is published by permission of the Most Honourable the Marquess of Salisbury.

APPENDIX VII

FINAL VERSION OF THE EXECUTION WARRANT OF MARY, QUEEN OF SCOTS, 1 FEBRUARY 1586/7: ROBERT BEALE'S TRANSCRIPT

The Text

Elizabeth: R:

Elizabethe by the grace of god Queene of Englande frau*n*ce & Irelande &c. To o*ur* right trustie and welbeloued Coosins George Erle of Shrewsburie, Erle marshall of Englande Henrie Erle of Kent, Henrie Erle of Derby, George Erle of Cumberlande, Henrie Erle of Penbroke greetinge. Wheras sithence the sentence geuen by yow and others of o*ur* Counsell, Nobilitie, and Judges against the Queene of Scottes by the name of marie the daughter and heire of James the fift late kinge of Scottes com*m*onlie called the Queene of Scottes and Douager of frau*n*ce, as to yow is well knowen: All the States of o*ur* late p*ar*lame*n*t assembled did not onlie deliberatelie w*i*th greate aduise allowe and approue the same sentence as iust and honorable, but did also w*i*th all hu*m*blenes and earnestnes possible at sondrie times require, solicite, and presse vs to proceade to the publishing of the same: and theruppon to directe such further execuc*i*on against her p*er*son, as they did adiudge her to haue duelie deserued, addinge therto, that the forbearinge therof was and would be dailie a c*er*taine and vndoubted danger not onlie to o*ur* owne life, but to them selues, their posteritie and the publyke state of this realme, aswell for the cause of the gospell and the true religion of Christ, as for the peace of the whole realme. Whervppon we did (though the same was w*i*th some delaye of time) publishe the same sentence by o*ur* p*ro*clamac*i*on and yet hitherto haue forborne to geue direction for the further satisfaction of the foresaid most earnest requestes made by the said Estates of o*ur* p*ar*lament, wherby we doe dailye vnd*er*stande by all sortes of o*ur* lovinge subiectes both of o*ur* Nobilitie and Counsell, and also of the wisest, grauest, and best deuoted of all other o*ur* subiectes of inferior degres how greatlie and deepelie from the bottome of their hartes they are grieued and afflicted w*i*th dailie yea howerlie feare of our life and therby consequentlie w*i*th a dreadfull doubt & expectac*i*on of the ruine of the p*rese*nt godlie and happie estate of this realme, if we shall forbeare the further finall execuc*i*on as it is desired and neglecte their gen*er*all and co*n*tinuall requestes, prayers, cou*n*sells and advises: And theruppon co*n*trarie to o*ur* owne naturall disposic*i*on in such a case beinge ou*er*come w*i*th the euident weighte of their counsells, and the dailie co*n*tinuau*n*ce of their intercessions, importinge suche a necessitie as appearethe directlie tendinge to the safetie not onlie of o*ur* self, but also of the weale of the whole realme: we haue condescended to suffer iustice to take place: And for thexecuc*i*on therof, vppon the speciall trust, experie*n*ce, and confidence, w*hi*ch we haue in yo*ur* loyalties, faithfullnes, and loue bothe towardes o*ur* p*er*son and the safetie therof, and to yo*ur* natiue cou*n*treye wherof yow are most noble & principall members: we doe will and by warrau*n*t herof doe directe and authorise yow assoone as yow shall haue time co*n*venie*n*t to repaire to o*ur* Castell of Fotheringhaye, where the said queene of Scotte*s* is in Custodie of o*ur* right trustie servau*n*t and Counsellor S*ir* Amys Powlet knighte, and there takinge her into yo*ur* charge, to cause by yo*ur* com*m*aundement execuc*i*on to be don vppon her p*er*son in the presence of yo*ur* selues and the said S*ir* Amys Poulet, and of suche other officers of iustice as yow shall com*m*aunde to be there, to attende vppon yow for that purpose, and the same to be don in such maner and forme and at suche time and place there, and by such p*er*sons as to yow five fower three or two of yow shalbe thought by yo*ur* discrec*i*ons co*n*venient, notw*i*thstandinge anie Lawe, Statute, or ordinau*n*ce to the co*n*trarie. And these o*ur* l*ett*res patente*s* sealed w*i*th o*ur* greate Seale of Englande, shalbe to yow and eu*er*ie of yow and to all p*er*sons that shalbe p*rese*nt, or shalbe by yow com*m*aunded to doe anie thinge app*er*teyning to the aforesaid execuc*i*on, a full sufficie*n*t warrau*n*t and discharge for ever. And further we are also pleased and co*n*tented, and by these p*ate*nts we doe will, com*m*aunde, and authorise o*ur* Chau*n*color of Englande at the requestes of yow all and of eu*er*ie of yow to deliu*er* vnto eu*er*ie of yow the duplicate of these o*ur* L*ett*res pate*n*tes to be to all purposes duelie made, dated, and sealed w*i*th o*ur* greate Seale of Englande as these p*ate*ntes are. In witnesse wherof we haue caused these o*ur* l*ett*res to be made pate*n*tes. Yeven at o*ur* manor of Grenewiche the first daie of februarie in the xxixth yere of o*ur* reigne.

The Manuscript

British Library, Additional MS 48027 (Yelverton MS 31), fols 645r-646r (see PLATE 7). A copy in the professional secretary hand of one of the principal clerks of Robert Beale (1541-1601), Clerk of the Privy Council; on three folio pages; docketed at the top in Beale's hand 'Her m*a*j*es*tys hand was also in the Copp*ie*'; docketed in the margin by the clerk 'Copy of the Com*m*ission vnder the greate seale of Englande for th'execuc*i*on of the Scotish Queen'; bound in a large folio volume of Beale's papers relating to Mary, Queen of Scots.

Other known copies

(i) Private collection. Another transcript in the hand of one of Robert Beale's clerks, also annotated almost certainly by Beale himself (including his bold heading 'Elizabeth R' and underlining of references to 'you'), and probably sent by him to the Earl of Kent, one of the commissioners for the execution. This manuscript was once part of the James Fairhurst Papers, which probably comprised state papers kept in the Commonwealth period by the jurist John Selden and which incorporated materials of the Earls of Kent. It was sold, with other related documents, at Sotheby's on 4 June 1946 (in lots 380-92) and again on 16 December 1996, lot 42, where the first page is illustrated in the catalogue (and see PLATE 8 above).

(ii) British Library, Additional MS 34218, fol. 185r-v: transcript (headed 'Her Ma*j*e*s*ties L*ett*eres patente*s* directed, for the Execution of the Queene of Scotts', with variants and omissions) in a compilation made for Sir Francis Fane, first Earl of Westmorland, M.P. (1580-1629).

(iii) British Library, Harley MS 290, fols 203r-204r: a contemporary transcript (with variants and omissions), subscribed 'A Copie of the warrant vnder the great seale of England for the execut*io*n of Marie Queene of Scotte*s* Dated at Greenwich 1° ffebruarij A^{o} 29 Elizabethe', endorsed in the hand of the antiquary Ralph Starkey (*c.*1569-1628) [and therefore possibly relating to his collection of papers of William Davison which was seized by the Privy Council in 1619],[37] in a volume of state papers (both originals and transcripts, some in Starkey's hand) relating to Mary, Queen of Scots. The text of this manuscript is edited in *Calendar of the State Papers relating to Scotland and Mary, Queen of Scots 1547-1603*, ed. William K. Boyd, IX (1915), 262-3.

37 See Peter Beal, *In Praise of Scribes: Manuscripts and their Makers in Seventeenth-Century England* (Oxford, 1998), p. 89.

(iv) British Library, Harley MS 4663, vol. II, fols 84v-87v: transcript (with variants and a substantial omission) in a compilation of late seventeenth- or very early eighteenth-century transcripts of state papers relating chiefly to Mary, Queen of Scots. An endorsement on fol. 87v reads: 'On the Back of this Copy is mark'd that it was penn'd by the Lord Treasurer [Burghley].'

(v) British Library, Sloane MS 650, fols 139v-141r: transcript (headed 'Her Ma*jes*ties Letters Patents directed for the Execution of ye Queen of Scots', with variants and omissions) in a compilation chiefly relating to disputes in the Church of Scotland, 1636-38.

A modern-spelling version of the warrant, from an unspecified source, is also printed in *Letters of Mary, Queen of Scots*, ed. Agnes Strickland, 2 vols (London, 1844), II, 239-41.

QUEEN ELIZABETH PRAYS FOR THE LIVING AND THE DEAD

Steven W. May

Rule by God's grace and in obedience to His will; rule founded on love for her subjects and confirmed by their reciprocal love for her. From the beginning of Elizabeth's reign, these were the very personal hallmarks of her sovereignty. Both themes dominated the myth of good Queen Bess as it developed after her death. Nostalgic elegies for Elizabeth gave way to plays, verse narratives, biographies, and countless references to her loving, godly rule in early Stuart correspondence, sermons, and political tracts. Scholars have traced the growth of her legend in the seventeenth century in numerous books and articles, most recently in John Watkins's *Representing Elizabeth in Stuart England* (2002) and in *The Myth of Elizabeth* (2003), a collection of essays edited by Susan Doran and Thomas S. Freeman.[1] These studies deal, however, almost exclusively with external influences on her myth. They analyse how later writers characterised the Queen in both literary and non-literary compositions. Yet the myth of Gloriana also received at least marginal nurturing from a small body of her own writings largely ignored in scholarly assessments of her reputation. These works nevertheless circulated widely in print and manuscript for half a century and more after her death. Their distribution and influence on her posthumous image is the subject of this paper.

Elizabeth's writings have come down to us in five principal genres of writing: speeches, letters, prayers, poetry, and translated prose and verse. With one exception, these last two categories of her work saw little or no circulation after her death. The Queen's image may, in fact, have benefited from the almost total neglect of her poetry during the seventeenth century, for her verse did not always express her most positive traits. Her attitude toward disloyal subjects in 'The doubt of future foes', for example, is harsh and menacing, while in another poem she composed in both Latin and English verses she complains of the onerous burden of rule in a manner not at all flattering to her subjects: 'I serve the rout, and all their follies bear.'[2] The one scrap of verse that did convey her authentic voice to later generations reveals her courage and determination in the face of persecution. In his *Acts and Monuments* John Foxe quoted the couplet 'Much suspected by me / Nothing proved can be' (STC 11222, 1563; four subsequent

1 Watkins (Cambridge, 2002); Doran and Freeman (Houndmills, 2003). See also Michael Dobson and Nicola J. Watson, *England's Elizabeth* (Oxford, 2002).
2 This is Poem 5b in my edition, *Queen Elizabeth I: Selected Works* (New York, 2004).

editions between 1610 and 1684). As Princess Elizabeth, she had inscribed this verse on a window at Woodstock Palace after Queen Mary confined her there in 1555-6, and this was the context in which it was regularly deployed in later publications. It was copied at sometime after 1606 by the scribe of Aberystwyth, National Library of Wales, MS Sotheby B2, fol. 59v, but I have no other evidence of its manuscript circulation. Thomas Heywood reprinted the poem in *Englands Elisabeth* (STC 13313, 1631; two more editions by 1641), and Samuel Clarke included it in *The Second Part of the Marrow of Ecclesiastical Historie* (1650, Wing C4556; 1683, Wing C4538). The couplet testifies to the Princess Elizabeth's courage and defiance in the face of persecution but so slight a work could have exerted little influence on the overall development of her myth.

Elizabeth's piety and love for her people endured as the dominant and persistent themes of her more substantial canonical works that circulated posthumously. Both themes emerge clearly in one of her most widely dispersed writings, her 'Golden Speech' to the House of Commons on 30 November 1601. This oration has come down to us in five different states only two of which saw widespread distribution in print and manuscript during the seventeenth century. I treat these compositions as Elizabeth's with some qualification. Their overlapping phrasing and sentiments coupled with the external evidence of how both texts were produced suggest that they both convey the Queen's words intermingled with words she did not utter on that November afternoon. More than two dozen manuscript copies of these two versions of the speech have survived along with a half-dozen printed texts between 1601 and 1682.[3] Both versions are unanimous in expressing the Queen's love for her subjects. In them she affirms that 'There is no jewel, be it of never so rich a price, which I set before this jewel, I mean your love.' As for the success of her long reign, she insists in the 'Golden Speech' on giving 'God the praise as a testimony before you and not to attribute anything unto myself'.[4] After her death, these themes were amplified and more specifically illustrated by her writings in two other genres, prayer and epistle. Some of her works in these genres circulated longer and even more widely than her 'Golden Speech'. Among her authentic writings, these alone could have contributed significantly to her reputation in the seventeenth century and beyond, although their nature, circulation, and influence have received little scholarly attention.

Of all the types of writing that might nurture an author's reputation, prayer must rank among the least promising genres with modern readers. Prayers are seldom considered the most memorable works in our English literary heritage. During the

3 T. E. Hartley, *Proceedings in the Parliaments of Elizabeth I* (Manchester, 1995), identifies nine manuscript copies of the third version of the speech (v.3.294), to which can be added those in Folger Library MS X.d. 152, fols 4r-8v; MS V.a. 142, fols 2r-4v, and Bodleian Library MS Rawl. D. 1045, pp. 84-91. In addition to the printed text in STC 7579, version three was reprinted in Wing E530 (1679). Hartley's version 4 is the text based on that in Townshend's *Journal* (published as *Historical Collections*, 1680, Wing T1991). Published texts of the speech include that in Simonds D'Ewes, *The Journals of All the Parliaments During the Reign of Queen Elizabeth* (1682), *A speech made by Queen Elizabeth* (Wing E533, 1688), and Wing E534, 1642. To Hartley's list of thirteen manuscript texts we can add the texts in British Library Lansdowne MSS 512, fols 37v-41r, and Lansdowne 515, fols 140r-144v.

4 *Elizabeth I: Selected Works*, Speech 11, pp. 84, 88.

Renaissance, of course, the age's spiritual intensity caused entire books of prayers to rank among the most popular genres of the book trade. In addition to the official liturgy of the Church of England, Elizabeth's government set forth prayers to be said on special occasions such as in time of plague, drought, or dearth. And book-length collections of prayers compiled by Edward Dering, Richard Day, Thomas Becon, and many others rolled from English presses in multiple editions (see PLATE 1).[5] Set prayers for personal use, popular as they were with our ancestors, are now of primary interest for what they reveal about the most intensely held beliefs and aspirations of historical persons. Queen Elizabeth, Supreme Governor of the Church of England, took prayer very seriously, none more so than prayers of her own composition. Moreover, she deemed her communications with the Deity highly personal and private forms of expression.

The most emphatic evidence that Elizabeth resented any public dissemination of her prayers emerges from documents connected with the prayer she drafted for the good success of the naval expedition against Spain in 1597. Her Archbishop of Canterbury, John Whitgift, obtained a copy of this prayer which he included in a pamphlet of state prayers on the same subject published under the title, *Certaine Prayers set foorth by Authoritie* (STC 16528a.5). Alas, the authority behind this volume did not pass royal muster. Sir Robert Cecil conveyed their sovereign's opinion of it in this letter to Whitgift:

> May it please your Grace,
> I have presented unto the Queen your book of printed prayers, and have read unto her three or four of them, of all which she taketh so great liking, as she hath willed me to give you many thanks for the same, and hath commanded some of them to be read in the chapel, as they were. But I must tell you withal, that she is much troubled that her own prayer is in print, and therfore hath commanded me to require you in any wise to make stay of it, and that the same may be taken out of all the books that are printed. This I hope your Grace will effect, and hereof I mean (when I shall see you) to speak with you further.

In a postscript, Cecil added: 'I assure you her Majesty requests this very earnestly to be done.'[6] It is worth noting that Whitgift had not published the Queen's prayer under her name. It appears in the tract on a page facing the royal arms and is set in a different font from the other prayers in the volume. Whitgift failed to confiscate all the offensive copies of the pamphlet, but he did reissue it minus the Queen's involuntary contribution. As a result, this book of prayers survives in four different states, two of which include Elizabeth's prayer. The compilers of the second edition of the *Short Title Catalogue* reasonably supposed that prayers were added to the tract in later editions, but Cecil's letter shows that material was instead deleted in the reprintings. Accordingly, the editions of *Certaine Prayers* appear in the *STC* in an order just the opposite of their actual publication.

5 Under 'Liturgies – Church of England ... Special Forms of Prayer on Various Occasions', STC2 lists 32 different prayers issued during Elizabeth's reign. Day's *Booke of Christian Prayers* saw four editions between 1578 and 1620; Dering's *Godlye Priuate Praiers for Housholders* saw nine editions (1574-1624), and Becon's *The Pomander of Prayer*, nine editions between 1558 and 1584.

6 Lambeth Palace Library, Fairhurst MS 3470, fol. 195, spelling normalized.

1 Woodcut depiction of Queen Elizabeth at prayer on the verso of the title-page of Richard Day's *A Booke of Christian Prayers*, 1578 (STC 6429)

From Elizabeth's standpoint it was bad enough that a few copies of the pamphlet escaped the bookstalls with her prayer intact, but much worse was to follow. Not only did this prayer circulate long and widely, its distribution actually lagged somewhat behind that of another of her private devotions. Only the year before, she had composed a prayer for the success of that summer's expedition against Spain, the so-called 'Cadiz Raid'. The title of one authoritative text of this work describes it as 'Her Ma^{tes} pryvate medytacion vppon th^{e} present Expedytion'.[7] Yet Secretary Cecil presumed to send a copy of it to the joint commanders of the venture, Lord Admiral Howard and the Earl of Essex. Cecil's letter to them emphasised the risk he had taken to acquaint them with the prayer:

> That wch was onely ment a secreat sacrifice to one, I haue presumed out of truste to particapat wth two, It came to my handes accidentally I dare scarce iustifie the sight, muche lesse the coppie.[8]

He concluded with a plea that they keep what he had shared with them in the strictest confidence. Someone, apparently, did not. Within the year, John Norden added the Queen's work to his popular devotional treatise, *A Pensive Mans Practise*. Elizabeth's prayer appeared in at least three editions of this book between 1596 and 1600. It was reprinted in Camden's *Annals* in 1634, in John Speed's *The History of Great Britaine* (1611), in Samuel Clarke's *The Second Part of the Marrow of Ecclesiastical Historie* (1650), and in a broadside as late as 1688 (*Queen Elizabeth's Opinion concerning Transubstantiation*). I have found twelve additional texts in seventeenth-century manuscripts.[9] But by far the most widespread dissemination of this prayer must be blamed on Thomas Sorocold, who printed it along with Elizabeth's Armada prayer and her prayer for the expedition of 1597 in his *Supplications of Saints*. The Queen's religious compositions first appeared in this book in 1612; by 1754 it had reached an astonishing 45 editions. Thus, readers from the age of Benjamin Jonson to that of Samuel Johnson were well acquainted with Elizabeth's piety and devout concerns for her subjects' welfare as expressed in her own words in these prayers. Measured by number of extant copies of any of her works, the 1596 prayer ranks as the best-known and most influential of her writings in the century and a half after her death.

In all three prayers, Elizabeth's humility before God and earnest supplication to Him find eloquent expression. She is intent as well in the prayers of 1596 and 1597 rather literally to justify the ways of man to God by assuring Him that the English are attacking Spain for defensive purposes only. The campaigns are, she writes, 'grounded on just defence from wrongs, hate, and bloody desire of conquest'.[10] And in both prayers, her devotion to her subjects emerges in her plea that the expedition return 'with the least loss of English blood'.[11] Thus her prayers give private testimony to the public expressions of piety and love for her people set forth in her 'Golden Speech'.

7 BL Lansdowne MS 82, fol. 161.

8 From Cecil's original letter, Bodleian Tanner MS 76, fol. 30. No text of the prayer itself accompanies this document.

9 These documents are listed in *Elizabeth I: Selected Works*, pp. 255-6.

10 *Elizabeth I: Selected Works*, Prayer 5, 1597, p. 257.

11 *Elizabeth I: Selected Works*, Prayer 4, 1596, p. 254.

Their transmission, however, creates one of the greatest ironies of the Queen's on-going career, for her private devotions became her most widely disseminated writings in the century and a half after her death.

Elizabeth's sense of privacy with regard to her prayers explains why so few of her writings in this genre survive in multiple copies datable from her reign. Even the prayers in English verse that she composed in response to the Armada crisis (poems 8 and 9 in my edition) were not published until 1637, and only the second of these survives in a contemporary manuscript copy. Elizabeth's proprietary attitude toward such works also calls into question the authenticity of the books of prayers and individual texts published under her name in 1563, 1569, and 1582.[12] The make-up of the 1569 collection strongly suggests that the Queen did not compose its prayers, most of which derive from Henry Bull's *Christian Prayers and Holy Meditations* published in the same year (STC 4028). Only the Lambeth Palace copy of the 1569 volume (STC 6428) was produced for the Queen's personal use, with some prayers specially composed in the first person. The most likely explanation of this anomaly is, I think, that Bull's collection was augmented with devotions that Elizabeth approved and used in her private devotions, but did not write. As Patrick Collinson has observed of other first-person prayers attributed to Elizabeth, the voice occurs in 'other prayers which we can be confident she did not compose herself', such as those in Bentley's *Monument of Matrones*.[13] I suspect as well that the other prayers published under the Queen's name designate royal use, not royal composition. Equally suspicious is the Queen's so-called prayer book, the lost manuscript volume of devotions in French, Italian, Greek, Latin, and English that survives now only as British Library Facsimile 218.[14] This document's foremost claim to royal authenticity is its handwriting, which has been consistently described as the Queen's holograph. Yet this hand's rounded script with its well-defined clubbed ascenders and descenders does not resemble any lettering Elizabeth is known to have used, least of all the plain angular italic that she wrote consistently from at least 1549 onwards. In any event, these sixteenth-century texts could have exerted scant influence on Elizabeth's seventeenth-century image. Instead, her authentic prayers amplified the pious sentiments she expressed in her 'Golden Speech' as they circulated long after her death in both manuscript texts and the printed and reprinted works of Camden, Speed, Clarke, and, above all, Sorocold.

Letters provide a far more promising genre than prayer on which to base a literary reputation. During the sixteenth century, letters in the sense of epistles written to others, gained recognition as an interesting and important type of composition. Still, few writers are remembered solely for their letter-writing abilities, and it is important to distinguish between letterbooks that served as models for letter writing – the so-called books of precedents – and collections of letters that are of interest primarily because of who wrote them and to whom they were addressed. Highlights in the

12 These are the *Precationes priuate. Regiae E. R.* (STC 7576.7), *Christian Prayers and Meditations* (STC 6428), and *Variae Meditationes et Preces Piae* (STC 17774, two prayers in Latin attributed to the Queen).

13 Patrick Collinson, *Elizabethan Essays* (London & Rio Grande, Ohio, 1994), p. 91.

14 The facsimile was edited by Adam Fox with a translation of its foreign-language prayers as *A Book of Devotions Composed by Her Majesty* (Gerrards Cross, 1970).

printed history of this latter genre begin with Johan Reuchlin's *Letters of Illustrious Men* (followed by its Erasmian parody, the *Letters of Obscure Men*), Roger Ascham's *Familiarum Epistolarum*, 1576, the *Cabala* of 1654, Dudley Digges's *Compleat Ambassador*, 1655, and *Scrinia Ceciliana: Mysteries of State & Government*, 1663. Elizabeth's words, however, were not conveyed to seventeenth-century readers in these printed collections. Although a number of the Queen's letters appeared in translation in the English editions of Camden's *Annals*, their texts bear little affinity with Elizabeth's original wording. I have found only one of Elizabeth's authentic English letters in a seventeenth-century printed book. Gilbert Burnet included a transcript of the Princess Elizabeth's letter to Queen Catherine Parr in his *Historie of the Reformation of the Church of England* (1679, Wing B5797). It is quite an early product of her pen, yet not quite so early as Burnet's description of it would have us believe: '... it will not be unacceptable to the Reader, to see this first Blossome of so great a Princess, when she was not full Four years of Age; She being born in September 1533. and this writ in July 1537' (p. 209). Is it possible that even Elizabeth's reputation for precocious learning could make this claim credible to Burnet's readers? The letter was, in fact, composed on 31 July 1548, when the Princess was almost fifteen.[15] In any event the lone edition of Burnet's *Historie* could have counted for relatively little in the formation of Elizabeth's late-Stuart reputation.

Meanwhile, seventeenth-century manuscript culture abounded with anthologies made up entirely or largely of copies of letters by eminent persons. The Queen joined Sir Walter Ralegh, the Earl of Essex, and Sir Francis Bacon among the most popular letter writers in these collections, scores of which were compiled between about 1600 and 1660. Two of Elizabeth's letters in particular joined with her prayers in contributing to the formation of her legend during the seventeenth century. The earlier of these epistles is Elizabeth's 1586 letter to Sir Amias Paulet. I have found nineteen copies of this text, all of which date from the first half of the seventeenth century.[16] I suspect, however, that this amounts at best to a slim majority of the surviving copies. In 1585 the Queen appointed Sir Amias guardian of Mary Queen of Scots, and in the same year he was sworn to the Privy Council. Mary's complicity in the Babington assassination plot was revealed in August of the following year, but it was late September before Elizabeth agreed that her rival should be brought to trial. In a letter to Sir Francis Walsingham on 22 August, Paulet may well refer to the Queen's letter to him when he thanks her Secretary that his 'partial report hath wrought in her Majesty [s]o good acceptation of my poor service, as hath appeared by her most gracious letters'.[17]

Above all, readers of this letter would perceive in Elizabeth's attitude toward her subjects her warm, personal regard for Paulet. 'If you knew (my Amias),' she writes, 'how kindly besides dutifully my grateful heart accepts your double labors and faithful

15 The original draft is BL Cotton MS Otho C. 10, fol. 236v; a copy is in the Bodleian, Smith MS 68, art. 50. The text appears as Letter 10 in *Elizabeth I: Collected Works*, ed. Leah S. Marcus, Janel Mueller, and Mary Beth Rose (Chicago, 2000).

16 The texts of this letter are cited in *Elizabeth I: Selected Works*, p. 174.

17 *The Letter-Books of Sir Amias Poulet*, ed. John Morris (London, 1874), p. 268.

actions ... it would ease your travail and rejoice your heart.' In addition, the Queen expresses in this letter her godly concern for two individuals. Of Mary she writes, 'Let repentance take place and let not the fiend possess her so as her better part be lost, which I pray with hands lifted up to Him that may both save and spill.' She opens this letter with the wish that God might reward Paulet 'treblefold in the double' for his service, and she concludes, 'With my most loving adieu and prayer for thy long life.'[18] Her words convey her esteem for this loyal officer in the context of her awareness that his actions and hers are judged by a higher power.

It was long ago suggested, of course, that Elizabeth's attitude toward the Queen of Scots was not wholly philanthropic. Mary's eighteenth-century apologist, William Tytler, cites the letter to Paulet in making the case for Elizabeth's desire to have her rival assassinated.[19] The Queen, Tytler affirms, 'had got over all scruples as to putting her rival to death, provided it could be done with secrecy; but had not the courage to avow openly her purpose, out of fear of endangering her popularity' (p. 318). He then quotes Walsingham's letter to Paulet informing him of the Queen's disappointment that 'you have not in all this time ... found out some way to shorten the life of the Scots Queen' (p. 322). Although Paulet eagerly anticipated Mary's execution, he had no stomach for murdering her himself. He protested to Walsingham, 'God forbid I should make so foul a shipwreck of my conscience, or leave so great a blot to my poor posterity, and shed blood without law or warrant.'[20] Walsingham's letter certainly expressed his will in the matter and may very well express Elizabeth's preferred means for doing away with Mary. If they faithfully transmitted her sentiments, however, they do not detract from Elizabeth's love for her subjects (or her political acumen). They become a liability only if, in this context, her letter to Paulet was a hypocritical attempt to lure him into killing his charge. But nothing in her letter of late August 1586 suggests such a purpose. And more than five months elapsed before Walsingham informed him, in a letter of 1 Febrary 1586/7, that the Queen was disappointed by his failure to dispatch Mary. If her earlier letter was intended as a hint to Sir Amias, it was far too subtle to be effective and nothing in his intervening correspondence suggests that he felt under any pressure to resolve the crisis through murder.

Elizabeth likewise expressed her love for her subjects in an epistolary sub-genre, the letter of consolation. So far as I can determine, she was the first English sovereign to send personal condolences to individual subjects on the deaths of their loved ones. In 1566 she addressed the earliest such letter I have discovered to Lady Elizabeth Hoby (née Cook), upon the death of her husband Sir Thomas, then ambassador to France. She also consoled her lady of the Privy Chamber Catherine, Lady Paget, on the death of her sister-in-law, Lady Crompton. She did the same for George, Earl of Shrewsbury, on the death of his son, Lord Talbot, in 1582. As late as 1598 she sent similar letters

18 *Elizabeth I: Selected Works*, Letter 28, pp. 172-3.

19 *An Inquiry, Historical and Critical, into the Evidence Against Mary Queen of Scots*, 4th edn (London, 1790), II, 318.

20 II, 322-3. Morris, *The Letter-Books*, pp. 354, 361-2, quotes the exchange between Walsingham and Paulet from Thomas Hearne's manuscript diary, vol. 85, 89.

to Edmund, third Baron Sheffield, to console him on the loss of a son and to Lady Elizabeth Southwell on the death of her husband, Sir Robert (PLATE 2).[21]

While most letters of this type were kept private, one of them entered the currents of manuscript circulation where, as with the Paulet letter, its widespread distribution no doubt influenced Elizabeth's seventeenth-century image. This is the letter of condolence the Queen addressed to Lady Margaret Norris on the death of her son, Sir John Norris. I list eleven manuscript copies of this letter in *Elizabeth I: Selected Works* (Letter 43) with the caution that many others no doubt remain to be found. Sir John, one of England's ablest military commanders, was serving in Ireland in September 1597 when he fell ill and died of gangrene. The Queen dictated her condolences to a scribe, then prefixed in her own handwriting the initial greeting to 'Mine own Crow'. This salutation, missing from many copies of the text, addressed Lady Norris by a nickname that Elizabeth apparently derived from the Norris family crest, a crow or raven, sable. As a further mark of respect to the Norris family, a gentleman in the Queen's service delivered her letter to them in person along with further expressions of sympathy that the Queen had personally entrusted him to convey. Elizabeth's strategy of consolation in the letter included praise of Lady Norris's son coupled with the assertion that she too honoured him with a maternal love. The Queen assured the grieving parents as well that 'nothing of this kind hath happened but by God's divine providence'. She conveyed both warmth and personal concern through her pledge to the Norris family to 'let these lines from your loving and gracious sovereign serve to assure you that there shall ever appear the lively characters [traits, characteristics] of you and yours that are left, in valuing all their faithful and honest endeavors'. Unfortunately those images did not last much longer. The Norrises lost five of their six sons by 1599. Lady Margaret died in that year, her husband two years later, and their last surviving son in 1603. Elizabeth's personal letter to the parents probably entered manuscript circulation in the subsequent legal disputes among the heirs to the Norris estates.

Of the three genres of Elizabeth's own writings that primarily shaped her image during the seventeenth century, only one could be termed royal propaganda. That is, only the 'Golden Speech' was designed to mould and enhance her public image. She certainly aimed in this speech to produce a strong and positive effect. She addressed it, after all, to those on whom she depended for extraordinary income at a time when the Irish campaign had drained the royal coffers. She even allowed a version of the speech to be published.[22] But as Elizabeth composed her prayers and private correspondence,

21 Henry Ellis transcribed Elizabeth's letter to Lady Hoby in *Original Letters, Illustrative of English History*, 1st Ser. (London, 1825), II, 229-30, from BL Harley MS 7035, fol. 161. I am grateful to Dr Peter Beal for directing my attention to the Paget letter; the holograph original is reproduced in the *Catalogue of the Lyttleton Papers* (London, 1978), p. 45. Elizabeth's letter to Shrewsbury is printed from BL Add. MS 15891, fol. 88v, in Sir Harris Nicolas's *Memoirs of the Life and Times of Sir Christopher Hatton* (London, 1847), pp. 267-8. The Earl's son, Francis Talbot, was buried 3 September 1582. The Southwell letter, scribal with the Queen's autograph heading and signature, is in the collection of the Elizabethan Club at Yale University. I am grateful to Dr Heather Wolfe, Curator of Manuscripts at the Folger Shakespeare Library, for acquainting me with this document.

22 *Her Maiesties most Princelie answere, deliuered by her selfe at ... White-hall, on the last day of Nouember 1601*, STC 7578.

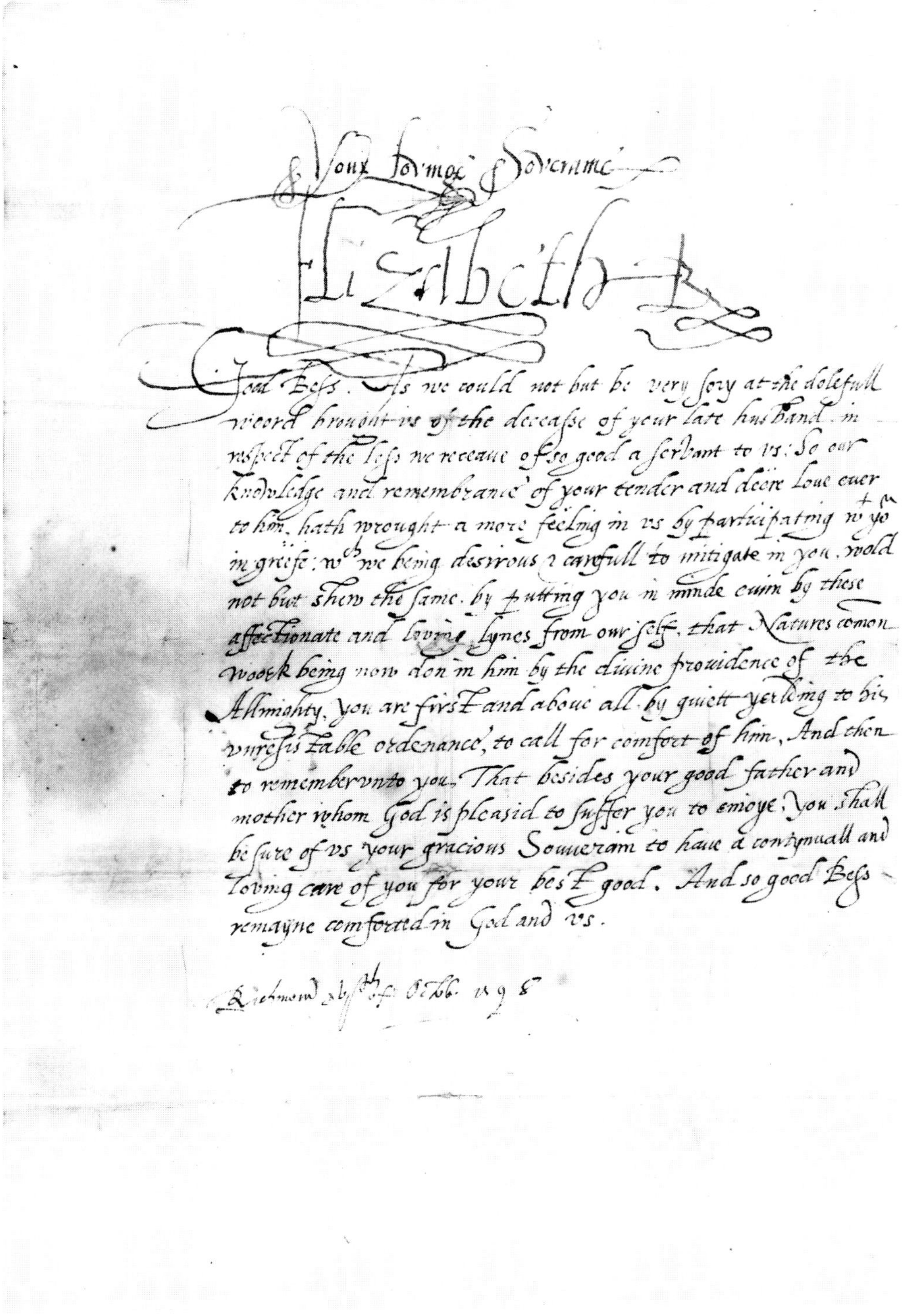
Your lovinge Soveraine
Elizabeth R

Good Bess. As we could not but be very sory at the dolefull record brought vs of the decease of your late husband, in respect of the loss we receaue of so good a seruant to vs: So our knowledge and remembrance of your tender and deere loue euer to him, hath wrought a more feeling in vs by participating wth you in greefe: wch we being desirous & carefull to mitigate in you, wold not but shew the same, by putting you in minde euen by these affectionate and loving lynes from our self, that Natures comon work being now don in him by the diuine prouidence of the Allmighty, you are first and aboue all by quiett yeilding to his vnresistable ordenance, to call for comfort of him, And then to remember vnto you, That besides your good father and mother whom God is pleased to suffer you to enioye, you shall be sure of vs your gracious Soueraine to haue a contynuall and loving care of you for your best good. And so good Bess remayne comforted in God and vs.

Richmond 15th of Octob. 1598

2 Letter of condolence by Queen Elizabeth, to Lady Elizabeth Southwell, in the hand of a scribe with the Queen's autograph superscription ('Your lovinge Soveraine') and signature, 15 October 1598

it is hard to believe that her eye was trained first on her broad public image. Instead, a few of these prayers and letters quite accidentally circulated in print and manuscript to influence her myth during the Stuart era. What is not accidental among these three genres of her writing is their consistency: her love for her subjects finds clear expression in all of these texts. In the speech and her prayers, the Queen professes her love for her people collectively. The letters, however, demonstrate her enactment of this principle as she communicates it to individual subjects. Aside from her concern for the salvation of Mary Queen of Scots, Elizabeth focused her expressions of godliness on her people and their welfare. Her prayers lack any specific requests to God to provide for her personal safety or prosperity. The Queen includes herself, merely one among the rest, in her concern for the nation at large. Accordingly, the ultimate source of the legend of good Queen Bess is, or should be, Elizabeth's testimony in her own words to her piety and devotion to her subjects. The myth was rooted in this testimony as it developed in the century after her death. Her own discourse, public and private, confirmed what was said about her in the writings of others. As for the result, we are left to wonder, was it only a myth?

GENERAL INDEX

INDEX OF MANUSCRIPTS